ENGLISH ZIONISTS AND BRITISH JEWS

ENGLISH ZIONISTS AND BRITISH JEWS

The Communal Politics of
Anglo-Jewry, 1895-1920

STUART A. COHEN

Princeton University Press
Princeton, New Jersey

For Tova

PROVERBS 31:28-29

Contents

Illustrations   ix
Preface   xi
Abbreviations   xv

Introduction   3

PART ONE: Opening Moves, 1895-1904
1. The Foundation of the English Zionist Federation, 1895-
   1899   25
2. The English Zionist Federation and Communal Strategy,
   1899-1904   47

PART TWO: The Politics of Zionism, 1904-1914
3. Storm over East Africa and Stress within the English Zionist
   Federation, 1904-1914   79
4. The Zionists and Communal Politics, 1904-1914   124

PART THREE: Anti-Zionism in Theory and Practice
5. Versions of the Past, Visions of the Future   155
6. Zionists and Anti-Zionists, 1914-1917   215

PART FOUR: Zionism and the Politics of Anglo-Jewry, 1914-1920
7. Anglo-Jewry and Zionism, 1914-1917   243
8. English Zionists and British Jews, 1917-1920   277

Conclusions   314

Bibliography   325
Index   341

Illustrations

Between pages 32-33

1. Handbill advertising Herzl's first public appearance in London, 1896. Courtesy of Mr. A. Schischa, London.
2. Col. A.E.W. Goldsmid (c. 1900). Courtesy of Central Zionist Archives, Jerusalem.
3. Herzl with delegates to the first English Zionist Federation Conference, London, June 1899. Courtesy of Central Zionist Archives, Jerusalem.
4. Israel and Edith Zangwill (1905). Courtesy of Central Zionist Archives, Jerusalem.

Between pages 96-97

5. Title page of Hermann Adler's sermon, "Religious versus Political Zionism" (1898). Courtesy of Mr. A. Schischa, London.
6. Herbert Bentwich (c. 1925). Courtesy of Central Zionist Archives, Jerusalem.
7. Ḥakham Moses Gaster (1898). Courtesy of Central Zionist Archives, Jerusalem.
8. Leopold Greenberg (1910). Courtesy of Central Zionist Archives, Jerusalem.
9. Jacob de Haas (1898). Courtesy of Central Zionist Archives, Jerusalem.
10. Sir Francis Montefiore (c. 1905). Courtesy of Central Zionist Archives, Jerusalem.
11. Lucien Wolf caricatured in the *Daily Graphic*, 1904. Courtesy of Central Zionist Archives, Jerusalem.
12. Delegates to the English Zionist Federation Conference, London, 1920. Courtesy of Central Zionist Archives, Jerusalem.

Preface

Jewish history is necessarily heterogeneous. The Jewish people does possess common traditions, but it has not inherited a common past. The only pivotal events in which the entire congregation of Israel is known to have participated were biblical: the receipt of the Law at Sinai, the entry into the Promised Land under Joshua, and the establishment of the Kingdom of David. Even the destruction of the second temple in 70 C.E. materially and immediately affected the everyday lives of but a portion of the Jewish people of the time. The subsequent dispersion—although undoubtedly the predominant theme of all postbiblical Jewish history—confirmed the fragmentary nature of the Jewish experience. Specifically, throughout their exile the Jews possessed few focal (and no all-embracing) political institutions. Individual communities developed distinctive patterns of political association which, despite their overall adherence to a recognizably Jewish political tradition, were framed as specific responses to the peculiarities of their different situations. Such divergences did not, of course, result in utter disintegration. Rabbinic law and lore continued to act as one unifying influence; the pervading phenomenon of persecution provided another. Nevertheless, the separate development of Jewish communities was persistently shaped by their diverse intellectual, political, economic, and migratory experiences. These perforce precluded total uniformity in the political reactions of all Jews to emergent situations over which they exercised no unitary control.

Political Zionism attempted to change all that. For Zionists, the notion that the Jews constitute one people, and therefore ought to act as such, is fundamental. The prescription is stressed in the first chapter of Herzl's *Der Judenstaat* and became a standard litany in the orthodox canon of Zionist literature thereafter. It is integral to the observation that a Jewish 'problem' is an inevitable feature of Diaspora life, for which the only solution is the establishment of an independent Jewish State. But the very force of this doctrinaire thesis tends to complicate the task of the historian who would wish to record and reconstruct any stage of Zionist progress. He cannot ignore the tension between the all-embracing diagnosis of the Jewish condition proposed by his subject and the forces of intra-Jewish particularism that it struggles to contain. Neither can he disregard the chronological discontinuities and geographical variations that have characterized the checkered chronicle of Zionist fortunes. The rise of modern Jewish nationalism cannot be regarded simply as an inevitable consummation of the Jews' ancient messianic yearnings. Traditional liturgies, legal codes, and legends undoubtedly preserved the link between the Jews and the Holy Land. Yet there remains a significant gulf between the orthodox version of Redemption as an act of God, marking a reconciliation between the Jew and his Maker, and the mainstream *political* Zionist concept that Jewish nationhood would essentially redress relations between the Jews and the nations of the earth, and largely be the work of man. Furthermore, not all of the signposts of modern Jewish history pointed toward political Zionism; several led down very different paths. In the West, the most pronounced of Jewry's responses to the intoxicating circumstances of the nineteenth century were acculturalization, assimilation, and religious reform. In eastern Europe, the dominant radical reactions to the intimidating events of the same period were migration westwards and/or revolutionary activity. The extent to which individual Jews were prepared to embark on a particular journey—and the fact that the vast majority, of their own volition, rejected the Zionist route—reflected several circumstances, not the least relevant of which were the cultural, social, and political atmospheres pervading their separate points of departure. Their behavior merely confirmed the degree to which the history of Zionism was tethered to the grainy particularity of various Jewish experiences.

Why individual Jews supported or opposed the Zionist claim to territorial independence is not, then, a question that would appear entirely amenable to generic analysis. To say that is obviously not to disparage the contributions of those scholars who have compiled synoptic accounts (the most helpful of which is David Vital's *The Origins of Zionism*, Oxford, 1975). Without their broad conceptualization, we would find it difficult to appreciate the comprehensive outlook of Zionism's founding fathers and the transcommunal impact of their movement. There is, however, a case to be made for a complementary, second-tier approach, one that might focus specifically on the mechanics of the process whereby what was universal in the appeal of political Zionism was welded to what was singular in the circumstances of particular Jewish communities. By postulating the idiosyncratic features of Jewish communal life, this perspective might facilitate our understanding of the interaction between the message that political Zionism proclaimed to the Jews as a collective and the response of Jews as members of different units. Such is the structure of argument underlying the present work. No claim is here made that the pattern followed by Anglo-Jewry was unique; readers will, no doubt, find analogous themes and trends elsewhere. But my own discussion has, deliberately, been less ambitious.

☐

As is so often said to be the case, the idea for this book originated in a conversation held in an Oxford Common Room. It was over a decade ago that Lord Alan Bullock, the Master of St. Catherine's College, asked me why political Zionism had taken such a long time to become a powerful force in Anglo-Jewish politics. Ill-equipped to answer him at the time, I was prevented from attempting to do so in an academic fashion during the following years by other pursuits and concerns. I trust, however, that the present belated reply will indicate the extent of my gratitude for his stimulation. The other debts that I have incurred during the course of my research are of more recent origin, but are equally substantial. Most obviously is this so in the case of the custodians and officials of the libraries and archives in which I received permission to work: in Israel, the Central Zionist Archives and

Preface

Jewish National Library (both in Jerusalem), and the Weizmann Archives (Reḥovot); in London, the Public Record Office, the British Museum, the Mocatta Library, the Board of Deputies, the United Synagogue, the Federation of Synagogues, the Sephardi Congregation, and the Jewish Board of Guardians (now the Jewish Welfare Board); in New York, the YIVO Institute for Jewish Research, the Jewish Theological Seminary, the New York Public Library, and the Zionist Archives; in Cincinnati, the American Jewish Archives. In each case, the unfailing patience and habitual courtesy of the staffs measurably increased the pleasures of historical research. Professor Basil Loewe, Miss May Maccoby, and Mr. Abraham Schischa (all of London) kindly allowed me to consult material in their private possession; Mr. Pinḥas Chen and Mrs. Chasya Kaplan (both of Jerusalem) helped with some of the research, and Miss Sarah Lederhendler with the typing.

Throughout, the Research Authority of Bar-Ilan University was most supportive, providing successive and generous grants between 1974 and 1977. Thanks are also due to the Memorial Foundation for Jewish Culture, and the Israel Commission for Basic Research.

Without in any way avoiding sole responsibility for the style and substance of my presentation, I record with gratitude the advice, encouragement, and—above all—the criticisms received from those scholars to whom I turned for information and guidance: Professor Chimen Abramsky (University College, London), Professor Lionel Kochan (Warwick University), Dr. Aubrey Newman (Leicester University), Professor Meir Vereté (The Hebrew University, Jerusalem), Professor David Vital (Tel-Aviv University), and Professors Daniel Elazar, Charles Liebman, Avrom Saltman, and Andrew Sharf (all of Bar-Ilan). Especially welcome, during the last tricky stages, was the valuable counsel—graciously offered and promptly rendered—of Mrs. Joanna Hitchcock and Ms. Marilyn Campbell, both of Princeton University Press.

My greatest debt, and one that is impossible to specify, is to my wife and our sons.

Bar-Ilan University, Ramat-Gan, Israel
May 1981 *Nisan 5741*

Abbreviations

AJA   Anglo-Jewish Association

CZA   Central Zionist Archives, Jerusalem, Israel

DEPS   Archives of the Board of Deputies of British Jews,
           London

Diaries   *The Complete Diaries of Theodor Herzl.* Edited by Ra-
           phael Patai. Translated by Harry Zohn. 5 vols. New
           York, 1960

EZF   English Zionist Federation

Ito   Jewish Territorial Organisation

JC   *Jewish Chronicle,* London

JQR   *Jewish Quarterly Review,* London

Letters   *The Letters and Papers of Chaim Weizmann. Series A:
           Letters.* Edited by Meyer Weisgal et al. 23 vols. Ox-
           ford, London, and Jerusalem, 1969-1980

TJHSE   *Transactions of the Jewish Historical Society of England,*
           London

WA   Weizmann Archives, Reḥovot, Israel

ENGLISH ZIONISTS AND BRITISH JEWS

Introduction

THE ZIONIST ORGANISATION
was founded in 1897 in order to secure the establishment (some
might have said the reconstruction) of "a Jewish homeland openly
recognised, legally secured." That remained its central purpose
until the foundation of the State of Israel in 1948. During the
intervening period, two major obstacles impeded the fulfilment
of Zionism's political ambitions. Broadly speaking, one was external: the relevant Great Powers were reluctant to sanction autonomous Jewish control over a portion of the Middle East; the
Arab inhabitants of the region were invariably, and often vio-
lently opposed to such a prospect. The second was internal: the
political Zionists were always a minority party within world Jewry.
Only a fraction of the entire Jewish people have emigrated to
Erez Yisrael ("The Land of Israel"); only since World War II have
most Jews—even in the free world—taken the more symbolic step
of contributing to Zionist funds or participating in the movement's
ancillary activities. A significant proportion remained either indifferent toward political Zionism or, in the more interesting
cases, avowedly opposed to its thesis. Ultimately, the internal
and external problems were clearly related. Zionist leaders could
best lay claim to a land "in the name of the Jewish people" if
they could demonstrate that they did indeed represent the main
body of world Jewry. But the order of priorities was usually reversed. Weizmann and Ben Gurion, no less than Herzl, largely
subordinated the campaign for the support of Jewry to the struggle
for international recognition. Given success in the diplomatic
arena, it was argued, domestic Jewish opposition was bound to
succumb.

Historians of Zionism have often followed that lead, particularly when recounting the relations between the Zionist move-

Introduction

ment and the British government. Several studies concentrate on the negotiations that led to the publication of the Balfour Declaration in 1917; many more elaborate on the subsequent record of contacts between the Jewish Agency and the mandatory regime in Palestine.[1] By comparison, very little attention has been paid to the ebb and flow of Zionist fortunes within Anglo-Jewry.[2] The omission is surprising. As is often acknowledged, the reservations of some Jews in Britain with regard to the propriety of political Zionism did occasionally threaten to influence the attitude of the British government.[3] It is also misleading. The intracommunal debate on Zionism was not detached from other contemporary currents in Anglo-Jewish life; it reflected, and fostered, the existence of exogenous conflicts and tensions. Representatives of all shades of communal opinion discussed the theme

[1] Always a popular subject of polemic, the prehistory and history of the Mandate period has attained the status of an industry with the opening of the relevant diplomatic archives. No bibliography can keep pace with the studies now pouring off the presses; for a recent attempt (necessarily incomplete, but nevertheless adequate) see Howard M. Sachar, *A History of Israel* (Jerusalem, 1976), pp. 846-61.

[2] Two exceptions, both very thin and now rather dated, are: Marvin J. Goldfine, "The Growth of Zionism in England up to the World War" (Master's thesis, Columbia University, 1939); and Paul Goodman, *Zionism in England, 1899-1949* (London, 1949). See also, Virginia H. Hein, "The British Followers of Theodor Herzl: English Zionist Leaders, 1896-1904" (Ph.D. dissertation, Georgia State University, 1978). Other communities in the Western world have merited much fuller and more comprehensive treatment: e.g., Jehuda Reinharz, *Fatherland or Promised Land: The Dilemma of the German Jew, 1893-1914* (Ann Arbor, 1975); Stephen M. Poppel, *Zionism in Germany, 1897-1933* (Philadelphia, 1977); Michael R. Marrus, *The Politics of Assimilation* (on France) (Oxford, 1971); Yonathan Shapiro, *Leadership of the American Zionist Organization, 1897-1930* (Urbana, 1971), and Melvin I. Urofsky, *American Zionism from Herzl to the Holocaust* (New York, 1975).

[3] One famous example is the furor caused by the Conjoint Foreign Committee's anti-Zionist manifesto in 1917 (on which see Leonard Stein, *The Balfour Declaration* [London, 1961], and below pp. 238-44). Another is hinted at in Winston Churchill's letter to Israel Zangwill of 13 July 1906. "Further there is the undoubted division among the Jews themselves, which seems to have impressed itself even upon some of those . . . who were strenuous in your support." Jerusalem, Central Zionist Archives [hereafter CZA], Files of the Jewish Territorial Organization [hereafter Ito files], A36/19a.

of Jewish nationalism, which was seen as impinging upon the widest spectrum of their religious, social, and political beliefs. Hence debates on the topic were usually uninhibited and—for many of the participants—crucial. They were rarely conducted in an intellectual or political vacuum. The English Zionist Federation grew out of a polygenetic communal background with which it reacted and which it also tried to shape. In many ways, the history of its supporters and opponents is that of the community at large. The purpose of the present introduction is not to compress a survey of either Anglo-Jewry or of Zionism into the space of a few pages. It aims, rather, to direct attention to those aspects of both considered relevant to an account of why some members of the community accepted, and others rejected, the principles and practices advocated by Herzl and his local lieutenants.

In Anglo-Jewry, as elsewhere, Love of Zion had been given practical expression some time before the advent of political Zionism. It had also assumed a degree of institutional form. Admittedly, the Jews of the British Isles made only a marginal contribution to the pioneering labors and writings which were ultimately to affect the course of their people's history. Intellectually, as much as geographically, the community hovered on the periphery of postmedieval Jewish life, its members reacting to Continental currents in Jewish self-consciousness rather than trying to shape them. But in matters affecting Zion Anglo-Jewry did possess the advantage of a uniquely favorable gentile environment. Influential segments of Christian society in Britain had long been receptive to the prospect of a revival of the historic connection between the Children of Israel and the Land of the Bible. The literary public of Victorian England was still affected by the residual influence of earlier millenarian visions of a Second Coming. Throughout the period, it was also supplied with more recent— and usually less eschatological—jogs to its scriptural memories. An entire school of travellers, Orientalists, archeologists, artists, and writers of fiction gave prominence to both the Holy Land and its ancient inhabitants. In so doing (according to some accounts) they generated a form of proto-Zionism which was to play an important role in the confluence of Israel's fortunes with those of Albion. Strategic considerations, it has been argued, pointed in much the same direction. Napoleon's campaigns in Egypt and southern Syria had provided startling evidence of the extent to which the movement of events in the Middle East might threaten British rule in India. The possibility that a friendly presence in Palestine—even a Jewish presence—might serve as a bulwark of Britain's position in the region had begun to play upon elements of the official mind long before the partition of the Ottoman Empire was seriously contemplated in Whitehall.[4]

More specific, if somewhat less operatic, was Anglo-Jewry's own tradition of association with the old and newer Jewish settlements in Erez Yisrael. As much is acknowledged by the standard Zionist genealogies. They all pay due homage to the projects and proposals initiated in Ottoman Palestine by Sir Moses Montefiore, the banker and communal worker who made the first of his seven journeys to the country in 1827 and the last, when he was ninety, in 1874. Honorifically designated a "great pioneer" in Naḥum Sokolow's *History of Zionism* (published in 1919), he has since been extensively memorialized in the State of Israel—most recently by having his portrait adorn a one-shekel note. Historians of Petaḥ Tikva, the "mother" of modern Jewish settlements in *Erez Yisrael*, also acknowledge the remarkable contribution of Zeraḥ Barnett. This sturdy and successful East End furrier was one of the four men to found the village in 1878; during the course of twenty-seven subsequent trips to London, he also man-

[4] The theme is outlined in Naḥum Sokolow, *History of Zionism, 1600-1918*, 2 vols. (London, 1919), and Barbara Tuchman, *The Bible and the Sword: England and Palestine from the Bronze Age to Balfour* (New York, 1956). On specific strands: Harold Fisch, *Jerusalem and Albion: The Hebraic Factor in Seventeenth Century Literature* (London, 1964); Marvin Scult, *Millennial Expectations and Jewish Liberties* (Leiden, 1978); Michael McKeon, "Sabbetai Sevi in England," *Association of Jewish Studies, Review* 2 (1977):131-70; Meir Vereté, "Why was a British Consulate Established at Jerusalem?" *English Historical Review* 85 (1970):316-45; idem, "The Restoration of the Jews in English Protestant Thought, 1790-1840," *Middle Eastern Studies* 8 (1972):3-50; and Norman Bentwich and John M. Shaftesley, "Forerunners of Zionism in the Victorian Era," in *Remember the Days: Essays in Honour of Cecil Roth*, ed. John M. Shaftesley (London, 1966).

aged both to replenish his own diminished fortune and to arouse some Anglo-Jewish support for his penurious fellow colonists.[5] The memory of Col. Albert Edward Williamson Goldsmid is generally revered somewhat less, possibly because Zionist historiography does not quite know where to place him. Goldsmid did not become aware of his Jewish identity until comparatively late in his life, and always had a highly personal view of the past and future of his coreligionists. He has been severely depicted as a frustrated philanthropist and a demonstrative romantic ("I am Daniel Deronda" was his opening gambit when first meeting Herzl). Perhaps it would be more charitable to say that Goldsmid combined a sentimental fixation on his own origins with a sophisticated appraisal of the necessity for coordinated—even tutelary— activity in order to improve the lot of the Jewish people. By profession an officer in the British army, he had a flair for administration and a long-standing interest in Jewish settlement overseas. He first visited Palestine in 1883 and was appointed Director General of Baron Hirsch's colonies in the Argentine in 1892. Between these activities, Goldsmid prodded the Chovevei Zion [Lovers of Zion] Association of England to adopt a written constitution; he also drew up a plan for its organization that was a cross between standard military practice and his own understanding of the framework employed by the Children of Israel in the wilderness of Sinai: affiliated societies were dubbed "tents" (junior societies, "cadet tents"); they were led by "commanders" responsible to a "headquarters," and placed under the overall direction of a "chief"—a position that Goldsmid himself held after 1893.[6]

Anglo-Jewry's Chovevei Zion Association was not, however, entirely Goldsmid's own creation. Its origins have been traced to the more modest activities of a small group of early east European immigrants, who established Lovers of Zion societies in the wake of the atrocities in Russia in 1881-1882. Three fledgling groups

[5] Y. Ya'ari-Polsky, *Sefer Ha-Yovel Limlot Ḥamishim Shanah le-Yesod Petaḥ-Tikvah* (Tel-Aviv, 1929); Gershon Kressel, "Eim Ha-Moshavot: Petaḥ-Tikvah," *Cathedra* 9 (1978):12.

[6] The full constitution, printed in both Hebrew and English, dated 1892, in CZA, Files of the Chovevei Zion Association of England, A2/7(ii).

of this sort functioned in Tredegar, Leeds, and Manchester in 1883, and two gentlemen (one of whom was Zerah Barnett) tangentially associated with an equally tiny London circle attended the European "conference" of Hovevei Zion at Kattowicz, in Silesia, in 1884. Thereafter, Palestinophile activities slowly gathered momentum and one milestone followed another with what appears to have been relentless, if uneven, regularity. The story has been fully chronicled elsewhere,[7] and can therefore be briefly summarized here. A short-lived Palestine Colonisation Association, consisting of about 250 members, was founded in London in 1885; a Kadimah ("Forward") society of some 150 younger spirits in 1887; a Chovevei Zion Society committed to more strenuous colonizing activity and largely composed of dissident elements from Kadimah followed in 1888; and the Chovevei Zion Association of England, amidst pomp and circumstance belying its nominal membership of about 450 families, held its first public meeting at the Jewish Working Men's Club in East London on 31 May 1890.

One significant feature of this unfolding record is the heterogeneous nature of the association's membership. The new movement was not an exclusively immigrant preserve; neither was Goldsmid the only native member of the community to venture into its fold. Recent arrivals, it is true, did provide whatever semblance there was of emotional commitment and numerical buoyancy. The East End Tent, always the largest, had a roll of over 1,500 members in 1893; they constituted much of the audience who came to hear the impassioned Chovevei Zion addresses regularly delivered by Rabbi Hayim Zundel Maccoby (the "Kamenitzer Maggid," come to London from Russia in January 1890), whose oratorical stamina soon became as famous as his Talmudic scholarship.[8] But Establishment figures, solidly rooted in the West End of London, also showed some interest. As much

---

[7] Most recently by Elhanan Orren, *Hibat-Zion be-Britanyah, 1878-1898* (Tel-Aviv, 1974); an anecdotal history was published in the first eight issues of *Palestina, The Chovevei Zion Quarterly* (October 1892-June 1894).

[8] Max Mansky, ed., *Imrei Hayim* (Tel-Aviv, 1929), introduction; and the obituary by Israel Shapotshnick in *Rashei Alfei Yisrael* 5 (1916):3-7.

is evident from the muster of names who graced the platform of the Chovevei Zion's foundation meeting in 1890. Sir Samuel Montagu was there: he was, after all, patron of the Jewish Working Men's Club, president of the Federation of Synagogues (the umbrella organization that united in uneasy partnership numerous immigrant Orthodox *chevrot* in the East End), an eminent merchant banker, and Liberal M.P. for Whitechapel, where much of the capital's Jewish immigrant population was concentrated. Still more impressive was the presence of Lord Nathaniel Rothschild, president of the United Synagogue of established metropolitan Orthodox congregations and, of course, scion of one of the most remarkable families in modern Jewish history. Aged fifty in 1890 (eight years younger than Montagu), Lord "Natty" had been created the first Jewish peer just five years earlier and stood at the very pinnacle of Anglo-Jewish society. He was to continue to do so for the next twenty-five years—despite Montagu's commercial, communal, and political attainments (Montagu was not created Lord Swaything until 1907). It was at Rothschild's urgings, so rumor had it, that Sir Benjamin Louis Cohen too had been induced to attend the meeting. This was an important addition. Besides being Conservative M.P. for East Islington, Cohen had since 1887 also been president of the Jewish Board of Guardians, the community's premier charity. By virtue of that office, he was almost as revered in Whitechapel as were Montagu and Rothschild. His presence provided yet another symbol of the West End's paternalistic interest in East End affairs. Perhaps it was in order to emphasize the links between the two worlds, and at the same time to stress the distance between them, that these lay dignitaries also brought to the meeting in their train a retinue of clerical luminaries: Rabbi Hermann Adler, who was very soon to succeed his late father as Chief Rabbi of the Ashkenazi community; Rabbi Moses Gaster, *Ḥakham* (principal minister) of the older, but smaller, Sephardi congregations; and Reverend Simeon Singer, the dignified minister of the New West End Synagogue in Bayswater Road, West London, who also served as court chaplain to the Rothschilds.

The imprimatur of these men seems to have provided the Chovevei Zion Association with the necessary impetus. By 1891, an emblematic tent had been established in West London, and a conspicuous amount of political activity had been initiated. On 23 May of that year, the Chovevei Zion arranged for a monster demonstration to protest against the situation in Russia, which was attended by 4,000 sympathizers. Soon thereafter, Montagu presented Lord Salisbury with a petition, addressed to the Sublime Porte of the Ottoman Empire, listing in considerable detail the improvements that were desired in the facilities offered to Jewish colonists in Palestine. As a result of the enthusiasm thus aroused and of Goldsmid's administrative innovations, twenty new tents were established; a journal (*Palestina*, edited by Dr. Samuel A. Hirsch, senior tutor at Jews' College) began to appear; 24,000 acres of land were purchased on the Golan; and the colonies of Castinie and Benei Yehouda were formally "adopted."[9] In 1893, the association drew up a second petition, albeit decidedly more decorous in tone and content than the first, which was duly presented to Lord Rosebery.

It is tempting to regard these developments as the harbingers of more momentous tidings. But no intellectual or functional line can easily be traced from the tame proceedings of the Chovevei Zion Association to the rigorous agitation later promoted by the English Zionist Federation. Whilst the first object of the former, as heraldically inscribed on its stationery, was "to foster the National Idea in Israel," few of its senior members seriously pondered the precise nature of the ideology that they were supposed to be cultivating. Of all the tents, only the B'nei Zion (a small but vocal group of East Enders who affiliated to the Chovevei Zion Association in 1894) attempted to undertake cultural and financial work with the avowed purpose of restoring the entire Jewish people to its ancient homeland.[10] Otherwise, the purposes of the Chovevei Zion were interpreted in a far more circumscribed fashion. This was particularly true of the West End membership which increasingly, and perhaps inevitably, came to dominate its affairs.

[9] See reports on the colonies, dated 1895, by J. Prag, in CZA, Files of the Chovevei Zion Association, A2/7(i).

[10] Orren, *Ḥibat-Ẓion*, pp. 82-83 and 112-13.

Introduction

Its spokesmen seem soon to have regretted their earlier activism and to shrink from suggestions that they repeat the efforts of 1891-1893. They wished the Association to invest far more energy in the promotion of proper English manners among its immigrant adherents, and far less in the propagation of abstract theories.[11] Furthermore, they insisted on working in conjunction with the apolitical Jewish Colonisation Association (Ica), established in Paris in 1894, and explicitly decried the maximalist program advocated by the firebrands of the B'nei Zion.

> Exaggerated statements have from time to time been put forward as to the aims of the Chovevei Zion societies [ran one circular], viz: that their object is to anticipate the fulfilment of prophesy by encouraging a wholesale immigration of Jews to Palestine. Such is not the aim or the idea of the Chovevei Zion.[12]

Accredited spokesmen for the movement hastened to stress that such statements did not imply any dimunition in their personal yearnings for Zion. But they did place definite limits on its official expression by the Association. Brazen claims to Palestine would merely arouse the suspicions of the Ottoman authorities, and thereby jeopardize the existing colonists in the country (said to be one untoward result of the 1891 and 1893 petitions). If articulated too specifically they would also implicitly conflict with other, more fundamental beliefs: that the condition of Jewry would improve with the universal diffusion of liberalism and emancipation (or, in some views, of social revolution); and that the Return to Zion would ultimately come about miraculously, and not as a result of an impatient and sinful dissatisfaction with the tardiness of the process. These were councils of restraint

---

[11] Paragraph six of the "Rules of the Chovevei Zion of England" specified that members "render cheerful obedience" to the laws of the land. See also the injunctions, in English and Yiddish, printed in a circular dated 26 May 1893, CZA, Files of the Chovevei Zion Association, A2/7(i).

[12] Circular dated February 1894, CZA, Files of the Chovevei Zion Association, A2/7(i). Also A.E.W. Goldsmid, "Modus Operandi," *Palestina* 5 (October, 1893):1-2.

which apparently explained why the vast majority of the community (native and immigrant) did not respond to the Association's appeals. They also accounted for the determination of its leaders to concentrate scrupulously on the attainment of minor ameliorations for the struggling pioneers in select Palestinian colonies.

Late nineteenth-century political Zionism presented the Jews of Britain, as elsewhere, with an entirely different ideology. As formulated by Theodor Herzl (the founder and first president of the World Zionist Organisation who, although not the first nor even the most intellectually distinguished proponent of the idea, was undoubtedly its most influential propagandist), modern Jewish nationalism disparaged the ethos of grim resignation enshrined in classic Orthodox immobilism. Exile, it claimed, was not a purgative experience; neither was deliverance to be a matter of grace. The advent of the millennium could legitimately be hastened by means that were not explicitly divine. At the same time, political Zionism also deflated the mythology of Diaspora messianism fostered by theorists of emancipation and religious reform. Pointing to the recrudescence of anti-Semitism in its racial and government-inspired forms throughout much of Europe, it argued the bankruptcy of the formula of cultural and social integration posited by Moses Mendelssohn in eighteenth-century Germany and advocated by subsequent devotees of a program of Diaspora *haskalah* (enlightenment). Instead, argued the Zionists, Jewry's situation was inherently unnatural: the Jew would not gain authentic citizenship by endeavoring to separate the religious from the national in his creed, still less by choosing (where permitted) the path of partial or total assimilation. Political independence within defined territorial boundaries represented the only relief. A multiplicity of scattered places of refuge, especially when dependent upon philanthropic condescension, would not meet the immense needs of the case. Jewish energies had to be harnessed to an avowedly national aim with the purpose of stimulating effective political action on an international scale.

Even thus baldly summarized, the doctrine was clearly an intellectual tour de force; it has properly been termed "revolutionary."[13] Left at the theoretical level, however, it need not have had the disruptive effect on Jewish communal life that it did. As much was evident from the muted reaction to the earlier writings of all the acknowledged Jewish "forerunners" of political Zionism (particulary Hess, Alkalai, Kalischer, and Pinsker). One lesson to be drawn from their experience was that the ventilation of innovative principles did not ensure that a significant number of Jews would respond to them—sympathetically or otherwise. Arguably, some allowance must be made for the passage of time;[14] still more for the pungent manner of Herzl's expression. Nevertheless, *Der Judenstaat*, as published, might have promoted nothing more than an inconsequential exchange of doctrinal set pieces: highly interesting in its own way and undoubtedly of importance to a limited circle, but essentially of little practical impact on the attitudes of most Jews toward their present and future condition. This was certainly so in Anglo-Jewry, where it was usual to observe certain formal niceties of debate. There was no linear progression from the sweet reasonableness which infused Herzl's initial reception in London to the intense personal distaste later aroused by his followers. Unless other catalysts are sought, his proposals alone do not adequately explain why all Jewish nationalists were eventually to be defined as "people with whom you never can argue & whom you never can trust," and anti-Zionists to be described as "men who have no honour or decency & must be watched at every turn."[15]

No single factor can explain why political Zionism became a cause of such friction. It was not the only, nor the first, source of tension within and across contemporary Jewish society. Modernism of various forms (a category that includes—where rele-

[13] Most recently by Harold Fisch, *The Zionist Revolution: A New Perspective* (Oxford, 1978); that, too, is the title of the Hebrew translation of David Vital's work.
[14] Hillel Halkin, "Zionism Revisited: The historic enterprise," *Commentary*, May 1973, pp. 74-77.
[15] 19 October 1921, C. Montefiore to L. Wolf, CZA, L. Wolf Papers, A77/3c; and 1 February 1918, J. Moser to C. Weizmann, Reḥovot, Weizmann Archives [hereafter WA], file 1918(2).

vant—the *haskalah*, emancipation, and the experience of migration and economic diversity) was already generating rifts in the
social and intellectual structure that characterized most medieval
communities.[16] From this perspective, Zionism did not represent
an autonomous outburst of radicalism. Rather, it was the out-
growth of contingent developments of varying importance clus-
tered around a rapidly growing—but divergent—mood of dissent.
Nevertheless, the Zionist Organisation, precisely because it was
an organization, played a seminal role in the process of change.
Inspired by Herzl's calculated theatricalism, it transformed an idea
into a movement and posited an agenda for communal action
that was as revolutionary as its ideology. It proclaimed its determination to convert Jewry to its cause, if necessary by a program
of institutional displacement; at various congresses (themselves
novel forms of Jewish association) it also established the bureaucratic machinery which potentially made such a transfer of communal authority possible. From the outset, the Zionists employed
slogans and images that deliberately created an atmosphere of
urgent clamor and thereby enhanced the immediacy of their appeal. They founded regional Zionist parties designed, not merely
to propagate the thesis of Jewish nationalism, but also to bring
into being the audience to which their appeals were addressed.
By doing all of this, they introduced a new pattern of alignment
into almost every community of the Diaspora. In Anglo-Jewry
the resultant rift was to be expressed in its most acerbic form
during the First World War.

> I should like to make clear the spirit and the purpose with
> which we approach your friends [wrote a leading local Zionist
> to a spokesman for the anti-Zionist camp]. We approach them
> as one power in Jewry addressing itself to another power in
> Jewry in the hope of securing a union of Jewish forces in this
> most critical hour of our people. We know that their coop-
> eration would be extremely useful. We know that their op-

[16] David Vital, *The Origins of Zionism* (Oxford, 1975) is essential reading; see,
too, Jacob Katz, *Tradition and Crisis* (Harvard, 1961) and *Out of the Ghetto*
(Harvard, 1968).

position would be a serious hindrance—as we are also convinced that it would be treason against the Jewish people. We are prepared to make great sacrifices in order to secure their cooperation. We are determined to go forward even without them and against them. If they stand aside it will be for the future historian of the Jewish people to pass judgment on them. If they oppose us we shall, however reluctantly, do what within us lies to destroy any authority they may claim in Jewry or beyond Jewry to speak for the Jewish people. We know we have the power to do it.[17]

So audacious was the Zionists' intention (and so conspicuous their success) that there has been a powerful tendency to select Jewish nationalists as subjects of detailed treatment, leaving their opponents in a state of oblivion. Significant gaps in the source material relating to Jewish anti-Zionism might provide one explanation. Much (although not all) of the opposition was latent and hence inarticulate, and therefore difficult to identify or analyze. But the key factor seems to be a conscious or unconscious type of Whig history. The "forces of innovation" are singled out for attention and examined with sympathy; the "forces of inertia" are neglected and their attitude hardly explored at all. This situation is to be regretted, not only because it produces a lopsided picture, but principally because it does violence to the *political* texture of the struggle between those who supported and rejected Herzl's program. An excessive concentration on the accelerators and a comparative lack of interest in the brakes have obscured the workings of the system as a whole. They have also distorted the strategies of both parties. The Zionists, after all, enthusiastically pitched themselves into a shrill contest for communal authority, and it is therefore within the context of the communal structure that their program has to be scrutinized.

At that level of analysis, the anti-Zionists would appear to dodge some of the more severe indictments regularly trundled out in Zionist demonologies. Anglo-Jewish resistance to the Zionists

---

[17] 1 December 1914, H. Sacher to L. Wolf, London, Board of Deputies of British Jews [hereafter DEPS], Zionism 1914-1916, E3/204(1).

is not necessarily to be equated with opposition to Zionism. The latter could reflect only a disagreement with a particular prognosis of the Jewish condition; the former could also entail a divergent commitment to the need for changes in the management of Jewish affairs. Programmatically, however, the two could converge. Anti-Zionism yoked together several competing, and even radically opposed, views of the meaning of the Jewish experience. What united its exponents, albeit in an uneasy and uncoordinated fashion, was their shared antagonism to the prospect of a Zionist domination over the community's affairs. Conversely, the Zionists often managed to overcome their own ideological and personal differences by clinging to the hope that they were on the way to attaining commanding communal authority. The tussle between the two camps and their respective fellow travellers was thus not always over categorical principles. The movement of events after 1897 was also influenced by the pragmatic attempts of the protagonists to reconcile their ideological rhetoric with their communal ambitions.

With such considerations in mind, the present study will attempt to serve three main purposes. The first, and most straightforward, is to chronicle the respective fortunes of the Anglo-Jewish Zionists and their opponents during the embryonic period of the movement. In so doing it will, secondly, aim to identify the various interests and groups within the community which chose either to facilitate or to obstruct the growth of political Zionism. Finally, and perhaps most important of all, it will attempt an analysis of the principal issues that the two sides considered to be at stake. These, we will suggest, were bifurcate. The Jews of Britain, as of other communities, did conduct several fundamental debates on the substantive merits of Herzl's thesis (which form the subject of the longest chapter in the present book). But such ideologically relevant dialogues were often influenced—sometimes decisively—by their perceived relevance to a simultaneous struggle for influence and prestige within the community at large. Hence, the study of Zionism in Anglo-Jewry is to some extent a study of the deployment of political argument and of political agitation within a communal setting of fissiparous tensions and shifting alliances.

The concentration on the intra-Jewish dynamics of the debate is, then, deliberate; and it has dictated the choice of terminal dates for this essay. Before the advent of political Zionism, the notion of Jewish nationalism played only a peripheral role in the affairs of Anglo-Jewry. Its advocates were few; their program was indeterminate. This was as true of their attitude toward their own society as of their policy with regard to Palestinian settlement. The Chovevei Zion Association did not formulate a thoroughgoing strategy of communal action; neither did it develop a systematic structure of social and political analysis which might have galvanized others into doing so. The reasons lie in the intentionally restricted perspectives of the Association's leadership. Not even at the height of their influence, in the mid-1890s, did the members of the Headquarters Tent project the image of men in possesssion of a comprehensive and independent view on those issues that were of major concern to the politically articulate sections of the community at large. They seemed to be curiously detached from several of the organic tensions which, by the end of the nineteenth century, were clearly affecting the quiescence of Anglo-Jewish life.[18] That, at least, was the contemporary impression fostered by an analysis of the composition of the Association's membership. Ḥibat Ẓion did attract some representatives of the native community's burgeoning middle class who had taken root in Hampstead and Bayswater: Joseph Prag, a pipe manufacturer who was elected vice-chief of the Association in 1892 is one example; Herbert Bentwich, a lawyer of whom considerably more will be heard, is another. But the organization did

[18] The standard work on the Anglo-Jewish community of the period remains Vivian D. Lipman, *Social History of the Jews in England, 1850-1950* (London, 1954); see too Israel Finestein's articles, "The New Community, 1880-1915," in *Three Centuries of Anglo-Jewish History*, ed. Vivian D. Lipman (London, 1961) and "The Lay Leadership of the United Synagogue since 1870" in *A Century of Anglo-Jewish Life*, ed. Salmond S. Levin (London, 1970). Supplementary family histories in Chaim Bermant, *The Cousinhood* (London, 1971). For the earlier community, Todd M. Endelman, *The Jews of Georgian England, 1714-1830* (Philadelphia, 1979).

not respond to the growing discrepancy between the professional, political, and personal interests of men of this type and those of the "Grand Dukes" of the City. Furthermore, the Chovevei Zion Association's leadership was entirely London-oriented. Its provincial constituency, although not insignificant, did not seem to exert an influence commensurate with the protean diversity of communal life in the northern and western parts of the country.[19] Most important of all, the Chovevei Zion did not offer a distinctive—or particularly imaginative—method of coping with the unprecedented rate of Jewish immigration to Britain from eastern Europe. Between 1880 and 1914 almost 150,000 Jews arrived from the Continent (approximately two-thirds before the passage of the Aliens Act in 1905); largely as a result of this influx, and of the high birthrate of the new arrivals, the existing Anglo-Jewish population of some 60,000 souls quintupled, with specifically immigrant Jewish quarters growing up in the East End of London and several provincial cities and towns. Long before the outbreak of World War I, these phenomena had begun to exert obvious strains on the entire cultural, social, and institutional fabric of the community; they had also provoked sporadic outbursts of anti-Semitism.[20] At a very shallow level, the Chovevei Zion did claim to constitute a bridge between Anglo-Jewry's two communities—the native and the immigrant.[21] But that was about all. As a body, the Association provided no recognizable alternative to the attitude of ambivalence habitually displayed toward the recent arrivals by the indigents; on the emergence of what was euphemistically termed anti-alienism in the press and at Westminster, its official pronouncements maintained an embarrassed silence.

[19] E.g., "The Manchester Questions," *Palestina* 5 (October 1893): 8-11.

[20] The authoritative and indispensable work on the immigrant is Lloyd P. Gartner, *The Jewish Immigrant in England 1870-1914*, 2nd ed. (London, 1973). On reactions to immigration see John A. Garrard, *The English and Immigration, 1880-1910* (London, 1971); Bernard Gainer, *The Alien Invasion: The Origins of the Aliens Act of 1905* (London, 1972), and Steven Bayme, "Jewish Leadership and Anti-Semitism in Britain, 1898-1918" (Ph.D. dissertation, Columbia University, 1977).

[21] Orren, *Ḥibat-Ẓion*, pp. 67-70.

Introduction

Altogether, the Chovevei Zion Association was never more than an insignificant—and potentially evanescent—cog in the far larger wheel of multifarious philanthropic, cultural, synagogal, and representative institutions with which the community abounded. The occasional activities of its members did not impinge upon proceedings at the councils of the United Synagogue, the Sephardi Congregation, the West London Synagogue of Reform Jews, or even the Federation of Synagogues where Maccoby was employed as an itinerant preacher.[22] Neither did their marginal subventions to small colonies in Palestine affect the preference of the Jewish Board of Guardians (founded in 1859) and the Russo-Jewish Committee (founded in 1891) for the alternative policies of outdoor relief for the immigrants or, more radically, of repatriating them to their eastern European countries of origin. Above all, the pale sentimentality of the Chovevei Zion did not intrude upon the sober deliberations of the Board of Deputies and the Anglo-Jewish Association. The former (founded as the London Committee of the Deputies of the British Jews in 1760, when Sephardim and Ashkenazim decided to repair the anomaly of their separate deputations to congratulate King George III on his accession) remained the community's only "parliament" of congregations; as such, it possessed a virtually exclusive commission to tackle the day-to-day issues of Anglo-Jewry's relations with its gentile environment. The Anglo-Jewish Association (founded in 1871 when, as a result of the Franco-Prussian War, the Alliance Israelite Universelle was in a state of temporary eclipse) similarly retained its position as the principal channel of

[22] Cecil Roth, *The Federation of Synagogues. A Record of Twenty-five Years, 1912-1937* (London, 1937), pp. 7-8. For the institutional structure of Anglo-Jewry see, in general, Maurice Freedman, ed., *A Minority in Britain* (London, 1955), and Vivian D. Lipman, "Synagogal Organisation in Anglo-Jewry," *Jewish Journal of Sociology* 1 (1959):80-93. Among the specific studies are: Vivian D. Lipman, *A Century of Social Service, 1859-1959: The History of the Jewish Board of Guardians* (London, 1959); Bernard Homa, *A Fortress in Anglo-Jewry* (London, 1953); Albert M. H. Hyamson, *The Sephardim of England* (London, 1951); and Aubrey Newman, *The United Synagogue, 1870-1970* (London, 1976). Full lists of individual institutions are provided in the *Jewish Year Book*, which began to appear in 1896.

political and educational aid to distressed Jewish communities overseas. This ad hoc collection of Anglo-Jewry's most prominent philanthropists evinced no inclination to relinquish its paternalistic hold on the community's foreign policy to the benefit of any other organization. On the contrary, representatives of both the Board of Deputies and the AJA regularly took council in the Conjoint Foreign Committee, which occupied a position roughly corresponding to that of a communal privy council—with the Rothschilds, who rarely attended any of these bodies, playing the role of a royal family. Whatever individual Chovevei Zionists may have thought of this institutional structure, they made no attempts to pose as the united critics of the existing arrangement, still less as the corporate vehicle of communal change. The majority did not challenge the prerogatives of the older organizations (even when they affected activities in *Erez Yisrael*[23]); we have no evidence of a concerted effort to form a distinct party within them.

This was no longer the case in 1920. By then, the English Zionist Federation was a cornucopia of political, cultural, and financial activity; it thus constituted, in its own right, one of Anglo-Jewry's most important communal organizations. Its leadership avowedly pursued communal power and its program insistently advocated changes in the form and structure of communal government. As will be seen, the Zionists were not the only group within Anglo-Jewry to strive for such ends; neither were they necessarily the most influential to do so. In many ways, it will be argued, Herzl's successors were not very much closer to a "conquest" of this community in 1920 than his supporters had been a quarter of a century earlier. Nevertheless, 1920 does represent a turning point, principally because it was in that year that the representatives of the major powers assembled at San Remo formally recognized Great Britain's position as the mandatory

---

[23] Report of a speech by Goldsmid to members of the Chovevei Zion in *The Jewish Chronicle* [hereafter *JC*], 6 October 1893, p. 13. *The Jewish Chronicle*, for all its limitations and biases, is an indispensable source for communal history throughout this period. See [Cecil Roth] *The Jewish Chronicle, 1841-1941* (London, 1941), p. 115.

authority in Palestine. Justifiably proclaimed a "great victory" for political Zionism,[24] that treaty culminated one phase of diligent diplomatic endeavor and ushered in another. Simultaneously, and consequently, it altered the dimensions of various Anglo-Jewish attitudes toward the movement. After San Remo, Zionist ambitions and Zionism's progress were no longer subjects of predominantly insular concern. They manifestly became (as, indeed, Herzl had originally intended them to become) issues of high policy—and ultimately of compelling international attention. The change was one of content as well as of context. As such, it necessitated a shift in the axes of communal concern and brought about a realignment of the forces that had hitherto helped to shape Zionist fortunes within Anglo-Jewry.

[24] Christopher Sykes, *Cross Roads to Israel* (London, 1965), p. 47.

PART ONE

Opening Moves,
1895-1904

1

The Foundation of the
English Zionist Federation, 1895-1899

THE INITIAL RECEPTION which the Anglo-Jewish community accorded to Herzl provided little inkling of the storm of opposition that the man and his ideas were later to arouse. During his first visit to the country in November 1895 he was neither shunned nor silenced; rather, he was received with courtesy and his proposals given an attentive hearing. For that, much of the credit must go to Israel Zangwill, the Anglo-Jewish author to whom he came armed only with a brief letter of introduction from their mutual friend in Paris, Max Nordau. Considering their differences, Herzl and Zangwill got off to a remarkably good start. Impressively handsome, Herzl generated an aura of refined civility and intense seriousness. That was not at all Zangwill's manner. Physically ungainly, he affected a witty rather than a profound style, his contrived idiosyncracy contrasting markedly with Herzl's cultivated Central European charm. But Zangwill did possess one crucial attribute. Whereas Herzl was a newcomer to the stratified labyrinth of intra-Jewish politics, Zangwill knew the territory intimately. He had written on the subject extensively, and had taken advantage of his resultant fame to widen the arc of his acquaintances within Anglo-Jewry. His contacts were immediately placed at Herzl's disposal. After hearing one brief summary of the idea of a Jews' state, Zangwill initiated a chain of interviews that introduced his unexpected visitor to some of the most eminent men in the community.

Despite the inadequacies of Herzl's English (much of the conversation with Zangwill was conducted in pidgin French), little more was needed. His urbanity and elegance, together with his status as a leading journalist on the Viennese *Neue Freie Presse*, eased his passage through the most exclusive of social circles. In quick succession he conferred with Rev. Simeon Singer, Chief Rabbi Hermann Adler, Asher Myers (the highly influential editor of the *Jewish Chronicle*) and Lt. (soon to be Col.) Albert Goldsmid. Meanwhile, and again through Zangwill's good offices, Herzl was also invited to lay his views before the prestigious Maccabean Club, whose members included many of Anglo-Jewry's leading artists, intellectuals, and professional men. Thereafter, as Herzl himself had envisaged, one thing led to another. The Maccabeans conferred upon him honorary membership of their society; Adler sent him to the House of Commons to meet Sir Samuel Montagu, and Myers commissioned a synopsis of Herzl's scheme for publication in his newspaper. Altogether, as Herzl recorded in his diary, it was not an unsatisfactory return for a trip that had lasted just one week.[1]

What is more, these bridgeheads were consolidated and expanded during Herzl's second visit to London the following July. By then, he had already begun to envision a possible community of interest between World Jewry and Great Britain; he had also made the first of his journeys to Constantinople and felt that he had some progress to report. Furthermore, he had begun to draft an agenda for an elitist "Society of Jews," whose task would be to draw up detailed plans for the Jews' state. Herzl was sure that in Anglo-Jewry he could identify men with the necessary talent for that purpose; all he had to do was approach them and enlist their support. Once again, therefore, he had an after-dinner session with the Maccabeans and what he considered to be "serious discussions" with Singer and Goldsmid. He also widened the circle of his personal acquaintances. He was introduced to Frederic Mocatta, a bullion merchant and one of the most generous and cultured philanthropists in the community; he strolled along

[1] *The Complete Diaries of Theodor Herzl*, ed. Raphael Patai, trans. Harry Zohn, 5 vols. (New York, 1960), 1:276-84.

Park Lane with Claude Montefiore, Anglo-Jewry's most venerated theologian. He was also interviewed for the *Daily Graphic* by Lucien Wolf, the journalist and historian, who was generally regarded as the community's oracle on diplomatic affairs. Furthermore, before his brief visit was over (this, too, lasted only ten days), Herzl had approached two sets of wider audiences. One was the immigrant community, several thousand of whose members crowded into the Jewish Working Men's Club to hear him speak on the afternoon of Sunday, 13 July 1896. The other was the Headquarters Tent of the Chovevei Zion Association, whose meeting he attended on the evening of the 14th. At the former he was demonstratively joined by Ḥakham Moses Gaster; after the latter he was contacted, more furtively, by Ephraim Ish-Kishor and Jacob de Haas, both members of the militant B'nei Zion group in the East End.[2]

But the impact that Herzl thus appears to have made on the community is somewhat misleading. Impressive though the range of his initial contacts undoubtedly was, he did not take the community by storm. Posthumous panegyrics, which retrospectively spoke of Herzl's "invasion of England," must be compared with Zangwill's more immediate and more sober assessment. Herzl's ideas had initially "startled" the community, he wrote in September 1896, but it had all been something of a seven-day wonder which "has rather simmered down now."[3] Admittedly, the Jews of Whitechapel did seem to be loudly enthusiastic, their encouragement suggesting possibilities for popular action which Herzl was quick to appreciate and tempted to exploit. Yet, as he himself realized, the sympathies of the immigrant masses were notoriously fickle and inchoate. Their support was probably less congenial to Herzl personally than that of the recognizably Anglicized leadership; in practical terms it was certainly less valuable. Herzl had

[2] Ibid., pp. 406-22, and 11 July 1896, Herzl to Gaster, in *Igrot Herzl*, ed. Alex Bein et al., 3 vols. (Tel Aviv, 1958), 1:123.

[3] 2 September 1896, Zangwill to M. D. Eder, in *Anglo-Jewish Letters, 1158-1917*, ed. Cecil Roth (London, 1938), p. 381; compare Louis Zangwill, "Herzl Invades England," in *Theodor Herzl, A Memorial*, ed. Meyer Weisgal (New York, 1929), pp. 41-43.

initially approached the grandees of London in November 1895, and it was their response to his project that he was most anxious to test in July 1896. But it was precisely at this level that he could make least progress. The prominent clerics and laymen of late Victorian Anglo-Jewry were rarely inclined to express hasty and extreme opinions; they usually preferred circumspection and restraint. Where specifically Jewish issues were concerned, they were especially prone to pursue a moderate and tentative policy. Sensible palliatives, broached during the course of diplomatic approaches to the Government through the Anglo-Jewish Association, were considered to be the most effective and proper means of dealing with "The Jewish Question"; grandiose panaceas, proclaimed at mass meetings (particularly when they concerned the turbulent Middle East) were thought to be alien to Jewish interests in particular and to the modulated tenor of British political life in general. After 1893, the leaders of the Chovevei Zion Association had avoided flamboyant displays; even so, as they informed Herzl, they had experienced considerable difficulty in getting people "even to hear the name of Palestine."[4]

Herzl, for all his urgency, could hardly have hoped to do much better. On the contrary, the very energy with which he attempted to communicate the magnitude of the Jewish problem—and the radical nature of his own solution—threatened to be counter-productive. It undermined his pose as a down-to-earth man of affairs and encouraged the impression that he was a romantic visionary. As late as August 1898, at least one lady of the community implored her husband: "Do not become a Herzlite. His motives may be of the best, but I fear he is not practical and is decidedly premature."[5] First impressions had been of a similar kind. Even Goldsmid, who had as good a claim as any to be regarded as an eccentric, had wondered whether Herzl possessed "sufficient stability" to serve the Jewish cause; Zangwill, who was from the first warned by Nordau of his visitor's "somewhat en-

[4] 7 July 1896, J. Prag to Herzl, Jerusalem, CZA, T. Herzl Papers, H VIII 658.

[5] August 1898, Mrs. Bentwich to H. Bentwich, quoted in Norman Bentwich and Margery Bentwich, *Herbert Bentwich: The Pilgrim Father* (Jerusalem, 1940), pp. 129-30.

thusiastic mind," later claimed to have been always frightened by his "fanatical passions." Mocatta seems to have echoed a broadly shared feeling: Herzl, he confided to Lucien Wolf, was undoubtedly "sincere and devoted," but nevertheless "seemed rather too much in a hurry to commit us to an expression of opinion."[6]

Hesitancy, rather than opposition, was thus the dominant tone of the response that the community, at its higher levels, evinced toward political Zionism. Reserve, the reaction that Herzl found most disconcerting, was that which he most often encountered. A minor but nevertheless indicative instance was provided by his reception at the Maccabeans. His first appearance, hastily arranged two days after Herzl's first arrival in the country in November 1895, was neither well-attended nor widely noted. Goldsmid, for instance, did not turn up; the *Jewish Chronicle* carried no report of the meeting; and Solomon J. Solomon (the current president of the club) had to promise that his members would undoubtedly receive Herzl "more fittingly" were he to inform them "in good time" of his next visit.[7] The second meeting, held in July 1896 in the French Room of the St. James Restaurant, Piccadilly, was indeed an altogether more august occasion. Speaking in carefully rehearsed English, Herzl delivered a well-pitched address, which contained a detailed exposition of his original plans and a suggestive hint of his interim progress in Constantinople. The subsequent debate (much of which was conducted in French and German) was, by most accounts, animated, prolonged, and wide-ranging. Admittedly, the evening was not an unqualified success. Herzl's ambitions were elegantly punctured by Zangwill's carefully constructed witticisms and somewhat trimmed by Prag's insistence on the superior merits of the old, cautious policy of gradual Jewish settlement in Palestine. On

---

[6] 1 December 1895, Goldsmid to Hirsch, private, London, Mocatta Library, University College, S. A. Hirsch Papers, AJ/28. 13 July 1906, Zangwill to C. Salaman, CZA, Ito files, A36/15a. Claude Montefiore, "A Diehard's Confession," in *Some Recollections of Claude Goldsmid Montefiore, 1858-1938*, by Lucy Cohen (London, 1940), pp. 226-27.

[7] 9 March 1896, Solomon to Herzl, CZA, Herzl Papers, H VIII 714.

balance, the response was more critical than favorable; according to the *Jewish Chronicle* fifteen Maccabeans spoke from the floor, of whom only three gave Herzl's scheme their unqualified support. Nevertheless, Herzl could be excused for his subsequent sense of satisfaction. After all, the Maccabeans had accepted one sugges- tion, moved by Lucien Wolf, that they establish a committee of inquiry; they had also noted another, moved by Herbert Bent- wich, that they organize a "Pilgrimage" in order to take a closer look at Palestine.[8]

But Herzl had misinterpreted the mood of the Maccabeans; his hopes that the Pilgrimage would advance the cause of political Zionism in England were particularly misplaced. Despite adequate publicity, the project evoked scant response, and some ridicule.[9] Ultimately, only twenty persons set out for Palestine in the spring of 1897, and of these only five were Maccabeans. Zangwill came (perhaps in order to visit his aged father in Jerusalem); so too did S. L. Bensusan (proprieter of the *Jewish World*) and Rev. George Emanuel, the minister of the Birmingham Hebrew Con- gregation. But, despite Bentwich's personal exhortations, Lucien Wolf declined to participate, as did such other prospective can- didates as Goldsmid and Gaster, and such respected Jewish ac- ademics as Solomon Schechter (reader in Rabbinics at Cambridge since 1892) and Israel Abrahams (who was to succeed Schechter when the latter departed for New York in 1902). Bentwich him- self tried to put a good face on things; these prominent person- alities might agree to lead subsequent pilgrimages. Meanwhile, there was something to be said for working as intensively as possible with the present band of stalwarts who could in turn exercise an influence on a larger number of the Maccabeans.[10]

[8] De Haas's subsequent recollection of the "childish" proceedings and "petty" questions ("Reminiscences of Zionism in England," p. ix, in CZA, J. de Haas Papers, A 224/3), must be compared with the fuller, and more immediate, ac- counts in *JC*, 10 July 1896, pp. 8-11; and Herzl's *Diaries*, 1:409-10.

[9] Letters to editor, *JC*, 26 March 1897, p. 10 and 9 April 1897, p. 10.

[10] 15 March 1897, Bentwich to Gaster, London, Mocatta Library, M. Gaster Papers. Bentwich's "Diary of the Maccabeans' Pilgrimage to Palestine," entry for 11 April, 1897, in CZA, H. Bentwich Papers, A 100/2, pp. 35-36. For an account of the Pilgrimage see Bentwich and Bentwich, *Herbert Bentwich*, pp. 110-17.

This, too, proved impossible. The Maccabeans had begun to regret their support for the Herzlian aspects of the Pilgrimage even before its departure. Their attitude had inspired Bentwich's public denial of the suggestion that the venture was in any way designed to serve the "political objectives" that Herzl had in mind. Replying to the latter's complaint, Bentwich pointed out:

> You will appreciate even more the necessity of the step I took when I tell you that at the Annual General Meeting of the Maccabeans held last Sunday a very innocent reference to the introduction of your famous scheme here by the Society was compelled to be modified in deference to the views of some of the old fashioned timid members, who refused to associate the Society in any way with your designs, and my Pilgrimage was assailed because it appeared in juxtaposition to the reference.[11]

The Maccabeans did subsequently host a dinner for the pilgrims on their return; but they did not implement the suggestion that they establish a "Maccabean Tent" of the Chovevei Zion Association. Neither did they accept the recommendation that the initiative be repeated and further trips to Palestine be organized under their auspices. Most of them seem to have found the entire idea, accompanied as it was by a fanfare of Zionist publicity, distasteful and best forgotten. They gave a far more enthusiastic and well-attended reception to Israel Abrahams when some twelve months later he returned from a journey to Palestine which, he stressed, had been "a private and personal affair." By 1902 they had virtually banned all mention of the topic at future meetings.[12]

The pattern thus set was emulated elsewhere; none of the other cultural societies of this class of Anglo-Jewry gave any sign of wishing to initiate the "earnest discussion" which Herzl had originally sought. Instead, as at the Association of Jewish Literary

[11] 25 March 1897, Bentwich to Herzl, CZA, Herzl Papers, H VIII 67. In the same letter, Bentwich refused to give "any pledge" as to his own attendance at the first Zionist Congress.

[12] The pilgrims' motion, dated 12 May 1897, in CZA, Files of the Chovevei Zion Association, A2/13; see also JC, 17 June 1898, pp. 12-13; and Maurice Wohlgelernter, *Israel Zangwill: A Study* (New York, 1964), p. 125.

Societies, Zionism was considered to be a subject of "too limited interest" to warrant a lecture.[13] In general, the upper classes of the community received Herzl's proposals in studied silence. When first published in the *Jewish Chronicle* in January 1896, his "Solution to the Jewish Problem" provoked only three letters to the editor (two of which were irrelevant). Sales of *The Jewish State*, issued in translation later that year, remained "very meager" as late as 1898. In reply to Herzl's anxious enquiries, the publisher reported that "Very few booksellers would take any copies . . . the regular Jewish booksellers simply refused to have anything to do with it."[14] Representatives of the non-Jewish press did ask Herzl for an interview; some even described the first Zionist Congress of 1897 as a "historical event."[15] Furthermore, individual gentiles in that year expected the Jews (of Bayswater and Hampstead, no less) to be "busy winding up [their] affairs" in preparation for their departure for Palestine.[16] The "prominent Jews" to whom some newspaper reporters turned, however, were far more hesitant. Several simply "refused to be drawn" on the entire question of Zionism; others felt that the subject had already been accorded all the attention it deserved. Asher Myers, having provided Zionism with an initial platform, soon felt that the importance of "local items" exceeded the necessity to publish Herzl's replies to his Continental critics. Even Zangwill, having laid about him with several cynical asides and mordant comments, in 1898 admitted that he really had nothing more to say on the topic.[17]

[13] *JC*, 18 July 1902, pp. 14-15. 7 August 1902, I. Abrahams to Zangwill; CZA, I.Zangwill Papers, A120/53.

[14] The detailed balance sheet showed that of the 500 copies printed, only 200 had been sold. Most of the remainder were lying about in various warehouses. 30 June 1896, D. Nutt to Miss Sylvie d'Avigdor and 21 April 1898, D. Nutt to Herzl, CZA, Herzl Papers, H VIII 618. Herzl's pamphlet was not reprinted in Britain until 1917, although the *Jewish Chronicle*'s special supplement on the Basle Congress soon became a collector's item, "double price," being paid for "unsoiled copies." *JC*, 19 November 1897, p. 17.

[15] Benjamin Jaffe, "The British Press and Zionism in Herzl's Time," *Transactions of the Jewish Historical Society of England* [hereafter *TJHSE*] 24 (1975): 89-100.

[16] 5 October 1897, Mrs. N. L. Joseph to Miss Bentwich, CZA, H. Bentwich Papers, A100/7a.

[17] 27 April 1897, Myers to Herzl, CZA, Herzl Papers, H VIII 315; and 8

A MASS MEETING

of EAST END JEWS will be held

ON SUNDAY JULY 12th 1896 AT 6 P.M.

— AT THE —

JEWISH WORKINGMEN'S CLUB, Gt. ALIE STREET, E.

to welcome

DR. THEODORE HERZL.

THE REV. DR. M. GASTER WILL PRESIDE.

M. EPSTEIN, Hon. Sec. of Reception Committee

א מאסס מיטינג

ווערד געהאלטען ווען אין דיא

דזוא"ש ווארפינגמענס קלוב, גרייט עלי סט. איסט

צו ווילקאממען דעם גרויסען וועלטבעריהמטען אידישען נאסט

דיא קטער הערצל

רעדאקטאר פון דיא גרויסע דייטשע ציטונג "נייע פרייע פרעססע" פון ווין
פערדאנסקי מאן דעם געניאלען ווערק, דיא אידישע מדינה.

דיזען זאנטאג דען 12-טען דזולי אום 6 אוהר אבענד

דאקטאר הערצל קומט יעצט פון קאנסטאנטינאפל וואו ער האט געהאט אן
אוידיענץ ביים סולטאן וועגען אפקויפען פאלעסטינא פאר דיא אידען. ער האט
אויך דאזו בעקומען דיא צושטימונג פון פיעלע גרויסע אייראפעישע סיניסטארין
דיעזער נדיבער מאן וועט ערשיינען זאמטאג אין חואיש ווארקינגמענס קלוב און
וועט שפרעכען איבער זיינע וויכטיגע ארבייטם און שמרעבונג פירים אייריש פאלק

רעוו. דר. מ. גאסטער וועם זיין אין דיא משעהר.

דר. הערצל וועט שפרעכען אין ענגליש און דייטש.

גרויסע און אבגעזעהענע מעננער פון אונזערע ענגלישע ברידער וועלען קומען צום מיטינג און
מאנכע פון דיא וועם שפרעכען, מערוואוסט גיט דיא נעלעגענהייט צו הערן דיזען גרויסען מאן

הדוקטריא פון א.ח. ראבביניאוויטש, 64 היא סטריט, וויטשעפעל.

1. Handbill advertising Herzl's first public appearance in London,
1896. The Yiddish text adds: "Dr. Herzl has just come from
Constantinople where he had an audience with the Sultan
regarding the purchase of Palestine for the Jews. He has also
received the approval of great European ministers. . . . Great
and illustrious personages from among our English brethren
will attend the meeting and some of them will speak."

2. Col. A.E.W. Goldsmid (c. 1900).

3. Herzl with delegates to the first English Zionist Federation Conference, London, June 1899. Herzl is standing in the third row, tenth from the right. To his right are Gaster, Bentwich, and Greenberg.

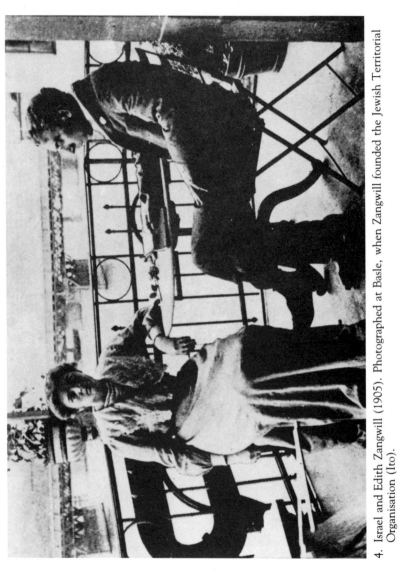

4. Israel and Edith Zangwill (1905). Photographed at Basle, when Zangwill founded the Jewish Territorial Organisation (Ito).

For some years thereafter, political Zionism retained the appearance of a fringe movement of Anglo-Jewry. Eleven Jews from Britain did participate in the first Zionist Congress, but, on their own admission, they "were not truly representatives of the Community."[18] Goldsmid and Singer, for instance, were notable by their absence (especially since they had received personal invitations from Herzl). Zangwill, who was present, no less demonstratively "sat upon the last seat in the Hall, merely an observer."[19] Altogether, the general reaction was tepid. Those members of the community who claimed to have "read the Basle proceedings with attention," considered that the congress had been an uninspiring affair. "The papers were all of a retrospective character and not one of them gave a glimpse of what the new State is to be like."[20] Even the fourth Congress, held in London in 1900, was admitted to be a failure; its location did little to make the movement as a whole more palatable to Anglo-Jewry.[21] Its opponents had already reached the logical conclusion that it would soon die of neglect. Singer, whose increasingly frequent derogatory references to Herzl's "noisy" supporters themselves reflected a wider communal feeling of distaste, had at an early stage advised that the Zionists be left "to prepare their own downfall." All the community had to do was sit tight and "await

---

February 1898, Zangwill to Hirsch, CZA, Files of Chovevei Zion Association, A2/86.

[18] See the account of S. B. Rubinstein's speech in Norman Bentwich, *Early English Zionists* (Tel Aviv, 1940); and compare *Stenographisches Protokoll der Verhandlungen des I. Zionisten-Congresses* (Vienna, 1897), pp. 45, 189. On attendance at the first Congress see Haiyim Orlan, "The Participants in the First Zionist Congress," *Herzl Year Book* 6 (1965):138; and for reports of the Anglo-Jewish delegation, *Jewish World*, 27 September 1897, pp. 4-5; and Ephraim Ish-Kishor, "Ait Alot ha-Shahar," in *Sefer Ha-Kongress*, ed. Leib Yaffe (Jerusalem, 1922), p. 98.

[19] Recalled by R. Gottheil in 17 November 1926 to L. Wolf, New York, YIVO Institute, David Mowshowitch Collection of Lucien Wolf Papers, folder 2, no. 85. On Goldsmid and Singer, see Herzl's invitations in *Igrot*, 1:240-42, 271, and 286-87.

[20] 7 September 1897, J. M. Levy to Gaster, CZA, Gaster Papers, A203/104.

[21] Note Weizmann's later criticisms in *Trial and Error* (London, 1949), p. 78.

events."[22] There was certainly no reason for recognized leaders of Anglo-Jewry to grace Zionists platforms. One standard excuse for declining to do so was that the Jewish people could not afford "a luxury of sentiment."[23] Another was the nationalists' apparently ambivalent attitude toward their own enterprise. N. S. Joseph (Chief Rabbi Adler's brother-in-law) gave voice to this particular taunt as early as 1899. "I shall believe in the sincerity of the leaders of this noisy movement when I see them leave their pleasant homes and profitable pursuits and make for themselves new homes in that Palestine which they profess to love so dearly." Meanwhile, he had decided to burn his invitation to a Zionist gathering. "It spluttered and flared and ended in smoke. So will end the Zionist movement."[24]

THE CHOVEVEI ZION ASSOCIATION AND POLITICAL ZIONISM, 1897-1902

One Anglo-Jewish body which could not permit itself the indulgence of reticence was, of course, the Chovevei Zion Association. Already committed to one program of Jewish self-help, the members of this organization felt no compulsion to adopt the defense mechanism of procrastination and indifference with regard to another. Many immediately recognized the kinship between Herzl's diagnosis of the Jewish predicament and their own. The clarity and strength with which he advocated his ideas was undoubtedly novel, but, in essence, they felt that he was only articulating conclusions toward which they had been themselves groping. If anything, Herzl's own ideas could be sharpened and his doctrinal errors corrected. One point in his scheme which demanded immediate clarification concerned the location of the Jews' state. Leaders of the Chovevei Zion were insistent that a Jewish haven could be established only in Palestine; Herzl's initial readiness to consider an alternative site therefore had to be quashed.

[22] 3 April 1899, Singer to Hirsch, private, CZA, Files of Chovevei Zion Association, A2/106/33.
[23] See, e.g., 18 April 1905, L. Magnus to Gaster, CZA, Gaster Papers, A203/137.
[24] 25 June 1899, Joseph to H. Bentwich, CZA, Bentwich Papers, A100/7a.

Ultimately, Dr. S. A. Hirsch (the secretary of the Chovevei Zion Association in England) felt this point important enough to warrant an official memorandum to the Zionist Actions Committee. Goldsmid, less formally, had throughout taken the same line. From the first he urged Herzl to exploit the "powerful lever of sentiment" provided by the unique ties that bound the House of Israel to its ancient homeland. Emphasizing the difference between a national idea and The National Ideal, he advocated that Herzl stress what was particularly Jewish about Zionism. "We have no need to copy modern Republics of yesterday's growth."[25]

That point apart, however, agreement seemed both possible and desirable. Initially, none of the leaders of the Chovevei Zion Association seem to have sensed Herzl's determination to play a wholly idiosyncratic role; in general, he was welcomed as a valuable recruit, whose felicity of expression could be put to good account on behalf of their movement. Typically, Hirsch was in 1896 instructed to ensure a good muster of his members for Herzl's second address to the Maccabeans since it might provide a good opportunity "to enlist support for the Chovevei Zion."[26] Subsequently, he readily echoed Herzl's calls for the wide diffusion of the national idea; less publicly, he also conceded the Zionist point that the establishment of individual settlements in Palestine had ultimately to serve a wider, avowedly political, purpose.[27] Goldsmid, with greater dispatch, had already proved far more forthright. Within three days of meeting Herzl for the first time he wrote: "As regards his idea of a Jewish State, I am as you are aware entirely of his opinion that the Jewish question will never be settled until one is established."[28]

---

[25] 13 March 1896, Goldsmid to Hirsch, Mocatta Library, Hirsch Papers, AJ/28. 8 August 1897, Goldsmid to Herzl, CZA, Herzl Papers, H VIII 285a. JC, 5 August 1898, p. 6. Also 28 January 1898, Hirsch to Herzl, CZA, Files of Chovevei Zion Association, A2/8.

[26] 26 June 1896, Goldsmid to Hirsch, Mocatta Library, Hirsch Papers, AJ/28.

[27] See his address "Israel: A Nation" (1898), in Samuel A. Hirsch, *A Book of Essays* (London, 1905), pp. 151-66; and 19 December 1895, Hirsch to Bodenheimer, CZA, Files of Chovevei Zion Association, A2/8.

[28] 1 December 1895, Goldsmid to Hirsch, Mocatta Library, Hirsch Papers, AJ/28.

This degree of affinity was not long sustained. Goldsmid was soon put out by Herzl's persistent criticisms of the Chovevei Zion's efforts at "infiltration" into Palestine and his public disparagement of their "puny" colonies there. Herzl's refusal to be dissuaded in July 1896 from addressing the mass meeting in the East End (which Goldsmid did not attend) seems to have contributed to his cool reception at the subsequent meeting of the Headquarters Tent and to the clipped manner of his dismissal ("Goodbye, Dr. Herzl"). For his part, Herzl was in August 1896 enraged by what he considered to be Goldsmid's "treacherous" refusal to commend him to Baron Edmond de Rothschild.[29] Thus, notwithstanding some early indications that the Chovevei Zion Association might adopt a singularly sympathetic attitude toward political Zionism, its leaders appeared to be falling into step with the more implacable of Herzl's Anglo-Jewish opponents. That, even while doing so, they continued to protest their attachment to Zion, lends their response its particular interest. Their persistent proclamations of fidelity to their original principles appear to have been delivered with sincere consideration. Unlike many members of the community, the leaders of the Chovevei Zion Association were at once powerfully attracted and repelled by Herzl's program. They did not make their choice without a considerable degree of widely publicized discomfort.

At issue, in the first instance, was a different idea of what ought to constitute the immediate purpose of Zionist activity. The Chovevei Zion did not doubt that for Herzl to emphasize the political nature of Jewish aspirations in Palestine would be "useful in its way. This appeals to the imagination of the masses and raises enthusiasm." But, in their view, the method was fraught with the danger of proving counterproductive. Recent Ottoman restrictions on the existing colonists in Palestine had already provided one indication of how this might be so (although hardly to the extent which Joseph Prag later maintained when complaining: "Everything was going on swimmingly until the arrival

[29] 28 August 1896, Herzl to Goldsmid, in *Igrot*, 1:140-141.

of Dr. Herzl on the scene")[30]. No less daunting, potentially, were the effects that Herzl's insistence on a loud publicity campaign might have on the Jewish public. The devotees, among whom the Chovevei Zion unquestionably included themselves, could of course be relied upon to give Zionism their unwavering support —but were consequently in no need of revivalist propaganda. If a wider audience were to be reached, a more circuitous route might be more effective. Basically this was because, in Goldsmid's words, "the Ideal was a high one and not immediately obtainable." In the necessary absence of quick results, popular support might, as Hirsch put it, "fizzle out" as quickly as Herzl could raise it to "fever heat" and thus leave the Zionist cause poorer than ever. Surely all true lovers of Zion would do far better to control their tendency toward high-minded theory and revert to the solid, practical program that had already won the favor of such a wealthy and influential body as the Ica. The "surest and safest" prescription was to buy up new tracts of land, "get fresh labourers who can filter into the country," and—above all else—generally adopt a lower profile and more moderate tone. Herzl's refusal to accept this advice, and his apparent inability to overcome what the Chovevei Zion regarded as his first flush of enthusiasm, accounted for the persistence of their objection to the "political colouring" of his program.[31] At best, the enunciation of his "Solution" could serve no more than a ceremonial purpose; at worst, its publication might prove an impediment to its realization. Majestic though Herzl's vision was it had to be opposed, wrote one sympathizer, "not because I do not consider it good, but because I am afraid that if we begin too largely we might not be able to do anything, and something ought certainly to be done, and that as soon as possible."[32] "Extreme Herzlism," in Solomon Schechter's words,

[30] Letter to editor, JC, 13 April 1900, p. 9.

[31] 30 March 1897, Goldsmid to Herzl, confidential, CZA, Herzl Papers, H VIII 285a. 28 November 1895, Hirsch to Goldsmid, private, Mocatta Library, Hirsch Papers, AJ/28.

[32] 1 March 1896, B. L. Freeman (Edinburgh) to Herzl, CZA, Herzl Papers, H VIII 246.

posited a mistaken order of priorities. "You must first have the colonies and then the nation."[33]

Eventually, the Zionists were themselves to adopt a policy that was virtually indistinguishable from that put forward by the Chovevei Zion. The tenth Zionist Congress, held at Basle in 1911, agreed to a "synthetic" program of practical work in Palestine with the avowed aim of obtaining piecemeal gains.[34] When proposed by Goldsmid in 1896, however, such a scheme had seemed indefensibly indeterminate. Consequently, it had been attacked by both supporters and opponents of political Zionism. Even those who had then criticized Herzl's aims had poured scorn on what they considered to be the Chovevei Zion's feeble attempts to restrain his ambitions. Israel Abrahams, for instance, maintained that Goldsmid and his colleagues had themselves done much to foster some of the worst excesses of political Zionism; they could now be accused of refusing to take responsibility for their actions. Their "philanthropic" attitude toward the Palestinian colonists had always been ambiguous; their timorous refusal to accept that their settlements might contain the germs of a future polity was hypocritical.

> While they have been playing with fireworks in the back garden [Herzl] has gone round to the front door and tried to set the house on fire. . . . He holds out the real thing before their eyes and they shrink from it as from a spectre.[35]

More damaging, in the short run at least, were the charges levelled by convinced supporters of Jewish nationalism. From their point of view, the awkward "yes-buts" of the Chovevei Zion would cause as much harm to the Zionist cause as the emphatic "noes" of Herzl's critics. Herzl had put forward a boldly simple plan that demanded an equally unequivocal response. Goldsmid's attempts

[33] 9 August 1898, Schechter to H. Bentwich, CZA, H. Bentwich Papers, A100/59.

[34] See the ironic comments in Samuel A. Hirsch, "Some Chovevei Zion Reminiscences," *Jewish Review*, 2 (March 1912):520-26.

[35] JC, 23 July 1897, p. 7.

to trim his sails to the prevailing winds of communal caution were both shameful and ill-conceived.

Significantly, criticisms of this sort were given their most forceful expression within the Chovevei Zion Association itself. There the lead seems to have been taken by the B'nei Zion Tent, of whom the most prominent spokesmen were Ephraim Ish-Kishor and Jacob de Haas. De Haas, who was at the time subeditor of the *Jewish World*, was elected to represent the B'nei Zion at Headquarters in June 1896 and promptly set out to make himself a power within the Chovevei Zion. Responding to the barrage of instructions that began to flow from Vienna as early as July 1896, he was soon offering to "capture" the Association for Herzl. De Haas's early promises to "precipitate a revolt" against Goldsmid were, it must be noted, premature. His progress reports were written in a conspiratorial style that encouraged hyperbole; moreover, they were laced with the occasional request for financial reimbursement that aroused Herzl's distaste.[36] But as the official minute books of the Association reveal, he did possess some influence. On behalf of the B'nei Zion Tent, de Haas was the first member of the Chovevei Zion to propose (in 1896) that "Headquarters should take up Dr. Herzl's scheme for the establishment of a Jewish State in Palestine." He was also the first to suggest, in 1897, that "Headquarters ought to pay more attention to the propagation of Jewish Nationalism." Admittedly, neither motion was carried; after some debate de Haas had to agree that both be "expunged."[37] Nevertheless, he persisted. He organized a round robin demanding a "special meeting for the purpose of discussing and deciding what steps the Chovevei Zion Association should take with regard to the Zionist Congress to be held . . . in August"; he also persuaded three other members at Head-

[36] Report of B'nei Zion election in CZA, Files of Chovevei Zion Association, A2/43, no. 21; for de Haas's reports see, e.g., 3 October 1896 and 16 October 1896, de Haas to Herzl, CZA, Herzl Papers, H VIII 513.

[37] Minutes for meetings of 5 October 1896 and 16 March 1897 in CZA, Files of the Chovevei Zion Association, A2/4; draft minutes for 2 November 1896 (not reproduced in official minute book) in ibid., A2/2.

quarters to vote in favor of accepting Herzl's invitation to that gathering.[38]

☐

The majority's decision to stay away from Basle was clearly a tactical error. An organized Chovevei Zion delegation to the congress would not have had much effect on its proceedings, but it might have enabled the Chovevei Zion Association in England to bask in some of the reflected glory. As it was, all the Headquarters could manage was an unconvincing attempt to suggest "the practical adherence of the Congress to *our* programme," and a tame motion, expressing "hearty approval of the moderate resolutions" passed at Basle.[39] Both actions merely emphasized the extent to which the Chovevei Zion had been overshadowed. "The air seems to be booming with Herzl's name," wrote S. B. Rubinstein, who had himself been to Basle. "It is evident that the Congress has created here in England many new adherents to the national idea, whom the Chovevei Zion have failed to influence uptil [sic] now. These, as well as some who are within our camp already, will for the future not be content with a simple colonisation programme."[40] De Haas himself continued to insist that he was "not anxious to split the camp"; but the "spirit of rebellion" which he and his friends reported (and perhaps fermented) was clearly beginning to spread. As early as March 1897, his opponents at Headquarters had felt it necessary to table a motion that "viewed with alarm the tendency on the part of certain tents to . . . attack the colonisation movement as at present carried on."[41] By the end of the year it was agreed that unity could be restored

[38] Minutes, 20 April 1897, ibid., A2/93 and 31 May 1897, ibid., A2/4; the voting was 8 to 4.

[39] 22 September 1897, Bentwich to Hirsch, ibid., A2/13 and minutes of 10 November 1897, ibid., A2/4.

[40] Rubinstein to Hirsch, 16 July 1897 and 3 October 1897, ibid., A2/106.

[41] Minutes of 16 March 1897; "after a discussion the motion was withdrawn by consent," ibid., A2/4.

only by a general meeting of all English Lovers of Zion, to which delegates from throughout the country would be invited.[42]

This was a forlorn hope. The "Conference of English Zionists" held at Clerkenwell Town Hall, London, on 6 March 1898, merely revealed the extent of the rift that Herzl's proposals had created. The assembled delegates, who represented various Chovevei Zion tents and an assortment of nonaffiliated societies (some of which had only been formed after the Basle Congress),[43] did agree on the sublimity of the national idea and the importance of Hebrew education. The several speeches on these largely ceremonial subjects were received in an atmosphere of general harmony. So too was Herzl's rather pontifical message of encouragement. However, a motion (proposed by Rubinstein) calling upon the conference "fully to cooperate with the Zionist Actions Committee" headed by Herzl, gave rise to "heated and passionate" discussion. As all the speakers appreciated, more was at issue than a theoretical choice between politics and philanthropy; the future leadership of the Chovevei Zion Association was itself in the balance. The matter could not be settled at Clerkenwell; instead a subcommittee, consisting of six delegates of the Chovevei Zion and six representatives of the nonaffiliated bodies, was established in order to formulate a program of federation.[44] However, despite

[42] Elhanan Orren, *Hibat-Zion be-Britanyah 1878-1898* (Tel-Aviv, 1974), pp. 143-46.

[43] The delegates represented twenty-seven Chovevei Zion tents; fifteen non-affiliated Zionist societies; two Palestinian charities; and two Hebrew education bodies. The Maccabeans, AJA, and Ica also sent observers. There is some doubt as to the exact number of participants: *Palestina* estimated them at about 150 ("Special Number," March 1898), but Israel Cohen states 116 ("300 Years of Anglo-Zionism," in *Aspects of Jewish Life, 1656-1956*, ed. B. Buill and W. Perry [London, 1956], p. 23). Orren, *Hibat-Zion*, who supplies a complete list of the societies represented (pp. 149-51), gives no figure of participants. Virginia H. Hein, "British Followers of Theodor Herzl" (Ph.D. dissertation, Georgia State University, 1978) p. 95, has 165.

[44] *Proceedings of the Conference of English Zionists Held at Clerkenwell Town Hall, 6 March 1898* (London, 1898), pp. 76-81; the episode, and its aftermath, is covered by Orren, *Hibat-Zion*, and Paul Goodman, *Zionism in England, 1899-1949* (London, 1949), pp. 19-20. See also the personal recollections of delegate S. Levy, CZA, Levy Papers, K11/96 (dated May 1959).

Goldsmid's professed interest in "a certain amount of give and take" no agreement was reached. In retrospect, it appears that none was possible. The "Herzlites," as they were now commonly called, insisted on allegiance to Vienna and absorption in Herzl's movement. Goldsmid and his aides (like their colleagues elsewhere in Europe) resented claims to preeminence on the part of a group of novices. They were irritated by Herzl's disparaging references to the work previously undertaken in Palestine by the international association of Chovevei Zion societies (some of whom they had consulted before rejecting his invitation to Basle); they were dismayed by his declared intention to bypass such bodies and forego their experience and advice. When they came to think of it, "there is no call for such an organization [as Herzl's] at all, as we have done all the work of Zionism here thoroughly and effectively."[45] After months of wrangling, the subcommittee established at Clerkenwell finally disbanded and the plans for an effective association of all parties were shelved. Herzl's supporters established their own English Zionist Federation which was inaugurated during a dinner at the Trocadero Restaurant, London, on 22 January 1899. Goldsmid did not attend.[46]

At the time, Goldsmid's action was attributed to the supposedly brittle nature of his *"amour propre."* Personal animosity was said to lie at the root of the entire affair. That such feelings did play some part is evident from the spate of recriminatory correspondence that passed between the Herzlites and the Chovevei Zion. Clearly, there was little love lost between Goldsmid, Prag, and Hirsch (of the Chovevei Zion) and, for the EZF, Bentwich, de Haas, and Leopold Greenberg (a printer and publisher of some ambition). The latter group had initially been annoyed by Goldsmid's refusal to attend Herzl's appearance at the Jewish Working Men's Club, and subsequently called attention to his "snobbish and sneaking ways."[47] Goldsmid, for his part, retorted that the

---

[45] 18 October 1899, J. Prag to Hirsch, CZA, Files of Chovevei Zion Association, A2/9.

[46] Goodman, *Zionism in England*, pp. 20-21. For a draft suggestion of the federation, dated March 1898, see CZA, Gaster Papers, A203/105.

[47] E.g., Herbert Bentwich in *JC*, 5 August 1898, p. 6; and the correspondence in CZA, Files of Chovevei Zion Association, A2/85 and A2/91.

split in the Zionist camp had been engineered by a clique of his personal opponents, who were motivated by a selfish desire to undermine his influence. They had manhandled his supporters at rowdy public meetings, and exploited his frequent absences from London on military duties to concoct a more extreme program of action than was either practicable or desirable. All this did not impair Goldsmid's regard for Herzl (with whom he was later to cooperate on the El Arish scheme). But it did lead to a feeling that he could not possibly work "with those whom I discovered playing an underhand game."[48]

This was a facile and not entirely fair view of events. In the final analysis, the outcome of the tug of war between Goldsmid and his opponents did not depend entirely upon personal squabbles at either the subcommittee or the Headquarters Tent. The future direction of Zionist work in Britain would eventually depend on the behavior of individual Chovevei Zion societies in London and the provinces. These therefore were the constituents whose allegiance both sides attempted to win throughout the period of their unsuccessful negotiations. The ultimate victory of the representatives of the English Zionist Federation cannot be attributed solely to the personal ambitions of a clutch of militants at the center of affairs. It was also the work of a larger number of scattered enthusiasts who were dissatisfied with Goldsmid's leadership of the national cause.

At the local level of Chovevei Zion affairs, Goldsmid was from the first at a decided disadvantage. Long before Herzl's arrival in England, several provincial tents had complained of the degree to which they had been neglected by the London leadership. Their appeals for literature, speakers, and information had often been ignored; so too had their requests that Headquarters meetings (to which they were entitled to send delegates) be held at a more convenient time than Wednesday afternoons.[49] The affairs

---

[48] 31 August 1899, Goldsmid to Herzl, CZA, Herzl Papers, H VIII 285a. For one gleeful account of the "smashing" of a public Zionist meeting, see 7 July 1899, Gaster to Herzl, CZA, Gaster Papers, A203/110. On the later relationship, J. Fraenkel, "Colonel Albert E. W. Goldsmid and Theodor Herzl," *Herzl Year Book* 1 (1958):145-53.

[49] For one typical post-mortem see 14 December 1898, A. Michelson (Stock-

of the Association were generally agreed to stand in need of some reform long before the Clerkenwell Conference at which, significantly, the provincial delegates had put forward some of the most vociferous demands for a "new spirit and order" of things.[50] In the aftermath of Clerkenwell, the mutual feeling of alienation between the Headquarters and the affiliated bodies steadily deepened. Reports from a variety of local tents reveal that veteran members of the Chovevei Zion were often at a loss to understand Goldsmid's dithering attitude toward the federation scheme; more recent converts to the national idea were frustrated by his seeming failure to appreciate the strength of Herzl's appeal. Admittedly, the sense of dissatisfaction was not universal. Some tents remained faithful to Goldsmid and to the old policy of gradual colonization. Birmingham, for instance, "saw no reason why the Chovevei Zion should merge its existence in that of the EZF. . . . We are against Political Zionism in any shape or form."[51] Other societies allowed their objections to Herzl's approach to ossify into prejudice against virtually all Zionist activity. A general meeting of the Cambridge University Tent had, early in 1898, returned its invitation to the Clerkenwell Conference. "In view of the present position of the Jews in Europe," the members recorded their "deep regret that H.Q. has summoned the Conference, as tending to prejudice the political and social standing of Jews in this country."[52] These, however, were exceptional statements which in any case emanated from small or intrinsically weak societies; the Cambridge Tent was wound up as early as June 1898, that in Birmingham in 1902. This was also the fate of the societies in Belfast, Hull, Glasgow, Norwich, and South London. All had voted to oppose association with the EZF, and

ton) to Hirsch, CZA, Files of Chovevei Zion Association, A2/55. "You must however do me the justice to remember that times and often I have written you explaining how absolutely necessary it was for someone of light and leading in the association to pay us a visit . . . but nothing was done."

[50] Which led Colonel Claude Conder to remark: "You seem now to have to guide rather than to create enthusiasm." Letter to Bentwich, 8 March 1898, CZA, H. Bentwich Papers, A100/7a.

[51] Report for 1899 in CZA, Files of Chovevei Zion Association, A2/18.

[52] 19 February, 1898, O. d'Avigdor-Goldsmid to Hirsch, ibid., A2/29.

all experienced a sharp decline in support. Unable to combat the "hold and appeal" of what they described as "local Zionist agents," they were each forced "to slacken the cords and pull up the stakes of our tent."[53]

The larger Chovevei Zion societies had reacted to Herzl's proposals somewhat differently; for that reason, they enjoyed better fortunes. Rather than wait for their supporters to melt away, they had revolted against the parent body of the Chovevei Zion Association and declared their allegiance to Herzl. Some tents, such as that in Southsea (154 members), had given warning of their intentions: "If different ideas prevail, the result will be disaster— Zionists, while supporting existing colonies, cannot see in this the Alpha and Omega of the movement. True Zionism is fixed on a broader basis, call it political if you will."[54] Others did not bother to do so. Jack Umanski, the secretary of the Leeds Tent (almost 200 members), simply informed Hirsch that he and his colleagues had been working independently of Headquarters "for some months. . . . There is no confidence here in the Headquarters tent since the unfriendly attitude of the latter towards the Vienna Committee & the Jewish Colonial Bank. . . . The strange proceedings at the meetings of the Zionist Federation Scheme have aggravated matters still more."[55] Under circumstances such as these, it was pointless for Goldsmid to expell the East London Tent (over 350 members) for their allusions to him as "the dead weight of an effete organisation" and for having affiliated themselves to the Zionists. Similarly without meaning were reprimands to Leeds for having bought shares in the Zionist Bank, and to Portsea for having passed resolutions "contrary to the principles of the Association."[56] De Haas's carefully planned journeys to the provinces were having a more decisive effect.[57]

---

[53] Reports in Files of Chovevei Zion Association, A2/29-A2/76.

[54] 2 July 1898, S. Levy to Hirsch, ibid., A2/53.

[55] 10 November 1898, ibid., A2/32; see also 28 July 1896, de Haas to Herzl, CZA, Herzl Papers, H VIII 153.

[56] Correspondence for October and November 1898 in CZA, Files of Chovevei Zion Association, A2/8, pp. 560-73.

[57] 21 May 1899, de Haas to Gaster, CZA, Gaster Papers, A203/109.

Characteristically, Goldsmid attempted to soldier on. In 1899, he even rejected the English Zionist Federation's offer of renewed talks on some form of association. In a blunt and rather patronizing letter he wrote that he could see no value in such discussions, and preferred to "trust that in future all parties will strive to seek where they may work in accord and where they cannot do so, agree amicably to differ without acrimony."[58] As a public relations exercise, this was an unwise move: for one thing, the English Zionist Federation had made its overture precisely in the hope that were it to be refused by the Chovevei Zion "then we can demonstrate that they are humbugs."[59] For another, Goldsmid had few assets with which to bargain. Some months earlier he had received a typical report from one of his personal friends in Manchester: "I think it would be useless to ask . . . Zionists to support any project emanating from the Chovevei Zion Association. . . . The large majority of Manchester Zionists are 'Herzlites.' "[60] The ground thus lost was never retrieved. In 1902 Goldsmid agreed to wind up the affairs of the entire body.[61]

[58] 2 December 1899, Goldsmid to Hirsch, CZA, Files of Chovevei Zion Association, A2/11(3); accepted *nem. con.* [without dissent] at special executive meeting of 10 December 1899, ibid., A2/4.

[59] 6 October 1899, de Haas to Herzl, CZA, Files of the Central Zionist Office (Vienna), Z1/243.

[60] Private letter from B. J. Belisha, 14 May 1899, CZA, Files of Chovevei Zion Association, A2/44. Belisha had in 1897 himself presided at a "crowded meeting" in Derby Hall addressed by de Haas, which had decided to send a delegate to the first Congress. JC, 6 August 1897, p. 11.

[61] 8 July 1902, Goldsmid to Prag, CZA, Files of Chovevei Zion Association, A2/11(4).

2

The English Zionist Federation and Communal Strategy, 1899-1904

T HE IMPORTANCE OF THE demise of the Chovevei Zion Association should not be exaggerated. From the perspective of the Anglo-Jewish community as a whole, that victory was rather marginal. It did not portend a general swing of sympathy toward political Zionism. As far as the upper classes of the community (in particular) were concerned, the resistance and antipathy which Bentwich had originally encountered at the Maccabeans remained the rule. Most particularly was this the case in the supposedly more representative forums of Anglo-Jewry, to whom the Zionists initially attempted to put their case. At the annual meeting of the Anglo-Jewish Association in July 1897, for instance, Bentwich and Gaster failed to stem the tide of invective against the Zionist Congress released by Chief Rabbi Adler's angry tirade. Their claim that "there could be no harm in meeting to discuss Zionism" was no match for Adler's references to that "egregious blunder" and "absolutely mischevous" project. When, the following year, the AJA debated an invitation to the Clerkenwell Conference of 1898, the results were equally disappointing. Overriding Gaster's objections, the council voted to accept the executive's recommendation that "opinion being so divided on the Zionist question, it is undesirable for the AJA as a body to take part in the Conference." Thereafter, the entire subject was virtually proscribed. As Claude Montefiore in his presidential address for 1898 warned the members, any form of contact with the Zionists would be impolitic. "For the work of the Association in conjunction with the Alliance [Israelite Universelle] . . . and for their relationship with the Governments of various countries, it was of cardinal importance that they should not seem to commit themselves to, or in any way be in relation with, the Zionist movement."[1]

Other communal institutions, which (unlike the AJA) had no prior commitment to political action on behalf of oppressed Jews, found a policy of obstruction even easier. In most cases, their senior officers simply claimed that the pressures of regular business prevented a time-consuming discussion of Zionist principles. This guillotine was regularly and effectively employed at the Board of Deputies, which "steadfastly" avoided the topic throughout the period of the Chovevei Zion negotiations.[2] It was similarly put to use at the United Synagogue, where some early attempts to provoke a debate on Zionism at the council (and at the annual general meetings of some constituent synagogues) were tersely ruled out of order.[3] The Elders of the Sephardi Congregation attempted to achieve an equally repressive effect. Ever since 1897, they had objected to Gaster's indiscriminate expressions of support for political Zionism, especially since he often voiced them in his official capacity as Ḥakham. In 1899 they took advantage of a debate over ministerial salaries to demand that Gaster refrain from further pulpit references to Zionism; they also insisted that whenever he spoke from a public platform, he state that his views were his own and not necessarily those of his congregants. This was a damaging and degrading motion which not even the opposition of Sir Francis Montefiore (the vice-president of the community) could avert. In fact, the latter had himself to give a similar pledge when he assumed the presidency of the Sephardi Congregation in 1902.[4] Finally, and as an indication of the extent

[1] Minutes of meetings of 11 July 1897 and of 13 February 1898 in London, Mocatta Library, University College, AJA Council Minute Books, Vol. 3, pp. 56-57 and 67. The meetings were fully reported in the *JC*, 16 July 1897, pp. 12-13 and 18 February 1898, p. 14.

[2] *JC*, 20 June 1902, p. 25.

[3] *JC*, 5 May 1899, pp. 22-23; and 7 February 1902, pp. 12-13.

[4] Minutes of Annual Meeting of Elders, 29 January 1899, London, Sephardi Congregation Archives, Elders Minute Book, 1891-1911, p. 175. For earlier complaints see J. M. Levy to Gaster, 7 September 1897 and 24 April 1898, CZA,

to which opposition to Zionism cut across otherwise clearly defined institutional boundaries, there was the situation at the Federation of Synagogues. In 1901, Zionist work in Palestine was
officially declared to be "outside the scope" of the Conference of
Provincial Congregations organized by that body. Here, too, the
trend of opposition had become apparent some time earlier.
Speaking in his presidential capacity, Sir Samuel Montagu had
in 1898 urged the members of the Board of the Federation "to
prevent the poor Jews of the East End from becoming involved
in [this] ill-judged scheme."[5] When English Zionists contemplated
this broad front of antagonism, some of the shine began to wear
off their victory over the Chovevei Zion. Indeed, according to
some accounts, that achievement had itself precipitated a "boy-
cott" against Zionism and "a dead set against the movement in
official and representative circles."[6]

Herzl's supporters had no doubt of the cause for this state of
affairs. From the first, they considered the behavior of their antagonists to be merely the selfish reaction of a ruling caste, whose
political opinions were essentially and necessarily subordinate to
their social pretensions. Anti-Zionists were quite simply "too
comfortable to appreciate the benefits a movement to Palestine
would have for the majority of the nation."[7] Their ideological
and theological objections were only camouflage. By virtue of his
name, wealth, and lack of occupation, Sir Francis Montefiore
was unquestionably a member of the Anglo-Jewish aristocracy—
despite his early adherence to Zionism. He was, therefore, perhaps
better placed than most people to appreciate the motives that
influenced the views expressed by members of his own circle.

Gaster Papers, A203/104 and 105. On Sir F. Montefiore, 17 February 1902,
Montefiore to Gaster, ibid., A203/124. This situation is totally distorted in Albert
M. H. Hyamson, *The Sephardim of England* (London, 1951), p. 410.

[5] Meeting of 23 October 1898, London, Federation of Synagogues, Minute
Book of the Board, Vol. 1, pp. 244-45; and *JC*, 8 November 1901, p. 13.

[6] 20 October 1898, A. A. Green to Bentwich, "private and confidential,"
CZA, H. Bentwich Papers, A100/71; and H. Bentwich, reported in *JC*, 14 April
1899, p. 15.

[7] 13 January 1897, Sylvie d'Avigdor to Herzl, CZA, Herzl Papers, H VIII 33.

They feared, he reported to Herzl, that "if Zionism should prevail it would make the Jewish people free and they would no longer be able to dictate to them as they now like to do in return for the money which they out of their superfluity give to our charities."[8] Zionists, he implied, would not break this hold until they had ousted their opponents from office.

This was precisely the policy advocated by Herzl himself. His own early experiences throughout Europe had proven the futility of attempting to win over the magnates of Jewry by the more conventional means of personal persuasion. By 1897, therefore, he had deliberately injected a novel—even revolutionary—element into Jewish communal politics when convening the first Zionist Congress. His declared intention, even then, was to take Jewish affairs out of the hands of private individuals and to establish "a forum before which anyone could be brought to give an account of what he is or is not doing in the matter of the Jews." His quest to demonstrate the extent of his popular mandate explains his persistent instructions that de Haas "stir things up" in London, and his desire to see a sizable squad of supposedly elected delegates turn up in Basle.[9] Although perhaps put out at "the army of *schnorrers*" who ultimately did so, he thereafter decided to take his program to its logical conclusion. In many respects, his failure to penetrate the thick crust of indifference with which the Jewish Establishment continued to surround itself left him with little choice. During his opening address to the second Congress in 1898, accordingly, he advised his supporters to raise themselves above the level of a fringe faction by capturing the highest offices that their communities had to offer:

> In all places where the official heads of the community are not with us, an election campaign must be started against them. Men who are worthy, and are capable of occupying communal posts, and are in accord with us, must be put into office in the name of the National Idea. . . . Thus I believe I am expressing

[8] 5 January 1900, Montefiore to Herzl, ibid., H VIII 577.
[9] David Vital, *The Origins of Zionism* (Oxford, 1975), p. 355.

your views if I place among our future aims the conquest of the communities.[10]

THE OPTIONS

As a practical guide to action, Herzl's program was in many ways ill-conceived. In no Jewish community of the late nineteenth century was government properly democratic. Some positions of authority were inherited; others were assumed; in a third category, they were conferred by gentile suzerains. Even where formal elections to office did take place, the circle of enfranchised persons was carefully circumscribed. Herzl's vision of a parliamentary situation, allowing for an orderly transfer of power from one party to another, was more suited to the French Chamber of Deputies (whose debates he had long reported) than to a Jewish forum. Not least was this so in Anglo-Jewry. There, most of the immigrants, who comprised the majority of the community, had no access at all to the ballot box. Comparatively few immigrant Jews could afford the annual contributions that would have entitled them to membership of either the Anglo-Jewish Association, the major synagogues, or, in a corporate capacity, the Board of Deputies. Fewer still had yet shown the inclination to devote their infrequent leisure hours to playing a significant role in the administration of such bodies. As the victory over the Chovevei Zion Association itself indicated, a cadre of well-placed militants was necessary. This fact, together with the imprecise nature of Herzl's own instructions, fostered various interpretations of what the "conquest of the community" really entailed. Although generally in agreement about the need to overcome their opponents within the Establishment, the leaders of the English Zionist Federation themselves considered a variety of methods whereby that objective might be attained. They gave expression to their differences during a protracted debate over tactics, which was not properly resolved until shortly before Herzl's death in 1904.

[10] Delivered on 28 August 1898, *Stenographisches Protokoll der Verhandlungen des II. Zionisten-Congresses* (Vienna, 1898), p. 5.

(51)

One school of thought proposed a radical program of Zionist action. Herzl's critics, it was argued, could not effectively be silenced by the ponderous electoral program that he had proposed. What was needed was a more flamboyant scheme, designed to transform the pattern of communal government in its entirety. Existing communal institutions ought to be bypassed, or neutralized, and new bodies established that would more properly reflect the popular will. The Anglicized Establishment was not to be outvoted, but overthrown by a popular "revolution." To many an outside observer, such as Max Nordau, the immigrant ghettos of London, Leeds, Liverpool, and Manchester seemed to be teeming with prospective Zionists, all eager to see "some smashing of heads."[11] Even those who supposedly knew the community somewhat better, such as de Haas, appeared to sense the advent of a communal "burst [sic] up." Claiming to have "organised" the East End on Herzl's behalf, he reported that he was attempting to persuade immigrant Jews to divert some of the funds accumulated in their Friendly Society accounts to the Zionist Organisation. A "tax" of this sort, he calculated, would assure the new movement of solvency and might even break the Establishment's stranglehold on the communal purse strings. A public meeting between Zionist leaders and the heads of the Jewish trade unions in London, it was suggested in 1900, might prove similarly beneficial.[12]

An alternative option was to reverse the order of the campaign. Instead of overthrowing the Establishment, the Zionists could undermine its resistance to Herzl by attaining a spectacular diplomatic victory. This, in its own way, was also a drastic course, since it would implicitly deny the claim of the major Anglo-Jewish organizations to constitute the only channels to the British government. In effect, the formula was simple: "Nothing would do so much to bring the Jewish plutocrats of Western Europe

[11] 6 July 1897, Nordau to de Haas, CZA, de Haas Papers, A224/6.

[12] 30 July 1897, de Haas to Gaster, CZA, Gaster Papers, A203/104; and 6 July 1900, de Haas to Actions Committee, CZA, Files of the Central Zionist Office (Vienna), Z1/243.

round as evidence that their own rulers supported" Zionism.[13] All that was needed was a direct and successful appeal to individual members of the British government; the blessing of the Jewish Establishment would follow as a matter of course. Highly publicized interviews with Lord Salisbury, Lord Rosebery, or even King Edward VII would thus serve a communal purpose, quite apart from the diplomatic benefits to which they might lead. Goldsmid altogether missed this point when attempting to instruct Herzl on "the peculiar constitution of this country" that precluded "any *practical* good" arising from a request that the King canvass the support of his ministers on Zionism's behalf. As was appreciated by Zangwill and Joseph Cowen (a friend whom Zangwill had introduced to Zionism), merely by taking place, an audience with the King or his ministers would demonstrate that gentile persons of the highest rank had "thrown the aegis of English society over the movement," thus obviating the need for a long campaign for communal authority.[14] These meetings might be hard to arrange (Herzl was refused an audience with Edward VII, and was unable to see either Salisbury or Rosebery); they might also involve some inconvenience (before a planned meeting with Cecil Rhodes, Cowen asked Herzl: "Can you shoot? This isn't asked with a view to entering the British army but perhaps grouse or partridge shooting will be on in Scotland"[15]). Nevertheless, some gains could be recorded. After all, despite Lord Rothschild's opposition, Herzl did obtain an invitation to appear before the Royal Commission on Alien Immigration in 1902; in 1904, as will be seen, he could also offer concrete evidence that the British government was prepared to consider assisting the foundation of a Jewish settlement in East Africa. Both were

[13] Vital, *The Origins of Zionism*, p. 282.

[14] Compare 12 February 1904, Goldsmid to Herzl, confidential, CZA, Herzl Papers, H VIII 285a with 1 January 1901, Zangwill to Herzl, ibid., H VIII 946, and J. Cowen to Zangwill, CZA, Zangwill Papers, A120/60. Herzl himself surmised that he "would ask the King to tell his big Jews that they could help me without prejudice to their *English patriotism*." *The Complete Diaries of Theodor Herzl*, ed. Raphael Patai, trans. Harry Zohn, 5 vols. (New York, 1960), 3:1161.

[15] 1 August 1901, Cowen to Herzl, CZA, Herzl Papers, H VIII 161.

"splendid strokes for the benefit of the movement," not least because they created "an immense sensation." The "upper" Jews might mutter about the consequences of these "cheap advertisements," but they had to admit that Herzl's movement could no longer be ignored.[16]

Despite such encouraging signs, the leaders of the English Zionist Federation rejected both of the extreme courses of action outlined above. After an initial period of indecision and debate, they chose not to pin all their hopes on the strength of their appeal to either individual gentile sympathizers or to the masses of Anglo-Jewry. Instead, they adopted a third strategy, and set out to "conquer the community" by the conventional electoral means that Herzl had suggested at the second Congress. In so doing, they did not entirely rule out the possibility of pursuing their other options. At this stage, the EZF was far too disparate an organization to permit distinct policy decisions and their implementation through an effective chain of command. Questions of communal strategy, in fact, were never formally decided by the Executive Committee, but bandied about during the course of informal meetings and exchanges, of which the records are necessarily incomplete. Nevertheless, it is clear that by 1904 the leaders of the EZF had, in Zangwill's phrase, chosen to sap the bastions of anti-Zionism from within rather than storm them from without. Tactically, in the sense of the ways and means to be employed, this involved a change of course. Zionists were to infiltrate—and thereby influence—the existing major institutions within the community. Support for Zionism at these bodies, rather than at public demonstrations in the East End or at fashionable clubs in Mayfair, was to be the true barometer of the movement's progress. In terms of purposes and consequences, which fell into the category of strategy, the change of perspective was more fundamental. In order to capture the community through the ballot box, the Zionists would have to arrange for something like a Zionist "ticket" at elections to the various political, charitable,

[16] 5 March 1902, Greenberg to Herzl, ibid., H VIII 291; and 5 June 1902, C. Emanuel (secretary of the Board of Deputies) to Herbert Bentwich, CZA, H. Bentwich Papers, A100/7a.

cultural, and synagogal bodies of Anglo-Jewry. Thereafter, they would have to form themselves into an influential—even if nebulous—"lobby" at such central institutions as the Board of Deputies and the Anglo-Jewish Association. In neither capacity could they limit their interests and responsibilites to the Basle Program. If they wished to widen the circle of their audience, they would also have to involve themselves in other issues of communal concern, however peripheral to the ideology of the Zionist cause. This might dissipate their strength; it would certainly force them into contentious alliances and sometimes painful controversies. Nevertheless, only a communal campaign of the broadest sort seemed capable of enabling the Zionists effectively to challenge the communal leaders and those who made them, and to discredit all those who scorned and libelled Zionism.

THE RESTRAINTS

Most of these considerations were only dimly perceived during the early period of the EZF's activity. When formulating their strategy of infiltration, few leading Zionists dared to predict either the extent or the form of the campaign upon which they embarked. Nevertheless, the sources suggest that they certainly possessed more than an inkling about some of the consequences of their actions. Even the earliest clashes at the Board of Deputies and the Anglo-Jewish Association had demonstrated that the conquest of both bodies would be a lengthy business; they had also provided an indication of the strength of the arguments which the Zionists would have to face. A superficial comparison, in fact, suggested that this course was both less attractive and more difficult than the alternative options of either gentile support or popular revolt. Therein, however, lies the interest of the EZF's ultimate preference for the slings and arrows of an electoral campaign. The most obvious considerations of feasibility do not appear to have been the most important in the formulation of the choice. Rather, feasibility seems to have been superseded by factors that were of primarily personal and programmatic relevance.

It is tempting to attribute the Zionists' choice of a moderate strategy of institutional infiltration to their failure in other spheres. Particularly is this so when note is taken of their numerical weakness. The immigrant quarters of the large towns did not provide the EZF with its expected natural constituency. De Haas's early assumption that "the East End is secure" was soon seen to be a gross exaggeration. More astute, it transpired, was Simeon Singer's simultaneous warning that "it is inexpressibly difficult to bring the [Zionist] Scheme into the prominence it requires for successful treatment or examination. The masses are either inert or absorbed in their own pursuits."[17] As was the case elsewhere, not until after World War I did Zionism attain the status of a truly popular movement within Anglo-Jewry. The initial growth of the EZF, although not insignificant, was hardly sufficient to indicate that the Zionist movement possessed the unswerving allegiance of a large proportion of local Jewry. This disheartening situation was only partially relieved by the occasional bursts of enthusiasm displayed whenever Herzl addressed an immigrant audience in Whitechapel (which he did almost annually after 1898). More to the point were the intervening periods of Jewish working class apathy and even opposition. As much is evident from the progress reports published by the Zionist themselves. Surveys of "Zionism in England" presented to early Zionist congresses contained statistics that suggested a growth of about 400 percent in the number of societies affiliated to the EZF at the turn of the century, and an increase in individual membership from some 4,000 in 1899 to 7,155 (almost two-thirds of whom lived outside London) by 1902. But, as was generally acknowledged, the picture nevertheless remained that of a small and frail enterprise, not a thriving concern. Despite their attempts at intense publicity (especially before and during the fourth Congress) the Zionists could claim the active support of no more than 4½ percent of the total population of Anglo-Jewry. The state of their organization was equally weak. Throughout the period, it remained true that the societies affiliated to the EZF "mostly consist only of commit-

[17] 19 February 1896, Singer to Herzl, CZA, Herzl Papers, H VIII 739.

tees."[18] Very few of them possessed either the funds or the prestige required to undertake extensive communal activity; some (such as the Glasgow Zionist Cycling Club) seem to have devoted at least some of their energies to other pursuits.

Leaders of the EZF found it relatively easy to identify the source and extent of their unpopularity within native Anglo-Jewry. As will be seen, among this section of the community public opinion was manifestly shaped, and reflected, by a series of formal sermons, scholarly essays, and newspaper comment—all of which readily yielded their message of antagonism and disdain. But the precise nature of the immigrant mood proved more difficult to ascertain. Consequently, why the bulk of the new arrivals were not more forthcoming in support of Zionism remained largely a matter of inference. In some quarters, the reserved attitude of the masses was attributed to their sheer physical and emotional exhaustion. Most sections of the Jewish working classes, it was argued, were simply too worn out by the mundane imperatives of their daily life and labor to play an active and consistent part in any communal cause, even one presumed to command as great a fund of latent sympathy as the movement for Jewish national regeneration.[19] Perhaps, too, as has been suggested in the North American context, Zionism was "by its nature . . . antipathetic" to the entire Jewish migratory experience. Having suffered the considerable hardships of their steerage passage from the European mainland, few immigrants—"even in imagination"—could bear the thought that they had taken the wrong route and would have to embark on another journey, this time eastwards.[20] To these

[18] Statistics in annual editions of the *Jewish Year Book*, and in *Protokoll der Verhandlungen des IV. Zionisten-Congresses* (Vienna, 1900), pp. 163-66, and *Protokoll der Verhandlungen des V. Zionisten-Congresses* (Vienna, 1901), pp. 48-49. See also Lloyd P. Gartner, *The Jewish Immigrant*, 2nd ed. (London, 1973), p. 265, and Marvin J. Goldfine, "The Growth of Zionism in England" (Master's thesis, Columbia University, 1939), pp. 29 ff.

[19] Ben-Eliezer [pseud.], "Man and Beast," *Der Vanderer*, no. 28, 6 March 1903; compare C. Russel, *The Jew in London* (London, 1900), pp. 106-114 with H. S. Lewis, "Another View of the Question," *The Jew in London*, p. 233.

[20] Irving Howe, *The Immigrant Jews of New York, 1881 to the Present* (London, 1976), p. 207.

might be added two other, more explicitly documented, barriers to Zionism's potential popularity. One was the Orthodox religious aversion toward a concerted attempt to regain the Holy Land by political means (see Chapter 5). Another was the conflicting demands for immigrant Jewish support made by libertarian spokesmen for left-wing movements of social protest and reform. Advocating a variety of pursuits from violent revolution to educational self-help, their appeal could often seem as urgent as that of the Zionists and, in the circumstances, more apposite. Most immigrants, after all, had wrested themselves from their east European environment in the hope of improving their individual lots. That few of them had managed to do so seemed the fault of the system that spawned the sweatshops—a proportion of which were owned by their coreligionists.[21] Under these circumstances, working class Jews could hardly be expected to share a sense of national unity with their exploiters. Indeed, the entire notion labored under the burden of anomalies avoided by the alternative doctrine of class consciousness advocated by Jewish socialist intellectuals.

Admittedly, the Jewish socialist, trade union, and anarchist circles in Britain were not themselves in complete command of immigrant sympathies. Laments in contemporary and memorialistic accounts (since substantiated by academic research) reveal that these groups, not unlike the Zionists, experienced lengthy periods of ideological controversy, factionalism, and fluctuating fortunes. But they had been the first in the field (Aaron Lieberman, a young writer from Vilna, had founded the Hebrew Socialist Society—the very first of its kind in Jewish history—in London as early as 1876). Moreover, some time before the advent of Herzl many of the left-wing groups had, in different ways, demonstrated a degree of organizational resilience, ideological vigor, and (especially during the halcyon days of the 1899 tailors'

[21] New York, YIVO Institute, no. 916644, Morris Myer, *Die Svetting system; vie vort mann fun ihr fotter* (London, n.d.), p. 9; E. Tcherikover, ed., *Geshikhte fun der Yiddisher Arbeiter Baveigung in der Faraynigte Shtotn*, 2 vols. (New York, 1943), 2:462-64; and Gartner, *The Jewish Immigrant*, pp. 67-93.

strike in London) effective militancy.[22] Equally relevant is the fact that some of their spokesmen had already mapped out the lines of their attack on the doctrine of Jewish nationalism. As early as 1886, the weekly *Arbayter Fraynd* (then socialist; after 1892 anarchist) had published a series of biting attacks on the "Golden Calf" worshipped by the Chovevei Zion. Written by Morris Winchevsky (a young writer from Central Europe who was constrained to find employment in a bank), the articles argued that the Jew was by nature cosmopolitan; the establishment of a Jewish "homeland" in Palestine was advocated by the Jewish bourgeoisie of Western Europe, whose members loathed and mal- treated their Polish-Russian brethren; even were it possible to "redeem" *Erez Yisrael*, the results would be regressive. The Lovers of Zion would merely re-create in Palestine a society dependent upon charity, and thus transplant the abysmal conditions prev- alent in the Pale. The Jewish working masses, like their gentile comrades, would attain relief only by adopting a program based upon socialist principles, and thereby helping to bring about the emancipation of humanity at large.[23]

Not unexpectedly, these themes were repeated and enlarged upon after Herzl's first visits to London. The *Arbayter Fraynd* then pilloried political Zionism as a bourgeois delusion and *idée fixe* that could only distract the Jewish proletariat from the struggle for its liberation. A typical reception for Herzl attracted (so one report ran) a heterogeneous turnout of "good-for-nothing laya- bouts and ignoramuses, on the one hand, and snobbish Jews who wished to rid themselves of the masses, on the other."[24] Such skeptics were not induced to change their attitude by the foun- dation of fragile Poalei Zion societies in London and Leeds in

[22] Gartner, *The Jewish Immigrant*, chap. 4 and William J. Fishman, *East End Jewish Radicals, 1875-1914* (London, 1975), pp. 97-227.

[23] Signed "Ben-Netz" (Winchevsky's pseudonym), the articles were published in the July, August, and September 1886 issues. In general see Elhanan Orren "Ha-Publizistikah ha-Yiddit bemizrah London beshanim 1883-1887; al parshat derakhim bein Sozialism ve-Hibat-Zion," *Ha-Zionut*, 2 (1971): 47-64.

[24] Y. Kaplan in *Der Arbayter Fraynd*, 7 July 1899, pp. 5-6 and 14 July 1899, pp. 5-6.

1904 and 1905; neither were they converted by the (intellectually) more robust advocacy of "Zionism from a Socialist Standpoint" by the disciples and colleagues of Kalman Marmor (a recent immigrant from Vilna). As the latter himself confessed, he could make little contribution to the progress of the EZF. Members of Poalei Zion societies in Britain were often as isolated from mainstream Zionists, who suspected their socialism, as from traditional socialists, who suspected their Zionism.[25] Their attempts to yoke the demand for Jewish national regeneration to the older struggle for proletarian emancipation seemed hardly to touch the mass of immigrants. That "Zionism and Labour are mutually antagonistic" continued to be a standard item of advanced left-wing propaganda; that "Zionism was engineered by the capitalists in order to draw off the attention of Jews from the general social question," remained a popular, and well-publicized, charge.[26] Hence the *Arbayter Fraynd* could claim that the anarchists had as much to say to the East End as did the Zionists; only half of the invited friendly societies and trade unions bothered to send representatives to a "Conference of East London Jewish Working Men" organized by the EZF in 1901. Even those who did so, although prepared to vote in favor of the mildly nationalist resolutions with which that meeting opened, refused to agree to the payment of regular contributions to the Zionist movement. They also appear to have ignored de Haas's call to "take upon themselves a larger share in the government of the community."[27] Despondently, de

[25] New York, YIVO Institute, no. 7/61874, K. Marmor, "Tsionisten-Sozialisten," *Di Yudishe Frayhayt*, 19 June 1905, pp. 2-7, and the reports of various societies on pp. 38-40 of the same issue. "Jewish Labour News" in the *JC* reported the foundation of Poalei Zion groups in trade union circles as early as 6 November 1903. See also Kalman Marmor, *Mein Lebens-Geshikhte*, 2 vols. (New York, 1959), 2:491-509.

[26] *Arbayter Fraynd*, 31 July 1903, p. 6; 2 October 1903, p. 7; and Herbert Burrows (president of the United Garment Workers Union), reported in *JC*, 27 November 1903, p. 6.

[27] *Arbayter Fraynd*, 14 October 1896, p. 2; *JC*, 4 October 1901, and 17 January, 1899, Englander to Gaster, CZA, Gaster Papers, A203/107.

Haas had already reported to Herzl that, in England, "instead of being an army, Zionism is becoming a guerilla band."[28]

Notwithstanding Herzl's hopes, this situation could not easily be repaired by direct appeals to the big names of gentile society. In fact, the leaders of the Anglo-Jewish community obstinately refused to be impressed by either Herzl's ostentatious appearances at fashionable garden parties or his extensive contacts with individual figures in British political life. Herzl's personal relations with Lord Rothschild did undoubtedly improve after their exchanges at the Aliens Commission in 1902, but the success was only partial. Rothschild continued to "view with horror the establishment of a Jewish Colony pure and simple." More important, he was not prepared to issue a public statement on Herzl's behalf.[29] Other influential figures remained equally reticent. In 1903 Claude Montefiore bluntly refused to see Herzl; the following year Chief Rabbi Adler was to find that the "peremptory orders" of his doctors prevented his attendance at a memorial service for the deceased leader.[30] For the majority of this class, Herzl's scheme remained (as it had been from the start) "an anathema": it challenged their religious beliefs in the nature of Israel's *mission civilisatrice* in the Diaspora, conflicted with their political preferences for the benefits of English citizenship over a Jewish nationality, and aroused their fears of a bout of anti-Semitic charges of Jewish ingratitude for the gift of emancipation. Altogether, they were convinced that "in the present state of the world political Zionism is likely to do us Jews more harm than good."[31]

Some prominent Christians, who observed Zionism from a different standpoint, claimed to have reached opposite conclusions. Those associated with the church missionary societies were particularly excited by the prospect of an Israelite return to Zion,

[28] 30 April 1901, de Haas to Herzl, CZA, Files of the Central Zionist Office (Vienna), Z1/243.
[29] 1 August 1903, Rothschild to Herzl, CZA, Herzl Papers, H VIII 708.
[30] *Diary*, 4:1395-96; and 12 July 1904, Adler to Gaster, CZA, Gaster Papers, A203/134.
[31] 19 April 1905, H.S.Q. Henriques to Gaster, CZA, Gaster Papers, A203/137.

and many regarded Herzl's program as a portent of the millennium.[32] But the Zionists found it difficult to translate such sympathy into active diplomatic support. Most particularly was this so at the parliamentary level, where they failed to organize an effective lobby. Such an attempt was made in 1900. On the eve of the general election of that year, the EZF issued a general circular to parliamentary candidates asking whether, if elected, they would use their influence "to secure the sympathetic consideration of Her Majesty's Government to the Movement and its good offices in favour of Zionist aspirations." At the same time, Herzl toyed with the idea of having Sir Francis Montefiore elected to the House of Commons as member for Whitechapel, in place of the sitting anti-Zionist Jewish incumbent, Sir Samuel Montagu.[33] Both moves failed. The election campaign was little short of a fiasco; only a fraction of the total number of parliamentary candidates replied favorably to the EZF circular, and the majority of those who did so were defeated at the polls. Montefiore himself refused to allow his name to be put forward, and even refused to address a letter of support to one of the very few Jewish candidates to have expressed sympathy for Zionism.[34]

Incidents such as these reportedly led Zangwill to comment that Sir Francis Montefiore was "too bound by etiquette and red tape to be a valuable conspirator."[35] Other leading figures in

[32] See, e.g., the Church Missionary Society's journal, *Jewish Missionary Intelligence*, October 1897, p. 3.

[33] 23 September 1900, Herzl to Cowen, copy in CZA, I. Cohen Papers, A213/7/46; and English Zionist Federation, *Opinions of Parliamentary Candidates on Zionism*, rev. ed. (London, 1901), p. 1.

[34] B. S. Strauss, letter to the editor, JC, 12 October 1900, p. 6. *Opinions of Parliamentary Candidates* listed favorable replies from only 114 candidates. Of these 46 were elected. Of the 21 Jewish candidates, the only 3 to reply favorably were all soundly defeated: Sir I. Hart in Central Hackney, B. S. Strauss at St. George's in the East (East London), and H. H. Raphael in South Derbyshire. Their lack of success stood in marked contrast to the fortunes of some prominent Jewish anti-Zionist candidates. Both Stuart Samuel (at Whitechapel) and B. L. Cohen (East Islington) were returned with huge majorities despite the ostentatious support of the EZF for their non-Jewish opponents.

[35] 15 November 1901, Cowen to Herzl, CZA, Herzl Papers, H VIII 161.

Zionist circles, however, were more understanding. In fact, it was not the absence of immediate results that alone dictated their decision to shift their attention from Whitechapel and Westminster. Rather, as their private correspondence reveals, their preference for a slower campaign of institutional "infiltration" was also influenced by their own perceptions of the consequences of the various options open to them. Their images of themselves and of their standing in Anglo-Jewry, while initially helping to arouse their support for Herzl, eventually circumscribed the sphere of activities that they were prepared to undertake on his behalf. Ultimately, they had to admit their ambivalence toward those of their potential supporters who were no more than on the fringe of established Anglo-Jewish society—if that. Despite their professions to the contrary, the senior members of the EZF essentially regarded both the recently arrived immigrants and gentile Zionist sympathizers as "aliens." They undoubtedly sympathized with the plight of the former, just as they sincerely admired the vision of the latter. But their personal inclinations toward political caution and their social backgrounds made them hesitate before combining with such forces against the accepted mainstream of the community of which they considered themselves a part.

Their attitude toward a program of parliamentary action provides a case in point. Senior Zionists in England were no less sensitive than their opponents to the danger of arousing anti-Semitism by a direct and sectarian appeal to a Jewish vote. Even before the returns for the general election of 1900 were known, many of Herzl's most influential English supporters had questioned the propriety of a specifically Zionist "ticket" in individual constituencies. Here, too, Sir Francis Montefiore's response had been typical. In declining Herzl's "flattering" invitation to stand for Parliament, Montefiore disqualified himself on grounds of principle, as well as personal shortcomings. A large number of Jewish Zionist representatives in Parliament, he held, would merely confirm "the danger of exciting jealousy. . . . Should Zionist questions ever come before the House they could be better dealt with by an independent, though sympathetic Christian."[36] In 1902, similar considerations appear to have influenced Gaster's attitude toward the possibility that Herzl would be invited to give evidence before the Royal Commission on Alien Immigration. This, he wrote to Greenberg, "is one point which affects wider circles, and if I had not heard from many and influential quarters as to the consequences which this departure may have for the future of the Jews and of Zionism here I would have kept silent." Even within unquestionably ardent Zionist circles, he claimed, the news of Herzl's invitation

> has caused widespread dismay and dissatisfaction, far more than one realises. And should he persist in following the advice which I am sorry to say has been given to him under a very wrong impression as to the effect it will have on the cause of Zionism, I am afraid it will be digging the grave of the movement here, at any rate. I am not exaggerating and I know full well the bearing of the words I am using! The Alien Commission is unfortunately already a Jewish Commission. We must take care not to make it a Jewish international Commission.[37]

Different influences precluded the adoption of the other extreme strategy, an exclusive appeal to the immigrant masses, not the least of which was the social composition of the leadership of the EZF itself. That body owed its foundation largely to the efforts of Bentwich, de Haas, Gaster, and Greenberg; among the more prominent and active members of its first executives were Sir Francis Montefiore, Joseph Cowen, and S. B. Rubinstein. They all unquestionably considered themselves part of the Anglicized section of the community, even though only Montefiore's family had lived in England for more than two generations. In neither their intellectual interests, professional pursuits, nor geographical habitat did they share the experience of the mass of first generation immigrants. Bentwich practiced law; Greenberg was a publisher; Cowen a clothing manufacturer; Rubinstein a

[36] 28 September 1900, Montefiore to Herzl, ibid., H VIII 577. Also Bentwich speech in *JC*, 12 October 1900, p. 8.
[37] 9 June 1902, Gaster to Greenberg, CZA, Gaster Papers, A203/239.

timber merchant; and de Haas a journalist who wrote almost exclusively in English. They could not fail to be aware of the social gulf that separated them, predominantly residents of fashionable West and North West London (in Rubinstein's case, Stoke Newington), from their coreligionists in the East End. Neither did their wives let them forget it.[38] Not unexpectedly, moreover, their paths to Zionism, and the expectations which they had of the movement, further distinguished them from Herzl's immigrant supporters. For the latter, Zionism provided a singular gleam of hope in an otherwise depressing world. But for many of the Anglicized Zionists, affiliation to "the cause" could offer much else besides: welcome relief from the lack of excitement of their daily lives (it is "such a change from blouse-making," mused Cowen); or a useful opportunity to extend their communal contacts and thus combine national duty with personal business.[39]

At one level, this explains why as early as the turn of the century some members of the immigrant community were forcefully criticizing the Zionists of the West End for their "cavalier assumption of the right to lead the Zionist forces throughout the country." Native Zionists undoubtedly deserved credit for having founded the EZF; but that did not excuse their subsequent misdemeanors. The native leadership, alleged Marmor, prevented immigrant Zionists from sending delegates of their own choice to annual Zionist congresses; Yeḥezkel Wortsmann (a Hebrew and Yiddish journalist who led the London "democratic fraction" in their call for practical work in *Ereẓ Yisrael* and the promotion

---

[38] See, e.g., Greenberg's lament to Wolffsohn, 16 March 1903, CZA, Herzl Papers, H VIII 292, and Norman Bentwich and Margery Bentwich, *Herbert Bentwich: The Pilgrim Father* (Jersusalem, 1940), pp. 129-30. For further biographical notes see: Joseph Cowen, "My Conversion to Zionism," in *Theodor Herzl: A Memorial*, ed. Meyer Weisgal (New York, 1929), pp. 104-106; Ruth L. Deech, "Jacob de Haas: A Biography," *Herzl Year Book* 7 (1971):321-53; Paul Goodman, *Zionism in England 1899-1949* (London, 1949), chap. 1; and, in greater detail, Virginia H. Hein, "British Followers of Theodor Herzl" (Ph.D. diss., Georgia State University, 1978), chaps. 3-7.

[39] E.g., 17 September 1897, Cowen to Zangwill, CZA, Zangwill Papers, A120/57; and Solomon Schechter's strictures on de Haas in 12 August 1902, Schechter to H. Bentwich, CZA, H. Bentwich Papers, A100/6a.

of Hebrew culture in the Diaspora) claimed that de Haas, Greenberg, and their cronies were ostracizing his group and attempting to undermine its influence.[40] However exaggerated these charges might have been, they cannot be entirely dismissed. The small caucus in whose hands the leadership of the EZF was first vested certainly did resist the call "to organise the poor against the *frum* and the rich" which was tentatively articulated at the Clerkenwell Conference in 1898. That gathering had not been convened with the intention of initiating such a drastic turn of events. Bentwich, who chaired the subcommittee which prepared the conference, deliberately steered a more moderate course. He was, for instance, quite explicit in his assurance that the proceedings would not commence until suitable precautions had been taken to "prevent the admission of any dangerous or undesirable elements."[41]

Once the EZF had been established, its founders were anxious to ensure that it would not be swamped by an East End "mob and rabble"[42] whom they might not be able to control. De Haas, for all his fiery oratory in public, privately wished to avoid a total split with the communal Establishment for as long as possible; Gaster, too, notwithstanding his public identification with the "foreigners" in the community, privately warned his fellow Zionist officers of the danger of launching anything like a "social crusade."[43] In general, the leaders of the movement in England appear to have agreed that an intemperate following would alienate them from the very type of person whose sympathy they ultimately hoped to gain. It is this consideration that explains the sorrow and pain with which Greenberg subsequently reported

[40] K. Marmor, "Die Elyen Bill fun der English Zionist Federation und Ihr Entshtehung," *Yudishe Frayhayt*, 1 (May-June 1905):13-20; and *Protokoll der Verhandlungen des VI. Zionisten-Congresses* (Vienna, 1903), p. 271; also Yeḥezkel Wortsmann, *Vos Villen die Tsionisten?* (London, 1901), pp. 24-31.

[41] 13 February 1898, Goldsmid to Hirsch, CZA, Files of the Chovevei Zion Association, A2/11.

[42] 25 November 1900, Loewe to Kessler, CZA, L. Kessler Papers, A143/2; 7 November 1900, Greenberg to Actions Committee, CZA, Files of the Central Zionist Office (Vienna), Z1/403.

[43] 1 April 1897, de Haas to Herzl, CZA, Herzl Papers, H VIII 513; 29 June 1898, Gaster to Bensusan, CZA, Gaster Papers, A203/113.

that the EZF was in danger of becoming no more than an "East End Committee." Cowen, too, thought that this eventuality would lead to disaster, and even talked about the possibility of a schism within the local movement.[44] Some months earlier, in November 1901, de Haas had resigned from the EZF precisely because he objected to the possibility that the Zionist movement in Britain would "be made wholly an East End one." In his view, progress could only be made if Herzl's supporters adopted a more diplomatic tone toward the anti-Zionist leadership of the community. "Our Jargon element, unfortunately, understands nothing of these things, and is suspicious of all not Jargonised, or Russified."[45]

THE PREFERENCE

There remained, then, the option of infiltrating the existing communal institutions. This was not an altogether forlorn policy. For one thing, some leading Zionists in Britain already possessed a foothold in those bodies. Gaster sat on the council of the Anglo-Jewish Association; Herbert Bentwich was a member of the Board of Deputies; Alfred Englander represented Vine Court Synagogue at the board of the Federation; Leopold Greenberg represented Hampstead on the council of the United Synagogue; Sir Francis Montefiore was in 1902 elected vice president of the Elders of the Sephardi Congregation, and in 1904 president. Men of lesser rank could obtain an entrance to other institutions, such as the Jewish Board of Guardians, simply by undertaking philanthropic work and donating small contributions to the main Jewish charities ("as the means to the end of mixing with the better classes").[46] Furthermore, these bridgeheads could be consolidated and expanded. Cowen, Bentwich, and Greenberg, for instance, attempted to widen the circle of Herzlite communal workers by

[44] 5 March 1902, Greenberg to Herzl, CZA, Herzl Papers, H VIII 291, and 3 March 1902, Cowen to Herzl, ibid., H VIII 161.

[45] 5 November 1901, de Haas to Herzl, ibid., H VIII 315; note the conciliatory speeches by Gaster and de Haas to the West Central Zionist Association, JC, 31 January 1902, pp. 17-18.

[46] 3 May 1900, L. Loewe to Herzl, CZA, Herzl Papers, H VIII 527.

disseminating Zionist propaganda in the more fashionable areas of London. In 1898 they established the first Zionist Society in the West End, and in 1901 attempted to persuade Herzl to talk there.[47] Gaster had a more ambitious program. Concentrating on the established institutions themselves, he attempted to present a carefully selected list of candidates for their offices. He prodded Francis Montefiore to become eligible for election to the council of the AJA, and enrolled "more subscribers so I can have a list of my own nominations for the elections." "Many a friend," he reported, "has faithfully promised to come to . . . the annual Meeting and to vote straight!" Subsequently, he also instructed several "Zionist" syngagogues in London on the methods of obtaining representation at the Board of Deputies.[48]

Even during its earliest and most tentative stages, this activity produced two important results. First, the presence of a group of vocal Zionists on the governing bodies of the more important communal institutions ensured that the Zionist case would not fail by default. As has been seen, their task was difficult and their progress slow. Nevertheless, their interjections on Herzl's behalf were sufficiently interesting to be recorded in the *Jewish Chronicle*. Despite the efforts of the chair, debates at the Anglo-Jewish Association and the annual meetings of subscribers to the Board of Guardians were occasionally dominated by Zionist speeches from Greenberg and Cowen; at the United Synagogue and the Federation, less frequently, lively Zionist snipings seem to have provided the only source of interest in otherwise humdrum proceedings.[49] Secondly, and no less noticeably, the small group of

[47] 16 September 1898, Bentwich to Herzl, ibid., H VIII 67; 25 October 1898, Cowen to Gaster, CZA, Gaster Papers, A203/106; and 21 April 1901, Greenberg to Herzl, CZA, Files of the Central Zionist Office (Vienna), Z1/242.

[48] 23 April 1899, Gaster to Greenberg, private, CZA, Gaster Papers, A203/110, and 27 April 1899, Gaster to F. Montefiore, London, Mocatta Library, Gaster Letter Book, 1897-1902, p. 267; 12 Janaury 1903, Goodman to Gaster, CZA, Gaster Papers, A203/133.

[49] E.g., annual meeting of AJA, 13 July 1902, Mocatta Library, Archives of the AJA, Council Minutes Book, Vol. 3, p. 165, and JC, 18 July 1902, pp. 14-16; annual meeting of the Board of Guardians, London, Jewish Welfare Board, Minute Book, Vol. 4, p. 75, and JC, 23 March 1903, pp. 10-12; council meeting

Zionist activists also provided a focus for other disaffected elements on those bodies by eagerly taking digs at the recognized leaders of Anglo-Jewry and the manner of their appointment. Greenberg, for instance, was one of the first to suggest (in 1898) procedural reforms at the United Synagogue council, "inter alia to prevent the virtual selection by the honorary officers themselves of their own colleagues"; Bentwich, likewise, was in 1903 the only member of the Board of Deputies to mar the conviviality of David Alexander's election as president of that body. "He thought it was time those offices were not life estates and were held only for a certain term, so that there could be a regular alteration of office-holders."[50]

Ultimately, it was by adopting this tactic that Herzl's principal lieutenants in Britain gained communal attention. More crucially, it was thus that they transposed the specific question of Zionism into the more general question of the state of Anglo-Jewry. Both purposes were entirely germane to their dispositions. Greenberg and Bentwich, together with Gaster, Cowen, Zangwill, and—at a different level—de Haas, Rubinstein, and Englander—revelled in their self-appointed role as communal mavericks. Perennially critical of established authority, they constituted a small but tenacious band of collaborators whose relish for the communal fray helped to sustain much of their nationalist fervor. Each in his own way was a tense and prickly character (one reason for their subsequent failure to work in harness at the head of the EZF's affairs); they were not satisfied with positions that were obviously subsidiary to those which the patrician "Cousinhood" tended to regard as exclusively their own. For this group, indeed, Herzl's call to "conquer the community," seems to have come at a propitious stage in their public lives. They were not, after all, novices to the scene of Anglo-Jewish politics. When Herzl issued his call in 1898, Gaster and Bentwich (both aged forty-one),

---

of United Synagogue, JC, 7 February 1902, pp. 12-13; and board meeting of Federation, 9 May 1904, London, Federation of Synagogues, Minute Book, Vol. 2, pp. 100-102, and JC, 14 May 1904, pp. 11-12.

[50] Greenberg, letter to editor, JC, 15 April 1898, p. 8; Bentwich, speech at meeting of Board of Deputies, reported in JC, 20 February 1903, p. 11.

Greenberg (thirty-six) and, most of all, Zangwill (thirty-four) had already attained various degrees of communal prominence. Each was also unabashedly avid for more—and perhaps, therefore, proportionately disappointed when their progress did not keep pace with the scope of their ambitions. They had, admittedly, risen far above the common ruck of congregational busybodies. But only occasionally, and grudgingly, were they being admitted to the elevated arena of Anglo-Jewish policy-making, and even then more as observers than as participants. They might have shared a sense that they had entered a cul-de-sac in communal life, seemingly condemned to hover on the fringes of a world whose positions of influence and power were reserved for men with a more distinguished pedigree than their own. Socially, as much as temperamentally and ideologically, they were thus poised to play the role of a "party of opposition" for which Herzl had unwittingly cast them.[51]

This context of pressures and motives would appear to account for much of what subsequently transpired. As Zionists, Greenberg, Cowen, Gaster, Bentwich, and Zangwill all enhanced their reputation for dissidence. Nevertheless, they deliberately avoided giving the impression that their interests were limited to issues of specifically Zionist concern. Implicit in their behavior was the assumption that, although Zionism might provide them with a worthy cause, it was simply not compelling enough to constitute the only issue of communal dissent. The pursuit of their ends (ideological, personal, and programmatic) demanded that they address themselves to a far wider range of interests. As Greenberg subsequently pointed out to Wolffsohn, he and Bentwich did not really aim to create fresh sources of tension within the community; they preferred to take advantage of the differences of opinion

[51] See the analysis in Hein, "British Followers of Theodor Herzl," pp. 170-72. Significantly, one interview with Bentwich was specifically entitled "The Opposition," *JC*, 23 December 1901, pp. 18, 21. R. N. Salaman later recalled: "To people like myself, who met him frequently on committees and casually outside them, it was always [Bentwich's] obstructionist and antagonistic attitude which came foremost." 22 November 1940, to N. Bentwich, CZA, N. Bentwich Papers, A255/606.

that were in any case developing within its native Establishment.[52] The object, throughout, was to exploit emergent situations adroitly (rather than ruthlessly), and thus to leave open the possibility of occasional collaboration with non-Zionists who shared many of their communal concerns.

At one level, this strategy demanded no more than that the Zionists note—and encourage—certain personal and professional tensions. Hermann Gollancz, for instance, might be induced to speak at a B'nei Zion meeting simply in order to snub the chief rabbi; he would thereby provide one further proof of his dissatisfaction with the manner in which Adler had refused to grant him the rabbinical diploma. As for Samuel Montagu, "there is just the chance that you can get him to serve our ends in order that he may take away a chance from Rothschild, whom . . . he hates like the devil does holy water."[53] At another level, existing disagreement over issues of communal policy could be put to Zionist use. This, admittedly, was more difficult since the senior members of the major institutional connections within Anglo-Jewry had during the nineteenth century established a tradition of broad agreement about their rather imprecisely defined political objectives. This had helped them to maintain the convention of infrequently interrupted harmony at the center of affairs. By the early twentieth century, however, matters had begun to change, with a range of pressing matters steadily undermining the attitude of empiricism which had hitherto obviated the need for communal debates on matters of principle. Prominent among the new issues that clamored for attention were the introduction of an Aliens Bill into Parliament, the growing expense of the policy of "repatriating" immigrants to Russia and Romania, the calls for a General Jewish Conference to discuss the plight of Jewry, and the Kishinev pogrom. All of these matters were, of course, tangentially related to Zionism, but it was not for that reason alone that they were of importance to the Zionists. Equally significant was the fact that they provoked communal debates over ends and

[52] 6 April 1903, Greenberg to Wolffsohn, CZA, Wolffsohn Papers, W78.

[53] 7 February 1900, de Haas to Gaster, CZA, Gaster Papers, A203/112; and 5 March 1902, Greenberg to Herzl, CZA, Herzl Papers, H VIII 291.

means, and thus produced some strains on the cohesiveness hitherto engendered by the supererogatory social benevolence of the
communal leaders. In a more local context, the proposal to establish a specifically Jewish hospital in Manchester, partly in order
to counter Christian missionary influence there, engendered controversy. At dispute was the willingness of the community to
reconstruct some of the barriers between Jew and gentile that an
earlier generation of fighters for emancipation had attempted to
break down.[54]

This, it must be stressed, was a carefully circumscribed debate,
in which the lower classes of the community (especially the immigrants) did not play a significant part. Prominent among the
Manchester group that eventually raised the money for a Jewish
hospital, for instance, was Counsellor Charles Dreyfus, the pro-
prietor of the Clayton Aniline Company; his principal local critics
included Nathan Laski.[55] On only one occasion did the poor
immigrant Jews of London attempt to influence decisions at the
AJA by forcing their way into one of its council meetings.[56] No
such scenes were reported at other bodies. Generally, differences
of opinion—such as they were at this stage—assumed the form
of a more restrained, and restricted, debate between groups of
individuals from similar social and cultural backgrounds.

For precisely that reason, leading Zionists in England felt that
circumstances favored the strategy of institutional infiltration which
they in any case preferred. Joseph Cowen, as early as 1898, had
specifically advised against too blatant an attempt to overthrow
the "money bags." Instead:

it seems to me that this [Zionist] question is above all one to
be treated as politics generally are. We must be diplomatic,
opportunists, everything and anything to gain our ends. It will
give us strange bedfellows but that is the way of big movements.

[54] E.g., Singer letter to JC, 14 September 1900, pp. 6-7.
[55] Significantly, Laski was not at the time a Zionist while Dreyfus, who provided
Weizmann with employment in Manchester, was.
[56] JC, 13 July 1900, p. 15.

Don't kick one man if you can help it—you never know when you may need him."[57]

One example of the workings of this policy is provided by the events of mid-1903, when public agitation over the Kishinev atrocities was at its height. Unlike the leaders of the Anglo-Jewish Association and the Board of Deputies, senior Zionists pressed for a public demonstration of the community's concern and horror. They did not, however, provoke an unrestrained onslaught on those bodies. At first they attempted to work through them. Sometimes they found it necessary to take the initiative in order to do so: Bentwich at the Board of Deputies and Greenberg at the United Synagogue were insistent critics of the inadequacies of the joint letter of protest which Claude Montefiore and David Alexander had sent to the *Times*.[58] Often, however, this was unnecessary. Other highly placed members of the community were equally vociferous in their demands for more effective action, and all the Zionists had to do was provide moral and vocal support. Most particularly was this so once the Conjoint Foreign Committee of the AJA and the Board of Deputies had virtually vetoed the AJA's earlier decision to hold a public demonstration under the chairmanship of the current Lord Mayor of London (himself a Jew). Responding to the demands of Zionists and non-Zionists alike, the EZF then organized its own "public *hesped*" at the Great Assembly Hall in East London on 6 July.[59] Nevertheless, the Establishment was not thereby ostracized; nei-

[57] 1 July 1898, Cowen to Gaster, CZA, Gaster Papers, A203/106.

[58] Published on 18 May 1903. For criticisms by Bentwich and Greenberg, see JC, 29 May 1903, p. 14, and 19 June 1903, p. 25 respectively.

[59] In Claude Montefiore's absence, the AJA Council had on 14 June 1903 recommended the public demonstration by 19 votes to 3; the motion had been introduced by Leopold Schloss and Delissa Joseph, neither of whom were Zionists. After a subsequent meeting of the Conjoint Foreign Committee, this decision was reversed by 12 votes to 7 on 22 June 1903; Mocatta Library, Archives of the AJA, Council Minute Book, Vol. 3, pp. 182-85. For other, non-Zionist, protests at the community's inactivity, see the Pentecost sermons delivered by A. A. Green, H. Gollancz, and S. Levy, reported in JC, 5 June 1903, pp. 24-25. For one call for the Zionists to take the initiative, see letter from M. Harris, in JC, 29 May 1903, p. 8.

ther was the sense of frustration and anger that the Conjoint's decision engendered allowed to provide an excuse for communal rebellion. On the contrary, Gaster lodged a

> protest against the use which will be made by speakers on a Zionist platform, to attack other institutions in the name of Zion. Any one who has a grievance to ventilate . . . ought in my opinion to call a special meeting solely for that purpose and not under the flag of Zionism.

In particular, the Zionists were concerned to keep themselves "clear from the East End excitement." Having considered their duty "very carefully" (in Cowen's words), they "decided only to work with the general community" and to avoid the mass demonstration, with its inevitable "much too strong language," which was being organized by the socialists and anarchists in Hyde Park.[60] Individual members of the Zionist executive (Englander in particular) did join the independent East End committees that were established in defiance of the expressed wish of the Board of Deputies and the AJA, but they often appear to have done so in order deliberately to "channel and manage" the emotions that such gatherings were bound to arouse.[61] As for the Zionists' own meeting, it was from the first to be kept strictly "to its character of a religious ceremony and Zionist manifestation, without the admixture of any compromising attack on the communal leadership." The speakers invited to the platform were selected for their moderation. Their brief, according to Gaster (the chairman), was not to stir up the community against its principal institutions, but to "try and conciliate and win the support and sympathy of all the other true Jewish bodies and thus work together for one common end."[62] On the night, Professor Hermann

[60] On which see Fishman, *East End Jewish Radicals*, pp. 250-52.

[61] 4/5 June 1903, Loewe to Gaster, CZA, Gaster Papers, A203/133. Note, in particular, Englander's restraining remarks at the meeting of the Kishinev Atrocities Relief Committee, reported in *JC*, 29 May 1903, p. 12.

[62] 13 May 1903, Gaster to Englander, private, CZA, Gaster Papers, A203/136; 16 June 1903, H. van Finkelstein (secretary of EZF) to Gaster, ibid., A203/133; 15 May 1903, Cowen to Herzl, CZA, Herzl Papers, H VIII 161; 21 May 1903, Cowen to de Haas, CZA, de Haas Papers, A224/5.

Gollancz did make one telling reference to the inactivity of the established leaders of the community "whose lines had probably fallen in pleasant places," but Gaster was carefully restrained. His object, throughout, had been to "try and *win over* to our cause those who hitherto for one reason or another are either antagonistic to our movement or still undecided."[63]

The management and tone of the Kishinev demonstration marked a significant stage in the development of a recognizable communal strategy on the part of leading Zionists in England. Its importance was both narrower and deeper than its initial impact might suggest. Narrower, because the EZF's decision to hold the demonstration did not herald a full-scale onslaught on the authority of the Anglo-Jewish Association or the Board of Deputies. Broader, because the demonstration did nevertheless indicate the extent of the role that Herzl's English supporters wished to play in their own community. By 1903, they were no longer content to restrict themselves entirely to the diffusion of their leader's nationalist theses through the medium of meetings and societies which had been called or created specifically for that purpose. Their own ambitions, their code of operational procedure, and their victory over the Chovevei Zion Association had all prompted senior members of the EZF to address a wider series of concentric and differing audiences. They sought to shed the image of a fringe faction, concerned exclusively with a topic of visionary proportions but marginal importance. Instead, they conspicuously pitched themselves—as Zionists—into the more obviously mainstream issues of communal concern, and set out to influence the established institutions by which Anglo-Jewry was governed. In so doing, they had an effect on both the direction of Zionist work in England and on the tone and form of debate throughout the community. Henceforth, the Zionist movement—although not necessarily its ideology—was to be inextricably linked to the entire spectrum of Anglo-Jewish life. Despite divisions within the

---

[63] 11 May 1903, Gaster to van Finkelstein, Mocatta Library, Gaster Papers, Letter Book, 1902-1903, pp. 565-66; for a report of the meeting see *JC*, 10 July 1903, p. 10.

EZF itself, Zionism was gradually to provide a testing ground for the strength of several competing, and sometimes radically opposed, elements within the community. Under cover of its name, new alignments were to be forged and old alliances broken. It became, in short, a political force in the community.

PART TWO

The Politics of Zionism,
1904-1914

3

Storm over East Africa and Stress within the English Zionist Federation, 1904-1914

T HE B A L F O U R D E C L A R A -
tion overshadows the early history of Zionism in Britain. Such
was the diplomatic and communal impact of that document that,
almost inevitably, there exists an impulse to examine and judge
the record for the period prior to 1917 in the light of that event.
If succumbed to, this temptation attaches importance to whatever
manoeuvers and stratagems might have brought about the Declaration—or, more precisely, might have contributed to the decision to work for its attainment; all else might be considered
subordinate. It is arguably legitimate to interpret Weizmann's
entire communal and diplomatic strategy after the outbreak of
World War I in terms of his search for official British recognition
of the Zionist claim to Palestine. A similar structure of analysis,
however, could be applied to the dozen years preceding 1914.
Such was the approach adopted in a letter of congratulation that
Herbert Bentwich sent to Gaster ten days after the Balfour Declaration was published. Not even during the dullest and most
uninspiring days of the prewar period, he wrote, had leading
English Zionists despaired of obtaining their Government's recognition of Jewish national claims. On the contrary, they had
persistently worked toward that end.[1] Weizmann, in this view,
was merely a catalyst. Both before and after Herzl's death, the

---

[1] 12 November 1917, Bentwich to Gaster, London, Mocatta Library, University College, Gaster Papers.

(79)

groundwork had been laid by other men with an equal call on their people's gratitude.

Some of the documentary evidence does appear to substantiate such contentions. Ever since the foundation of the EZF, most of its leading members (although Bentwich himself perhaps less than most) had supported Herzl's diplomatic efforts to attain an international charter for a Jewish homeland. In theory, their emphasis on political work had caused their break from the Chovevei Zion Association. Although reluctant to reduce Zionism to a sectarian issue in British party politics, they did agree with Herzl's more discreet excursions into the field of high diplomacy. They were particularly eager to help where British statesmen were concerned. As early as 1898, Herzl had himself referred to England as "the Archimedan point where the lever could be applied"; subsequently, his lieutenants considered London to be his "proper sphere of operations," where they wished him to establish his headquarters.[2] They were particularly put out by the fact that Herzl "lives for 50 weeks out of every 52 practically under the advice of those ignoramuses in Vienna," and was therefore unaware of the possible advantages of playing upon the Protestant fundamentalism which seemed to infuse British society.[3] The ears of England, they informed him, "are pricked up on the question of the return of the Jews to Palestine, and any approach . . . will be regarded mythically." He ought, they advised, to parade his program "boldly as a plan of Jewish Salvation" and put his case before a prominent member of the Cabinet ("If you can see two so much the better").[4]

As is well known, Herzl accomplished precisely that. He had his first meeting with the secretary of state for the colonies, Joseph Chamberlain, on 22 October 1902. The latter arranged for him

[2] Herzl's statement to the Clerkenwell Conference, dated 18 February 1898, in Paul Goodman, *Zionism in England, 1899-1949* (London, 1949), pp. 18-19; see also 16 January 1902, Cowen to Herzl, CZA, Herzl Papers, H VIII 161 and 5 November 1903, Zangwill to Herzl, ibid., H VIII 946.

[3] 22 May 1903, Cowen to de Haas, New York, Zionist Organization of America, de Haas Papers, microfilm 1.

[4] 2 May 1903, Cowen to Herzl, CZA, Herzl Papers, H VIII 291.

to meet with the secretary of state for foreign affairs, Lord Lansdowne, on the following afternoon. With both men he discussed
the possibility that the British government might grant the Zionists a territory in Cyprus or, which seemed preferable to all
parties, in the Sinai Peninsula. These moves were closely followed
by Lord Rothschild (who, although impressed by Herzl's somewhat breathless accounts of the conversations, nevertheless refused to be hurried into putting 5 million pounds sterling into
such schemes). Herzl was more sympathetically supported by senior Zionists in Britain, who had greater hopes of a fruitful outcome. Leopold Greenberg played a particularly prominent role.
It was he who arranged Herzl's introduction to Joseph Chamberlain (Greenberg and Chamberlain both came from Birmingham where they may have had some earlier contact); subsequently, as the discussions dragged on, Greenberg acted as Herzl's
ambassador in London, performing various wearisome tasks on
his behalf. With more panache and independence (a fact that
aroused Herzl's suspicions) Greenberg also bore the brunt of the
negotiations with Lord Cromer (Britain's agent and consul-gen-
eral in Cairo) and the Egyptian government in 1902, when it
appeared that a concession for El Arish might be in sight. Despite
his awareness of the snags involved in the project, Greenberg did
not question the underlying strategy that justified its pursuit.
Essentially, the line to the British government had to be kept
open. "If we are careful," he reflected, "we shall be so able to
work things, that a Jewish Settlement will become not alone a
Zionist question but also a question in which the British Gov't.
is involved and which for their credit's sake they will have to see
through." Zionist policy, therefore, ought to be directed toward
getting ministers "so involved in our project and so virtually
pledged that they must see us through somewhere."[5]

That is precisely what seemed to have occurred in the summer
of 1903. After further negotiations between Chamberlain and

[5] 6 March 1903, Greenberg to Herzl, ibid., H VIII 292. On the El Arish
negotiations see: Raphael Patai, "Herzl's Sinai Project—A Documentary Record,"
Herzl Year Book 1 (1958):107-144; and Oskar K. Rabinowicz, "Herzl and England," *Jewish Social Studies* 13 (1951):25-46.

Greenberg, the British government then promised "to entertain favourably proposals for the establishment [in East Africa] of a colony or Jewish settlement, on conditions which will enable its members to observe their national customs."[6] By any standards, this was a diplomatic coup, the enormity of which is not reduced by either the truncated form of Lord Lansdowne's offer or the limited interpretation that (from the first) he chose to give it. For whatever motives, and in however oblique a manner, he had confirmed the impression that Herzl had already formed in 1902: "The British Government had recognized him, and the movement represented by him, as a negotiating party."[7] In so doing Lansdowne had revolutionized Zionist fortunes. Hitherto, Herzl had made little progress. He had failed to clinch a bargain with Cromer, and had received very little recognition from either the sultan, the kaiser, or the Russian minister of the interior. In the last resort, and very much against his own inclinations and intentions, his diplomatic approaches had assumed the air of petitions rather than negotiations. As such, they had smacked of the traditional intercessionary methods practiced throughout the Diaspora by a long line of cautious *shtadlanim*. The East Africa offer was something entirely different; for the first time, the government of one country proposed to enter into a formal and territorial relationship with a movement representing Jews of several others, without apparent regard for either immediate financial profit or short-term civic return. Instead, the basis for negotiation had been the thesis which Herzl had throughout claimed to be proper and relevant—the common interest of both parties in seeking a political solution to a humanitarian and social problem. Compared to this lofty plain of apparent agreement, differences over details—the form of the constitution and size of territory— seemed paltry. What counted was that the British government— no less—had made an offer to the Jewish people at large, and

[6] 14 August 1903, Sir Clement Hill to Greenberg, reproduced in Robert G. Weisbord, *African Zion: The Attempt to Establish a Jewish Colony in the East Africa Protectorate, 1903-1905* (Philadelphia, 1968), pp. 79-80. Weisbord's book covers the entire subject.

[7] Quoted in Alex Bein, *Theodore Herzl*, (Philadelphia, 1943), pp. 425-26.

not to certain Jewish individuals in particular. As Greenberg, once again, immediately grasped:

> The value of the proposal . . . is politically immense. . . . It will for the first time since the Diaspora[,] almost [,] be a recognition of the necessity for aiding our people as a whole— not a mere local section as was the case in the Berlin Treaty for instance—and hence will be the first recognition of our people as a Nation.[8]

That, of course, was precisely the claim that iconoclast anti-Zionists found so objectionable. They had from the first denigrated the notion that autonomous Jewish settlements ought to be created anywhere in the world. Consequently, they took no direct part in the highly charged debates which ensued within Zionist circles as to the respective merits of the locations loosely referred to as "Zion" and "Uganda."[9] Indeed, from their point of view, whichever was ultimately preferred was really immaterial; the crucial question was the extent to which "the general public of the Anglo-Jewish community" (for instance) considered the entire idea of Jewish self-government to be either desirable or justifiable. One man who had no doubt of the answer was Lucien Wolf, now honorary secretary of the Conjoint Foreign Committee of the Board of Deputies and the Anglo-Jewish Association. Ideologically opposed to the very notion of Jewish nationalism (and perhaps irritated by Herzl's assumption of negotiating prerogatives properly reserved to his committee), he had seized upon the East Africa debate as an opportunity to attack Zionism in general. To this end, he had reached for his pen even before the internal Zionist wrangle had drawn to its exhausted close (not improperly, since its outcome was irrelevant to his argument). He would, he announced in the *Times* in 1903, readily give the East Africa project "the most favourable consideration" were it merely a remedial scheme of emigration. But there was more to it than that. The "inner meaning" of the proposal was the "invincible unas-

[8] 7 June 1903, Greenberg to Herzl, CZA, Herzl Papers, H VIII 292a.
[9] On which see Michael Heymann, ed., *The Uganda Controversy*, 2 vols., (Jerusalem, 1970; Tel Aviv, 1973).

similability of the Jews." As such, it already constituted "a comprehensive capitulation to the calumnies of the anti-Semites"; if implemented, it would undoubtedly rear "a monument to our civic incapacity" throughout the Diaspora. Privately, said hostile hearsay, Wolf exploited his influence in official circles in order to persuade the Government to climb down.[10] His public utterances were themselves damaging enough. Little was added to the prestige of either camp by his prediction that: "The only 'national customs' which the scheme would perpetuate are the disagreeable habits of life which have unfortunately grown up among the Eastern Jews."[11]

As will be seen, such themes (together with their more dignified variations) were to be given full rein at a later stage. Meanwhile, they were largely subordinated to the more salient matter of choice. The East Africa offer threw Zionists and anti-Zionists into an emotional turmoil which was further complicated by Herzl's sudden death in April 1904. After considerable heart-searching and much high drama at the sixth (1903) and seventh (1905) Congresses, the Zionists formally allowed the British proposal to lapse—much to the relief, incidentally, of some ministers. David Wolffsohn, who succeeded Herzl to the presidency of the Zionist Organization in 1905, was anxious to retain the tradition of Zionist diplomacy, and himself twice conducted negotiations in Constantinople. Weizmann, as is well known, put out an even earlier line to Arthur Balfour, with whom he conferred informally in 1905. But neither effort produced immediate results, and the Zionists found no means of exploiting the opportunities supposedly provided by either the revolution of the Young Turks in 1908, the Italo-Turkish war of 1911, or the Balkan wars of 1912-1913.[12] Instead, the movement increasingly, and perhaps inevitably, tended to concentrate its attention on steady "practical" work in Palestine and "cultural" activity in the Diaspora. In so doing, it seemed to lose something of its glamour. Wolffsohn,

[10] 8 September 1903, Cowen to Herzl, CZA, Herzl Papers, H VIII 161.

[11] Wolf's letters to the *Times*, 8 July and 9 September 1903.

[12] Pinḥas A. Alsberg, "Ha-Orientatẓiah shel Mediniut ha-Hanhalah ha-Ẓionit erev Milkhemet ha-Olam ha-Rishonah," *Ẓion*, n.s. 22 (1957):149-76.

even though deserving of more credit than many of his contemporaries were prepared to allow, was conspicuously lacking in the dynamism and charisma which many Zionists craved. His most substantial achievement, the fact that he held his disparate movement together and provided it with a more workmanlike and less personalized structure than his predecessor had permitted, was itself prosaic. Harmony, it seemed, could only be achieved by lowering Zionist ambitions and reducing the tempo of Zionist activity.[13] There seemed little of Herzl's grandeur, still less of his brazenness, in the repetitive agricultural reports and financial statistics ritually presented to Zionist congresses during the prewar period.

ZANGWILL'S CHALLENGE TO THE ENGLISH ZIONIST FEDERATION

While the momentum of Zionist diplomacy visibly slowed, a far more vigorous pose was struck by Israel Zangwill. Dismayed by the manner in which the majority at the seventh congress had spurned East Africa, he had broken with the official Zionist movement in 1905 and, together with other disaffected elements, founded the Jewish Territorial Organisation (Ito). As its president, he attempted to revive the British government's original offer and, when that failed, cast about for an alternative site.[14] He took pains to ensure that his efforts were made known to as wide an audience as possible. Not the least of Zangwill's objectives was to cultivate the image of a resolute—even aggressive—man of the world. His interest in the denizens of the ghetto, he claimed, extended far beyond the bounds of literary curiosity; his concern for their national welfare entitled him to support as well as acclaim. In pursuit of both, Zangwill flamboyantly followed up every

[13] Compare Louis Lipsky, *A Gallery of Zionist Profiles* (New York, 1956), p. 28; with the judgment of Wolffsohn's latest biographer, Mordekhai Eliav, *David Wolffsohn, ha-Ish u-Zemano* (Tel Aviv, 1978).

[14] *Protokoll der Ersten Konferenz der Judisch-territorialistischen Organisation, Basel 30 Juli-1 August 1905* (Geneva, 1905); and the correspondence with Lord Lyttelton (Chamberlain's successor as secretary of state for the colonies) in *Ito Pamphlets*, no. 1 (London, 1905), p. 5.

lead and flagrantly titillated the imaginations of the Jewish public by dispatching high-sounding "Commissions of Enquiry" to various parts of the globe. The contrast with the drab and somewhat timid appearance of the Zionist Organization was deliberate and, in the specific case of Anglo-Jewry, largely successful. Although the Ito boasted of federations and sympathizers in several countries, the headquarters of its International Council was in London and it was in Great Britain that Zangwill achieved some of his most gratifying successes. By 1914, the British Ito Federation possessed almost twenty branches in London and over thirty in the provinces; its total membership was estimated at some five thousand. Faced with this challenge, the English Zionist Federation could not claim to be the only group in the community representing the forces of Jewish progress.

From the Zionist point of view, the Ito represented an especially insidious threat. Even while attacking the decisions of the seventh Congress, Zangwill continued to proclaim his allegiance to the underlying tenets of Jewish nationalism. His conflict with the Zionists—although very much complicated and embittered by clashes of personality and reciprocal charges of perfidy[15]—was basically over means, not ends. Pragmatic considerations, rather than ideological postulates, constituted the brunt of his arguments. As Ito's very first *Manifesto* (issued on 18 August 1905) made plain, the new body agreed with the Zionist diagnosis that the Jewish question would not be solved until the Jews possessed a land of their own.[16] Furthermore, and likewise in strict con-

---

[15] Zangwill charged that Greenberg had failed to keep his promise of an early introduction to British ministers (7 December 1908, Zangwill to Wolf, CZA, Wolf Papers, A77/4); Greenberg, for his part, reported that, from the start, Zangwill and Wolf had simply put their heads together in order to seek a means of tapping Zionist enthusiasm (15 December 1905, Greenberg to Wolffsohn, CZA, Wolffsohn Papers, W78).

[16] Reprinted in *Speeches, Articles and Letters of Israel Zangwill*, ed. Maurice Simon (London, 1937), pp. 242-48. Nevertheless: "I cannot too strongly draw your attention to the fact that political Zionism run by freethinkers is *not* what the Jewish people had been dreaming of for 19 centuries; and therefore it is a mockery and a false pretence to say that the modern development can only be in Zion. As for the Zionism run by your orthodox gang, it is even a dirtier form of the Messiah." 10 January 1908, Zangwill to Cowen, CZA, Ito files, A36/135.

formity with Herzl's analysis, Zangwill and his International Council castigated with unconcealed contempt the puny efforts of both the Chovevei Zion in Palestine and the Jewish Colonisation Association in Argentina. Where they parted company with the Zionists was in their insistence that, as a *practical* proposition, "Zion" Zionism had reached an impasse. The Kishinev pogrom, which was followed by further outbreaks of anti-Jewish violence in southern Russia, had underlined the necessity for a solution which would have to be radical in its immediacy no less than in its scope. In its readiness to accept East Africa, the Ito, at least, could offer the survivors of such massacres a tangible prospect of a "fertile territory of 18,000 square miles." After the seventh Congress, all the Zionists possessed was a forlorn hope that the sultan might one day be induced to relinquish the Ottoman title to Palestine, and a pious conviction that the Jews, by improbably herculean labours, would ultimately be able to change the inhospitable face of their Holy Land.

This was not an altogether original line of attack. Zangwill had himself shown signs of becoming a "territorialist" *avant la lettre*. In 1898 he had wondered aloud whether Zion was "the only possible centre of a restored Jewish nationality"; in 1899, after noting the climatic and administrative obstacles already impeding the progress of Palestinian settlement work, he had been "tempted to say that Zionism would be practicable but for Zion."[17] Admittedly, Zangwill had been consistently inconsistent. Refusing to take up a clear position in either the Zionist or anti-Zionist trenches, he had developed the annoying habit of sauntering across the battlefield and happily waving to friends and associates on both sides of the lines. There was, it seems, some justification in the charge (made by all parties) that his vacillations were designed merely to display his large portfolio of witticisms and thus gain publicity.[18] But in thus drawing attention

---

[17] See the "Appendix" (published London, 1898) to his *Dreamers of the Ghetto*; and "Zionism," *The Contemporary Review* (October 1899), reprinted in *Speeches*, pp. 100-110.

[18] E.g., Singer, letter to the editor, JC, 2 November 1900, p. 6; and 18 November 1903, S. Schechter to H. Bentwich: "You know that I never trusted him. . . . I enjoyed his jokes as [did] everybody else, but I refuse to recognize

to the alleged impracticality of Zionism, Zangwill had throughout been in respectable company. From the moment Herzl had placed his ideas before the Anglo-Jewish community, some of its most respected members had voiced their doubts as to the trustworthiness of the sultan, the efficacy of Great Power guarantees to a "tiny" state in the Middle East, the advisability of Jewish control over Christian and Moslem Holy Places, the fertility of Palestine, and even the "ruffianism" of the local Arab population.[19] Searching "practical questions" of this nature had formed the core of the *Jewish Chronicle*'s first editorial comment on Herzl's proposals in April 1896 and had taken up most of the discussion at the Maccabeans the following July. Before long, they had become standard features of all discussions of the topic.

Prior to the trauma of the East African offer, many Zionists in England had professed to see some advantage in public debate, even along such lines. After all, they maintained, Herzl's critics could hardly quibble with him on points of detail without at the same time giving prominence to the entire range of theoretical propositions that he had raised. "Opposition," ran the argument, "is to be preferred to indifference."[20] Experience, however, showed that such optimism might be misplaced. Most critics implied that it was pointless to debate the desirability of a Jewish state until they had been convinced that its establishment was even faintly feasible. Let the Zionists first produce evidence of sufficient agricultural and industrial resources within Palestine and of substantial diplomatic and financial backing elsewhere. The latter was precisely what Herzl had sought from the leading Anglo-Jewish bankers; but they had been similarly deflating. Samuel Montagu, as early as 1896, had skirted the central theoretical

---

him as a guide or leader in Judaism." CZA, N. Bentwich Papers, A255/444, p. 20.

[19] For early fears of the reaction of the Moslem peasantry see: 8 April 1898, Col. C. Conder to Bentwich, CZA, H. Bentwich Papers, A100/7a; and A. Carliph, letter to editor, JC, 5 July 1901, p. 7.

[20] See, e.g., "E.Z.F. Bulletin," no. 5 (29 November 1900), CZA, Files of the Central Zionist Office (Vienna), Z1/402; and 7 February 1912, I. Cohen (Actions Committee) to S. Cohen (Liverpool), ibid. (Berlin) Z3/956.

issue by producing a string of practical reasons for refusing to countenance Herzl's pleas for cash and confidence.[21] Rothschild, even while more courteously summarizing why he would "view with horror the establishment of a Jewish Colony pure and simple," emphasized similar drawbacks. Rothschild himself harbored various (even large-scale) plans, "but all these undertakings could easily be wrecked at the outset by schemes which are ambitious, and which the public would consider illjudged and rash. Of one thing I am convinced—that the dream of Palestine is a myth and a will-of-the-wisp." Finally, "let one and all of us beware of the impossible."[22]

Herzl's own attempts to rebuff the consequent charge of romantic utopianism had been unavailing. Little impression seems to have been made by either his detailed analysis of the possible process of economic growth (in *The Jewish State*), or his more enthusiastic assessment of the future Jewish use of modern science (in *Altneuland*). Some geographic authorities did contemplate a possible "restoration" of Palestine to its biblical prosperity. But their reports were infrequent, and often inconsistent.[23] Most evidence appeared to indicate, conclusively, that "Palestine is not a country to which Jews should emigrate." As much seemed painfully obvious to those already associated with existing settlements there, who felt it their duty "to prevent the Jewish population from investing their money and energy in undertakings

[21] "Among them," according to Singer, "(a) the European impetus must come from one of the three Emperors among whose subjects is the most numerous of the Jews; (b) England just now is in. no great favour with the Sultan and the intervention of a British subject would raise opposition rather than lead to concession; (c) Turkish suspicion is invincible; a resettlement in Palestine will only be possible when the division of Turkey is resolved upon by the Powers." Disarmingly, Singer concluded, "If you think you can successfully combat these views, you should write to M. yourself." 11 May 1896, Singer to Herzl, CZA, Herzl Papers, H VIII 739.

[22] Rothschild to Herzl, private and confidential, 29 July 1902 and 18 August 1902, ibid., H VIII 708.

[23] Zionists made great play with the supposedly favorable reports issued on behalf of the Palestine Exploration Fund by Col. Claude Conder, R.E. For examples see: Naḥum Sokolow, *History of Zionism, 1600-1918*, 2 vols. (London, 1919), 2:iii-viii.

which, from our knowledge of the country, appear doomed to failure."[24] Similar conclusions were drawn by occasional visitors. Many Maccabean pilgrims (Bentwich included) had to admit that a tour of Palestine could dampen the most ardent of spirits.[25] Other assessments were more forthright:

> You talk of the Holy Land. In God's name what do you know about Palestine? I have been there and a more God-forsaken place there does not exist on this planet. How can a land thrive without water and whence can you find a supply for irrigation [?] The whole thing is pernicious nonsense, and what is more the advocates of the plan know it to be impossible. . . . I warn you sir that you misuse your undoubtedly great talents by deluding those poor creatures who have not yet got sense enough to save themselves, that you incur a heavy responsibility if you add to their *damnosa hereditas* the additional curse of utterly evil counsel, conceived in the narrowest spirit of racial pride and delivered to them with the recklessness of a Mahdi of the desert.[26]

□

In "territorialism" Zangwill claimed to have found a fitting retort to such criticisms. The Ito, he persistently argued, deserved support precisely because it was businesslike and appealed to the heads as well as to the hearts of its adherents. It shared the Zionist ambition to liberate the Jews from their resigned immobilism in the face of anti-Semitism; but it surpassed the older organization in demonstrating how practical use might be made of the nationalist passions thus released. "By a territory the Ito *means* a

[24] See the impressive article, "Palestine," by Olga D'Avigdor and Walter S. Cohen in *JC*, 9 March 1900, p. 23.

[25] I. Zangwill, "Zionism" (October 1899), in *Speeches*, p. 160; S. L. Bensusan, letter to editor, *JC*, 14 May 1897, p. 8.; Rev. G. Emanuel, "Zionism and the Jewish Question," sermon delivered at New West End Synagogue, *JC*, 26 November 1897, p. 27.

[26] H. A. Stacke (Cleveland Gardens, Hyde Park), to Zangwill, 2 February 1902, CZA, Zangwill Papers, A120/78.

territory, and not nationalistic speeches, debates, clubs, branches, picnics and dances. We exist to get a land, not to promote an 'ism.' "[27] The charge that East Africa (or any of the various successor territories that Zangwill was soon to consider) would divert enthusiasm from the true Zion was hardly to the point; the essence of the issue was whether the long wait for Palestine would not cause such harm to the Jewish spirit that there would not be any enthusiasm left. Besides, the chosen territory was designed solely to satisfy present Jewish needs; it need not replace *Erez Yisrael* as a focus of future affections. Instead, it could be portrayed as a useful, perhaps essential, "rallying point for Zionism, a training school in self-government, a fulcrum of political influence and a nursery of agriculture for Palestine when obtained."[28] Dreams were for dreamers; "men of science" appreciated that action—brisk in style and utilitarian in conception—was the stuff of which a Jewish state would be made.[29]

The buoyant pose was, of course, deliberately struck. It suggested a contrast between the cheerful confidence of the Ito and the gloomy desperation of the Zionists. The latter, maintained Zangwill, clung to Palestine with a grit born of helplessness. Unable to jettison ancient conventions, they had manoeuvered themselves into a bigoted and forlorn position. The Ito, by contrast, was blithely pragmatic, its progress toward the inevitable day of Redemption unimpeded by either sentimental commitments or timeworn aspirations. Moreover, and as always in the world of business, flexibility implied strength. The Ito was not

[27] "A Land of Refuge," speech delivered at Manchester Hippodrome, 8 December 1907, in *Speeches*, p. 238.

[28] "The East Africa Offer," speech at Derby Hall, Manchester, April 1905, in *Speeches*, p. 212. That, at least, was the public line; in private, Zangwill had from the first appreciated that East Africa also "dodges all the religious and political difficulties of the Old Palestine," 5 June 1903, Zangwill to Herzl, CZA, Herzl Papers, H VIII 946.

[29] 21 December 1908, Zangwill to Marmorek, CZA, Zangwill Papers, A120/72; similarly, 21 November 1906, Zangwill to Claude Montefiore; "Even our much discussed autonomy clause springs from no fantastic source, but from a conviction that this is the only scientific way of ultimately solving the problem." (CZA, Ito files, A36/133).

(91)

bound to accept the East Africa offer—or any other. On the contrary, it would refuse to do so without prior assurances that the land in question was sufficiently large and fertile to support mass settlement. Consequently there was no need to approach the Ottoman, Portuguese, Brazilian, or Australian governments (all of whom Zangwill regarded as reasonable candidates) with cap in hand. Since most of these countries manifestly needed Jewish capital and labor, the Ito could threaten each with the possibility that it might opt for the other. By the same criterion even Weizmann's negotiations with the British government after 1917 could be subjected to critical scrutiny.[30]

Until such time as the Zionists could indeed demonstrate material progress on the diplomatic front, Zangwill's several arguments had forced them into a defensive position. Especially was this so in the arena of communal politics. Zangwill, like Herzl before him, had soon realized that the support of Jewry for his schemes was an essential prerequisite to their consideration by gentile governments. One basic reason was financial: Jewish philanthropic sources—whether individual or institutional—had to be persuaded to put up the funds necessary for the efficient functioning of the Ito's various offices and commissions. Another was more properly diplomatic: statesmen were most likely to be impressed when confronted with a display of solid Jewish support for an Ito scheme. As much had been stated, with disarming candor, by Churchill in 1906 when he informed Zangwill of his government's thinking on East Africa:

> There is the undoubted division among the Jews themselves, which seems to have impressed itself even upon some of those who, like Lord Percy, were strenuous in your support. . . . If you were able to come to us with a long list of powerful names guaranteeing a great sum of money, I would do my very best to further your wishes.[31]

[30] 8 January 1919, Zangwill to J. Schiff, Cincinnati, American Jewish Archives, J. Schiff Papers, box 187.

[31] 13 July 1906, Churchill to Zangwill, private, CZA, Ito files, A36/19a.

The deliberate reference to powerful names was not lost on Zangwill. No more than the leaders of the EZF did he wish to lead a "popular" revolt against the aristocracy of Jewry. That explains why Zangwill did not measure the Ito's success solely by the yardstick of an "African fever" in the East End, nor even by its estimated influence over Jewish voters in the provinces.[32] Such manifestations of popular support were of course encouraging, but he aimed at a more exclusive target. Indeed, it was the essence of his strategy that the Ito be regarded as responsible by the leading men of affairs in Jewry. He hoped to gain their support by projecting an image of political acumen and discretion. By demonstrating the unnecessary impulsiveness of the Zionists (as represented in Britain by the EZF) over East Africa, he planned to stake a competing claim to communal influence.

Thus reduced to a question of public appeal, Zangwill's communal strategy did not differ very much from that adopted by the leaders of the EZF. From the first, the Ito and the EZF had to jockey for very much the same patch of communal ground. Neither organization felt capable of accomplishing its aims without the help of the existing communal institutions; on the contrary, each wished to harness the strength and prestige of the Establishment to its own cause. Most obviously was this so at the level of world Jewry's financial elite. In 1907, Zangwill went to the High Court in an unsuccessful attempt to establish the Ito's right to a share in the estate of Baron Maurice de Hirsch, the Austro-Hungarian philanthropist, who had left enormous sums to the Ica. Throughout the prewar period, he assiduously cultivated the personal goodwill of the American banker and industrialist, Jacob Schiff, participating (albeit with some initial reluctance) in the latter's project to settle immigrant Jews in Galveston, Texas.[33]

---

[32] On which see Weisbord, *African Zion*, pp. 233-35; immigrant views in *Der Idisher Zhurnal*, 1, 6 and 8 June 1908; *Der Idisher Ekspres*, 3 June 1908; and *Der Arbayter Fraynd*, 11 January 1907, pp. 6-7.

[33] On Zangwill's High Court litigation over the Hirsch estate, which commenced in July 1907 and dragged on for over a year, see CZA, Files of the Central Zionist Office (Cologne), Z2/300, nos. 356-57. For a recent view of the Galveston project see: Garry D. Best, "Jacob H. Schiff's Galveston Movement. An Exper-

But the Ito's search for support had particular implications for Anglo-Jewry. From the first, so Greenberg believed, Zangwill had deliberately set out to "tap the enthusiasms" generated by the Zionists (a judgment that exaggerated the importance of the latter); he certainly seemed to be competing for the favors of the very same bodies, or at least their leading figures, as the EZF.[34]

At this level, Zangwill was initially the more successful. Admittedly, the territorialists did not win the allegiance of some of the men who were thought to occupy the very top drawer of Anglo-Jewish society. Some clothed their opposition in ideological garb, self-righteously informing the readers of the *Times* that they objected to the Ito's pessimistic forecast of the permanency of gentile antagonism toward the Jews. Others, with what appears to have been more honesty, bluntly admitted that they "would have nothing to do with it because Z. is its leader."[35] Among those who refused invitations to join the Ito's International Council were Claude Montefiore, because he remained opposed to any scheme that smacked of autonomous Jewish aspirations; H.S.Q. Henriques (a member of one of the most distinguished Sephardi families in Anglo-Jewry, and himself an eminent barrister and vice-president of the Board of Deputies), because he claimed that his sense of legal propriety was outraged by Zangwill's "irresponsibility"; Lord Nathan Rothschild, "on practical grounds"; and Samuel Montagu because (according to Zangwill) he was "too old and set in his ways."[36] But these failures were to an extent offset by an impressive roster of persons only one remove from either the most wealthy or influential in the community. Among the men who agreed to serve on the Council of the British Ito

---

iment in Immigrant Deflection," *American-Jewish Archives* 30 (April 1978):43-79.

[34] 15 December 1905, Greenberg to Wolffsohn, CZA, Wolffsohn Papers, W78/1.

[35] The *Times*, 8 December 1905, p. 4, published a manifesto against the Ito signed by eight prominent Jews in Britain; see also the diary kept by Miss Phillips (Zangwill's secretary), entry for 22 February 1906, in Mocatta Library, AJ/9.

[36] 21 November 1906, Zangwill to Montefiore, CZA, Ito files, A36/133; 29 April 1907, Henriques to Zangwill, CZA, Zangwill Papers, A120/69; 1 November 1905, Leopold de Rothschild to Zangwill, CZA, Ito files, A36/24; and 13 March 1906, Zangwill to O. Straus, CZA, Ito files, A36/40.

Federation were Mr. (later Sir) Meyer A. Spielman, a respected educator and founder of a reformatory for Jewish boys; Leopold de Rothschild, treasurer of the Jewish Board of Guardians; Mr. (later Sir) Osmond D'Avigdor-Goldsmid, who was subsequently to become president of both the Board of Deputies and the AJA; Sir Lionel Abrahams, financial secretary at the India Office (after 1911, assistant undersecretary of state); and Laurie Magnus, son of Sir Philip, the M.P. for London University. These, as Greenberg ruefully admitted, were all "prominent men" whom the Zionists had failed to reach. So, too, was Lucien Wolf who—after much characteristic circumlocution—allowed his itch for the great game of diplomacy to overcome his aversion for the notion of Jewish nationalism.[37]

No less disconcerting, from the Zionist point of view, was the opportunity which the Ito seemed to provide for the coalescence of otherwise mutually hostile elements. Zangwill's organization in fact seemed to bring into association erstwhile antagonists, making it difficult for the Zionists to exploit the differences between their opponents. The Ito also helped to produce a measure of coherence from the jumble of themes implicit in Anglo-Jewish opposition to Zionism. By concentrating on the common denominator of Palestine's political and agricultural deficiencies, it attracted many members of the community who questioned the practicability of Zionist ambitions. Others, who disputed the ideology behind Zionist aims, were meanwhile disarmed by the Ito's claim that its territory was designed only for such Jews "as cannot or will not remain in the lands in which they presently live" (a very different matter from Zionist talk of a home for "the Jewish People"). Altogether, in fact, Zangwill skillfully played on several different themes, and in so doing managed to put together an otherwise remarkable coalition of ostensibly unlike-minded persons as some native Reform ministers and the Orthodox rabbis

---

[37] Wolf's correspondence with Zangwill, dated September 1905, in *Ito Pamphlets*, no. 1, pp. 9-13; and 28 September 1906, Zangwill to C. Salaman, confidential, CZA, Ito files, A36/15a.

of individual immigrant communities in the provinces.[38] Similarly, their common distaste for the extreme views of the "Zion" Zionists could place in common harness such embattled personalities as Philip Hartog, the registrar of London University, and Lady Kate Magnus, wife of the institution's M.P. The former joined the Ito because he believed Palestine to be too sensitive an area of international intrigue to ensure Jewish security; the latter, because she could not bear to see the Land of the Bible turned into

> a dumping ground for sad, soiled rubbish. I *ache* for those poor refugees—but I *can't* help put them where the prophets trod—it isn't fair to our memories nor our hopes that Zion should be repeopled except by our *best*.[39]

Zangwill does not seem to have risen to that patronizing bait, but some Zionists were less restrained. They taunted that the Ito was dominated by a clutch of antinationalists, who intended leading Zangwill himself by the nose toward yet another exercise in philanthropy.[40] Such charges, however, were both inaccurate and unfair. Contrary to Gaster's repeated assertions, Zangwill did not "sell the pass" and move into the antinationalist camp. Notwithstanding his persistent warnings of the imminence of an "Arab Question" in Palestine,[41] he continued to occupy ground some way between the Zionists and their opponents; if anything, he inclined both intellectually and temperamentally toward the former rather than the latter. One possible advantage of this inter-

[38] "Divisions in the Community," *JC*, 27 December 1907, p. 18; and on international support, Ben Halpern, *The Idea of the Jewish State*, 2nd ed. (Cambridge, Mass., 1969), p. 155. See also reports of support for East Africa from Rabbi Y. Herzog, of Dublin, and Rabbi Y. Rabinowitz, of Edinburgh, in *JC*, 21 September 1960, pp. 24-25.

[39] 5 May 1903, Lady Magnus to Zangwill, CZA, Zangwill Papers, A120/55 (m), and 7 May 1906, Hartog to Zangwill, CZA, Ito files, A36/46b.

[40] E.g., 23 November 1905, Greenberg to Zangwill, private, CZA, Ito files, A36/128; and Gaster speech in Leeds, reported in *JC*, 2 January 1906, pp. 38-39.

[41] See: Hani Faris, "Israel Zangwill's Challenge to Zionism," *Journal of Palestine Studies* 4 (1975):74-90.

The NORTH LONDON PULPIT

A Special Series of Sermons delivered at the
NORTH LONDON SYNAGOGUE.

No 10.

"Religious versus Political Zionism."

**A SERMON
PREACHED AT THE
NORTH LONDON SYNAGOGUE.
— ON —**

Sabbath. November 12th 5659 · 1898.

— BY THE —
Rev. Dr Adler,
CHIEF RABBI.

Printed for the Wardens of the North London Synagogue,
FOR PRIVATE CIRCULATION.

5. Title page of Hermann Adler's sermon, "Religious versus Political Zionism" (1898).

6. Herbert Bentwich (c. 1925).
7. *Ḥakham* Moses Gaster (1898).
8. Leopold Greenberg (1910).

9. Jacob de Haas (1898).
10. Sir Francis Montefiore (c. 1905).
11. Lucien Wolf caricatured in the
   Daily Graphic, 1904.

12. Delegates to the English Zionist Federation Conference, London, 1920. Since the first gathering in 1899 (see fig. 3), the EZF had substantially increased and widened its appeal to include all ages, both sexes, and a sprinkling of the strictly Orthodox.

mediate position was that Zangwill himself could pose as a prospective partner to either side; he was, indeed, courted by both. Thus, notwithstanding the allegedly antinational influence of his gentile wife, Edith Ayrton,[42] Zionists in England made several attempts after 1906 to bring Zangwill back into their fold. When those failed, they subsequently attempted to enlist his help in their efforts to dispose of the "dead-weight of the self-appointed leaders of the community on the neck of tortured Jewry."[43] Apparently aware of the threats implicit in precisely that alignment, anti-Zionists simultaneously sought to prolong the benefits that they derived from Zangwill's persistent differences with the Actions Committee. Even as late as 1918, and despite the imminent closure of the Ito,[44] Lucien Wolf tried to convince Zangwill of the continued need for an independent territorialist approach to the Palestinian issue.[45]

Nevertheless, Zangwill's attempts to straddle some of the ideological fences of Anglo-Jewry did cause him some discomfort. This was especially so once his negotiations with the British government over East Africa had finally fallen through in 1907; having lost its original focus, the Ito was forced to seek a new raison d'être for its separate identity. As critics of the Ito pointed out, Zangwill had to find a new project that would be sufficiently different from that of the Zionists to warrant the sympathies of

[42] "Zangwill I am afraid is 'verloren' so far as the movement is concerned. If you want to know the cause look at 1st Kings chapter 11 verses 3 and 4. In Solomon's case it took 700; in Zangwill's one has been enough." 22 March 1905, Greenberg to Wolffsohn, CZA, Wolffsohn Papers, W78.

[43] 20 November 1914, Weizmann to Zangwill, CZA, Zangwill Papers, A120/60. For earlier attempts at reconciliation, see e.g., 9 May 1906, Cowen to Zangwill, CZA, Ito files, A36/135; 12 January 1908, Kessler to Zangwill, ibid., A36/137; and 5 June 1914, M. Myers (EZF) to Actions Committee, CZA, Files of the Central Zionist Office (Berlin), Z3/807. Before World War I, the only occasion for cooperation was provided by the Bialystok massacres, concerning which Zangwill and Greenberg issued a joint protest. JC, 22 June 1906, p. 24 and correspondence between EZF and Wolffsohn in CZA, Files of the Central Zionist Office (Cologne), Z2/266.

[44] On the ultimate decision to end the Ito, see Zangwill's circular to all members in CZA, L. Wolf Papers, A77/3.

[45] 26 February 1918, Wolf to Zangwill, JC, 8 March 1918, p. 12.

"practical" men, and yet sufficiently visionary to justify its precedence over a string of less ambitious schemes which were vying
for public attention and funds.[46] This combination of pressures
and contexts was certainly conducive to calculated ambiguity,
which became an even more emphatic hallmark of Zangwill's
rhetorical style after 1907. More subtly, but no less significantly,
it would also seem to have given rise to a situation in which
Zangwill was tempted to play the game of communal politics for
its own sake. A new tone was thus injected into the struggle for
communal influence in which the Ito, no less than the EZF,
became involved. Without abandoning his undoubtedly sincere
concern for the plight of east European Jewry (a point worth
stressing since it is often taken for granted in the documents),
Zangwill's calculations became political as well as humanitarian
in form. The need for a refuge was not the only factor to influence
the timing, form, and even location of his choice for a suitable
territory. Also at stake was Zangwill's concern that the Ito remain
a powerful force in Jewish affairs. As was once said of Disraeli,
some of Zangwill's efforts give the impression of being designed
to ensure that he stayed in the driving seat; precisely where the
coach was headed sometimes seemed to have been of subsidiary
importance.

☐

One illustration is provided by the Ito's project for Jewish settlement in Mesopotamia. He publicly launched the proposal in a
series of speeches during the summer of 1909, and did not finally

[46] E.g., "Rothschild against Zionism," *Die Welt*, 22 December 1905; and 30
December 1908, Schiff to Zangwill, CZA, Ito files, A36/17. Also Weizmann's
comment: "Zangwill unearths millionaires, thereby saving himself and his party."
18 September 1905, to Vera Khatzman, Chaim Weizmann, *The Letters and Papers
of Chaim Weizmann. Series A. Letters* [hereafter *Letters*], general ed. Meyer Weisgal
et al. 23 vols. (Oxford, London, and Jerusalem, 1969-1980), Vol. 4, *January
1905-December 1906*, ed. Camillo Dresner and Barnet Litvinoff (Jerusalem, 1973),
p. 157.

abandon it until 1913.[47] The fact that the Mesopotamia project is often neglected in the literature would seem to justify a fairly detailed review of its context and character. Superficially, and especially when outlined with Zangwill's customary skill, the scheme seemed eminently attractive. During the early twentieth century, the region between the Tigris and Euphrates was popularly believed to possess limitless commercial potential. It was also considered to require a large number of skilled immigrants in order to extract and develop its mineral and agricultural resources.[48] Were the Jews to provide such manpower, British authorities (in particular) might not be displeased. For one thing, there was the perennial mirage of supposed Protestant sentiment: "You must know," reported Clement Salaman, "that among a very large section of sentimental Christians, Mesopotamia has always been considered as a settling place for Jews prior to their final restoration in Palestine."[49] Of greater importance was the strategic significance of the region. As the current Anglo-German negotiations concerning the Baghdad Railway concession indicated, Britain considered Mesopotamia to lie within the defensive perimeter necessitated by her interests in the Persian Gulf and her concern to protect the overland route to India. All Zangwill had to do—so he claimed—was to convince the Government that the Jews would faithfully guard that gate.

Finally, and more particularly, there seemed a chance that his coreligionists could be persuaded to assume responsibility. After all, with only a slight effort of imagination, Mesopotamia could be described as "the cradle of the Jewish race"—an argument

[47] The subject is considered in greater detail in my article, "Israel Zangwill's Project for Jewish Colonization in Mesopotamia: Its Context and Character," *Middle Eastern Studies* 16 (October 1980):200-208.

[48] E.g., Sir Valentine Chirol, *The Middle Eastern Question* (London, 1903); David G. Hogarth, *The Nearer East* (London, 1905); Paul Rohrbach, *Die Bagdadbahn* (Berlin, 1903); Sir William Willcocks, *The Re-Creation of Chaldea* (Cairo, 1903). For official and equally enthusiastic reports see evidence presented to the Committee of Imperial Defence subcommittee on the Baghdad Railway and the Persian Gulf, March 1908, London, Public Record Office, Committee of Imperial Defence records, CAB 16/10.

[49] 11 March 1909, Salaman to J. Fels, CZA, Ito files, A36/38.

once put to Herzl.[50] Furthermore, when looked at from an atlas in London, the area appeared sufficiently near to Palestine to interest the Zionists, and yet sufficiently distant to constitute a legitimate field of enterprise for those Jewish relief organizations who feared the political and particularist implications of the "Zion" Zionist project. It might in fact provide a unique opportunity for cooperation between these two wings. Various reports indicated that this aspect of Zangwill's thinking had already been antici-pated. Between 1908 and 1909, the possibility of Jewish settle-ment in Mesopotamia had formed the subject of several conver-sations between representatives of the Young Turk government and a significantly wide variety of Jewish organizations: Victor Jacobson's recently established Zionist Agency in Constantinople; Alfred Nossig's para-Zionist Allgemeine Juedische Kolonisations-Organisation, and the anti-Zionist Jewish Colonisation Associ-ation (Ica).[51]

Zangwill hoped to coordinate these efforts and eventually to orchestrate the entire project. As early as 1908, he had ap-proached Claude Montefiore, Leonard Cohen, and George Lou-sada, the three British representatives on the Ica Council, with an offer of cooperation on Mesopotamia. During the course of his public addresses a year later, he invited the Zionists in England to add their weight to the scheme. Meanwhile, in the spring of 1909, he had taken preliminary soundings with several Jewish financiers: the Rothschilds, Jacob Schiff, the Sassoons (the An-glo-Indian merchants whose family originated in Baghdad), and Sir Ernest Cassel (Edward VII's "court Jew" whose National Bank of Turkey was the British financial institution most closely con-cerned with Mesopotamian ventures). Largely in the hope that these efforts would prove successful, Zangwill had also launched a diplomatic campaign. At the end of April 1909 he wrote to

[50] Correspondence between Herzl and Cyrus Adler in Cincinnati, American Jewish Archives, C. Adler Papers, box 1071; also 9 May 1903, Cowen to Herzl, CZA, Herzl Papers, H VIII 161 and Zangwill, "Zionism," *Contemporary Review* 76 (October 1899):510.

[51] Neville J. Mandel, *The Arabs and Zionism before World War I* (Berkeley, 1976), pp. 94-95; also reports in, e.g., JC, 25 December 1908, pp. 16-17.

Ahmed Riza Bey, the president of the Ottoman Chamber of Deputies, offering to enrich the Ottoman exchequer and to develop Mesopotamia "provided Turkey was ready to set aside a definite territory there within which the Jews should be able to form the predominant majority."[52]

But these auspicious appearances were deceptive. Ito's Mesopotamian project, almost from its inception, was impracticable. What is more, Zangwill himself seems to have known as much. As early as 1907 an Ito report had compared Cyrenaica and Mesopotamia for territorialist purposes, and had provided ample evidence of the climatic and financial difficulties that Jewish settlers in the latter region would have to face. There was no reason to think that the Ica Commission (which investigated Mesopotamia during the winter of 1909-1910, and upon whose report Zangwill seems to have pinned some hopes) would reach any other conclusions; in fact, the Ica confirmed the Ito's earlier findings.[53] Secondly, and again as early as 1907, Zangwill had been explicitly informed—by no less a figure than Lord Rothschild—that Mesopotamia was far too close to the center of international intrigue to attract serious financial investment. Before Zangwill launched his public appeal this judgment was seconded by Cassel, who therefore refused to have anything to do with the scheme.[54] Similar conclusions could have been drawn from the discouraging reactions of the governments to whom Zangwill appealed. The Young Turks publicly deprecated the idea of Jewish settlement in Mesopotamia (some Arab deputies to the Ottoman Chamber, perhaps understandably confused by the plethora of Jewish organizations interested in their regions, took Zangwill's project as a sign that "the Zionists aspire not only to Palestine, but to Syria and Iraq as well");[55] the British Foreign Office point-

[52] 30 April 1909, Zangwill to Ahmed Riza Bey, CZA, Ito files, A36/64.

[53] Minutes of 17th meeting of the Ito International Council, 3 July 1907, and of the British Ito Council, 26th July 1907, both in CZA, Ito files, A36/46b, file 51. For the Ica report, minutes of 39th meeting of International Council, ibid.

[54] Rothschild's views in 9 August 1907, Zangwill to O. Straus, ibid., A36/40; Cassel's in 21 April 1909, Wolf to Zangwill, CZA, Wolf Papers, A77/4.

[55] Mandel, *The Arabs and Zionism*, p. 95.

edly refused to send the Ito a copy of an official, and confidential, report on the trading possibilities of Mesopotamia. Obviously unimpressed by Zangwill's vision of an Anglo-Jewish alliance, some officials reverted to conventionally anti-Semitic themes: "The Jews," ran one minute, "are not agriculturalists but parasites. They will settle in the towns and as usurers gradually acquire the earnings and estates of the peasantry, when there is a peasantry in Mesopotamia."[56]

Other obstacles, of more direct relevance to the project itself, should have been equally apparent. One was the attitude of some prominent British Zionists, who as recently as 1908 had spurned an offer to cooperate with Zangwill and who in 1909 rejected the Mesopotamian scheme out of hand.[57] Another was the discouragement that Zangwill had already received from the anti-Zionists. Montefiore, not unexpectedly, had from the first warned that he would not support the idea of Jewish autonomy in the region. Narcisse Leven, the president of the Ica, in March 1909 also wrote that "notre Société n'obeit à aucune preoccupation d'ordre national." Leonard Cohen pronounced "with an air of finality" that the only object of the Anglo-Jewish Association, too, was "to make Jews free citizens of free countries"; and Schiff, who had all along made his support conditional on the attitude of such "senior bodies" as the Ica, ultimately declared that "I would have Jews go to Mesopotamia as they do to America—I am in no sense a Jewish nationalist."[58] Given this formidable barrage of concerted opposition, the entire scheme was doomed to failure.

In retrospect, the bitterness with which Zangwill greeted this verdict would appear to have been unwarranted. As has been seen, he could himself have predicted most of the objections

[56] Minute on 31 August 1910, Sir G. Lowther (H. M. ambassador in Constantinople) to Sir E. Grey (foreign secretary), Public Record Office, Foreign Office Files, FO 371/992, file 177, no. 32231.

[57] *Jewish World*, 21 May 1908, pp. 8, 10.

[58] Schiff interview in *JC*, 28 May 1909, p. 7; 27 April 1909, Leven to Zangwill, CZA, Ito files, A36/121; 25 November 1907, Zangwill to H. Bentwich, CZA, Ito files, A36/133.

some time before the summer of 1909; some of his colleagues did so. Under these circumstances, the really intriguing question to arise from the entire episode is why—despite his foresight—Zangwill ever attempted to fly this particularly inept kite. A charitable view might suggest that the Mesopotamian project merely indicates the lengths to which he was prepared to go in search for a solution—any solution—to the Jewish question. The documentary evidence, while not contradicting this version, suggests a supplementary motive. Not the least of Zangwill's concerns was the continued independent existence of the Ito as a force on the communal map. The desire to remain in the public view had, in fact, played some part in each of the enterprises upon which the Ito had embarked after the failure of the East Africa negotiations. Thus, as early as 1906, Zangwill admitted that Schiff had virtually "forced" him to participate in the Galveston scheme; "for if another body undertakes it, public attention will be drawn to their work and we shall be comparatively ousted."[59] Of Cyrenaica, in 1907, he said: "Any choice is better than wobbling eternally."[60] Once a specially appointed commission had reported unfavorably on that region in 1909, similar motives would appear to have directed him toward Mesopotamia. As Zangwill told the members of the Ito's International Council, without a further project the organization would find itself in an ideological and financial crisis; Mesopotamia was attractive principally because it was there. His real concern seems to have been not that the project might fall through, but that in applying for a Mesopotamian concession the Ito would have to subordinate itself to some other organization. Hence Zangwill's insistence that he, rather than Jacobson or

[59] 14 September 1906, Zangwill to Straus, CZA, Ito files, A36/40. Note, too, Zangwill's reported "insistence that the Ito be given all credit for the program and that if that were not the case the project 'had better not be done at all.' " Quoted in Best, "Jacob H. Schiff's Galveston Movement," pp. 52-53.

[60] 12 July 1907, Zangwill to M. Eder, CZA, Ito files, A36/22. In fairness, it must be pointed out that such calculations were not restricted to Zangwill's Ito period. Excusing himself for raising Mesopotamia in a 1903 address, Zangwill told Herzl: "I do not believe Sinai is lost yet, but I spoke of Chaldea to prepare the way for some large scheme *anywhere.*" 15 May 1903, CZA, Herzl Papers, H VIII 946.

Narcisse Leven, take the lead in negotiations in Constantinople
(a suggestion which Schiff soon scotched); hence, too, his otherwise far-fetched efforts to persuade Oscar Straus (the American
ambassador to the Porte) to support a Mesopotamian Development Company which would bypass the Ica altogether. Unless
the Ito could lay claim to a position of unique importance, it
would be "cut out . . . of the whole business."[61]

This, of course, did not happen. Instead, even when deprived
of Mesopotamia, Zangwill ostentatiously turned the Ito's attention to Western Australia, British Honduras, Brazil, and—with
more good fortune than elsewhere—Angola. (Significantly, he
had begun to consider each of these territories even while claiming to concentrate all his efforts on Mesopotamia.)[62] That none
of these schemes ever came to fruition must not be allowed to
detract from their importance. Zangwill himself seems to have
considered that his impact and influence depended as much upon
what he promised as upon what he actually achieved. In terms
of the specific struggle for the support of the Anglo-Jewish community, the results were soon apparent. Zangwill's flair for publicity helped to deflect attention from the EZF, and thus to add
to its burdens. That is precisely what Greenberg, from the first,
had been afraid of. The real danger in the Ito, he informed
Wolffsohn in 1906, was that it might "tap the enthusiasms" of
the same elements in the community that the Zionists were attempting to win over. "We have not such a lot [of the community]
with us that we can allow him to take any."[63] For a good deal of
the subsequent decade Cowen's complaints were equally relevant:

[61] 17 March 1910, Zangwill to Schiff, CZA, Zangwill Papers, A120/28; and
21 January 1910, Zangwill to Straus, CZA, Ito files, A36/40.

[62] 29 June 1909, Spielman to Zangwill, CZA, Ito files, A36/42; 18 May 1909,
Zangwill to his wife, CZA, Zangwill Papers, A120/49; and 7 April 1910, Zangwill
to Rothschild, CZA, Ito files, A36/138. On the Angola project see: David I.
Marmor, "Ha-masa u-matan ha-diplomati shel ha-histadrut he-teritorialistit ha-
yehudit (Ito) u-mesibat kishlono," *Zion*, n.s. 11 (1946):175-94.

[63] 5 October 1905, Greenberg to Wolffsohn, private, CZA, Wolffsohn Papers,
W78.

Until the Ito came along, here was the position:
Unorganised, indifferent, material or charitable Jews,
no plans, no brains, no ideas
　　Vs Zionism.
Now it is　Unorganised etc.
　　Vs Zionism and Itoism.[64]

THE EZF, 1904-1914

It was unfortunate for the progress of Zionism in England that
the leaders of the EZF failed to close ranks in order to meet the
threat posed by the Ito. Instead, the period of Zangwill's most
conspicuous territorialist activity coincided with that of the EZF's
least edifying internal crises. Zangwill, not unexpectedly, exploited this state of affairs—most provocatively by occasionally
offering to cooperate with one or the other of the contending
Zionist factions. But, in the majority of cases, he was not responsible for or involved in the internal squabbles that plagued
the EZF before 1914. His part was that of a foil. His claims to
represent a dynamic and united party were designed to accentuate
the listless and divided picture presented by the EZF.

The contrast was not, of course, perfect. The territorialists
were not always at one; neither were the Zionists always at odds.
Although most of the EZF's early records have not survived, it
is clear that some steps were taken before 1914 to provide Zionism
in Britain with a unified nationwide institutional framework. The
EZF acquired modest offices (first in Commercial Street, East
London, then in Chancery Lane, Holborn), and employed some
salaried clerks. After 1899 it also convened annual conferences,
where a national executive—consisting of London and provincial
representatives—was elected. In turn, this body promoted the
establishment of "regional centres" and, although never able to
support a popular and regular newspaper of its own, did issue
occasional bulletins and help to distribute local Zionist journals.
More effective were the attempts made to reach an audience

[64] 5 July 1906, Cowen to Zangwill, CZA, Ito files, A36/135.

through the medium of the existing Anglo-Jewish press. De Haas, for instance, provided frequent features on Zionism for the *Jewish World*, which he edited until 1901; throughout the period, *Ha-Yehoodi* (the Hebrew-language weekly edited on a shoestring by Isaac Suvalsky) regularly received items of specifically Zionist interest, as did *Di Tsayt* (the most popular of the Yiddish dailies, edited by Mauriss Myer) after 1913. Potentially, Leopold Greenberg's acquisition of the *Jewish Chronicle* in 1907, for which some of the funds first came from the Jewish Colonial Trust, provided the Zionists with an even better platform. Admittedly, Greenberg insisted that he intended to run the paper as a business venture, not an act of Zionist faith. Consequently, and despite complaints from Gaster and Wolffsohn, he continued to publish items that did not always reflect credit on the movement; he specifically promised Zangwill that he would adopt a "balanced" attitude toward the Ito, and explicitly instructed his overseas correspondents to give Zionism "its fair share, but not more."[65] Nevertheless, the ultimate sympathies of the *Chronicle*, and its undiminished influence in the community, were rarely in doubt. That was why, by the end of the war, Anglo-Jewish opponents of Zionism considered it so necessary to produce a newspaper of their own.

Steps were also taken to extend the range and form of Zionist activities throughout the country. Few of these ventures were directly initiated by the EZF executive; some of them in fact were of peripheral importance in propaganda terms, since they reflected a desire for Jewish, rather than strictly Zionist, fare. Nevertheless, they were important in keeping the Zionist idea alive at the grassroots level. Thus, the EZF attached some importance to the propagation of Zionist Joint Share Clubs in the East End, to the spread of Hebrew study circles throughout the country, and to the establishment of Hebrew language schools (although the latter in fact owed their foundation and existence almost entirely to

[65] 10 September 1908, Greenberg to B. Richards (New York), New York, Jewish Theological Seminary, B. Richards Papers; and 30 December 1907, Greenberg to Wolffsohn, CZA, Wolffsohn Papers, W79(ii). On the purchase of the JC, see correspondence in CZA, Files of the Central Zionist Office (Cologne), Z2/281-2.

the individual efforts of Rev. J. K. Goldbloom at Redman's Road, London, and to J. S. Fuchs in Liverpool).[66] Occasionally, such enterprises were supplemented by "mass" demonstrations at which local and continental leaders exhorted their followers to purchase more *shekalim*, and thus entitle British Zionists to a greater representation at the periodic congresses of the World Zionist Organization. Nominally, all Zionist activities in the country were coordinated by annual conferences of the EZF's own Central Committee, where matters of ideology and organization were regularly discussed.

When reported to the Actions Committee, all this bustle could be made to seem very impressive. Nevertheless, its ultimate effectiveness appears to have been limited. By the outbreak of war in 1914, the EZF possessed no more than 4,000 fully paid-up members, sprinkled through over fifty local societies; even at its peak, it has been calculated, the body represented no more than 6 percent of the entire prewar Anglo-Jewish population.[67] Admittedly, allowance must be made for the larger number of unaffiliated sympathizers, many of whom could be relied upon to turn up in force to hear such popular visiting orators as Naḥum Sokolow (in 1905 and 1912) and Shemaryahu Levin (in 1914). Nevertheless, the occasional bursts of enthusiasm which these men could generate did not compensate for lengthy periods of apathy ("There is little life now in the whole affair," was a standard complaint. "I am trying my best to keep up our Society, but it is very hard to find any material support"[68]). Neither did their elaborately staged tours produce the required sales of *shekalim*, which were always disappointing, nor repair the EZF's own chronic shortage of funds. One typical financial report noted that while the movement's expenses were steadily increasing, its income from donations was "vanishing"; another pointed out that "an urgent letter about *shekalim* sent to all Societies . . . produced

[66] Lloyd P. Gartner, *The Jewish Immigrant*, 2nd ed. (London, 1973), pp. 236-37; Joseph S. Fuchs, *Merkaz Ivri: An Hebrew Centre* (London, 1909).

[67] Marvin Goldfine, "The Growth of Zionism in England" (Master's thesis, Columbia University, 1939), pp. 40-48.

[68] 24 January, 1907, Daiches to Gaster, CZA, Gaster Papers, A203/154.

but one reply, and that was from a Society to which the letter had gone by mistake, as it had already sent in its shekel money."[69]

To many an outside observer, such as Chaim Weizmann initially was, this sort of haphazard ineptitude simply reflected the generally despondent state of Anglo-Jewry. Many of the immigrants, he reported soon after his arrival in Manchester, were merely "a mob and a rabble"; as for the more established classes, their Zionism was, at best, "empty, a mere amusement."[70] This was an atmosphere that tended to temper Weizmann's own appetite for any local Zionist work; it also had the effect of stifling the creative impulses of other, more sensitive personalities. One such example was Yosef Hayim Brenner, the Hebrew novelist, who lived in virtual obscurity and abject poverty in the East End between 1904 and 1908. Another was Ahad Ha'am (Asher Ginzberg), the justifiably more renowned essayist, who commenced an unhappy stay of fifteen years when he came to London as the representative of the Wissotsky Tea Company in 1907. Neither man found in the English capital either the congenial ambiance or (especially in Ahad Ha'am's case) the leisure that they had originally sought. Despite their very different temperaments and outlooks—their first meeting in Ahad Ha'am's rooms in Belsize Park was a disaster—both men shared a feeling that they were "fish out of water" in Anglo-Jewry. Their respective outputs suffered, although not necessarily in equal measure. Brenner was unable to sustain his Hebrew literary journal (*Ha-Me'orer*, which appeared intermittently between 1907 and 1908); Ahad Ha'am sorely missed the inspirational atmosphere that had fueled his work in Odessa. His incisive mind found little scope in the tame "cultural" proceedings of those who occasionally sought to benefit from his presence. Many of the Hebrew study circles who invited him to their meetings were ephemeral; others, to judge by their linguistic attainments, were ineffective. The first "Hebrew Conference," held in Manchester in 1909, was marred by an unfor-

[69] 22 August 1912, L. Simon to Actions Committee, CZA, Files of the Zionist Central Office (Berlin), and *Protokoll der Verhandlungen des XI. Zionisten-Congresses* (Vienna, 1913), pp. 44-46.

[70] 1 September 1905, Weizmann to Vera Khatzman, *Letters*, 4:143.

tunate wrangle over whether the proceedings would be conducted in Hebrew or Yiddish. Budding London Hebraists could do no better. Their circulars, written in English, provoked particular scorn from Aḥad Ha'am, who steadfastly continued to practice his self-denying ordinance against public appearances throughout his stay.[71] The mere fact of his residence in London therefore did nothing to repair Greenberg's earlier lament that "we here in England are in an awful situation so far as Zionism is concerned."[72]

Much of this unfortunate situation could, perhaps, be attributed to faults of a structural nature. The early mushroom growth of the EZF had resulted in a confused and inefficient situation; each of the societies formed during the movement's initial years jealously insisted on retaining its independence. Consequently, three or four societies often existed in small provincial centers, where one would have been less wasteful and more efficient.[73] A chronic dearth of competent movement workers in Britain increased the difficulties of repairing this situation. Concerned principally with keeping their individual societies alive, most local leaders possessed neither the inclination nor perspective necessary to propose far-reaching projects of reform. At the center, matters were even worse, especially after 1902, when Jacob de Haas left England to become the first paid official of the Federation of American Zionists. For all his faults,[74] de Haas had at least possessed a rudimentary interest in organization. Most of his colleagues lacked even that. The majority of prominent Zionists in London were businessmen whose time was limited; invariably they tended to transact Zionist business in a rush, or, like Greenberg, "over a cup of tea in a Lyons' tea shop."[75] A staff of clerks might

[71] Leon Simon, *Ahad Ha'am* (London, 1946), pp. 24-28; on the Manchester Hebrew Conference, *Hayehoodi*, 10 June 1909, p. 5.

[72] 23 January 1906, Greenberg to Wolffsohn, CZA, Wolffsohn Papers, W79(i).

[73] See the personal recollections of this situation in, e.g., Zvi Hirsch Masliansky, *Ketavim*, 3 vols. (New York, 1929), 3:133.

[74] E.g., 29 March 1900, Sir F. Montefiore to de Haas, New York, Zionist Organization of America, de Haas Papers, microfilm 1; also Richard Gottheil's early strictures, quoted in Yonathan Shapiro, *Leadership of the American Zionist Organization 1897-1930* (Urbana, 1971), p. 35.

[75] Israel Cohen, *A Jewish Pilgrimage* (London, 1956), p. 77.

have compensated, but the EZF also lacked adequate secretarial assistance. As late as 1913, most of the correspondence was left to the honorary officers who, as they often complained, "were far too busy to cope with anything but the bare essentials."[76] One obvious exception to this rule was Sir Francis Montefiore, who was altogether an unhurried person. But he did less than most to rectify the situation. As president of the EZF (from 1899-1907), he proved utterly incapable of providing the organization with either an efficient structure or a commanding lead. Once elevated to the position of honorary president, in 1907, he became little more than a ceremonial figurehead.

Many of these difficulties might have been overcome had Montefiore's nominal subordinates been united. In fact, however, internecine dissension seems to have been endemic to the EZF. The organization, which had been born in an atmosphere of intrigue occasioned by the split from the Chovevei Zion Association, could never completely rid itself of the blight of personal rivalries. As early as 1898, when the need for unity within the infant body was universally acknowledged, it had taken de Haas, Bentwich, Cowen, and Gaster three hours just to agree upon a name for the organization; only after a further nine meetings did they finally draw up a draft constitution. Even then, as several letters to Herzl reveal, the difficulties were not entirely ironed out. "There is a tendency to split off into trifles," ran one report for 1899, and "an atmosphere of dissent," another for 1900.[77] A decision, taken in 1900, to entitle the members of the executive committee to act in turns as sessional chairmen did ease some of the rivalries for place and prestige, but it could not completely eradicate others. Most obviously was this the case where Greenberg and Gaster were concerned. The two men first seem to have clashed over the propriety and usefulness of Herzl's appearance before the Royal Commission on Alien Immigration in 1902; it was the East Africa offer, however, that exacerbated their relationship. Greenberg, as has been seen, was from the first in favor

[76] 24 February 1913, P. Goodman to Action Committee, CZA, Files of the Central Zionist Office (Berlin), Z3/806.

[77] 8 June 1899 and 7 July 1901, CZA, Herzl Papers, H VIII 291.

of acceptance; Gaster, with equal promptness, declared himself very much against and accused Greenberg of betraying Herzl's trust. Thereafter, charges of double-dealing sped back and forth until—in a rather contrived exhibition of good will—both parties professed their desire for harmonious cooperation.[78]

Greenberg and Gaster were too incompatible for their differences to be so easily patched up. They soon picked new quarrels and began to organize coteries of rival supporters. The formation of two distinct camps within the EZF was clearly apparent when the movement's executive met in July 1906. Ostensibly, discord was then occasioned by the form and tone of the EZF's public protest against the latest round of massacres in Russia. Gaster complained that Greenberg had "minced the words" of the manifesto to the national press; together with Sir Francis Montefiore, he had also acted unconstitutionally in not consulting the executive before deciding to invite Zangwill's cooperation on the matter. In effect, however, more was at stake. Gaster's supporters on the executive (the most prominent of whom were Herbert Bentwich, Percy Baker, and Chaim Weizmann) alleged that Greenberg was generally maintaining too close a contact with Zangwill; they also accused him of attempting to impose his will and views upon the movement as a whole. Greenberg's supporters (notably Joseph Cowen and some of the East End members) retorted that the Ḥakham was temperamentally incapable of suffering opposition; he planned, they claimed, to secede from the EZF and found an independent organization over which he could "more easily rule."[79] These were recurring themes. Throughout the period, each side was to accuse the other of attempting "to whittle down our movement into a little family party" and maintained that "the whole of the trouble has arisen through miserable petty jealousy and dirty ignominious intrigue." As late as 1913, Gaster continued to assess developments within the EZF in terms of "slights and grudges" on the one hand, and "loyalties" on the

[78] See the reported exchange in *JC*, 16 July 1905, pp. 16-17.

[79] Report of the meeting in *JC*, 27 July 1906, pp. 18-20; see also correspondence between P. Baker and Gaster in CZA, Gaster Papers, A203/194 and between Greenberg and Wolffsohn in CZA, Wolffsohn Papers, W79(i).

other. "We must," he insisted, "eliminate all those objectionable persons who have proved a snare and a curse to the movement."[80]

In his jubilee house history of the EZF (*Zionism in England, 1899-1949*), Paul Goodman took a deliberately charitable view of this wrangling. Peering through the barrage of mutual vituperation and abuse (much of which he must have himself remembered), he claimed to discern some genuine differences over policy. To an extent, his analysis is substantiated by the official record. The alignment of Zionist factions in Britain did represent a pale reflection of the contemporary division of the Zionist movement as a whole into what were loosely referred to as the "political" and "practical" parties. Greenberg and Cowen, as befitted Herzl's earliest diplomatic lieutenants, declared themselves to be "politicals." In that capacity, they followed the lead of Wolffsohn, Nordau, Marmorek, and Jacobus Kahn in insisting that international recognition of the Jewish claim to Palestine was the essential prerequisite to any activity within Palestine itself. Small-scale colonies or experiments would merely squander the movement's meager resources. On the other hand, Gaster, as befitted a staunch opponent of East Africa, claimed to support the "synthetic" or "practical" approach advocated, in particular, by the Russian Zionei Zion. A concerted effort at land reclamation and colonization within Palestine, he argued after visiting the country in 1907, would strengthen the Zionist hand in any future diplomatic negotiations. Likewise, a cultural program of education in the Diaspora, as well as the eventual establishment of a Jewish university in Jerusalem, would help the movement to win over the educated elements of Jewry as a whole.

But that was not the entire story. Influence and position (and the one was impossible without the other) were as avidly sought as was the Jewish state that all parties professed—not insincerely—to desire. Moreover, the controversies within the EZF resulted as much from a clash of personalities as from differences over policy. Gaster, especially, possessed an uncommonly irras-

[80] 11 August 1913, Gaster to Moser, CZA, Gaster Papers, A203/202; see also 19 March 1909, Greenberg to Wolffsohn, CZA, Files of the Central Zionist Office (Berlin), Z3/311; 21 June 1910, J. Israel to Wolffsohn, Files of the Central Zionist Office (Cologne), Z2/415.

cible temperament. A man of monumental irritability, he was prone to quarreling irreconcilably with persons of all types. Even in his clerical capacity, an inordinate portion of the Ḥakham's life was taken up with feuds; he infused his Zionist relationships, too, with an intense personal animosity. As his vast correspondence reveals, he rarely supported any cause without from time to time turning savagely on its founders and backers, always charging that he had been betrayed and tricked and never admitting that he had been in the wrong. From that point of view, his opponents within the EZF were equally culpable. Greenberg and Cowen emerge from the archives as men who were just as obstinate, often simply for obstinancy's sake; they were also just as careless about the damaging effect of their squalid and often ludicrous squabbles on the community's image of Zionism. What is more, they did not possess Gaster's saving intellect or dynamism, nor even the bluster and pomposity that impressed friends and foes alike. This is not to suggest that the protagonists in either camp were stupid or malevolent. Generally successful in their chosen professions, they were in fact rather adept at the inelegant sort of manoeuvre that the hurly-burly of communal politics seemed to call for. Within these parameters, indeed, they were to achieve a measure of personal gratification. It was largely thanks to the (separate) efforts of Greenberg, Cowen, Bentwich, Gaster, and their collaborators that Zionism came to play any part in the day-to-day politics of the Anglo-Jewish community. But the advantages were not evenly spread. On balance, Anglo-Jewry probably benefited from the communal activities undertaken by local Zionists; but the Zionist movement, as a body, gained comparatively little from such a close involvement in the affairs of Anglo-Jewry. It is difficult to avoid the impression that the Gaster-Greenberg feud (and the ancillary skirmishes it provoked) was primarily responsible for retarding Zionism's development within the community throughout the period under review.

☐

Chaim Weizmann was the single exception to the rule of Anglo-Zionist mediocrity and small-mindedness. Always aware of the fact, he had from the first instinctively attempted to steer clear of the intrigues that (as he immediately appreciated) plagued the EZF.[81] He had come to England in 1904 in order to further his budding scientific career, and his earliest letters from Manchester indicate that he pursued professional advancement with an intensity born of single-minded ambition. They also suggest that Weizmann suffered from a despondency characteristic of many lonely expatriates (he did not marry Vera until August 1906). England, generally, was an initial disappointment; even more so was Anglo-Jewry, whose materialism and superficiality he found such a contrast to the "spirituality" which he recollected in Russia. Unable to work up much enthusiam for Zionist work (for which he anyway had limited time), he seems to have been engrossed in the "quiet and hard-working drudge of the laboratory."[82] Nevertheless, even during his earliest and most difficult years in Manchester Weizmann kept in mind the possibility that England could become a convenient second-line base for the Russian Zionei Zion. With this end in view, he involved himself in local Zionist affairs.[83] In January 1905 he was elected as delegate of the Manchester Zionist Association to the EZF's annual conference at Leeds; there, he was appointed to the national Federation Committee.

In terms of the alignment within the EZF, Weizmann was from the first a member of the Gaster camp. The two men had apparently struck up a relationship when serving together on the cultural commission established by the third Congress in 1899. Their friendship was furthered when Gaster generously helped Weizmann to find his feet in England, providing advice, contacts and—often more to the point—small loans. Their common op-

---

[81] 17 July 1904, Weizmann to Ussishkin, *Letters*, Vol. 3, *September 1903-December 1904*, ed. Gedalia Yogev (London, 1972), pp. 288-90. In general see I. Sieff, "The Manchester Period," in *Chaim Weizmann: A Biography by Several Hands*, ed. Meyer Weisgal and Joel Carmichael (New York, 1963); and Barnet Litvinoff, *Weizmann: Last of the Patriarchs* (New York, 1972), pp. 57-62.

[82] E.g., 20 May 1905 and 20 June 1905, Weizmann to Vera Khatzman, *Letters*, 4:92-94 and 110-111.

[83] 29 January 1905, Weizmann to Ussishkin, ibid., 4:20-21.

position to East Africa and their agreement on the need for "practical" Zionism cemented the alliance. Initially, Gaster was undoubtedly the senior partner, but the relationship was never totally unbalanced. Weizmann had gained some prominence in Zionist affairs before his arrival in England and, as his keynote speech on "synthetic" Zionism at the eighth Congress of 1907 was to confirm, could command an international reputation, quite independent of his local constituency. In fact, he owed much of his subsequent influence in England to his election to the Actions Committee, even though his increasing familiarity with the country did much to help too. ("I believe I know the movement in this country. . . . I know London, know the provinces, which I have toured several times. Since the Congress I have had over 60 meetings in various towns."[84]) By 1907 he was powerful enough to lobby heavily on behalf of Gaster's election to the presidency of the EZF and to try to arrange for an accommodation between the Ḥakham and his opponents. Largely as a result of Weizmann's efforts, at the annual conference that year Sir Francis Montefiore was elected to the ceremonial post of honorary president. Gaster became president and Weizmann himself provincial vice-president; to balance the forces, Cowen was elected London vice-president and Greenberg a member of the executive.[85.]

There followed two years of uneasy tension, during which both Greenberg and Gaster manoeuvered for position. Relations were still tense; Greenberg threatened to resign from the executive, and Gaster refused to address public meetings to which Greenberg had been invited. The 1908 Conference, accordingly, had to be held *in camera*.[86] The storm broke, however, at the Annual Conference of January 1909 held in Sheffield under Gaster's chairmanship. There, Greenberg's party—despite their leader's con-

---

[84] 24 July 1906, Weizmann to Wolffsohn, ibid., 4:319-23. On the relationship see Josef Fraenkel, "Chaim Weizmann and Haham Moses Gaster," *Herzl Year Book* 6 (1965):183-238; and Virginia H. Hein, "British Followers of Theodor Herzl," (Ph.D. diss., Georgia State University, 1978), pp. 377-81.

[85] Report in *JC*, 8 February 1907, p. 24.

[86] 10 April 1908, S. Cohen to Gaster, CZA, Gaster Papers, A203/171, and *Idisher Ekspres*, 3 February 1908, p. 4.

spicuous absence—launched a deliberate attack on their opponents. During the opening session, Gaster was roundly criticized for the inertia of the movement; he was also accused of failing to consult with the executive and of neglecting to give due respect to the honored veterans of the movement (a clear reference to Cowen and Greenberg). Despite a conciliatory speech from Weizmann, the executive's report was only passed by twenty-six votes to twelve. It soon became apparent that the parties were even more finely balanced. In the elections for London vice-president (which Gaster allowed despite Bentwich's protests of jiggery-pokery) Greenberg defeated Bentwich by twenty-two votes to twenty-one. When the result was announced, Gaster himself (reelected president), Weizmann (now provincial member), Moser (provincial vice-president), and Salis Daiches (London member) all resigned from the executive. This action provoked scenes of utter and unedifying disorder. Greenberg attempted to continue the EZF's business; but Gaster refused to hand over the keys, books, and papers of the office. After futile appeals for Sir Francis Montefiore's intervention and a good deal of untoward publicity, Greenberg finally accepted Wolffsohn's advice to hold a conference at Leeds in March 1909. Since most of Gaster's supporters (with the exception of Harry Sacher) boycotted this meeting, it was a more orderly affair. Mr. Charles Dreyfus, a supposedly "neutral" candidate, was elected president, and Greenberg London vice-president (his majority over Bentwich this time being thirty-two votes to eight). But the EZF was now too weak to be stable. Dreyfus resigned the presidency in 1910, and his successor, Joseph Cowen, refused to stand for reelection in 1912. "No one was willing to take his place," and only after much lobbying was Leopold Kessler prevailed upon to assume the thankless task.[87]

Meanwhile, Gaster's supporters—who had regrouped after their defeat at Sheffield in January 1909[88]—had decided to muster their

[87] I. Cohen's circular to all societies in EZF files for 1909-1910, London, Mocatta Library, AJ/133; also JC, 2 April 1909, pp. 25-27; and Goodman, *Zionism in England*, p. 31.

[88] See Sacher's report of various conclaves in 10 March 1910, letter to Gaster, CZA, Gaster Papers, A203/187.

forces under different auspices. They did not have to establish a
new organization of their own in order to do so. Instead, they
increased their collective influence over the Order of Ancient
Maccabeans, a "nationalist" body which had been in existence
since 1896. The records of this organization have unfortunately
not survived, and it is therefore impossible to trace its early history
in any detail. Its origin seems to have been similar to that of the
EZF (which was a younger body), in that it was founded by a
group of erstwhile Chovevei Zionists who were dissatisfied with
Goldsmid's temperate reaction to Herzl. In fact, the twelve founding members, led by Ephraim Ish-Kishor, may have been influenced by Herzl's own suggestion that de Haas form a "Knights of
Zion" group who would be independent of Goldsmid; significantly, they were all members of the B'nei Zion Tent of East
London.[89] Other influences were at work too, however. The
Maccabeans adapted the model of the Chovevei Zion Association
and organized themselves into "beacons," under the overall direction of a "grand commander" (and the inspiration of the slo-
gan: "For our people and the cities of our Lord.") They also had
the distinction of constituting a Friendly Society, in which strictly
Zionist activities could be combined—when necessary—with the
distribution of mutual social benefits. That was one reason why,
even after the foundation of the EZF, the Order of Ancient
Maccabeans retained its separate identity. Its activities were not
as widely reported as were those of the EZF; neither were the
majority of its members (who were largely drawn from the working
classes and who numbered almost 2,000 by 1909) particularly
active in Anglo-Jewish communal affairs in London and the provinces. Nevertheless, for the purposes of the Gaster group, the
Order of Ancient Maccabeans possessed two distinct advantages.
First, it was a particularly well-knit body (as befitted a Friendly
Society); secondly, and perhaps even more important, in 1909
the grand commander of the Order was one of their own number:
Herbert Bentwich.[90]

[89] 27 July 1896, Herzl to de Haas, *Igrot Herzl*, ed. Alex Bein et al., 3 vols.
(Jerusalem, 1958), 1:129-30.
[90] This account, largely based on CZA, Ish-Kishor Papers, K11/1; 20 November

Bentwich willingly pitched his forces into the battle. Immediately after the Sheffield conference, he wrote to the commanders of every Maccabean beacon, exhorting them "to act on behalf of true Zionism."[91] At the same time, he took more practical steps to ensure that the order as a whole could challenge the EZF's claim to speak at Zionist congresses on behalf of all English supporters of the movement. Referring to the rule that allowed a congress to recognize nonterritorial bodies under the appellation *Sonderverbände* provided they represented 3,000 shekel-holders, he applied for permission to sell *shekalim* and—when the required number was reached—for independent status at congress. The EZF, of course, protested. Israel Cohen (the honorary secretary) complained that independent sales of *shekalim* by the Maccabeans was depriving the EZF of sorely needed commission fees and causing damage to the status of Zionism in Britain. Greenberg charged that "the Order . . . is only being used by Bentwich to undermine the Federation because he was not elected as Vice-President. It has not in any way adopted the Basle programme."[92] But these allegations did not prevent a shift of power within Britain itself. By the time the ninth Congress met at Hamburg in December 1909, Weizmann (prompted by Moser and Gaster) had secured the election of his own Maccabean nominees as delegates; by 1910, he had also persuaded the order's own Annual Conference to reiterate its claim for independent status.[93] Con-

---

1912, M. Simon to Actions Committee, CZA, Files of the Central Zionist Office (Berlin), Z3/907; and JC, 11 October 1901, pp. 18, 19; and 8 November 1901, p. 29. See also, Elḥanan Orren, *Ḥibat Ẓion be-Britanyah, 1878-1898* (Tel Aviv, 1974), pp. 132-33 and Goldfine, "Growth of Zionism," p. 48.

[91] 18 February 1909, copy in CZA, Gaster Papers, A203/197.

[92] 14 May 1909, Greenberg to Wolffsohn, CZA, Wolffsohn Papers, W79(ii). Formally, this was true. The rules of the order were explicit that "no person shall be admitted as a member of a Beacon who is deaf, dumb, paralysed, maimed or suffering from a rupture," but merely asked for a general statement that "he is in agreement with the Zionist movement." *Constitution of the Order of Ancient Maccabeans* (London, 1907), para. 5. See also *Idisher Zhurnal*, 6 October 1911, p. 2.

[93] 12 December 1909, Weizmann to Gaster, *Letters*, Vol. 5, *January 1907-February 1913*, ed. Hanna Wiener and Barnet Litvinoff (Jerusalem, 1974), pp. 162-63; and JC, 1 April 1910, pp. 23-24.

sequently, even Wolffsohn, who had managed to stall on the *Sonderverbände* issue at Hamburg, was forced to seek an accommodation. He himself presided at one all-day meeting of the two factions in London in May 1910, and promoted another in June. A further series of discussions was held in August 1911, when the tenth Zionist Congress convened at Basle.[94] None of these gatherings, however, managed to reconcile the parties. The influence wielded by Cowen and Greenberg as board members of the Jewish Colonial Trust and the Anglo-Palestinian Company was sufficiently strong to prevent the dissolution of the EZF, but they could not stop the grant of independent status to the Order of Ancient Maccabeans. Instead, in February 1912 they had to agree to the Action Committee's suggestion that Zionist affairs in England be managed by a Joint Council of both sides. Although Samuel Hirsch (who had largely retired from Zionist affairs since the demise of the Chovevei Zion Association) chaired this body with impeccable impartiality, he was powerless to prevent its subjection to the Gaster group. Greenberg's influence, by contrast, was marginal.

The establishment of the Joint Zionist Council cannot be explained solely in terms of the growing influence of the "practical" faction within the Zionist Organization. Undoubtedly, the latter's victory at the tenth Congress (symbolized by Wolffsohn's resignation and his replacement by Warburg) did have an effect on events in England. But so, too, did internal developments that were of specific relevance to Anglo-Jewry. Of these, perhaps the most important was the growing confidence of provincial Zionists and their increasing readiness to challenge the prerogatives and power of the London leadership. This was not an entirely new

[94] Reports in 17 June 1910, Executive Committee of the EZF to Wolffsohn, CZA, Files of the Central Zionist Office (Cologne), Z2/415; 21 June 1910, OAM to EZF ibid.; and Proceedings of the Maccabean Delegation to the 10th Zionist Congress, private and confidential, CZA, Gaster Papers, A203/193. On Wolffsohn's visit to London, see Mordekhai Eliav, *David Wolffsohn* (Tel Aviv, 1978), pp. 260-62. On the later negotiations for a Joint Council, CZA, Files of the Central Zionist Office (Berlin), Z3/524 and WA, file 134; *Die Welt*, 23 February 1912, pp. 242-43.

development. It will be recalled that Herzl's earliest supporters in England (although principally Londoners) had themselves benefited from provincial dissatisfaction with the behavior of the London officers of the Chovevei Zion Association. They had, in fact, managed to organize a revolt against the Headquarters Tent largely by exploiting such sentiments. By the time the EZF entered upon the second decade of its existence, however, that process seemed to be repeating itself—only now to the disadvantage of the executive of the English Zionist Federation. Gaster, it seems, was the first to feel the effects. Early in 1908 (when still president of the EZF), he was faced with a demand that provincial Zionists be allowed to convene and coordinate their views before the regular annual conference of that year; subsequently, he had to agree to a suggestion put forward by Leon Simon and Harry Sacher (two of the more prominent Mancunians) that the provinces be allowed a greater share of the EZF's propaganda funds. By 1909, he was openly complaining of a "provincial campaign" against the London executive—a charge that would appear to be substantiated by the highly particularist motions presented to the 1909 Annual Conference.[95]

Characteristically, Gaster did not hesitate to take advantage of the strength of provincial feeling once he had himself resigned the presidency in 1909. In fact, he then advised that the provincial societies "should seriously take into consideration the advisability of forming small alliances and a properly constituted Federation of their own, so as to become entirely independent of that London element of which the least said is best."[96] But in thus causing trouble for Greenberg (which was obviously the object of the exercise), the Ḥakham was merely exploiting an existing trend. Quite independently of Gaster, provincial delegates to the Leeds Conference of March 1909 proposed the transfer of the EZF's headquarters to Manchester—a move which,

[95] 23 January 1908, S. Harris to Gaster , CZA, Gaster Papers, A203/160; and 1 July 1908, L. Simon to Gaster, ibid., A203/173; Swansea proposed "district committees" Manchester, special conferences of provincial societies; Leeds, separate representation for every town; and Dublin, more interest in the provinces.
[96] 4 February 1909, Gaster to Sacher, ibid., A203/183.

according to Sacher, Greenberg "took good care" to have rejected. (As Greenberg himself informed a somewhat bemused Wolffsohn: "There is a great local jealously as between Manchester and other towns which is reflected in the ideas of our people. . . . I am afraid that the London people will be very angry at the prospect."[97]) Even the later attitude of the Maccabean beacons—whose headquarters, significantly, were located in Manchester—can perhaps be better understood in this context. The willingness of their members to constitute the *arbeitsgruppe* with which Weizmann might challenge Greenberg in some respects reflected their concern with issues of local importance. Their independent attitude toward the EZF, especially after 1910, seems to have owed as much to provincial pride as to personal animosities and policy differences. That was one reason why Charles Dreyfus, although himself a Mancunian, wished to retire from the presidency of the EZF in 1910. Once he had shown himself incapable of combatting the London leaders, his life in his home town—as even Greenberg admitted—became "utterly unbearable."[98] Clearly, the formation of a "Manchester group," which figures so prominently in many accounts of wartime Zionism, did not depend solely on the fortuitous coincidence of the neighborly proximity of Weizmann to Sacher, Simon, and Israel Sieff.[99] As will be suggested below, their strength seems to have reflected—and owed much to—a steady growth of provincial influence which was affecting many other areas of Anglo-Jewish life.

Weizmann was far better placed to exploit this trend than was Gaster. Indeed, by 1912 the latter's influence in Zionist circles was already beginning to decline. In part, this was due to an unfortunate run of illnesses in his family during 1910 and 1911,

[97] 19 March 1909, Greenberg to Wolffsohn, CZA, Files of the Central Zionist Office (Cologne), Z2/311.

[98] 20 July 1910, Greenberg to Wolffsohn, CZA, Wolffsohn Papers, W79(ii). Also, 7 July 1910, Dreyfus to Wolffsohn, CZA, Files of the Central Zionist Office (Cologne), Z2/415.

[99] See, especially, Chaim Weizmann, *Trial and Error* (London, 1949), pp. 115-16; and Harry Sacher, *Zionist Portraits* (London, 1959), pp. 18-19; also 10 February 1911, P. Goodman to Actions Committee, CZA, Files of the Central Zionist Office (Cologne), Z2/415.

which necessitated Gaster's frequent absences from many Zionist meetings and reduced his effectiveness at others. Equally important, however, was a growing feeling in several quarters that the Ḥakham's pride was doing the movement more harm than good. His refusal to accept the chairmanship of the Joint Zionist Council in 1912 was a political mistake. So, too, was his proposal (in 1913) that the EZF be disbanded and replaced by an entirely new "English Zionist Association," which he proposed to lead. Even though that suggestion had the initial support of some of his friends on the Actions Committee, their backing merely confirmed the extent of Gaster's isolation from his erstwhile colleagues in the local movement. The latter were still to treat him with deference, as befitted his status, and to make use of his extensive contacts (most notably in 1917, when the first meeting between the Zionists and Sir Mark Sykes took place at Gaster's house). But they nevertheless defeated his proposals at the 1913 annual conference of the EZF and elected, by acclaim, Joseph Cowen to the presidency.[100]

Weizmann, in particular, had been deliberately circumspect. The more his scientific and Zionist status grew, the freer he felt to dissociate himself from Gaster. In fact, he did not correspond with the Ḥakham at all between the summer of 1911 and the spring of 1913—a silence that contrasts strikingly with both the quantity of their previous exchanges and the increasing warmth of Weizmann's letters to Aḥad Ha'am. By the time the relationship was resumed, Weizmann's work on behalf of the Jewish University in Jerusalem had taken him far beyond the stage of dependence on the older man's capricious patronage. His search for support for the project had taken him into salons whose doors were closed to Gaster (most critically, that of the Rothschilds); his growing reputation also enabled him to build up a core of personal followers in both London and the provinces.[101] As early

---

[100] On these events see 13 October 1912, Moser to Gaster, CZA, Gaster Papers, A203/194. 15 April 1913, Weizmann to Smaller Actions Committee, *Letters*, Vol. 6, *March 1913-July 1914*, ed. Barnet Litvinoff (Jerusalem, 1974), pp. 34-37; JC, 6 June 1913, pp. 29-32; and *Idisher Ekspres*, 26 February 1913, p. 4.

[101] 3 December 1913, Actions Committee to L. Stein, WA, file 161; and 18 May 1914, I. Sieff to Weizmann, ibid., file 169.

as 1911, Weizmann had given notice of his intention to act independently when agreeing to serve as provincial vice-president under Joseph Cowen. He retained his poise in 1913, despite his disappointment with the EZF's unfavorable reaction to his suggestion that Gaster be elected president of a "homogenous" executive. He continued to associate with his political opponents, partly in order to tether them, and at the 1914 Conference held in Leeds, he again agreed to serve as vice-president under Cowen.[102] In this capacity, he was well placed both to impress his views on the Federation and to substantiate his claim to represent the senior body of English Zionists. Within three years (in February 1917) he was to assume the presidency of the EZF.

[102] 6 June 1913, Weizmann to Gaster, *Letters*, 6:86-7; and 16 February 1914, Weizmann to Smaller Actions Committee, ibid., 6:256-57.

4

The Zionists and Communal Politics, 1904-1914

Eventually, WEIZMANN'S leadership of the EZF was to inaugurate a period of conspicuous Zionist progress within Anglo-Jewry. During his presidency (which lasted until 1924), the Federation at last began to gain communal prestige. But that development could not have been reasonably foreseen before 1914. Rather, throughout the decade that preceded the outbreak of World War I, the EZF was more often villified than praised. The failings of the organization's leaders were paralleled by similar deficiencies throughout the local movement. Both official memoranda and personal memoirs have bequeathed an entire dossier of minor squabbles at every level and within virtually every branch of the EZF. These skirmishes, although neither as intense nor as prolonged as the central clash between Gaster, Greenberg, and their accomplices, were hardly less harmful to the general image of Zionism. Their overall effect was demoralizing, even on committed adherents to the notion of Jewish nationalism. Latent sympathy for the Zionist idea, it might be argued, remained widespread, but the EZF was in no position to harness that emotion. Purity of conviction and uniformity of purpose (if, indeed, they had ever existed) seemed everywhere to have been replaced by lassitude, ineptitude, and, above all, contentiousness.

This situation necessarily impeded the progress of the Zionist movement as a force for change in the structure and political affiliation of Anglo-Jewry. As a body, the EZF continued to proclaim its adherence to a program of communal "conquest"; in effect, it seemed to possess very little ability to pursue the extensive activities that this policy would have required. Particularly was this the case where the immigrant section of the community was concerned. It became increasing unlikely that the Zionists might dislodge the incumbent native leadership by a direct appeal to the sympathies of the immigrants. That option had in any case been virtually discounted before 1904. The EZF still did not possess the necessary degree of organizational cohesion to deploy a mass movement; neither could it yet muster the popular following which might have tempted its leaders to do so. Statistical comparisons with other contemporary movements of communal and social protest (anti-Zionist and non-Zionist) even if possible, would probably be misleading, especially since those movements too possessed relatively few committed followers in immigrant Jewish quarters. But some of the prominent left-wing groups do seem to have attracted many of the more vibrant, sensitive, and politically active inhabitants of those areas. Their personal qualities, it has been argued, compensated for their limited quantity. By contrast, the leaders of the EZF generally convey a banal and even squalid impression. No local Zionist personality (especially not in retrospect) matches the charisma of Rudolf Rocker, the unique mentor of East End Jewish anarchism, who edited the *Arbayter Fraynd* after 1903. Similarly, British Zionists failed to produce a doctrinal and institutional program that might have deflected increasing Jewish participation in the general (non-Jewish) trade union movement.[1] Scattered observations in the Yiddish press indicate that very few Poalei Zion societies remained afloat in the poorer areas of London and the provinces during the prewar period; those which did manage to do so were often far too debilitated by the effort to constitute the stuff out of which

[1] On the fortunes of Jewish anarchists and socialists during this period see William J. Fishman, *East End Jewish Radicals, 1875-1914* (London, 1975), pp. 229-309; and Lloyd P. Gartner, *The Jewish Immigrant*, 2nd ed. (London, 1973), pp. 132-41. See also reports on Jewish trade union activity in *Der Idisher Trayd-Yunionist* (New York, YIVO Institute, microfilm, 66-y-728) 14 July 1910 and 12 August 1910; on the Free Workers' Ring, *Idisher Zhurnal*, 11 April 1911 and 1 November 1911.

a "communal revolution" on Zionism's behalf might have been made.[2] Their eclectic formulations of doctrine (which markedly decreased in originality once Marmor left for the United States in 1906) merely provoked the derision of austere left-wing critics;[3] their occasional attempts to organize "mass demonstrations" provided no justifiable grounds for hope in less hostile quarters. As Joseph Cowen wryly commented to the Actions Committee in 1914:

> You state that you have received a number of letters from England proving that there is great enthusiasm for our cause here. Perhaps you would put me in touch with your correspondents, as I have not been able to find much sympathy.[4]

No senior members of the EZF quibbled with that judgement. It is, however, a tribute to their resourcefulness and resilience that most nevertheless continued to seek a wider degree of communal influence. The conquest of Anglo-Jewry remained their avowed policy, even in 1909 and 1910 when the organization which they claimed to represent was itself on the verge of bankruptcy and disintegration. Such steadfastness of purpose cannot be attributed exclusively to compelling Zionist faith. As has already been noted, most leaders of the EZF evidently sought communal prestige and influence, whether at a national or at a local level, for its own sake. The effects that their activity might have on the status of Zionism in Britain was, although not a subordinate consideration, certainly not the only one. To say this is not to question the sincerity of their Zionist convictions, but merely to call attention to the influence of less explicitly ideological ambitions. The first generation of native Zionists in Britain, not unlike their North American counterparts,[5] may have discovered

---

[2] E.g., *Idisher Ekspres*, 6 September 1911, p. 6; and 11 January 1912, p. 5; and *Idisher Zhurnal*, 12 October 1911 and 7 December 1911.

[3] Particularly the *Arbayter Fraynd*. See, e.g., 22 August 1902, p. 11; 14 June 1907, p. 6; 21 June 1907, pp. 6-7.

[4] 6 February 1914, Cowen to Hantke, CZA, Files of the Central Zionist Office (Berlin), Z3/807.

[5] Yonathan Shapiro, *Leadership of the American Zionist Organization, 1897-1930* (Urbana, 1971), chaps. 2 and 3.

(126)

in the Jewish national movement a doctrine that would clearly distinguish them from most members of the Anglo-Jewish Establishment; by extention, it also supplied a form of political rhetoric that justified the foundation of a rival institution under their own control. Hence, they could regard their roles in the EZF as a convenient, and perfectly justifiable means of reconciling their personal ambitions (which were unabashedly parochial) with their Jewish national consciences.

The ambivalent attitude of the EZF's leadership toward its immigrant following was in some measure related to such considerations. Notwithstanding their repeated attacks on the indifference of the Anglo-Jewish Establishment, they were themselves not altogether immune from similar criticisms. The native officers of the EZF continued to keep a tight hold on the reins of executive position,[6] and made comparatively few efforts to attain massive immigrant support. With the exception of sporadic "synagogue campaigns" (which were not very successful), we have very little evidence of a concerted effort to generate popular support in the East End or any comparable district; occasional suggestions that the EZF establish its own nationwide Yiddish newspaper were regularly shelved. The reasons were not entirely functional, in the sense of being the result of organizational inefficiency and financial stringency. No less relevant was the fact that the immigrant community was, in any case, not the primary target of the activity of the EZF's leadership. Socially and professionally, it is worth repeating, most of the men who set the tone of Zionist communal work in Britain were themselves far too closely associated with native Anglo-Jewry to encourage what was grandly termed a "revolt of the masses." They generally preferred to advance the national idea by a strategy more gradual and more circumscribed in its implications. In his own way, Weizmann shared this perspective.[7] Consequently, neither he nor any other

[6] Jacob Fuchs, *Merkaz Ivri* (London, 1909), pp. 27-28.

[7] E.g., 6 October 1912, Weizmann to Smaller Actions Committee, *Letters and Papers of Chaim Weizmann Series A. Letters* [hereafter Letters], general ed. Meyer Weisgal, et al. 23 vols. (Oxford, London and Jerusalem, 1969-1980) vol. 5, *January 1907-February 1913*, ed. Hanna Wiener and Barnet Litvinoff (Jerusalem, 1974), p. 319.

leaders of the EZF sought to reopen their organization's earlier and protracted debate over the form and direction of Zionist tactics in Anglo-Jewry. Despite their squabbles over other matters, these men broadly agreed that their movement had to advance by cultivating the sympathies of the advantaged. In practical terms, what this involved was the continuation, and if possible intensification, of their campaign to bring Zionism into association with the most important of Anglo-Jewry's established institutions. This was a strategy that several native Zionists were still well-placed to pursue. It also possessed two other, immediately recognizable advantages. First, it seemed to depend very little on either organizational ability or financial resources (of which the Zionists had very little). Secondly, and no less crucially, it appeared to offer ample scope for the gratification of personal ambitions (of which they had a surfeit).

The process of institutional infiltration did not await a formal policy decision. It gathered a momentum that was virtually independent of whatever transpired within the EZF. In 1905, for instance, Gaster arranged for Naḥum Sokolow to be received by the Conjoint Foreign Committee, ostensibly with the purpose of acquainting its members with the Jewish situation in Russia and obtaining their advice on possible measures of relief. Despite his opposition to East Africa, he also attempted to exploit the AJA's hesitant acceptance of David Wolffsohn's invitation to discuss the report of the commission of enquiry to the region. "Now that you have convinced yourself to send a delegate to a quasi-Zionist Conference," he urged members of the council, "you may just as well commit yourself to be present at a truly Zionist meeting."[8] Notwithstanding his personal differences with Gaster, Greenberg pursued a parallel course: in 1906 he pressed the Board of Deputies to accept Wolffsohn's invitation to a General Jewish Conference in Brussels on the east European situation; significantly, he also asked members of the EZF to "do their best to influence their representatives on the Board" to support his appeal.[9] Similar

[8] E.g., 16 April 1905, Gaster to Henriques, CZA, Gaster Papers, A203/147.
[9] 23 March 1906, circular, CZA, Files of the Central Zionist Office (Cologne), Z2/411.

attempts at conversion were made elsewhere. Individual Zionist societies began to seek affiliation with the Union of Jewish Literary Societies as early as 1906. In 1907, and again in 1909, Norman Bentwich and Leon Simon proposed that the union's Annual Conference grant such Zionist societies formal recognition. At the same time, and with more success, they asked that the union support the establishment of the proposed Jewish University in Jerusalem.[10]

Altogether, the EZF would appear to have made a deliberate effort to attain the support of the more prosperous, and hence the supposedly more influential, members of the community. There was nothing irregular in the call to arrange meetings at private houses "to which well-to-do Jews might be attracted." By 1913, it was taken for granted that societies would make every effort to inject their speakers into "the drawing-room circuit" of the community, and that rising barristers such as Leonard Stein would best work through " 'round-table conferences' of prominent people."[11] Of a piece with this policy were the equally determined attempts to propagate Zionism among Anglo-Jewish university students. As early as 1907 Joseph Cowen had specifically marked down as prospective Zionists "all the young intelligence—Varsity men, etc.—that is growing up around us."[12] By 1914, Zionist societies had been established at the major universities, and although their membership was small, their very existence was considered to be one of the EZF's most prestigious gains. Ultimately, these efforts bore more substantial fruit. For one thing, some of the second generation of native Zionist leaders first attained prominence at the university societies (Norman Bentwich at Oxford, Selig Brodetsky at Cambridge, and Leon Simon in

[10] Minutes of executive meeting on 13 March 1906, Minute Book of Union of Jewish Literary Societies, 3:17 (London, Mocatta Library, University College, AJ/12); report of annual conference in JC, 28 June 1907, p. 20 and 2 May 1909, pp. 19-21.

[11] 15 May 1913, Simon to Weizmann, WA, file 152 and 21 November 1913, EZF to Actions Committee, CZA, Files of the Central Zionist Office (Berlin), Z3/807.

[12] 27 December 1907, Cowen to Zangwill, CZA, Ito files, A36/135.

London being the most obvious examples). For another, Zionism at the universities became altogether more respectable. At its third Annual Conference in 1920, the Inter-University Jewish Federation was persuaded to reverse its previous ruling against discussing politics. Instead, on Brodetsky's motion, it unanimously agreed to "welcome" the British mandate in Palestine and express "great gratification at the facilities now afforded for the reconstruction of Erez Israel."[13]

Whether or not these advances warranted the extravagant self-congratulations of the Zionists is debatable. Zionist activities at the universities aroused sufficient opposition for twenty-five "graduates and members of Oxford, Cambridge and London Universities" to publish in April 1909 a sharply worded attack on Jewish nationalism which was publicly supported and perhaps privately inspired by several members of the lay and clerical establishment.[14] Despite all the Zionists' efforts to conquer the community, Anglo-Jewry's traditional leadership had neither been converted nor replaced. Convinced that they still enjoyed the confidence of the community—and, of course, that their objections to Zionism were valid—they saw no reason to be afraid. The EZF, after all, still represented only a minority of the community. As for Anglo-Jewry at large, "the leaders for the most part seem still to be where they were; and one is permitted to doubt whether a movement which embraces only a fraction of the race—and that the least powerful—ever can effect a sweeping revolution."[15]

THE COMMUNAL CONTEXT

Considering the EZF's limited corporate impact on Anglo-Jewish affairs, such disdain was unquestionably justified. But from the wider perspective of communal politics, patrician compla-

[13] JC, 13 August 1920, p. 21.

[14] The original letter in JC, 9 April 1909, p. 6; for later support (by Adler and Morris Joseph, for example), see JC, 23 April 1909, p. 11 and 30 April 1909, pp. 16-17.

[15] JC, 29 November 1901, p. 27.

(130)

cency of that nature was less warranted. The position of the communal Establishment was not entirely secure. The decade before the outbreak of World War I was already witnessing the incubation of several social, political, and regional tensions which were subsequently to bring about substantial changes in the style and personnel of communal government. As much is evident once attention is shifted from exclusively Zionist concerns, and a survey is made of other topics of communal contention. From this more lateral perspective, it becomes clear that the leaders of the EZF were not operating in an atmosphere entirely devoid of dissent. Neither did they constitute the only, nor indeed the most effective, opposition to the community's established leadership. The senior officers of Anglo-Jewry's principal institutions could certainly rely upon overwhelming support for their publicized anti-Zionist statements, but on many other issues they were confronted with an increasing barrage of criticism from their own constituents. The latter usually adopted such attitudes quite independently of Zionist pressure; indeed they were invariably opposed to the principles and practices of the EZF. Nevertheless, many of them contributed to the institutional pressures and tensions for which the Zionists were subsequently to claim some credit.

In order to substantiate this analysis, a certain amount of digression is necessary. Specifically, note must be taken of the major issues and topics that gave rise to discord in native Anglo-Jewry before the war, and of the principal figures who generated institutional debates on those matters. Often, the record leaves a frankly disagreeable taste. A review of various forms of communal dissent (the spectrum ranges from the utterance of an unhappy protest in closed meetings to ostentatious public pronouncements) uncovers a welter of minor feuds, the surviving traces of which reveal a confusing and wearisome trail of trivial vendettas and faceless individuals. Nevertheless, the story is not entirely a catalogue of personal rancor.

Out of the cluster of subordinate grumbles, more substantial complaints affecting communal government do emerge. Two interrelated issues constantly recur, and both were purported to stand in need of urgent attention. One was the "undemocratic" manner whereby honorary officials were elected to positions of communal responsibility; the other was the "inadequate" representation accorded to the provinces in the major councils of Anglo-Jewry. These complaints gave rise to confrontations with the incumbent leadership of the community in several forums and at various opportunities. Very occasionally, the debates were generated by contentious issues of international Jewish importance: the Kishinev pogrom and its successors, the East Africa offer, or the Beilis trial. More often, they were sparked by essentially parochial matters: pending government legislation (especially the Aliens Act of 1905, the Slaughter of Animals Bill of 1910, the Insurance Bill of 1911), sporadic outbursts of anti-Semitism (both violent, as in South Wales in August 1911, or genteel, as in the writings of Chesterton and Hillaire Belloc), the procedure for the election of a new Ashkenazi Chief Rabbi in 1912-1913, or the initiation of liturgical changes in various synagogues. Each instance was thought to provide a suitable opportunity for the ventilation of conflicting religious and political ideologies; each also uncovered successive layers in a more pragmatic tussle for communal authority.

As much would seem to be evident from the regularity with which complaints of a broadly similar *constitutional* nature recurred at several Anglo-Jewish forums during the early twentieth century. Despite their dissimilarities of function and organization, most of the community's principal institutions were faced with strikingly similar demands that they reform the methods whereby they managed their affairs. The development had roots in the recent past. Anglo-Jewry of the Victorian era, as several studies point out, was a malleable society. By the closing decades of the nineteenth century, the rising commercial and professional classes (an amalgam of native and German-immigrant success stories) had already won substantial concessions from the "Grand Dukes." Hence the extension of the franchise in the United Synagogue, the provisions for provincial representation at the Board of Deputies, and the tolerance extended toward the Federation of Synagogues.[16] Nevertheless, by the early twentieth century the move-ment toward institutional reform seems not only to have gathered momentum, but also to have changed its character. In response to further shifts in the community's economic and demographic map, what are referred to as "the perennially burgeoning upper middle classes" sought to protect and extend their gains. In ad-dition to representation, they now demanded the right to con-sultation. Their quarrel, to put it another way, was with the practice of communal government rather than with its structure. Their contention was that many of those who had established a claim to express their views on pressing Jewish affairs at home and abroad were being muzzled by a range of institutional con-ventions. Charges of a similar kind were, it has been seen, levelled at the same time against the Zionist leadership. The executive of the EZF, no less than the Headquarters Tent of the Chovevei Zion Association before it, was persistently accused of being self-elective and out of touch with its provincial constituents. But there is no reason to treat these as special cases. Instead, the existence of such pressures merely emphasizes the degree to which internal divisions among the Zionists might have mirrored wider communal tensions between groups not inappropriately defined as "ins" and "outs."[17] A survey of the reports (official and un-official) of proceedings at the better-known of Anglo-Jewry's non-

[16] These developments are best outlined in Vivian D. Lipman, *Social History of the Jews in England* (London, 1954), and touched upon in Israel Finestein, "Arthur Cohen, Q.C. (1829-1912)," in *Remember the Days*, ed. John M. Shaftesley (London, 1966); see also, idem, "The Lay Leadership of the United Synagogue since 1870," in *A Century of Anglo-Jewish Life*, ed. Salmond S. Levin (London, 1971); and Vivian D. Lipman, "The Development of London Jewry," in ibid. For comments on the later history of the Grand Dukes: Cecil Roth, "The Court Jews of Edwardian England," *Jewish Social Studies* 5 (October 1943):355-66; and John Camplin, *The Rise of the Plutocrats: Wealth and Power in Edwardian England* (London, 1978).

[17] Thus Gaster's remark that some people in the community adopted positions of "factious opposition . . . only and solely with the object of thwarting those that are in for they are 'outs.' " 1 May 1914, to Weizmann, private, WA, file 168. The conceptual structure is expressed by Robert K. Merton, "Insiders and Outsiders: A Chapter in the Sociology of Knowledge," *American Journal of Sociology* 78 (July 1972): 9-47.

Zionist institutions suggests that the clamor and contention prevalent at the EZF differed only in degree from that apparent elsewhere. Non-Zionists, no less than Zionists, claimed to feel that contemporary cultural and economic pressures, together with the contiguous phenomenon of mass immigration, were undermining the social unity and hierarchical harmony of Anglo-Jewry, and thus necessitating a fundamental overhaul of the mechanisms of communal government.

Demands for constitutional changes during the early twentieth century were especially rife at the Board of Deputies. There, moreover, the movement toward reform seems to have been generated quite independent of Zionist pressure. Briefly summarized, the story is one of progressive—although minority—discontent. In 1904, for instance, only two deputies of the fifty-three present had supported a motion to disband the Conjoint Foreign Committee, the self-styled communal "cabinet" (composed of representatives of the Board and the Anglo-Jewish Association) on the grounds that "that body tends to be too secretive and to stifle discussion."[18] But the number of critics had risen to half a dozen by 1907 and to twenty-three in October 1909.[19] By that time, moreover, a new group of (non-Zionist) communal dissidents had begun to emerge. Prominent among them was Simon Rosenbaum (later Rowson; deputy for Exeter since 1907), a statistician and one-time lecturer in physics at University College, London, who had gained a reputation for meticulous attention to detail when working on Joseph Chamberlain's tariff commission. Ambitious, energetic, and professionally successful, Rowson emerges from the Board's records as a somewhat brash man, who kept a close watch on the effects of his various public pronouncements and could quickly recognize and learn from his mistakes. Thus, although forced to withdraw a motion calling for a review of the conjoint arrangement with the AJA in 1909, he did gather enough support for his attacks on its "undemocratic" character to be

[18] Minutes of 15 June 1904, London, DEPS, Minute Books, A15:34-35.
[19] JC, 22 October 1909, p. 12.

loudly supported by several deputies in 1910.[20] In turn, these criticisms of the "sham" discussions and "farcical" proceedings at the Board were echoed in several pungent editorials in the native Jewish press, some of which specifically supported Rowson's suggestion that the "adoption of the 'party system' into the . . . election of deputies would introduce a greater zest and clearer direction into its deliberations."[21]

Such gestures did not precipitate fundamental changes at the Board itself; numerically, those deputies who advocated reform were still in a minority. But the complaints thus articulated did contribute to a climate of opinion in some quarters in favor of the establishment of a parallel, but more representative institution. The initiative was taken in June 1909, when a representative of the American Grand Lodge of the Independent Order of the B'nai B'rith addressed an invited audience of prominent Anglo-Jewish communal workers in London. Initially, the suggestion that a sister branch be established in Britain was received coolly; only nine participants in the gathering supported the idea. Claude Montefiore (in whose house, curiously enough, the meeting took place) predictably alluded to the prior claims of the community's veteran political and philanthropic organizations; other pundits similarly doubted whether Anglo-Jewry was in need of yet another body committed (as was the B'nai B'rith) to "developing and elevating the moral and material condition of the people of the Jewish faith."[22] But independence of the existing framework was precisely the aim that less conservative spirits hoped to achieve by establishing a London branch. As Walter Schwab, the historian of the First Lodge of England records, the body owed its

[20] Minutes of meeting of 28 November 1909 and of annual general meeting of 26 June 1910, London, DEPS, Minute Books, A16:25-26, 37-40. Rowson, who was eventually to become president of the B'nai B'rith, also had much to say on other aspects of communal affairs; see his article, signed S. Rosenbaum, "The Jewish Question in England," *Jewish Review* 2 (1911):106-119.

[21] E.g., *JC*, 17 December 1909, p. 7; *Jewish Review*, 1 (1910):287-89; *Hayehoodi*, 8 June 1911, pp. 2-3.

[22] E.g., J. Lesser in *JC*, 26 November 1909, p. 31; and the account of the early history of the Order in the draft of its first annual report (1910), in Mocatta Library, Gaster Papers, vol. 28.

establishment to the dissatisfaction felt by several members of the emergent middle class with the "oligarchy, autocracy, traditionalism and narrow insularity" which (he cautiously adds) "may have characterised the communal leadership of the time."[23] By 1910, the original nine felt they had enough support among their own class to apply for a Charter of Association in the international Order; within another year their list of members—most of whom were already active in local or national communal affairs and very few of whom were not business or professional men—ran to over two hundred prominent names. Moreover, the Lodge and its officers soon established a commendable record of political activity, much of it successful. The Insurance, Slaughter of Animals, and Shops Bills, as well as the question of legal representation for aliens and the Russian government's reluctance to issue passports to prospective Jewish visitors to its east European territories—all became areas in which the B'nai B'rith claimed to possess expertise. On these subjects, Lodge members were sufficiently well-versed to make representations to the relevant departments of Government, and sufficiently effective to rebuff charges of irresponsible "encroachment" on the demesne of the Board of Deputies. By 1912, the B'nai B'rith, as a body, had won the Board's reluctant agreement to the establishment of a joint committee for the purpose of dealing with the most pressing of those questions.[24]

The success of the B'nai B'rith stimulated more forceful criticisms of the Board's executive. In 1911, Simon Rowson (himself one of the original applicants for the Lodge's charter) felt sufficiently confident to take the unprecedented step of proposing a motion of censure against David Alexander. His indictment was: "That the actions of the President of the Board in relation to the evidence before the Divorce Commission, the Shops Bill, the Insurance Bill, the Slaughter of Animals Bill, and the provision of legal aid for Alien Immigrants, have had the effect of severely

[23] Walter M. Schwab, *B'nai B'rith, The First Lodge of England: A Record of Fifty Years* (London, 1960), p. 16.

[24] Minutes of Board of Deputies meetings of 21 January 1912 and 14 July 1912, London, DEPS, Minute Books, A16:90, 108.

damaging the authority and influence of the Board as the accredited representative of Jewish Institutions in this country."
From the available reports, it appears that the debate which
ensued was more "involved and stormy" than is initially suggested
by the margin of Alexander's victory (over fifty votes).[25] Further
revisions of the Board's constitution and procedures were proposed
in the remaining years before the outbreak of war, and popular
criticism of the Board's structure remained rife. "What the community needs," concluded the *Jewish Chronicle* in February 1914,

> is an elected body which shall be representative of the com-
> munity in the broadest and completest manner practically pos-
> sible. The Community needs a representative body which will
> voice its opinions either in defence or in defiance, armed with
> the backing of popular representation and popular support. It
> does not require . . . a mere dunghill on which chosen cocks
> may crow to their sweet content.[26]

Significantly, charges of executive inefficiency and electoral
underrepresentation were not restricted to the Board of Deputies.
To cite similar instances is not to exaggerate their importance;
overt dissatisfaction with the prevailing state of affairs was still
the exception rather than the rule. The climate of communal
discourse was usually quiescent to the point of being somnolent.
Nevertheless, the prevalent mood was interrupted sufficiently often
to indicate that the spirit affecting the Board of Deputies was
beginning to penetrate other organizations too. Council meetings
of the United Synagogue, for instance, were occasionally inter-
spersed with protests against "the virtual selection by the honorary
officers of their own colleagues." Representatives of some constituent congregations also lodged complaints against the "ef-
fortless superiority" with which a small coterie of officials attempted to "railroad" important business through monthly meetings,
while snubbing suggested innovations and insisting—above all

[25] Minutes of meeting of 19 November 1911 in ibid., p. 82 and JC, 24 November 1911, pp. 15-17; and *Idisher Zhurnal*, 16 November 1911, p. 3.
[26] "Mentor" (usually Leopold Greenberg), in JC, 20 February 1914, p. 11.

else—on financial solvency.[27] Far more notable (and better documented) is the resentment aroused by the manner in which Lord
Nathan Rothschild insisted on the election of Dr. Joseph Hertz
as successor to the late Chief Rabbi Adler in 1913. Led by Sir
Adolph Tuck, (another member of the B'nai B'rith), an influential deputation of dissidents waited upon the elderly peer (only
to be told: "Go away; leave me alone. I am sick and tired of you
all!"). Subsequently, the presentation of a strongly worded written protest was only averted by the somewhat desperate plea that
"if further action on our part would involve the alienation of
Lord Rothschild from the U.S. we should not only remain without
the guidance of a Chief Rabbi but also lose that of the lay leader,
who has for more than 40 years safeguarded the interests of Anglo-
Jewry with dignity and wisdom."[28]

Proceedings took a different form at the Federation of Synagogues, where Sir Samuel Montagu (who was created Lord
Swaythling in 1907) had established an even more intimidating
tradition of presidential superiority. There too, however, there
were signs of comparable protest, particularly once the second
Lord Swaythling succeeded his late father in 1911. Altogether,
the new president of the Federation was less devoted to its affairs
than his predecessor; his personal standards of religious orthodoxy
also left more to be desired. Perhaps for both reasons he inspired
less respect among what had, potentially, always been a turbulent
and truculent membership. Neither Swaythling's name nor his
purse prevented the outbreak of two serious revolts against the
manner of his rule. His unilateral decision to withdraw the Federation's delegates from the Chief Rabbi's Conference of 1912
provoked one motion "against the manner in which the executive
refused to consult with its members"; his alleged refusal to attend

[27] E.g., *JC*, 24 December 1909, p. 21. References to such tensions in Aubrey
Newman, *The United Synagogue* (London, 1976), chaps. 7-9.

[28] 14 February 1913, S. Japhet to Sir A. Tuck, copy in New York, Jewish
Theological Seminary, E. Adler Papers, Box 3; and Newman, *United Synagogue*,
pp. 100-101.

a public demonstration of sympathy for Beilis in 1914 almost occasioned another.[29]

At the Sephardi Congregation, to cite the third of the metropolitan community's main synagogal bodies, complaints of that kind were more muted, but they had been voiced even earlier. A sizable bloc of so-called "democratic *Yehidim*" (ordinary members) seems to have taken shape at Bevis Marks during the contentious Ramsgate College affair of 1896. Thereafter, their spokesmen repeatedly demanded "adequate power in the management of the Congregation's affairs," and issued well-publicized protests against the *Mahamad* for "framing laws for themselves so as to protect their own self-appointed privileges, to the possible detriment of the Congregation."[30] In 1900 they resolved that the Finance Committee of the *Yehidim* be allowed to inspect "all or any of the books, documents or papers of the Congregation to which they may wish to have access"; in 1908 they insisted that the power of electing delegates to the Board of Deputies be transferred to their hands.[31]

The records of the Anglo-Jewish Association provide substantial evidence of the simultaneous and contiguous call for more provincial consultation in communal policy-making. Such demands can be traced as far back as 1900 (when the Manchester branch of the AJA resolved on the need for further information on proceedings at the council), and appear to have gathered steam in the wake of the controversy aroused by the Association's inept handling of the Kishinev demonstration in 1903. In April of that year the Executive Committee received a blunt warning that the Glasgow branch would cease its contributions unless assured of

[29] London, Federation of Synagogues, Minute Book, 2:146, 173-76: fuller accounts in *JC*, 1 March 1912, pp. 38-39, and 13 February 1914, p. 32; and *Idisher Ekspres*, 29 October 1913, p. 4.

[30] *JC*, 2 June 1905, p. 20, and minutes of annual meeting of *Yehidim* for 1902 in London, Sephardi Congregation Archives, Elders Minute Book, p. 218.

[31] Minutes of special meeting of 2 December 1900 in Sephardi Congregation Archives, Elders Minute Book, p. 216; and annual meeting of 1908 in *JC*, 3 April 1908, p. 16.

"wider representation" for the provinces on the council; in December 1904 it had to promise to hold alternate annual meetings in the provinces.[32] A local revolution within the Manchester branch in 1905 provoked further change. It was largely in response to a petition of the newly installed Manchester executive that the council of the AJA reluctantly accepted Wolffsohn's invitation to a General Jewish Conference on East Africa; in 1906 it agreed to a change in its own constitution that enabled provincial branches to propose action for the consideration of the council without sending accredited delegates to its meetings.[33] Shortly thereafter, Barrow Belisha and Joseph Duhlberg, both prominent exponents of Mancunian aspirations and institutional reorganization, advocated the formation of a representative "parliament" for Anglo-Jewry and a more robust Shechita Board for Manchester.[34]

These demands, too, were not entirely innovative. As several local and regional studies have shown, a "provincial consciousness" had been forming throughout the nineteenth century. Reflecting, albeit a little belatedly, a general trend within English society, Jewish communities in several parts of the British Isles had developed institutions and traditions that were peculiarly their own.[35] By the early twentieth century, the variety of pro-

[32] The first of which was held in Birmingham in 1906; see also Mocatta Library, Archives of the AJA, Executive Committee Minute Book, 4:383.

[33] Ibid., p. 430, and JC editorial, 19 January 1906, p. 5.

[34] Letters calling for an Anglo-Jewish parliament, from Belisha and Duhlberg, appeared in the JC, 23 February 1906, pp. 16-17; 16 March 1906, p. 26; 11 May 1906, pp. 23-24 and 6 July 1906, p. 29. See also report of Special General Meeting of the AJA on 13 January 1907 in Mocatta Library, Archives of the AJA, Council Minute Book, 3:273. On the Manchester Shechitah Board, whose influence was far greater than its name suggests, see JC supplement on Manchester, 15 June 1906, p. vi.

[35] The purpose of the present work is to trace the effect of these developments on the central (London-based) institutions, and not their local course. On the latter see (for gentile English society) Donald Read, *The English Provinces c. 1760-1960: A Study in Influence* (London, 1964) and (for an earlier period of Anglo-Jewish history) Cecil Roth, *The Rise of Provincial Jewry, 1740-1840* (London, 1950). On specific communities, see, for example, Bertram B. Benas, "Later Records of the Jews in Liverpool," *Transactions of the Historic Society of Lancashire*

vincial experience already formed an essential attribute of Anglo-Jewish life as a whole. Nevertheless, some sort of apotheosis seems to have been attained, with Manchester (in particular) achieving a position of unparalleled influence. No movement toward "provincial independence" took place, but there was an adjustment of the imbalance between London and other communities. Consequently, the case against overcentralization put to the AJA and, in a different context but at the same time, to the English Zionist Federation, was also extended to other spheres of Anglo-Jewish life. The community's ministry, for example, was said to be laboring under the burden of a London-tied bureaucracy which did little to take account of unique provincial needs. The Conference of Anglo-Jewish Ministers repeatedly recommended the establishment of "provincial communal councils" of local rabbis and reverends. When these proposals were disregarded, some congregations demanded that their delegates take no part in the election of the new Chief Rabbi.[36]

Far more forceful—and effective—were the complaints against "anti-provincial discrimination" voiced at the Board of Deputies. Representatives from Manchester were particularly loud in their indictments of the Board's failure to adapt its cumbersome ma-

---

and Cheshire 45 (1929):33-35 and "A Survey of the Jewish Institutional History of Liverpool and District," *TJHSE* 17 (1953):23-28; Philip Ettinger, *'Hope Place' in Liverpool Jewry* (Liverpool, 1930); Arnold Levy, *History of Sunderland Jewish Community* (London, 1956), especially pp. 195-97; and Ernest Krausz, *Leeds Jewry, Its History and Social Structure* (Cambridge, 1964), pp. 4-27. The latest, and most substantial of the local Jewish histories indicates that the independence of spirit shown by the Manchester community had a lengthy pedigree: Bill Williams, *The Making of Manchester Jewry, 1740-1875* (Manchester, 1976). See also *Provincial Jewry in Victorian Britain, Papers of a Conference at University College, London, Convened by the Jewish History Society of England*, prepared by Dr. Aubrey Newman, (London, 1975).

[36] Reports of meetings of the Standing Committee of the Conference of Anglo-Jewish Ministers in *JC*, 27 January 1911, pp. 18-19, 5 January 1912, pp. 21-23, and 12 June 1914, pp. 20-24. On the election of the new Chief Rabbi, see, e.g., 11 February 1913, S. Myers, hon. sec. Manchester Central Synagogue, to P. Ornstein, secretary of the United Synagogue, London, United Synagogue Archives, Conference on the Chief Rabbinate, file 137b; and unanimous resolutions of the Manchester Shechitah Board, *JC*, 24 January 1913, p. 24.

chinery to the quickening pace of provincial experience. One test case occurred in 1908, when agitation over the harsh administration of the Aliens Act was at its height at the Board, and when a parlimentary by-election was called for the North-West (Cheetham) district of Manchester where the proportion of Jewish voters was comparatively high. In an unsuccessful attempt to influence the result, what was reported to be "an influential deputation" of Manchester Jews ostentatiously canvassed on behalf of Winston Churchill, the Liberal candidate, whose attitude toward Jewish aliens they considered to be more sympathetic than that of his Conservative rival, William Joynson-Hicks. During the course of the hue and cry that ensued at the Board (and elsewhere), Manchester deputies angrily repudiated charges that they had acted unconstitutionally as well as irresponsibly. Instead, they put up a spirited defense, not only of their wisdom in calling into being a "Jewish vote," but of their right to take political initiatives usually reserved to the Law and Parliamentary Committee of the Deputies. "The Board is too affected with Londonism," they claimed to be the feeling of their constituents; it would not truly represent provincial interests until its character and composition had been altered.[37] This was precisely what they then set out to accomplish. Led by Louis Kletz (deputy for the Higher Broughton Congregation, which had been founded in 1905 by a group of bourgeoisie, intent on retaining their Orthodox practices and "suburban distinctiveness"[38]), Manchester deputies in 1912 launched a campaign for the "adequate" representation of provincial members on the Board's most influential committees; in 1913, and once again led by Kletz, six of their number formed

[37] Minutes of Board of Deputies meetings of 17 June 1908, 19 July 1908 and 30 December 1908 in DEPS, Minute Books, A15:213-16; see also correspondence between J. I. Loewy (of the Manchester delegation) and David Alexander (president of the Board) in JC, 3 July 1908, p. 9. For the general background Randolph S. Churchill, *Sir Winston Leonard Spencer Churchill, 1874-1965*, 6 vols. (London, 1966-1977), Vol. 2, *Young Statesman, 1901-1914*, pp. 253-61.

[38] On which see Samuel Davies, *The Higher Broughton Hebrew Congregation: The First Fifty Years, 1907-1957* (Manchester, 1957). Louis Kletz wrote an impressive series of articles on communal affairs, entitled "Representation, Charity and Education," which commenced in the JC, 17 April 1912, pp. 19-20.

an independent committee to act as "an agency and intelligence Department of the Board." This group then framed a list of specific proposals, of which the most radical were: a residence qualification for provincial representation, longer regular meetings of the Board, and a more "balanced" membership in its committees. After a series of informal meetings with leading members of the London executive, the Manchester group was persuaded to trim many of its demands. But on others it got its way. In June 1913, the Board set up a special committee to review the bylaws; in October the committee recommended that the executive agree to hold every Board meeting on a Sunday, provide deputies with regular reports of the Conjoint Foreign Committee's activities, and drastically curtail the amount of time usually devoted to matters of a purely formal or ceremonial nature.[39] Whether or not these reforms could meet the needs of the case remained a matter for debate. One thing, however, seemed clear:

> Anglo-Jewry today is not being looked at, or judged, or estimated, or its history being made, nor its future destiny being appointed out of Metropolitan Jewry. It is arising from Anglo-Jewry as a whole, of which provincial Jewry is a large component proportion.[40]

ZIONIST COMMUNAL STRATEGY

It is tempting to posit an organic connection between each of these instances of dissent and the program of institutional infiltration pursued by several leading members of the EZF. Two tangential circumstances, both already noted, might appear to support that contention. One is the fact that anti-Zionists overwhelmingly dominated the executives of those institutions (syn-

[39] Correspondence between Louis Kletz (on behalf of the Manchester group) and David Alexander in *JC*, 9 May 1913, p. 21; and minutes of deputies' meeting of 26 October 1913 in DEPS, Minute Books, A16:155.

[40] "Mentor" in *JC*, 12 September 1913, pp. 11-12; on demands for further changes see the letter from D. G. Baker (deputy for Liverpool) in *JC*, 31 October 1913, p. 16; report of the meeting of the executives of Manchester synagogues in *JC*, 14 November 1913, p. 37, and *Di Tsayt*, 30 January 1914.

agogal and nonsynagogal) that were under sporadic but progressive attack during the period. Another is that some leading figures
in British Zionism, acting in their individual capacities, took part
in the more acerbic of the debates which punctuated institutional
proceedings. In effect, however, the movement of events was
more subtle than might be suggested by a one-dimensional analysis
of cause and effect. Although dissent and protest were becoming
an increasingly conspicuous motif of native Anglo-Jewish institutional life before World War I, the leaders of the EZF did not
play a commanding role in that development. At most, as members of a particularly ambitious lobby, they could help to articulate
many of the complaints against the reigning Anglo-Jewish Establishment. But they did not thereby manage, as some of them
had hoped, to transform their own movement into the vehicle
whereby the changes thought necessary in communal government
would be brought about. Their own organizational weaknesses,
in addition to the conflicting ambitions of some of their intended
allies, forced them to set their sights somewhat lower.

Advocates of communal reform did not look to the Zionists
for either inspiration or approval. Anglo-Jewry's native dissidents
cannot all be dragooned into categories drawn along an axis of
their attachment to the principles of Jewish nationalism enunciated by the EZF. The opposition of the community's established
leadership to political Zionism does not appear to have dictated
either the tactics or the arguments of most of the men who called
for changes in the style and structure of Anglo-Jewish government. No evidence has been found to indicate that Zionism—
or, more precisely, the anti-Zionism of Claude Montefiore and
David Alexander—constituted a plank in the reform program
gradually formulated at either the AJA or the Board of Deputies.
Some of the Manchester group of dissidents on both bodies did
have contact with individual Zionists at an early stage of their
campaign.[41] But the association was generally unobtrusive and,
in terms of institutional proceedings, the results were inconse-

[41] See. e.g., 26 March 1905, Belisha to Gaster, CZA, Gaster Papers, A203/140.
Weizmann had some disparaging things to say about Belisha in *Trial and Error*
(London, 1949), p. 104. Both Belisha (an uncle of Hore-Belisha and Nathan
Laski) and Duhlberg were active Itoists.

quential. Even at the Sephardi Congregation, where Gaster's outspoken involvement in the affairs of the EZF undoubtedly rankled, Zionism does not seem to have lain at the root of the tensions that developed within the community. Once they had got over the showdown of 1899 (involving Gaster's salary), the Hakham and his congregants thereafter reached a *modus vivendi*. Their relationship improved, or at least was quiescent, until the outbreak of World War I, with both sides showing a willingness to let bygones be bygones and to benefit from the aura of conviviality engendered by the celebration of Gaster's Silver Jubilee as Hakham in 1912. It is indicative of the prevailing atmosphere at Bevis Marks that Zionism was not an issue in the earlier election of Sir Francis Montefiore to the presidency of the *Mahamad*. As Gaster admitted, the subject was considered to be so peripheral (and Sir Francis himself so ineffectual a proponent of the idea) that most members of Bevis Marks could afford to adopt an attitude of indifference to that aspect of the case.[42]

So, too, at the Council of the United Synagogue and the Board of the Federation of Synagogues. No complaints were voiced at either forum when accredited officials of both bodies publicly supported the "university petition" against Zionism addressed to the *Jewish Chronicle* in March 1909. In 1912-1913, when the machinery for the election of a new Ashkenazi chief rabbi was set in train, the subject was similarly ignored. The main criteria for the selection of the successful candidate were said to be Hertz's scholarship and his potential for bridging the gulf between immigrant and native Jewry. That the new Chief Rabbi was also a Zionist (a fact that he in any case tended to play down during his early years in office)[43] does not seem to have influenced the election one way or the other. After his appointment, Zionism

[42] Thus the *Mahamad* regularly granted Gaster increases in salary and made him a rent-free grant of a house large enough to accommodate his growing family; for his part the Hakham refrained from commenting on the Congregation's decision to cease its financial contributions "to any portion of H. M. the Sultan of Turkey's dominions." See, Sephardi Congregation Archives, Elders' Annual Report, 12 January 1907, in Minute Book, p. 304.

[43] Even when interviewed by the *Idisher Ekspres* (14 August 1912, p. 1) he was reticent on the subject. See, too, pp. 190-91 below.

continued to remain virtually taboo at the United Synagogue
Council, and "out of order" in various constituent synagogues.
In 1914, not even as influential a local figure as S. B. Rubinstein,
who had been treasurer of the EZF's executive, could place on
the agenda of the Stoke Newington Synagogue's annual meeting
a motion that called upon the congregation to express support
"for the National Idea." As was the case elsewhere, the rank and
file of Rubinstein's audience, even those who dabbled in Zionism,
regarded his outburst as irrelevant to the more pressing need for
remedial action at the basic, day-to-day level of institutional
management.[44]

This perspective necessarily affected the impact of occasional
attempts to introduce Zionist issues into the major communal
councils. At best, these could be dismissed as "snipings"; more
often, they proved counterproductive. Most members of the AJA
and the Board of Deputies, despite other differences with their
executives, continued to maintain that the Jewish problem in
Russia and Romania would have to be solved locally, by measures
of economic reform and political emancipation. They clearly resented the efforts of a few noisy Zionists to hustle them into a
"nationalist" solution. In fact, the tolerance with which such
interjections had originally been treated was soon replaced by a
more abrasive response. Increasingly, it became true to say that
"most criticisms of the Zionist movement are personal. People
object to the blatant, and arrogant attitude of its leaders."[45] Sporadic efforts to intrude Zionist matter into debates on other subjects aroused particular indignation. In 1908, for instance, Greenberg and Bentwich were accused of trying to make undeserved
Zionist capital at the Board of Deputies out of the wrangle provoked by the supposed appearance of a Jewish vote during the
North-West Manchester by-election. Throughout 1911, Gaster
and Samuel Daiches were upbraided for gratuitously introducing
Zionist polemics into communal debates on the Chief Rabbi's
evidence to Royal Commission on Divorce and the deputies' own

[44] Minutes of AGM of 2 May 1914, in United Synagogue Archives, Stoke
Newington Synagogue, Minute Book.

[45] 27 September 1906, C. Salaman to Zangwill, CZA, Zangwill Papers, A120/28.

representations on the Slaughter of Animals Bill. In 1913, the EZF as a whole was called to order for attempting to "stampede" the Board into persuading Jewish Members of Parliament to support a public demonstration against the arrest of Beilis. None of the issues involved, claimed non-Zionists as well as anti-Zionists, could properly be assessed from the narrow perspectives of an obvious minority within the community. Each raised substantive issues of Anglo-Jewish policy, and the manner in which they were to be handled had to be judged by the widest standards of propriety and responsibility. Measured against such criteria, the advice tendered by a rowdy bunch of irresponsible fanatics, most of whom had little experience in communal management, was really irrelevant. In fact, they and their movement had best be ignored.[46]

Criticism of that sort did not shame the Zionists into withdrawing from the communal fray. Greenberg, Gaster, Bentwich, and Cowen, all veterans of several years of communal campaigning, refused to be easily silenced. If anything, and with a consistency that smacked of sheer contrariness, they intensified their public attacks on the communal Establishment. What is more, they did not do so alone. This seasoned (if usually disharmonious) quartet of Anglo-Jewish mavericks reared a younger, but equally vociferous chorus. During the second decade of the twentieth century an increasing share of the communal limelight was captured by the brothers Samuel and Salis Daiches (both rabbis, both Zionists, and the former also deputy at the Board for his congregation in Sunderland), Norman Bentwich (who had already won several legal laurels), Israel Cohen (a young writer who was transferred to the central Zionist offices in Germany and was beginning to develop extensive contacts with a range of minor officials in Anglo-Jewish public life), Paul Goodman (who was to hold executive office in the Sephardi Congregation, the B'nai B'rith,

---

[46] For samples of these criticisms see (for 1908) DEPS, Letter Book, B3/32; (for 1911) minutes of 22 October 1911, DEPS, Minute Books A16:75-76; JC, 27 October 1911, pp. 26-27 and 28 March 1911, R. Cohen to H. Sacher, CZA, I. Cohen Papers, A213/16(i); and (for 1913) JC, 17 October 1913, p. 13 and 12 December 1913, p. 9; and New York, YIVO Institute, Mowshowitch Collection of L. Wolf Papers, folder 85.

(147)

and the EZF), and Albert Hyamson (the budding historian and English civil servant). These men did not always operate in concert. Tarred with the same brush of disaffection as their Zionist seniors, they often quarrelled. Nevertheless, they shared certain characteristics, and these may have accounted for the fact that they tended to react to the communal situation in which they found themselves in a broadly similar style. Each member of this group, for instance, was a native Englishmen; all had received a good formal education, although some better than others (a point that tended to rankle where Israel Cohen was concerned). Collectively, they were also in a hurry to attain positions of communal influence and, so some of them felt it necessary to insist, eager to see the consummation of their Zionist aspirations. For both reasons, they enthusiastically pitched themselves into the communal campaign.

□

The story is not, however, one of unadulterated continuity. Older Zionist hands, possibly influenced by their younger collaborators, did initiate some changes in the nature of their movement's local strategy. Without entirely overhauling the policy initiated before 1903, they nevertheless altered its scope, direction, and form. The prevalence of non-Zionist issues of communal debate, together with the internal crises that had discredited the EZF as a respectable communal organization, virtually left them with no choice. Consequently, instead of attempting to transform the Zionist organization into the principal focus of communal dissent, they began to take more modest (and in the circumstances more realistic) advantage of the existing climate of institutional disaffection. Theoretically, what was involved was nothing more than a change in the chronological order of anticipated events. The propagation of Zionism would not precipitate a change in the communal structure; rather a change in the communal structure was an essential prerequisite to the successful propagation of Zionism.[47] From a programmatic perspective, however, the shift

[47] For early assessments of this nature, 15 August 1906, W. Nathan to Smaller Actions Committee, CZA, Files of the Central Zionist Office (Cologne), Z2/411.

of emphasis was more substantial. The fortunes of the EZF, was the assumption, would not be furthered were its leaders to concentrate exclusively on topics of specifically Zionist content. Instead, as was formally decided at a specially convened conference of Zionist activists in 1912, "Zionists in England should take part in all matters Jewish in this country *and especially in Jewish communal politics.*"[48] This might occasionally require them to subordinate their nationalist ambitions to concerns of a less sublime kind, and hence to subsume their particularist aspirations within the wider movement for local communal reforms. But as a prescription for communal prominence, the departure possessed distinct and compensatory advantages. It attempted to mask the EZF's quantitative and qualitative weaknesses by encouraging its members to forge alliances of convenience with native interests and individuals who had hitherto proven immune to a more explicitly ideological appeal. As such, the campaign was imaginative and—in its audacity—pregnant with possibilities for the future shape of communal politics.

The strategy thus outlined was not accepted unanimously; neither was it implemented consistently. Only after a "lengthy and heated discussion" did the conference of 1912 agree ("by a small majority") to pass the resolution quoted above. Even then, the fragmented state of the EZF prevented its comprehensive translation into policy. Thus, Zionists in Britain could never pursue their program with the intensity, cohesion, and radicalism which seemed to have become the hallmark of their German colleagues.[49] Nevertheless, the change was there and it merits at-

[48] As reported in JC, 29 November 1912, p. 33. Similar sentiments in Dr. S. Daiches, presidential address to the London Zionist League (JC, 19 November 1909, p. 19) and J. Cowen, presidential address to the EZF annual conference (JC, 16 February 1912, p. 34).

[49] See, for example, the charges made by prominent German anti-Zionists in their country's national press in February 1914: "Zionists have entered non-Zionist organisations not to co-operate peacefully, but to gain control over them. Consequently, strife and disharmony have been generated. The methods used by these elements have never been practised in German Jewry before. By presenting facts in a manner suitable to their purposes and through wilful misrepresentations of the opinions of those who oppose them, they seek to strengthen their position."

tention. A shift of perspective would appear to explain the diversity of the communal activities undertaken by several of the more prominent Zionist veterans in Anglo-Jewry during the four or five years that preceded the outbreak of war. Greenberg increasingly devoted himself to his expanding newspaper empire (he resigned from the Board of Deputies in 1908 and acquired the *Jewish World* in 1913); Gaster and Bentwich invested much of their time in the B'nai B'rith; Louis Kletz, who resigned from the EZF in 1909, immersed himself in Mancunian Jewish affairs; and Weizmann, by now thoroughly disgusted with both Zionists and anti-Zionists in Anglo-Jewry, concentrated almost exclusively in 1913 on winning influential converts to the idea of establishing a Jewish University in Jerusalem. Of all these pursuits, only the last can properly be described as Zionist work. Greenberg, for instance, continued to resist all suggestions that he place his newspapers at the service of the Zionist Organisation; Kletz did not put forward any specifically Zionist claims in his approaches to the executive of the Board of Deputies; and the B'nai B'rith did not include even a hint of the Basle Program in its list of objectives.[50] Significantly, those Zionists who were most active in the London Lodge (Bentwich was the first president; Gaster, Sir Francis Montefiore, and Albert Hyamson were members of its first council) did not attempt to change this situation. Indeed, it was of the essence of their attitude that the Lodge not give the impression of acting at the behest of the Zionists. Only by posing as the spokesman for a broader cross section of native communal opinion could they hope to attract the sympathies of

Quoted in Jehuda Reinharz, *Fatherland or Promised Land: The Dilemma of the German Jew, 1893-1914* (Ann Arbor, 1975), p. 219.

[50] Formally, the Order was devoted to: "(a) promoting Jewish philanthropic work; (b) assisting the victims of persecution; (c) furthering the cause of Jewish learning; (d) encouraging the cultivation of Science and Arts among Jews; (e) providing opportunities for the discussion of matters affecting general Jewish interests." *Constitution of the First Lodge of England 1663* (London, 1911), p. 2. Gaster put it somewhat differently. The objects of the B'nai B'rith, he claimed, were to show that "character and determination go further than mere money." 15 September 1911, to H. Bentwich, Mocatta Library, Gaster Papers, Letter Book, 1909-1911, p. 711.

other prominent dissidents in Anglo-Jewry; only by addressing themselves to communal interests that were not specifically Zionist could they possibly exert some leverage over the direction of policy. That was why they placed such store by the affiliation to the B'nai B'rith of such Anglo-Jewish personalities (not otherwise associated with the Zionists or the EZF) as Sir Adoph Tuck, Simon Rowson, and the Revs. A. A. Green (of Hampstead Synagogue) and Joseph Hochman (of the New West End).[51]

Notwithstanding these successes there was, from the outset, a danger that this communal strategy might backfire. Diversification, as practiced by the EZF's native leaders, would only pay explicitly Zionist dividends if it could ensure its practitioners of greater communal prestige and influence. But quite the opposite might occur. In part, this was because those Zionists who transferred (or returned) their communal energies to the non-Zionist arena seemed to take with them some of the worst excesses of their behavior at the EZF. Relationships within the B'nai B'rith provided a case in point. Gaster was soon being accused—not without good cause—of using his new platform in order to settle old scores, and thereby bringing the Order as a whole into disrepute.[52] No less insidious, certainly in the long run, were the effects that the new departure might have on the corporate status of Zionist fortunes within Anglo-Jewry. Every communal alliance, as Joseph Cowen had long appreciated, carried its price; the Zionists, as organized in the EZF, were in too weak a position to drive a particularly hard bargain.[53] Collaboration with individuals who had no commitment to the ideology of Jewish nationalism, but who shared the Zionist itch to criticize (or even embarrass) the incumbent communal leadership, could only serve limited tactical ends. At the institutional level, it might impart a veneer

---

[51] E.g., 30 October 1911, Gaster to Bentwich, Mocatta Library, Gaster Papers, Letter Book, 1909-1911, p. 992a.

[52] See the letter signed "Ben Berith" in *JC*, 25 July 1913, p. 29 and the "private and confidential" circular subsequently published in *JC*, 8 August 1914, p. 10. Also, 11 August 1913, Gaster to Moser, CZA, Gaster Papers, A203/202.

[53] 1 July 1898, Cowen to Gaster, CZA, Gaster Papers, A203/106; quoted above pp. 72-73.

of aggression to the EZF's otherwise undistinguished record; on the personal plane (often the more important) it might also provide the movement's leaders with an outlet for their otherwise frustrated communal energies. But the search for such opportunities did not ensure that the Zionists would attain greater influence over Anglo-Jewish affairs. As subsequent events were to demonstrate, the flow of communal pressures could be multilateral; the EZF, even while benefiting from the process of interaction with other bodies, could become a subordinate partner in the wider political formation.

PART THREE

Anti-Zionism in Theory
and Practice

5

Versions of the Past,
Visions of the Future

COMPARISONS BETWEEN
Zionists and anti-Zionists in Anglo-Jewry can never be entirely
exact, or entirely fair. Principally, this is because the two parties
were so unevenly matched in style, temperament, and intention.
The Zionists (and especially the leaders of the EZF) were by and
large an overtly ambitious group of men. However glaring their
faults, they must be credited with having seized the communal
initiative; they insisted that Anglo-Jewry take note of the stirrings
of Jewish nationalism and they pestered their coreligionists into
some consideration of their proposed solution to the Jewish problem. Moreover, and especially once they had got the bit of communal ambition between their teeth, the Zionists give the impression of having pursued their personal and institutional ends with
grit, gall, and not a little courage. The fact that they ultimately
emerged victorious (notably by capturing the highest offices of
the Board of Deputies during the Second World War) tends to
color perceptions of earlier events, but even had they gone down
to defeat it seems probable that their style of communal activism
would have left its mark on any chronicle of the period. They
possess the enormous advantage of having been crusty and lo-
quacious characters, whose genius for self-advertisement is no less
conspicuous than their devotion to political Zionism.

By contrast, the anti-Zionists within the community give the
impression of being a more limpid and latitudinarian circle. There
was, indeed, hardly any reason for them to be otherwise. Anglo-
Jewry was not split down the middle on the merits of Herzl's

scheme. The prevailing attitude of the vast majority of the community was one of bland unconcern. As Gaster appreciated as well as anyone else: "Zionism is not fashionable enough and many circles believe that it is a sign of being select by showing indifference, I do not like to say animosity."[1] Under these circumstances, it is not surprising that Sir Samuel Montagu did not feel it necessary to repeat his one early effort to unite the more prominent of Herzl's opponents. Neither, before World War I, was there any response to the call to found a less exclusive "Anti-Zionist Congress."[2] On the European continent and in the United States (as is well known) specifically anti-Zionist lobbies were recognizable in several communities as early as the end of the nineteenth century. But in Britain, organized Jewish opposition to Zionism was a later development, which did not take formal shape until the publication of the Conjoint Foreign Committee's manifesto in May 1917 and the foundation of the League of British Jews the following November.

Comprehensive statements of ideological opposition to the notion of Jewish nationalism had, nevertheless, preceded those developments. Anti-Zionists in Britain were not altogether dormant before 1917. Their much maligned actions of that year cannot be regarded as the sudden and nervous reactions of a few hitherto silent individuals, driven by Weizmann's diplomatic progress to lengths of thought and behavior which had no intellectual foundation or precedent. Critics of Herzl's theses within Anglo-Jewry had in fact stated their philosophical objections to his scheme as promptly as the *protestrabbiner* in Germany, the Central Conference of American Rabbis, and many of the Orthodox sages of eastern Europe. From the first, several scholars within the community had understood that political Zionism's empirical objectives were allied to a spiritual purpose, of which the messianic impulse formed an integral part. Their objections to Herzl's program had never,

[1] 27 November 1908, Gaster to N. S. Burnstein, CZA, Gaster Papers, A203/183.

[2] In 1898 Montagu arranged for a meeting of communal dignitaries "to consider the question of political Zionism"; letter to S. A. Hirsch, private, London, Mocatta Library, University College, Hirsch Papers, AJ/28. Also A. L. Carliph, in JC, 13 September 1901, p. 9.

therefore, been entirely restricted to points of detail. Reform and Orthodox thinkers, in particular, had recognized that the idea of political Zionism challenged many of their most cherished beliefs. Whether or not it constituted a consummation of Jewish history and teachings, or a rebellion against the fundamentals of the faith, was not a question which they wished to avoid. Rather, in their different ways, spokesmen for both schools of thought sought to analyze the relationship between the vision presented by the new Jewish nationalism and their separate versions of the Jewish past. Arguably, some of the debate that ensued can be classified as political rhetoric, designed to polarize and to rationalize a spectrum of communal conflicts which did not owe their origin to either Herzl or his thesis. But note must also be taken of the range and force of various anti-Zionist ideologies. To an extent, indeed, such a perspective is essential to an understanding of the movement of events during the critical years 1914-1920.

From the ideological perspective, mainstream anti-Zionists in Anglo-Jewry, as elsewhere, possessed an important advantage. Of the two cases, the nationalist and the anti-nationalist, the latter appeared to be the more consistent with traditional Jewish practice and the more soothing to contemporary Jewish consciences. There existed no respectable precedent in modern Jewish history for the Zionist doctrine that the Jewish people should foster its national self-awareness, and no universally accepted authority for the Zionist claim that the Jews had to work in concert toward the establishment of their own state. Any attempt to implement such ideas smacked dangerously of a reversion to the traumatic wave of pseudo-messianism unleashed by Shabbetai Zevi in the seventeenth century, and was bound to be attacked accordingly. The anti-Zionists were the sitting tenants where Jewish political theory was concerned. They would not be displaced by strident disquisitions on the supposedly organic irradicability of anti-Semitism. References to the marginally less debatable social and cultural abnormality of Jewish life in the Diaspora were likely to prove equally ineffective. Such arguments overlooked far too many of the successes of post-exilic Jewish history. The very survival of the Jews and their religion, in however cramped and adulterated a form, provided one testimony to the virtues of the conventional (nonnationalist) approach to public affairs. A second was to be found in the substantial, and often remarkable political achievements of numerous communal intercessors (*shtadlanim*), none of whom had ever put forward recognizably national claims on their coreligionists' behalf. Jewry had yet to be convinced that Herzl's rush to statehood constituted a more viable program. If anything, it might place in jeopardy the progress already made. There was, indeed, something inherently irresponsible in his call to abandon the proven paths of steady incremental gains. As much was appreciated by some English Zionists themselves. Not even the leaders of the cause, in its embryonic stages, could predict with any certainty the movements of the hare that they had started. Joseph Cowen, for one, was "appalled for the moment at the audacity of the handful of us. . . . What a Frankenstein we have created. . . . Can we guide it? or will it swamp us?"[3]

It was possible to argue, of course, that the impulsiveness of the Zionists was an inevitable consequence of the Jewish predicament. Only the boldest of solutions, Gaster was fond of saying, had any chance of success. Nevertheless, there remained an uncomfortable whiff of rashness about Herzl's entire scheme. Their own consciousness of this factor may possibly account for the hesitant, even defensive, tone of many of the Zionists' arguments. Certainly, and notwithstanding their need to convince the Jewish public of the justice of their case, prominent Zionists seemed reticent to advance comprehensive statements of ideological intent. In the main, the clearest and most intellectually aggressive home-grown expositions of doctrine emanated from the anti-Zionists, who also provided the more comprehensive discussions of the principal issues to which the Jewish national idea gave rise. By contrast, the Zionists in Britain were uninformative and, as polemicists, unimaginative. Invariably averse to what Herzl once disparaged as abstract "theologising discussions," they adopted an attitude of empiricism in matters of theory. Only the initial clash with the Chovevei Zion Association does not fit this pat-

[3] 5 February 1903, Cowen to Zangwill, CZA, Zangwill Papers, A120/57(c).

tern. Otherwise, to read the records of the EZF is to gain an impression of infrequently relieved doctrinal poverty. Internal divisions over the merits of the East Africa offer, or the respective advantages of a "political" and "practical" course—even when not overshadowed by personal rivalries—essentially dwelt on means rather than ends. Neither debate gave rise to the intense sort of intellectual huffing and puffing which was occasioned elsewhere in Europe; neither, therefore, contributed toward Zionism's campaign for the collective mind of the community.

From an ideological perspective, then, Anglo-Jewish Zionists were a barren assemblage, who paid no more than intellectual lip service to the ideal in which they professed to believe. Many leaders of the EZF, for instance, seemed to be in some doubt as to the ultimate aims of their own movement, and very few devoted serious thought to the possible implications and consequences of the Zionist ideal. Admittedly, they did all unhesitatingly proclaim their allegiance to the basic tenets of "Jewish nationalism," but this simple formula hardly did justice to the intricacies of Herzl's thesis. Significantly, the EZF did not produce a vernacular compendium of Zionist thought and rationale until 1916; its earlier literary output had been principally confined to edited translations of those pamphlets which had gained some popularity in other countries or to cheap Yiddish playlets of questionable heuristic and artistic value.[4] In fact, throughout the period under review, the leaders of the EZF made virtually no independent contribution to Zionist theory, and hardly participated in the seminal debates on cultural, political, and social policy conducted in prewar Zionist congresses. They made no concerted attempt to construct a cohesive theory of Jewish nationalism consistent with local conditions, and produced no intellectual activist group which might compare with the "democratic fraction" in Russia or Kurt Blumenfeld's circle in Germany. Invariably, even sympathetic enquiries regarding the relationship between Zionism and Judaism were answered by reference to the doctrines supposedly enshrined

[4] One example is Z. Frimkas's *Nach Tsion Brudder* (London, 1904); New York, YIVO Institute, no. 7/40143; the flyleaf contains a list of other works of the same genre.

in the Basle Program (hardly an informative source); questions as to the future shape and form of a possible Jewish government in the Holy Land were fobbed off with equally unhelpful allusions to "the first principles of Zionism."[5]

Somewhat curiously, leading Zionists in Britain contrived to derive some advantage from their prevailing pragmatic attitude. Without the encumbrance of an explicit canon of their own thought, they attempted to circumvent, or at least gloss over, some of the more trenchant objections that their opponents put forward to the underlying philosophy of the Zionist movement. In effect, while desisting from an abstract analysis of their own position, they attempted to dismiss the intellectual credentials of the anti-Zionists. By and large, their preferred strategy was to concentrate on the social context of their detractors' views, and not their ideological content. By focusing attention on the sociological composition of the anti-Zionist alignment in England, they could avoid an analysis of its ideological implications. A priori, it was possible to argue, the contentions of the anti-Zionists could not possibly possess any intellectual substance or theoretical justification. Indeed, there simply were no anti-Zionist theories worthy of consideration. If, as Gaster admitted, "the great names of so-called English Jews (forsooth)" were opposed to Zionism, this was

> not because they are against the principle but because they are not at the head of the movement and because they imagine nothing can be done, and for that matter ought to be done, which has not first obtained their sanction. The weapons which are used are therefore not of argument, they cannot offer any real argument, but the usual ones here I am sorry to say, of open or covert intimidation, slander and denunciation.[6]

[5] See e.g., the complaint in 28 April 1899, B. L. Abrahams to H. Bentwich, "I cannot but think that the questions which I have ventured to raise demand a more adequate answer." CZA, H. Bentwich Papers, A100/71. As late as 1921, the *Jewish Guardian* asked: "Would Dr. Brodetsky permit his dullest student to use language so extraordinarily loose as he permits himself in writing about Zionism?" (6 May 1921, p. 10).

[6] 28 October 1898, Gaster to S. Wise, CZA, Gaster Papers, A203/113.

Anti-Zionists were themselves prone to a similar level of analysis. At moments of acute tension, they were goaded into describing all Zionists in England as "foreign Jews, having no quality to speak for the native Jews of the United Kingdom with whom, for the most part, they do not co-operate in the affairs of the community."[7] Zionists posited a more comprehensive theory. From the very outset of Herzl's campaign, their entire perspective had been colored by the assumption that their opponents were quite simply "too comfortable to appreciate thoroughly the benefits a movement to Palestine would have for the majority of the nation."[8] Ultimately, the objections to Zionism expressed no more than the selfish reaction of a plutocratic clique, whose opinions were essentially and necessarily subordinate to their social preferences. Stripped of its doctrinal camouflage, the case of the anti-Zionists could consequently be reduced to a transparently selfish formula: "England is the Paradise of the Jew—Why help to lose it or be driven from it? "[9] Clearly, this was a counsel of and for only the most privileged members of the community. In fact, as Weizmann was repeatedly to inform influential gentiles during the war, anti-Zionism had necessarily to be the preserve of "those Jews who by education and social connection have lost touch with the real spirit activating the Jewish people as a whole. . . . Zionism was never meant for those people who have cut themselves adrift from Judaism, it is meant for the masses who have a will to live a life of their own." Even the most perfunctory examination would show, therefore, that there was nothing ideological about the anti-Zionists and their views. They were simply a bunch of "assimilated cosmopolitan Jews, mostly belonging to the *Haute finance*, who have lost contact with the development of Jewish life and ideas."[10]

[7] 21 April 1917, Wolf to L. Oliphant, confidential, London, DEPS, General Correspondence, C11/12/54.

[8] 13 January 1897, Sylvie d'Avigdor to Herzl, CZA, Herzl Papers, H VIII 33.

[9] "We need not chafe for the freedom of tomorrow while we are enjoying the freedom of today." Lady Alice Sassoon, presidential address to the Butler Street Club for Jewish Girls, JC, 1 March 1907, p. 17.

[10] 2 October 1917, Weizmann to Balfour, private and personal, *Letters and*

At the most basic—and perhaps least interesting—level, Weizmann and his colleagues may have been correct. Differences of background, occupation, and status did appear to influence the alignment of the parties to the Anglo-Jewish debate on Zionism. But, as will be seen, these determinants were not universally, or uniformly, effective. Many anti-Zionists (to be fair, like some of their nationalist opponents), sought to be assessed by the criteria of the intellectual respectability and responsibility of their case. To judge from the evidence of their theoretical statements, they deserve to be so. The erudition and consistency, and sheer quantity, of their arguments reveal that in many cases their positions were deeply considered and honestly felt. It was not only a narrow perception of their presumed social status that led anti-Zionists to incur the opprobrium of many fellow Jews; neither can their allegedly callous attitude toward their less fortunate coreligionists adequately explain the ridicule that they were prepared to suffer from some gentiles.[11] Rather, it may be suggested, they seem to have acted in accordance with their intellectual convictions, as well as their personal interests and their social customs. This is not to deny that their ideology was functional, in the sense that it was formulated in parallel with, and sometimes in the train of, ongoing communal activity. Nevertheless, their rhetoric should not be dismissed prima facie as nothing more than a form of manoeuver, designed to provide their private fears with a veneer of public respectability. That opponents of political Zionism in England have not been given the same credit (and academic attention) occasionally accorded to their Continental and transatlantic counterparts[12] is therefore misleading. Artificial circum-

---

Papers of Chaim Weizmann. Series A. Letters [hereafter *Letters*], 23 vols., general eds. Meyer Weisgal et al., (Oxford, London and Jerusalem, 1969-1980), Vol. 7, *August 1914-November 1917*, ed. Leonard Stein (London, 1975), pp. 521-22; 7 October 1917, to P. Kerr, ibid., pp. 526-28, 15 October 1917, to Sir M. Hankey, ibid., pp. 533-34.

[11] See, for example, Oliphant's minute: "Mr. Wolf's charge against the Zionists of intending to go 'the whole hog' seems a trifle severe from one Jew to another." 29 April 1915, London, Public Record Office, Foreign Office Files, FO 371/2488, no. 51705.

[12] See, e.g., the collection of articles on United States Jewry in *Herzl Year*

stances such as these have helped to sustain the impression that the anti-Zionists merely paid lip service to the canons of their belief. They have also perpetuated the standard Zionist taunt that the opponents of the movement were inspired, to the exclusion of all else, by an unrelenting and inexpiable "desire to destroy the distinctive characteristics which recalled their origin."[13]

NATION OR RELIGIOUS COMMUNITY?

Blanket imputations of this sort were most frequently, and ceremoniously, levelled against the prominent anti-Zionists of the Reform and Liberal persuasion in Anglo-Jewry.[14] Even in their case, however, the charges may be judged misleading. They revealed an unwillingness to appreciate that, in this case, anti-Zionism was a logical consequence of a wider framework of thoughts and ideas.

Claude Montefiore and Israel Abrahams, the twin pillars of this particular school of British anti-Zionism, provide two cases in point. They deserve to be treated in tandem, partly because they considered themselves to have so much in common. They were of the same age (both were born in 1858, the year of Jewish

---

Book 5 (1963), which includes Joseph Sternstein, "Reform Judaism and Zionism, 1895-1904"; Herschel Levin, "The Other Side of the Coin"; Moses Rischin, "The American Jewish Committee and Zionism, 1906-1922." Also Naomi W. Cohen, "The Reaction of Reform Judaism in America to Political Zionism (1897-1922)," *Publications of the American Jewish Historical Society* 40 (June, 1951):361-94; Michael R. Marrus, *The Politics of Assimilation* (Oxford, 1971), pp. 243-81; Stephen M. Poppel, "German Zionism and Jewish Identity," *Jewish Journal of Sociology* 18 (December 1976):115-22, and Jehuda Reinharz, "Consensus and Conflict between Zionists and Liberals in Germany before World War 1" in *Texts and Responses: Studies Presented to Nahum A. Glatzer* (Leiden, 1975).

[13] Naḥum Sokolow, *History of Zionism 1600-1918*, 2 vols. (London, 1919) 1:194; and Chaim Weizmann, *Trial and Error* (London, 1949), pp. 226-27 and 252-62.

[14] On which see: Michael Leigh, "Reform Judaism in Britain (1840-1970)," and Michael J. Goulston, "The Theology of Reform Judaism in Britain," both in *Reform Judaism*, ed. Dov Marmur (London, 1973). For a more personal account of the foundation of the Liberal Synagogue in Britain see Lily H. Montagu, *The First Fifty Years: A Record of Liberal Judaism in England* (London, 1950).

Emancipation in England, in itself a circumstance of symbolic importance by which they both set some store); cofounders and coeditors of the *Jewish Quarterly Review* during its early heyday; two of the prime movers behind the establishment of the Jewish Religious Union (from which the Liberal Synagogue developed); and, together, the most prolific academic writers in Anglo-Jewry. Abrahams is usually referred to as a student of rabbinics (he was Reader in Rabbinic and Talmudic Literature at Cambridge) and a historian of medieval Jewry; Montefiore is conventionally categorized as a theologian. But these labels are unhelpful. They suggest artificial differentiations in their works, which were in fact influenced by a common desire to advocate and enhance Liberal Judaism, and the more popular of which occasionally contained flattering cross-references.[15] Of the two, Montefiore was considered to be the more intellectually talented—the only member of the Anglo-Jewish Establishment, it was said, who deserved to be tutored by both Benjamin Jowett and Solomon Schechter.[16] By comparison, Abrahams's schooling was more pedestrian: Jews' College and a year as a visiting student at Oxford. Nevertheless, if the critics and eulogists are to be believed, Abrahams's works (especially *Jewish Life in the Middle Ages* [1896] and *Studies in the Pharisees and the Gospels* [Vol. 1, 1917, Vol. 2, 1924]) uniformly displayed the careful scholarship and substantial research to which his students aspired and which his peers respected. In this respect, at least, they are said to stand comparison with Montefiore's principal contributions: *Lectures on the Origin and Growth of Religion as Illustrated by the Religion of the Ancient Hebrews* (1892), *The Synoptic Gospels* (1909), and, with H. Loewe, *A Rabbinic Anthology* (1938).

More obvious were the differences in their social backgrounds

[15] Claude G. M. Montefiore, *Liberal Judaism* (London, 1911), pp. 303-304, quoting Abrahams, and Israel Abrahams, *The Union and the Festivals* (London, 1909), p. 5, quoting Montefiore.

[16] It was Montefiore who first brought Schechter to England from Berlin in order to be his private tutor in rabbinics. See Norman Bentwich, *Claude Montefiore and His Tutor in Rabbinics* (London, 1966); subsequently, however, their relationship appears to have soured, and Schechter claimed that he had made his name in England without Montefiore or Adler "and largely against them." 14 Adar 5662 (1902), Schechter to H. Bentwich, CZA, H. Bentwich Papers, A100/60.

and public activities. Abrahams (the grandson of an immigrant) was not born to the same degree of fame and fortune as was Montefiore, who was a grandnephew of Sir Moses and, through his mother (to whom he owed his first interest in Judaism) a member of the equally influential Goldsmid family. As the son of a principal of Jews' College, Abrahams was decidedly on the fringe of the Anglo-Jewish Establishment—a position which his marriage to Simeon Singer's only daughter did much to confirm. Neither was Abrahams as overtly active in Jewish public affairs as was Montefiore. He did agree to appear on Chovevei Zion platforms (after the split with the Herzlites) and, after some hesitation, he and his wife applied for Ito membership, "without a very confident belief in the prospects of success. But we can no longer reconcile ourselves to standing aloof from a movement which does promise to do something and which is free from some of the most objectionable features of political Zionism."[17] More promptly, he later joined the executive committee of the League of British Jews. In the main, however, Abrahams's communal activities were restricted to the cultural arena: the Maccabeans, the Association of Jewish Literary Societies, and the Jewish Historical Society of England—all of which he helped to found. These were institutions that Montefiore, by contrast, patronized infrequently (the only occasion during the entire prewar period on which Montefiore agreed to chair a meeting of the Maccabeans was at a dinner in honor of Abrahams). His public concerns were more explicitly political and philanthropic. As president of the Anglo-Jewish Association, a member of the Council of the Jewish Colonisation Association, and a regular preacher to Reform congregations, Montefiore moved restlessly between the worlds of action and introspection. Perhaps for that reason he was sometimes at home in neither. On at least one occasion he felt tempted to "chuck all Jewish work and retire to Coldeast [his country home near Southampton] and live exclusively as an ordinary Englishman among my English neighbours—my own *people*, as I call them."[18]

[17] 13 November 1905, Abrahams to Zangwill, CZA, Ito files, A36/19.
[18] 15 April 1917, Montefiore to S. Blank, S. Blank Papers, Cincinnati, American-Jewish Archives, Box 625.

Of the two men, Abrahams comes through as a more likable personality. His prose style, as in his letters from Palestine, could be light and fluid; his lectures, as befitted a one-time tutor in homiletics, were witty and popular. Montefiore, on the other hand, invariably wrote in a grave and decorous vein, and delivered sermons that were remembered as being "scholarly, lengthy & highbrow."[19] Moreover, Abrahams exhibited the occasional eccentricity (such as his passion for cricket) which amused his pupils and endeared him to his friends.[20] Montefiore seems to have been intensely, even obsessively, formal. In his case, one searches in vain for the *bon trovato* anecdote, not to mention the disarming quirk or oddity, which might relieve his grave style and manner. He undoubtedly inspired respect among an entire generation of his own class and background, but others proved less amenable to his scholarly posture and self-consciously beatific eminence. Herzl dismissed him as a "stupid ass who affects English correctness"; the young Lewis Namier wrote him off as a "learned old humbug."[21]

Despite their differences, there was never any doubt that Montefiore and Abrahams equally abhorred the notion of political Zionism. Montefiore had, during the summer of 1896, personally informed Herzl that national aspirations had no proper place in Judaism; even earlier, he had publicly disparaged the "fantastic schemes" of the Zionists, and had urged the congregants of Berke-

[19] 5 March 1955, L. G. Montefiore to S. Blank, ibid.; compare Phyllis Abrahams, "The Letters of Israel Abrahams from Egypt and Palestine in 1898," *TJHSE* 24 (1975):1-23.

[20] Albert M. H. Hyamson, *Israel Abrahams: A Memoir* (London, 1940), and Herbert Loewe, *Israel Abrahams: A Biographical Sketch* (London, 1944).

[21] *The Complete Diaries of Theodor Herzl*, ed. Raphael Patai, trans. Harry Zohn, 5 vols. (New York, 1960), 3:1165, and Julia Namier, *Lewis Namier, A Biography* (Oxford, 1971), pp. 96-97; compare B.L.Q. Henriques, *The Indiscretions of a Warden* (London, 1937), p. 21 and L. L. Loewe, *Basil Henriques: A Portrait* (London, 1976), pp. 136-37. Similarly sympathetic accounts of Montefiore in Lucy Cohen, *Some Recollections of Claude Goldsmid Montefiore* (London, 1940); W. R. Mathew, *Claude Montefiore: The Man and His Thought* (London, 1956); and the "Claude Montefiore Centenary Number" of the *Liberal Jewish Monthly* 29 (June 1958).

ley Street Synagogue, London, to "set against the political idea of Jewish nationalism the religious idea of Jewish universalism, which shall solve the Jewish question according to the prophetic aspirations of the 87th Psalm." Before the year was out, Abrahams had likewise asserted that "the religion was never less stable than when Jewish nationalism was strongest."[22] Thereafter, more outspoken condemnations—many of which were faithfully reported in the *Jewish Chronicle*—followed thick and fast. Zionism, proclaimed Abrahams, was a conception "which has no roots in the past and no fruits to offer for the future"; "the Jewish State is more likely to harm Judaism than to destroy anti-Semitism"; the entire idea "will once more create or rather strengthen a modern Hellenising movement similar to the one fostered by the Maccabean nationalists in the past." Simultaneously, Montefiore warned that the Zionist movement constituted "a blow and an injury to the development of Judaism as a religion"; "in the long run, [it] will be prejudicial and deleterious to the best interests and truest welfare of the Jews themselves."[23] Moreover, these leading voices were supported and echoed by an entire chorus of other pulpit, platform, and pamphlet addresses, all of which proclaimed the same message. Rev. Morris Joseph, the respected minister of the West London (Reform) Congregation of British Jews; the members of the Magnus family (Sir Philip, Lady Kate, and Laurie), who held administrative positions in that community; Oswald J. Simon and Lily Montagu, who were both instrumental in founding the Jewish Religious Union; all described Zionism, variously, as a "travesty of Judaism," "a mistake," "a peril," and "a restoration of primitiveness."[24]

[22] Montefiore, "One God, One Worship," in *JC*, 14 February 1896, pp. 19-20; Abrahams in "Books and Bookmen," *JC*, 20 November 1896, p. 17.

[23] Israel Abrahams, *Jewish Life in the Middle Ages* (London, 1896), p. xxiv; letter to the editor, *JC*, 11 June 1897, p. 19; 10 November 1897, Abrahams to Zangwill, CZA, Zangwill Papers, A120/53(a); Montefiore, presidential address to the AJA, *JC*, 8 July 1898, pp. 12-14.

[24] E.g., Morris Joseph, *Judaism as Creed and Life* (London, 1903), pp. 170-71; Sir Philip Magnus, "The History and Obligations of Judaism," *JC*, 1 May 1896, p. 8; letter to the editor, the *Times*, 30 August 1897; Laurie Magnus, *Aspects of the Jewish Question* (London, 1902); Oswald J. Simon, "The Return of the Jews

That few of these critics ever revised their opinions speaks for the strength of their convictions, and not merely the sluggishness of their thought. Whichever the case, the views of this circle of anti-Zionists rarely altered, notwithstanding the impact of the events that occurred between Herzl's first appearance in England and the foundation of the League of British Jews. Montefiore and Abrahams, as late as 1918, believed that the anti-nationalist arguments which they had enunciated a quarter of a century earlier still represented their best thoughts on the subject.[25] So did Laurie Magnus, who simply reprinted an earlier anti-nationalist essay (*Aspects of the Jewish Question*, 1902) under a new title (*Zionism and the Neo-Zionists*, 1917). Lucien Wolf, too, was consistent. Admittedly, he had been somewhat slow off the mark; his personal sympathy for Herzl initially clouding his ideological distaste for Zionism.[26] But, as has already been noted, all that had changed by the time of the East Africa offer. His letters to the *Times* on that subject were preceded by a disparaging article on Zionism in the *Encyclopaedia Britannica* (where he described the movement as "artificial and doomed to extinction"); they were followed by a spate of equally forthright statements in Jewish and gentile journals. To all intents and purposes, Wolf had said his piece by 1904, when he published "The Zionist Peril" in the *Jewish Quarterly Review*.[27] His subsequent articles and speeches, even his memoranda to the Foreign Office, were merely elaborations on the same theme. Those who sought to study the subject further were explicitly referred back to the 1904 article which, even a decade later, Wolf saw "no reason to alter or modify."[28]

---

to Palestine," *The Nineteenth Century* (September 1898), pp. 437-47; and Lily H. Montagu, *Thoughts on Judaism* (London, 1904), p. 118.

[25] E.g., Abrahams, "Palestine and Jewish Nationality," *Hibbert Journal* 16 (April 1918):464; and Montefiore, "Zionism," *The Inquirer*, 24 November 1917, pp. 463-64.

[26] It was to Wolf, then foreign editor of the *Daily Graphic*, that Herzl owed his first invitation to express his ideas in a non-Jewish journal; on the relationship between the two men see: Josef Fraenkel, "Lucien Wolf and Theodor Herzl," *TJHSE* 20 (1964):161-88.

[27] First delivered as a lecture to the Central Jewish Literary Society (*JC*, 27 May 1904, pp. 13-15); and published in *JQR* 17 (October 1904):1-25.

[28] 19 January 1914, Wolf to Dr. P. Nathan, CZA, Wolf Papers, A77/3a.

In the heat of the rumpus caused by the events of World War I, the members of this circle were disparagingly referred to as "assimilationists." Similar epithets were later bandied about by Zionists whenever the activities of the League of British Jews were discussed. If assimilation is taken to mean the absorption, or reabsorption, of the Jewish people as a collectivity into the society of nations, then the charge was perhaps misdirected. After all, it was not the anti-Zionists who exhorted the Jews to abandon their distinctiveness. Rather, it was the Zionists who revived the ancient call that the Jews become a nation like all others. "Religious" Zionists apart, most members of the movement could be accused of neglecting to provide for the specifically *Jewish* character of their future homeland. It was the anti-Zionists who had best reason to claim that "this 'modern nationalism' is the most extraordinary instance of assimilation which the Jews have ever experienced."[29]

So, too, in the case of individual assimilation. Montefiore and Abrahams, for example, undoubtedly strove for a high degree of acculturalization; that the literature, language, and mores of their birthplace were imprinted upon their characters was as much a source of pride to them as it was a cause of envy to some of their opponents.[30] Yet neither they, nor their Reform colleagues, ever denied their Jewish identity or consciously advocated the abandonment of their Jewish distinctiveness. Their labors on behalf of specifically Jewish cultural and philanthropic causes, as much as their social habits and intellectual interests, indicate that the preservation of both Judaism and the Jews was one of their prime concerns. They insistently, proudly, and not altogether incorrectly contended that they were probably more attracted to the traditional religious customs "on historical, ethical and spiritual grounds" than were many Zionist leaders; consequently, they argued, they were "quite as good Jews . . . and have as excellent a title to be so regarded." Abrahams, for instance, demanded that they be understood as "a class . . . who retain a deep Jewish

---

[29] Abrahams, "Palestine and Jewish Nationality," *Hibbert Journal* 16 (April 1918):457.

[30] 22 February 1897, Schechter to H. Bentwich, CZA, H. Bentwich Papers, A100/59.

sentiment, yet are not Zionists"; Montefiore, likewise, refused to concede that "there is no middle term between Assimilation (in the sense of complete religious disappearance) . . . and Zionism 'a Nation.' "[31] The essential distinction, argued Montefiore, was between "good" and "bad" assimilation. Within the latter category came mixed marriages, the transfer of the Sabbath to Sunday, the reduction of Hebrew studies to the curious dissection of a fossil—in fact, all the drastic steps that might have sacrificed Jewish distinctiveness and turned Judaism into "a pale reflection of Christianity." "Good" assimilation had always consisted of the process whereby Jews might absorb, without pain, coercion, or compromise, the undoubtedly beneficial elements and characteristics of the cultures and societies in which they lived, in the hope that the resulting contact would prove uplifting to both parties: "We may have much to give, but something also to receive; much to teach, but something also to learn." That, indeed, had always been the Jewish attitude:

> The Babylonian Talmud (as its name implies) was not developed on Palestinian soil. It grew up in what is now glibly called an "alien environment." Within the Talmud are elements derived from many cultures. After its close we find Judaism again and again flourishing in non-Jewish countries, assimilating, to some extent at least, the good of those countries, and yet growing fuller, richer, and even more influential, just because of its wider horizon."[32]

The appeal to the bar of Jewish history was a recurring motif throughout the debate. In many ways, it reflected the purposes of the protagonists as well as their academic interests. Their object was an evaluation of the past and the enunciation of a philosophy of Jewish history that would quicken the anti-nationalist sensibilities which Herzl and his followers had attempted to numb by tendencious raids into the Jewish past. They aimed to reveal the

[31] 2 December 1899, Abrahams to Zangwill, CZA, Zangwill Papers, A120/63(a); and 18 February 1903, Montefiore to Zangwill, ibid., A120/79.

[32] Claude Montefiore, "Assimilation: Good and Bad," *Papers for the Jewish People*, no. 9 (1909), p. 16.

perennial "essence" of Judaism, that which remained static whatever the vicissitudes of time and of place and whatever the force of occasional waves of anti-Semitism. The gulf that divided the Zionists and their opponents was not, therefore, limited to differing estimates of the relationship between the Jews and the Holy Land. As Montefiore himself admitted, even at the height of the controversy over the Balfour Declaration, no other region of the globe could supplant a Jew's intense regard for "a country in which long ago his ancestors lived, where the prophets spoke, the Psalmist sang, the sages taught."[33] At issue, rather, was the entire character and ethos of the Jewish people, from which the Zionists monopolistically claimed to derive so much inspiration.

Fundamentally, the anti-Zionists posited the incompatibility of nationalism and religion in Jewish thought. The Jews, they claimed, constituted a religious community, not a nation; their distinctiveness derived from their particular beliefs and practices, not from their alleged national or racial characteristics. Herzl's apparent desire to alter this emphasis, and "to drive the religion into a national corner," was considered to be his greatest error. Conversely, Claude Montefiore's celebrated description of the history of Jewish advance was long regarded as the greatest of all his contributions to the anti-Zionist cause. His address, "Nation or Religious Community? " (which was printed in the community's two most prestigious academic journals and extensively quoted in numerous speeches and articles)[34] was deliberately intended to lay down the guidelines for all later discussions. In conjunction with his extremely popular *Bible for Home Reading* (1st edition, 1896; seven further editions by 1920) and his *Outlines of Liberal Judaism* (1911), it attempted to demonstrate the process, uneven but inevitable, whereby "the word Jew came to have a religious, rather than a racial or national, connotation." It was also designed to illustrate that, even during the periods of

---

[33] "Liberal Judaism and Jewish Nationalism," *Papers for the Jewish People*, no. 16 (1917), p. 7. Unlike Abrahams, Montefiore never visited Palestine, although he did plan to do so in 1904. According to one account, "his heart was not in it." L. Cohen, *Recollections*, p. 265.

[34] *TJHSE* 4 (1903):1-15 and *JQR* 12 (1900):177-94.

independent Jewish statehood, "the religion, in its deeper essentials" had always been "too universal to be satisfied with, or happy in its nationalist institutions." Even the Davidic era, claimed Montefiore, had witnessed tendencies that sapped an ordinary, secular nationalism at its roots. "The germs of universalism," apparent in many of the Psalms, then began to overshadow "the glow of patriotism" induced by the original "lawless disposition" of the land of the Canaanites.[35] This trend had been hastened during the "Persian period" of Jewish history (the first exile), and brought to fruition during the "Greek period" that followed Ezra's return. The book of Ruth indicated the extent to which Judaism held fidelity to be wider than race; the teachings of Philo claimed that "kinship is not merely measured by blood, but by agreement in deeds and by the common pursuit of the same ends"; the festival of Ḥanukah (associated with the victory of the Maccabees, and to which the Zionists attempted to give explicitly nationalistic overtones)[36] was primarily a tribute to the victory of the monotheistic idea. "The mere national aspect of the matter is very small and trivial. . . . Chanukah is a *religious* festival."[37]

Exile, in this scheme of things, was not the unmitigated disaster of Zionist polemic. On the contrary, "the religion became in many respects purer and freer when separated from the national soil." The Dispersion purged the Jews of the tribal, secular "chauvinism" that had blighted their biblical history; it also arrested the sorry record of spiritual decline and moral decay that had characterized the Maccabean kingdom. Only the bloody circumstances that had accompanied the fall of Jerusalem to Vespasian's legions had retrospectively surrounded that event with an aura of disaster. "If the Temple could have been quietly destroyed without any embittered struggle with Rome," the Jews might have

[35] *The Bible for Home Reading*, 2 vols. (London, 1896), 1:106.
[36] The EZF frequently proclaimed the eighth (last) day of the festival to be "Zion Day"; e.g., *EZF Bulletin*, no. 6, 6 December 1900, CZA, Files of the Central Zionist Office (Vienna), Z1/403.
[37] *The Bible for Home Reading*, 2:740; in fact Montefiore's connotation was in strict keeping with the traditional Jewish attitude. See e.g., *Babylonian Talmud*, Shabbat, folio 25a.

been able to regard the Diaspora in a more benign light. The logic of the universalistic beliefs taught by the prophets had in any case unfitted Judaism to be a purely national creed; the religion itself was compelling "the nation to be other than a nation. By its power it transformed the nation into the religious community." The Dispersion, painful though it initially was, merely emphasized the concept of God "as the one . . . Deity of the entire world." This was its greatest benefit. If Jews cherished hopes of a Restoration, they had in mind the reaffirmation of their religious purity, not the revival of their state.[38] The new Jewish National Movement, which taught otherwise, was (in Wolf's words) "a traitor to the Jewish past which it misreads and misinterprets." From a religious, as well as an ethnographical point of view, all post-exilic attempts to revive a Jewish nationality were anachronistic.

> There is a Jewish race, there is a Jewish religion, there are Jewish customs which took their rise in a Jewish theocratic state and have consequently been all the more easily invested with an exclusively spiritual meaning. But there is no Jewish nationality. To say that it is necessary to restore the nationality in order to observe these customs is—well, it has no justification.[39]

□

From this crucial view of Jewry and Judaism, three supplementary arguments appeared logically to follow. One was that the struggle for emancipation represented the continuation of a specifically

[38] Which was why, according to Abrahams, Maimonides had not included the latter in his Thirteen Principles of Faith (*JC*, 6 August 1897, p. 6). Inconsistently, however, when describing the destruction of the Northern Kingdom, Montefiore wrote: "The Israelite exiles in Assyria could not maintain their religion outside their land. They became absorbed in the population among whom they dwelt, and we hear of them no more." *The Bible for Home Reading*, 1:367.

[39] Lucien Wolf, "The Jewish National Movement," *Edinburgh Review* 225 (April 1917):15-16; and 28 September 1903, letter to Zangwill, CZA, Zangwill Papers, A120/53.

Jewish religious development as much as it constituted the fulfilment of a secular and humanitarian ideal.[40] In seeking the removal of the various disabilities that emphasized their distinctiveness and in demanding across-the-board equality before the law, the Jews had explicitly stressed that they constituted nothing more than a religious brotherhood. Political Zionism, by positing the existence of a separate Jewish nationality, threatened to undermine this position and thereby to rob equality of its justification. Even at its crudest level, this argument was not nurtured solely by the fear of the charge of dual loyalty. For that reason, the excessive energy that various Zionist spokesmen expended in demonstrating the compatibility of Zionism and British patriotism was somewhat unwarranted.[41] Admittedly, according to one typical editorial in the *Jewish Chronicle*, "English Jews decline to associate themselves with a movement which, in however remote a degree, might seem to call in question—not their loyalty, for that could never be questioned—but the absoluteness of their English citizenship and nationhood."[42] Yet neither the force, nor the influence of that particular approach (common though it was) need be exaggerated. Indeed, with the obvious convergence during the war of Zionist ambitions and British Imperial interests, this aspect of the polemic became self-evidently irrelevant. Montefiore, for instance, ultimately admitted that "if H.M. Government is anxious to publish this formula [the Balfour Declaration] for the sake of *this* country as well as for the Jews, I would, of course, subordinate my Jewish feelings, wishes and interests to

[40] Thus Israel Abrahams: "The whole story of Jewish emancipation in Europe is one of the noblest pages in Jewish, or any other history. The best impulses of the Jewish heart and mind were devoted to the struggle, and those impulses were responded to by the best impulses of the heart and mind of Christian Europe." JC, 8 March 1901, p. 8, and *Jewish Life Under Emancipation* (London, 1918).

[41] And not altogether wise; the stress on British patriotism clearly compromised the position of German and Austrian Jews; see memorandum in CZA, M. Rosenberg Papers, A150/152; Hertz sermon, JC, 2 October 1914, p. 16; Samuel Daiches, *Zionism and Patriotism*, (London, 1909) p. 7; Harry Sacher, *Zionism and the State* (London, 1915).

[42] 17 August 1900, p. 11.

the interests of England and the Empire."[43] By the same logic, the League of British Jews did not hesitate to criticize the Balfour Declaration once it had been issued, and thereby risk the charge of disloyalty of which they were presumably so afraid. Their actions, it might be argued, owed much to their concern to preserve the status of the *principle* of Jewish emancipation in England. For one thing, "Jews could not have it both ways. They could not have their status in Palestine on one theory of Nationality, and then claim equality in the world on an altogether inconsistent theory."[44] For another, their emancipation had become a matter of honor. Ahad Ha'am might spurn the gift; Israel Abrahams (with whom he corresponded on the matter) could not.[45] Therein lay the difference.

Some indication of the Reform attitude toward the emancipated status of Anglo-Jewry is provided by the treatment accorded to the history of the Act for the Removal of Jewish Disabilities. The jubilee of Jewish emancipation in England (celebrated in 1908) provided an obvious topic for Anglo-Jewish academic discussion during the early Zionist period. Nor surprisingly, the subject formed a constant theme in the lectures delivered to the Jewish Historical Society of England, and was referred to during the course of numerous debates at other intellectual forums.[46]

[43] 12 October 1917, Montefiore to Sir M. Hankey, London, Public Record Office, War Cabinet Papers, CAB 21/58; similarly, Edwin Montagu never once threatened to resign from the Cabinet over the issue.

[44] Abrahams, *The Future of Palestine* (London, 1918), p. 5; see also Claude Montefiore, "The Dangers of Zionism," *Papers for the Jewish People*, no. 20 (1917), p. 7: "You claim that a Russian citizen, if he become converted to Judaism, should not forfeit any fraction of his national and civic rights, and are you going to make a Jewish citizen lose any fraction of his national and civil rights in Palestine, if he become converted to Christianity? "

[45] 21 February 1910, Ahad Ha'am to Abrahams: "If we, the *nationalist* Jews of Russia were asked to subscribe to all that is written in [Macaulay's speech on Jewish disabilities] in return for all the rights enjoyed by Western Jews, I and my colleagues would reply 'No!' " Ahad Ha'am, *Igrot*, 6 vols., 2nd ed. (Tel Aviv, 1956-1960), 4:252. See also the longer, and better known, "Slavery in Freedom" (1892), translated in his *Selected Essays* (Philadelphia, 1912).

[46] The topic formed the subject of seven of the lectures for the session 1902-1905 (*TJHSE* 5 [1908]:xi); and for three more in the session 1908-1910 (*TJHSE*

The record of those discussions indicates that the relevance of the emancipation episode for the contemporary Zionist debate was fully appreciated. Consequently, the lessons to be derived were on occasion tendentiously suited to the terms of the nationalist controversy. One favorite argument (put forward by Wolf and Abrahams, in particular) was that their forebears had won social respectability before they had attained full political equality; in fact, they had made use of their individual acceptability in order to obtain that communal right.[47] Their emancipation, in other words, had been the result of their claim to be regarded as essentially honorable persons, who could be expected to preserve the "trust" of which Macaulay (in 1833) had deemed them worthy. Far from displaying an "inept [*sic*] understanding of the British mind and of the British political and social make-up,"[48] the anti-Zionists—at this level—considered themselves to be attuned to the traditional British values of honesty and fair play. "While we enjoy and exercise all the civil rights of Englishmen," Jews could not "flaunt our doubts as to whether we ought after all to condescend to regard ourselves as Englishmen."[49] Having

---

6 [1912]:viii-xi). In addition, it constituted roughly 20 percent of the program of some of the Jewish Study Societies. See Minute Books of the Union of Jewish Literary Societies, Mocatta Library, AJ/12. The subject was also covered in H.S.Q. Henriques's *The Jews and the English Law* (Oxford, 1908), pp. 290ff; and in the preface by I. Abrahams and S. Levy, to *Macaulay's Essays and Speeches on Jewish Disabilities* (London, 1908), which ran to two editions within the space of as many years. This degree of attention might be contrasted with the lack of notice generally accorded to the Jubilee in the immigrant press. Thus, *Hayehoodi* carried no report of the Commemoration Dinner of November 1908. See, however, Raphael Mazin, *History of the Jews in England* (Yiddish), (London, 1915), esp. p. 1.

[47] Henriques, *The Jews and English Law*; see corroboration of this view in Ursula R. Q. Henriques, "The Jewish Emancipation Controversy in 19th Century Britain," *Past and Present* 40 (1968):126-46.

[48] Isaiah Friedman, "Dissensions over Jewish Identity in West European Jewry," in *The Role of Religion in Modern Jewish History*, ed. Jacob Katz (Cambridge, Mass., 1975), p. 137.

[49] B. L. Abrahams, "Sir I. L. Goldsmid and the Admission of the Jews of England to Parliament," *TJHSE* 4 (1904):129; originally delivered as a paper to the Jewish Historical Society on 17 February 1901, entitled, "The Struggle for Jewish Emancipation in England." See JC, 12 April 1901, pp. 20-21. Israel

won emancipation on the grounds that the bonds that united Jews were not those of race but of religion, they could not now unilaterally deny the validity of that theorem.

There was, therefore, more to this case than the traditional, and generally applicable, injunction to "pray for the welfare of the country" in which Jews lived.[50] The inescapable conclusion of the pamphlet debates and parliamentary discussions of the 1840s was that the removal of Jewish disabilities had been dependent upon an explicit code.

> What, then, does this loyalty to England demand of us? It demands service . . . it demands the sharing of its ideals and the readiness to give of one's utmost towards their realisation. . . . This loyalty is owed to England by the Jews. It is the just recompense of even-handed justice. England has given to the Jews liberty, equality, fraternity. One's blood boils if these great gifts are not answered by a single, an undivided and a complete allegiance, if the loyalty paid towards England is other than profound and pure.

Essentially, and most banefully, Zionism threatened to alter the terms of the original contract entered into freely and wholeheartedly. It was therefore as dangerous to Jewish self-respect as it was damaging to Jewish self-interest.[51]

Besides, in gaining emancipation, the Jews of England had not merely benefited themselves. The had also, it was claimed, helped the gentile world to demonstrate the possibility of its own enlightenment. Here lay the second reason for this school's oppo-

---

Abrahams, in a later address to the same body, stated: "With Jews victory is never the end of a campaign . . . we are never secure in the enjoyment of a right if we do not go on earning it." "Report of the Commemorative Dinner of the Jubilee of Political Emancipation," 30 November 1908, *TJHSE* 16 (1912):93. See also: Laurie Magnus, *Zionism and the Neo-Zionists* (London, 1917), p. 6.

[50] Jeremiah 29:7; although that, of course, was repeatedly invoked; e.g., Joseph, *Judaism*, pp. 484, 491.

[51] C.G.M. Montefiore and B.L.Q. Henriques, *The English Jew and His Religion* (London, 1918), pp. 1-2; and I. Abrahams, "Nationalism and Emancipation in England," *Jewish Opinion*, August 1919, pp. 5-6. For a Zionist reply see: Harry Sacher, *Jewish Emancipation: The Contract Myth* (London, 1917).

sition to the nationalism of their opponents. Zionists, by maintaining that anti-Semitism would persist for as long as the Jews continued to live in the lands of their dispersion, were in fact exacerbating the very "Question" to which they claimed to have found a solution. Whether or not anti-Semitic movements and governments would make use of the ammunition thus conveniently placed at their disposal was, of course, an important question. (What, indeed, was to prevent the anti-Semites from exploiting the Zionist thesis and using it as a pretext for helping the Jews—even forcibly—to leave their existing homes?) But this was not the only consideration. In the anti-Zionist mind, it was largely superseded by the feared effect that Herzl's doctrines might have on the ongoing battle between the forces of progress and reaction within the *gentile* world. At this level, argued the anti-Zionists, the relationship between Jews and gentiles had to be regarded as nothing less than the yardstick of the liberal progress of European civilization. The ethical evolution of societies, in other words, could be evaluated by the extent of their tolerance toward the Jews: persecution reflected a retarded, barbarian society; emancipation was the sign of an advanced, humane environment. Conceived in dialectic terms, anti-Semitism constituted the thesis and liberalism the antithesis. The victory of the latter was dependent upon the eradication of the former. Decent, healthy—even stable—orders were inconceivable as long as the blight of the persecution of the Jews persisted. That was the lesson of the Dreyfus Affair.[52]

Up to a point, some Zionists were prepared to agree with this analysis. Gaster, who was himself familiar with the Hegelian terminology thus employed, was one such instance. He, too,

[52] For a clear exposition of these arguments see Lucien Wolf's articles on "Anti-Semitism" and "Zionism" in the *Encyclopaedia Britannica*, 11th ed. (Cambridge, 1910). Wolf himself suggested a limit of four or five columns to his article on Zionism, "because Zionism after all is a purely Jewish movement whereas Anti-Semitism is a large piece of the political history of our times. Still, five columns in the Encyclopaedia Britannica will be handsome acknowledgement of the dignity of the movement." 10 March 1902, Wolf to Zangwill, CZA, Zangwill Papers, A120/58.

(178)

taught that "the struggle for Emancipation was not one between Jew and Gentile; it was between right and wrong, between liberty and persecution, for the position which a Jew occupied in any country was the touchstone of its moral conception and political elevation."[53] The two camps differed, however, in their conception of the role that the Jews ought to play in this struggle. According to the anti-Zionists, Jewish history constituted a glorious chronology of commitment to the liberal elements in the gentile world. In fact, "whenever periods of enlightenment such as the present have come, Judaism has always managed to find refuge in the great world-ideas of its environment."[54] Zionism, however, threatened to reverse this process, and to place its adherents in unethical harness with reactionary movements and ideas. Thus Lucien Wolf:

> The characteristic peril of Zionism is that it is the natural and abiding ally of anti-Semitism and its most powerful justification. It is an attempt to turn back the course of modern Jewish history, which hitherto, on its political side, has had for its main object to secure for the Jewish people an equal place with their fellow citizens of other creeds in the countries in which they dwell, and a common lot with them in the main stream of human progress.[55]

Proclamations of Jewish separatism, therefore, had to be condemned. By retreating (physically and ideologically) to some rarified "refuge" on the periphery of contemporary history, the Jews would desert the forces of decency and thus do considerable harm to Western civilization as a whole. "What we have to do is to buckle on our armour and fight the good fight, not to turn tail and run away."[56]

The optimism with which the anti-Zionists thus prepared to do battle with the forces of anti-Semitism was one of their most

[53] Speech at the Commemorative Dinner of the Jubilee of Jewish Emancipation, 30 November 1908, *TJHSE* 6 (1912):98.

[54] 10 November 1897, Abrahams to Zangwill, CZA, Zangwill Papers, A120/53(a).

[55] "The Zionist Peril," *JQR* 17 (October 1904):12-13.

[56] 27 May 1903, Wolf to Zangwill, CZA, Zangwill Papers, A120/58.

outstanding characteristics (which is not to deny that it was tragically misplaced). Nor surprisingly, therefore, the contrasting pessimism of the Zionists formed a constant, and dominant, theme of this branch of polemic. "We . . . still refuse to become, as Herzl told me that he became, Nationalists through despair," wrote Claude Montefiore.

> It is, I admit, easy for an English Jew who lives in comfort, liberty and toleration . . . to put forward the specious plea that he does not think so basely of human nature. . . . I admit that; I feel that. And yet I must combat this doctrine of despair. . . . I still believe that what has happened in England can happen even in Poland. The night is long, but it may be—I for my part, believe that it is—the divine will that at last the dawn will come, the dawn of liberty and of enlightenment.[57]

In private conversation, Montefiore may have sometimes admitted his doubts concerning the prospect of continued Jewish survival in eastern Europe. On at least one occasion Wolf, too, confessed that "I do not know that there is anything to be said except the usual banalities about the sun of freedom rising in Russia as soon as this awful night of war comes to an end." Even in public, both men constantly urged the need for "patience, self-discipline and courage."[58] Nevertheless, the overwhelming majority of their speeches and writings (and, indeed, actions) indicate that, from their point of view, Zionism continued to be reprehensible because it lacked faith in deliverance. Resistance to the movement by anti-Zionists was the result of a conviction born of irrepressible confidence. Not even the Kishinev pogrom altered their absolute belief that "manliness and faith together

[57] Claude G. M. Montefiore, *Outlines of Liberal Judaism* (London, 1905), pp. 307-308; and "A Diehard's Confession," lecture to the Jewish Religious Union, October 1935, in L. Cohen, *Recollections*, pp. 226-27.

[58] 14 January 1908, C. Salaman to Zangwill, CZA, Zangwill Papers, A120/28, reporting a talk with Montefiore "last night on the way home from a meeting." 1 February 1916, Wolf to Zangwill, New York, YIVO Institute, Mowshowitch Collection of Lucien Wolf Papers, folio 45, no. 4120; and reports of the general meeting of the Anglo-Jewish Association, 3 July 1898, pp. 12-14; and JC, 15 December 1911, pp. 33-34.

will find the way, and laugh the doubters and the cowards to scorn."[59] Neither did their distaste for revolution restrain the joy with which, in 1917, they greeted the news that "in Russia the chains have been removed . . . the 'Jewish problem' in Russia has been solved, as so many of us longed and prayed that it would be solved, *in* Russia itself and by the Russians themselves. Five millions of our co-religionists are emancipated at a stroke." At both extremes of experience their message was the same: "Whatever befall, let us have faith. . . . Anti-Semitism is not forever. Let us have faith in human nature, created in the divine image."[60]

The conviction that the Jews could survive the physical trials of the Diaspora was closely associated (in the anti-Zionist mind) with a belief that they had a moral duty to do so. As the custodians of a unique spiritual heritage, their ultimate mission was to impart the sublime teachings of Judaism to the entire world. Like its predecessors, this—the third—pillar of Reform anti-Zionist thought was founded in a teleological view of Jewish history. The Almighty had originally selected Abraham to be the instrument whereby He would reveal eternal values to all mankind. ("Through thee shall all the families of the earth be blessed" [Genesis 12:3] was, by a statistical count, one of Montefiore's favorite biblical quotations.) The same beneficial Providence had released the Children of Israel from Egyptian bondage in order that they might provide a collective example of the virtues of freedom and the triumph of justice. Passover, therefore, provided an occasion for celebrating the liberty of all humanity and not simply the liberation of one people. Indeed, that the "human and religious aspects" of the Passover might "dominate and overshadow the purely national aspects of that ancient and picturesque festival" had been indicated by the rabbis themselves. By way of allegory they had stressed the Almighty's own discomfiture at the destruction of so many of His creatures at the Red Sea, and in so doing

[59] Montefiore, "Assimilation: Good and Bad," p. 10; 27 May 1903, Wolf to Zangwill, CZA, Zangwill Papers, A120/58.

[60] Claude G. M. Montefiore, "Liberal Judaism and Jewish Nationalism," *Papers for the Jewish People*, no. 16 (1917), pp. 16-17; Laurie Magnus, *Old Lamps for New* (London, 1918), p. 8.

had tempered the primitive urgings of chauvinism with the spiritual concept of universalism.[61] The Sinaitic revelation, too, had been accompanied by the distinct injunction to be "a holy nation and a kingdom of priests," and the period of Israel's greatest physical strength had witnessed the teachings of Israel's spiritual power. As expressed by the prophets, the Jew was—above all else—to be God's servant and messenger, charged with "diffusing and teaching throughout the world the knowledge and the worship of the one and only God."[62] Dispersion, therefore, was essential to the divine plan; it provided the Jews with an opportunity to fulfil their "mission" and to prove, by their fortitude in the face of tribulation, that they were worthy of doing so.

Redemption had to be of a piece with this scheme. It could not be diluted to the mundane notion of a physical return of a small portion of the House of Israel (for, as had been the case in Ezra's time, no more than a small proportion would—or could—return). To have meaning, the messianic age had to be a matter of universal and transcendent significance, auguring a millennial situation in which every human being would be restored to a state of total harmony with his Creator. The Jerusalem for whose

[61] "The work of my hands is drowning in the sea, how can you sing songs of praise? " *Babylonian Talmud*, Megillah, folio 10b and Sanhedrin, folio 39b. Significantly, this was one of the only two instances in which Montefiore did quote from a rabbinic text in his *Bible for Home Reading* (1:61); the identical quotation in Israel Abrahams, "The Hallel," *Festival Studies* (London, 1906), pp. 156-66; for similar views of Passover see: Joseph, *Judaism*, pp. 217, 221; Montagu, *Thoughts on Judaism*, pp. 90-96; Mrs. N. L. Cohen, *Addresses to Children* (London, 1922), pp. 114-15. For the contrary, nationalist meaning attached to the festival by the Zionists see, e.g., J. de Haas, "The Spirit of the Festival," *Jewish World*, 12 April 1895, p. 7; Gaster's introduction to *The Book of Prayer and Order of Service According to the Customs of the Spanish and Portuguese Jews*, ed. M. Gaster, 6 vols. (London, 1901-1907), 6:xiii; Isaiah Raffalovich, "Passover 1917," *Our Inheritance* (London, 1932), pp. 241-44; and F. S. Spiers, *Zionism and the Jewish Religion* (London, 1919), p. 7.

[62] See, e.g., Montefiore's commentary on Isaiah, chaps. 23; 42: 1-9:49:1-13 (omitting verse 12); 50:4-9; 52:13-15; and 53:1-12, in *Bible for Home Reading*, 1:502ff and 2:360ff. Conversely, chap. 11:11-16 was dismissed as a "later interpolation," ibid., 2:336. The argument was later summarized in Claude G. M. Montefiore, *Liberal Judaism: An Essay* (London, 1903), pp. 182-92.

restoration the Jews prayed was not, therefore, a city but an *idea*; its place as the former capital of a kingdom would be absorbed and swallowed up by its new, metaphysical position as the religious metropolis of the world. In preparation for that age, the Jew had to devote himself to his task—wherever he might be. "The whole earth may be his real home, since his true destiny lies in cultivating that ample domain."[63] However virtuous some Zionist stimulants to Jewish culture might be—and the anti-Zionists were initially generous in their praise for such incidental offshoots as the idea of a Jewish university[64]—they could not compensate for the regressive nature of Herzl's central program. If they contributed toward the dwindling, rather than the dissemination, of the religious influence of the Jews, they would ultimately contradict and frustrate their own purpose. "Isolation . . . even though it be isolation in Palestine and accompanied by national independence, would mean failure for Israel's mission."[65] Political Zionism, within this context, was nothing more than a betrayal.

> The sphere of the Jew is the universe, the birthright of the Jew is his religion, his message is the moral law, and his secular instrument is the right—a right imposing obligations—to live with his neighbours on equal terms. To exchange our religious heritage for a dubious political status, which only a tenth part of Israel's host could embrace, seems to me a degradation of the ideal, a mockery of revealed Judaism, and a surrender to temporary passions, inflamed by this terrible war, of the noble, permanent and abiding principles, the truth of which we live to spread.[66]

[63] Abrahams, *JC*, 6 August 1897, p. 10; C.G.M. Montefiore, "What Would You Have Us Do?," *Papers for the Jewish People*, no. 7 (1913); I. Mattuck, "Liberal Judaism and the Religion of the Jew," *Jewish Religious Union: Bulletin* 1 (June 1914):1-2.

[64] Abrahams's support for the project in *JC*, 28 February 1908, p. 16; on his later withdrawal, 19 January 1914, C. Fox to Weizmann, WA, file 163.

[65] Joseph, *Judaism*, pp. 170-71.

[66] L. Magnus, *Old Lamps for New*, p. 16.

Anti-Zionism in Theory and Practice

ORTHODOX RESISTANCE TO POLITICAL ZIONISM

Political Zionism gained very few converts among Reform elements within Anglo-Jewry. Claude Montefiore's poignant vision of a far-flung missionary people appealed far more to this section of the community than did Solomon Schechter's acid disparagement of the entire notion; it was certainly more persuasive than the abrupt Zionist retort that "only a free, independent, creative nation can fulfil a mission."[67] Although individual Reform preachers did occasionally advocate a more sympathetic attitude toward Herzl's "heroic efforts," these exceptions were few, far between, and largely uninfluential.[68] They did little to counter the generally hostile impression fostered by the prevalent doctrine that "modern Reform Judaism . . . teaches to eliminate those ceremonies and beliefs which are less compatible with a universal than a racial religion." Overwhelmingly, Montefiore's disciples concurred in his opinion that certain scriptural passages (such as those dealing with Joshua's wars of conquest) had "no place" in a modern edition of the text. They also accepted his suggestion that the Jewish Religious Union expunge all references in its prayers to the Ingathering of Exiles, and thus bring its liturgy into line with that of advanced Reform congregations on the Continent and in the United States.

Traditional Orthodox Jews could not sanction any such tamperings with sacred practices and beliefs. This was as true of the native community as of the immigrants. Chief Rabbi Hermann Adler, many of whose mannerisms and opinions were criticized

[67] E.g., Samuel Daiches, "The Mission of Israel" (1910), in *Essays and Addresses*, ed. Maurice Simon and Isaac Levy (London, 1955), pp. 133-37; and Salis Daiches, "The People of Israel, Past and Present," *Beit Va'ad la-Hakhamim* 1 (February 1902):34-38. Montefiore later complained bitterly when Schechter referred to his doctrine as a "sickly platitude." Letter of 12 December 1900, New York, Jewish Theological Seminary, Schechter Papers.

[68] For some exceptions see: H. S. Lewis, "The Past and the Present," *Addresses Delivered at the Services of the Jewish Religious Union* (London, 1904), pp. 27-40; Jacob Strauss (Bradford), "Zionism," *Essays* (London, 1911), pp. 245-64; Solomon Levy, *Zionism and Liberal Judaism* (London, 1911); and on Rev. A. Wolf, P. S. Goldberg, *The Manchester Congregation of British Jews, 1857-1957* (Manchester, 1957), p. 64.

in the East End, nevertheless elicited widespread support when proclaiming his strict adherence to the "Old Paths." The lay officers of the United Synagogue, notwithstanding the laxity of their private religious practice, in public also protested their un-qualified—if not punctillious—respect for the ancient codes of law.[69] Such attitudes had originally contributed to the ostracism of the West London Synagogue of Reform Jews (founded in 1849); in 1902 they also led to the immediate condemnation of the Jewish Religious Union. It was one thing to sanction female choristers, vernacular prayer-readings, or even to consider a trien-nial cycle for the reading of the law.[70] Although such modifi-cations severely compromised native orthodoxy in immigrant eyes, they could nevertheless be described as peripheral attempts to attain a modicum of modernity. It was quite another to contem-plate a more thoroughgoing revision of hallowed tenets and doc-trines.

Ostensibly, the belief in the Return to Zion came within the latter category. Israel's links with the Holy Land were sanctified by both Jewish practice and Jewish thought. This was self-evident from the sizable body of biblical and talmudic law that appertained exclusively to actions performed in or on *Erez Yisrael (mizvot ha-teluyot ba'arez)*; it was also apparent from the more mystical doc-trine—in itself an extension of the legal code—that that partic-ular portion of the globe had been divinely endowed with spiritual qualities unmatched anywhere else. "It is a land," states Deuter-onomy 11:12 (a favorite Zionist text), "which the Lord your God tends and on which His eye rests from year's end to year's end." Religious observance elsewhere, even of the strictest kind, nec-essarily had an attenuated appearance. Repeated references to the

[69] An example of east European praise for Adler in *Ha-Meliz*, 29 May 1897, p. 3; his sermon "The Old Paths" in JC, 12 December 1902, p. 8. Abrahams complained: "The lay leaders who denounce reform do not themselves obey one percent of the ritual laws. They are consciously hypocrites." To D. Philipson, 1 March 1903, Cincinnati, American Jewish Archives, D. Philipson Papers, Series A, Box 1.

[70] An interesting example in the six volumes of *Evidence of the Committee on the Triennial Cycle*, presented to the board of the New West End Synagogue in 1912, London, United Synagogue Archives, file 1723.

Return to Zion in the everyday liturgy (which were retained in
every Orthodox synagogue) simply underscored the message. So,
too, did pulpit exhortations. Prior to the advent of Herzl, Adler
had explicitly professed his religious attachment to the Holy Land
and, to prove the point, had himself visited Palestine and contributed financially to the Chovevei Zion Association. He had
also publicly stressed the centrality of Zion in traditional Jewish
thought, a thesis that he supported by invoking the authority of
several rabbinic authorities.[71]

The EZF continually attempted to exploit these sentiments.
Its leaders considered that the Orthodox elements were those
"best worth winning"—not least since they were, in any case,
far more numerous than were the Reform.[72] That Herzl "bow
diplomatically to the wishes of the conscientiously Orthodox"
was, accordingly, an early piece of advice. His English lieutenants
themselves invested some energy in the task. De Haas, for instance, cultivated a relationship with the spiritual leader of the
pietist Machazike Hadath synagogue, Rabbi Abba Werner—"a
nice old man" whom he hoped to entice to Basle in 1898 "to
show that ultra Orthodox Talmudism stands for the Congress.
There will be wailing in some quarters if this comes off."[73] After
the turn of the century and the foundation of the English Zionist
Federation, "synagogue campaigns" became a sporadic feature of

[71] Hermann Adler, *A Pilgrimage to Zion* (preached at the Great Synagogue)
(London, 1885); and CZA, Files of the Chovevei Zion Association, A2/105.

[72] 7 March 1917, A. Lewis (organizing secretary, EZF) to Weizmann, WA,
file 213; attendances at JRU services were never very high, and attempts to hold
them regularly in the East End were soon abandoned. By contrast, membership
rolls of the United Synagogue increased throughout the period (Aubrey Newman,
The United Synagogue [London, 1976], Appendix 1); so too, more dramatically,
did those of the Federation of Synagogues (Cecil Roth, *The Federation of Synagogues* [London, 1937], p. 6); and of the numerous independent *chevrot* in
London and the provinces (successive issues of the *Jewish Year Book*). Of course,
some members of the community might have belonged to more than one synagogue. Sir Samuel Montagu probably held the record; he *paid subscriptions* to
forty.

[73] It did, and there was. 15 July 1896, de Haas to Herzl, confidential, CZA,
Herzl Papers, H VIII 513; and 27 July 1898 to Gaster, CZA, Gaster Papers,
A203/137.

Zionist activity in Britain. Individual sympathizers were charged with the task of convincing, and where necessary converting, the spiritual leaders of their congregations; the EZF, more cohesively, attempted to gain recognition for the seventh day of the Passover festival as "Zionist Day." At the approach of spring, therefore, most wardens were requested to "arrange with the Minister of your Synagogue to devote his Sermon on that day to calling the attention of his Congregants to the National Revival in Jewry, and the hope that subsists of our re-establishment in Palestine as a Nation." The ministers themselves were asked to believe that "a Zionist Society in your town would also act as a rallying centre for Jewish and social life among your people."[74]

Somewhat more determined were the efforts made during the war years, when the Zionists sought to produce substantial evidence of the extent of their communal support. They then organized Conferences of Rabbis, both native and immigrant. Most such gatherings were private affairs, designed (in the words of one invitation) "to adjust the differences prevailing between the parties"; others took the form of public meetings. One, held at Philpot Street Synagogue, East London, in 1915, gave rise to the hope that "valuable propaganda will be conducted throughout the East End"; another, held at Toynbee Hall in January 1916 (and attended by eighty laymen and ten rabbis), elected a committee to consider "practical" steps in the same district. Altogether, the EZF determined that "we must have in view a systematic and organized scheme to win over the Synagogue to our cause."[75]

This aim was not fulfilled. Admittedly, highlights of the Zionist calendar did win wider synagogal recognition: on the anniversaries of Herzl's death, in particular, EZF spokesmen were virtually given the run of most congregational vestries. Less regularly, Zionism became a subject of pulpit addresses delivered to the

[74] One such circular, dated 1904, in CZA, Gaster Papers, A203/137; another dated 1910, in Mocatta Library, Files of the EZF, AJ/133.

[75] S. Lipton memorandum, 3 February 1918, CZA, Files of the Central Zionist Office (London), Z4/692(ii); see also the records of meetings in ibid., Z4/679, and H. J. Morgenstern minute, 14 October 1917, ibid., Z4/674.

congregation at large. "The synagogue is a place of worship, it is not the battleground of rival political factions," thundered the *Jewish Chronicle*. Nevertheless Jewish nationalism (or various associated themes) was intermittently discussed in ponderous sermons designed for the ears of acculturated audiences and in intricate discourses aimed at predominantly immigrant congregations.[76] But the pulpit, it transpired, was a two-edged weapon which could be used as effectively against Herzl's scheme as the Zionists hoped that it would be employed on their behalf.

From the Zionist point of view, matters were most obviously disconcerting where the native Orthodox clergy was concerned. Among this circle, the tone had very decidedly been set by Chief Rabbi Hermann Adler. Although prepared to discuss Zionism with Herzl in 1895, Adler had not been converted to the cause. On the contrary, he had soon publicly aligned himself with the *protestrabbiner* of Germany and such opponents of the movement as Claude Montefiore in England. The first Zionist Congress, Adler claimed, was a "premature effort"; Herzl's program was an "illusory scheme" which aroused his "unfeigned concern, because I regard it as opposed to the teachings of Judaism, as impolitic, aye as charged with the greatest peril."[77] Other native ministers, who had been less instinctively abrasive, soon felt it necessary to follow this forthright lead. A. A. Green at Hampstead Synagogue and Simeon Singer at the New West End, the two London ministers who most obviously approximated an Anglo-Jewish clerical ideal, provided the prime examples. Both had initially been supportive: Singer was at one stage considered by Herzl to be his "chief representative" in England. Yet both were soon regarded (Singer with perhaps better reason than Green) as enemies of the cause.[78] Throughout their ministries (Singer died in 1906 but

[76] See my article "The Reception of Political Zionism in England. Patterns of Alignment Among the Clergy and Rabbinate, 1895-1904," *Jewish Journal of Sociology* 16 (December 1974):171-85.

[77] Speech at AJA in JC, 8 July 1898, pp. 12-14, and *Religious Versus Political Zionism* (London, 1898).

[78] Compare Herzl's *Diary*, 1:284, and 19 April 1898, Goldsmid to Hirsch, CZA, Files of the Chovevei Zion Association, A2/11(2); and 22 November 1900,

Green did not retire until 1930), both men candidly informed their congregants of their misgivings: Zionism was not necessarily the *only* cure for anti-Semitism; neither were the leaders of the movement entirely reassuring. Particularly galling, to both men, was the fact that many Zionists "seemed to sneer at the mission of Israel and failed to appreciate how much the English Jews owed to England." Moreover, as Green privately intimated to Gaster as early as 1898, matters had to be examined candidly:

> If my information is correct then Herzl is too fast. . . . If we do not moderate the political part of the Herzl programme, I fear we may be creating new problems which we shall find it hard to solve and new trouble which we shall find it difficult to palliate. Excuse my being frank. We must be honest with each other.[79]

Few of Green's colleagues were so considerate. In many cases they simply, and obsequiously, followed the tone set by Chief Rabbi Adler's pseudo-episcopal directives. Michael Adler (no relation) at Hammersmith, Fay at the Central Synagogue, Stern in East London (each of whom ministered to constituents of the United Synagogue), as well as Emanuel in Birmingham and Friedeberg in Liverpool, all echoed Adler's celebrated comparison of religious and political Zionism. Unkind rumor had it that they were virtually "commanded" to do so by the Chief Rabbi, whose tendency to pull rank in this way was notorious. Indeed, his baneful influence was reported to extend to those immigrant rabbis whom he enlisted in his service, and with whose help he hoped to bolster the sagging image of his own establishment. The *dayyanim* Spiers, Hyamson, and Chaikin, it was remarked, were

---

EZF Bulletin, no. 4, CZA, Files of the Central Zionist Office (Vienna), Z1/403. On Singer, see Israel Abrahams, "Memories of Simeon Singer," in *The Literary Remains of Simeon Singer*, 3 vols. (London, 1908), 1:xxii-xxiii; and Ephraim Levine, *The History of the New West End Synagogue* (London, 1929), pp. 18ff. On Green, Raymond Apple, *The Hampstead Synagogue 1892-1967* (London, 1967), pp. 46-55.

[79] 31 October 1898, CZA, Gaster Papers, A203/106.

all profuse in their praise for the virtues of the Anglicanization of immigrants, and cool in their attitude toward Zionism.[80]

There were exceptions: some members of the clerical establishment who ministered to predominantly native congregations were recalcitrant supporters of Zionism. Ironically, Chief Rabbi Adler's antagonist views were not shared by his only son, Rev. Alfred S. Adler; more abruptly, they were explicitly contradicted by his successor, Joseph Hertz, and by his Sephardi counterpart, Ḥakham Moses Gaster. These, of course, were significant accretions to the Zionist movement and yet—for various reasons—not always effective props to the emergent cause. Alfred Adler, although profuse in expressions of "love" and admiration for Herzl, refused to buy a Zionist *shekel* or to attend a Zionist congress in anything but an "unattached" capacity. This, quite apart from his early death, appears to have robbed his advocacy of much of its effect.[81] Hertz, admittedly, was more forthcoming. He had established impressive Zionist credentials during his earlier career in South Africa and the United States, and the EZF quite properly gave him an enthusiastic reception when he assumed office in 1913. In 1917 he won additional laurels when opposing the Conjoint Foreign Committee's manifesto and supplying a crucially favorable response to the British government's questionnaire on the Palestine issue.[82] But these were exceptions rather than the rule. For most of his early period in office, Hertz tended to keep

---

[80] Isaac I. Black, *Shevilei ha-Yahadut be-Angliah* (London, 1903), p. 91; *Hayehoodi*, 20 February 1902, p. 4. For some examples of relevant teachings see: Avigdor Chaikin, *The Celebrities of the Jews* (Sheffield, 1899), and interview in *JC*, 11 August 1916, p. 10; Moses Hyamson, *The Oral Law and Other Sermons* (London, 1910), pp. 3-10. Baruḥ Spiers, *Divrei Devash: Ethical Sermons Delivered to the Working Classes at the Great Synagogue and Other Places of Worship* (London, 1901), p. 85, no. 11 (1898).

[81] Alfred S. Adler, *The Discipline of Sorrow* (London, 1911), pp. 145-47. For Zionist hopes and disappointments, see: *Hayehoodi*, 13 February 1902, p. 4, and 24 May 1903, p. 3; and 29 September 1904, L. Loewe to Gaster, CZA, Gaster Papers, A203/134.

[82] Samuel Landman, "Origins of the Balfour Declaration: Dr. Hertz's Contribution," in *Essays in Honour of the Very Rev. Dr. J. H. Hertz*, ed. Isidore Epstein, Ephraim Levine and Cecil Roth (London, 1942), pp. 261-70.

his support for Zionism to himself. In 1916 he "declined to be drawn" by an eager activist group in Manchester; in 1917 he refused to allow Sokolow to speak from one London pulpit, "afraid of it being said that a propagandist address was delivered in the Synagogue"; and in 1918 opposed the preamble to a motion, put to the Board of Jewish Religious Education, which attempted to present Zionism as a logical outcome of the course of Jewish history.[83] Although he did have some intermittent contact with Weizmann in 1917, Hertz was far too sensitive to the prevailing communal atmosphere to be as supportive as Weizmann wished. Possibly because he was afraid of opening new wounds when he had so many old sores to heal, Hertz preferred to maintain a diplomatic—but discouraging—silence.

Gaster, of course, had no such qualms. As early as 1896 (when he had been the only member of the established clergy to appear alongside Herzl at the Jewish Working Men's Club), he had pledged his support for the cause. As his sprawling correspondence indicates, he was subsequently as good as his word; there was hardly a year when he did not travel the length and breadth of the country on behalf of the Zionist cause, often in order to address pitifully small audiences, at great cost to his health and scholarly pursuit of Semitic studies. Nevertheless, he too was a doubtful asset. Partly, this was because he was a notoriously difficult man to work with. No less consequential, however, were his simmering relations with the lay authorities at Bevis Marks. Clashes of temperament and policy between the *Ḥakham* and his community had erupted before Herzl's arrival in England and were to remain an ubiquitous feature of the Anglo-Jewish scene until the tie was messily severed in 1918. Gaster's outspoken support of Zionism did nothing to temper the asperity of his exchanges with the lay authorities of his community. On the contrary, he drew so much fire from his congregants that Zionists

[83] See respectively, *Di Tsayt*, 6 October 1916, p. 3; 5 July 1917, A. L. Weis (acting secretary, EZF) to Sokolow, CZA, Files of the Central Zionist Office (London), Z4/674; and JC, 22 February 1918, p. 13. In his first interview with an immigrant newspaper, Hertz had pointedly omitted all mention of Zionism; *Idisher Ekspres*, 14 August 1912, p. 1.

themselves sometimes wondered whether their cause did not suffer more than it gained from being associated in the public mind with such a stormy petrel.[84] As much was also apparent to Simeon Singer who, with tongue gleefully in cheek, in 1898 demanded that Gaster subject his nationalist contentions to the *vox populi*. The Hakham was for once effectively silenced when Singer offered to stand for reelection at his synagogue (as an anti-Zionist) if Gaster did likewise, on a Zionist platform, at Bevis Marks.[85]

With one of the ecclesiastical giants of Anglo-Jewry thus embroiled in controversy at the center of the stage, most of the more reserved, and often less significant, figures opted to stay in the wings. Impervious to Zionist appeals, they preferred to skirt the entire nationalist issue altogether. One indication of this tendency toward reserve—which was necessarily harmful to the Zionist cause—was provided as early as 1898, when preparations for the convention of the Clerkenwell Conference were set in motion. Considering the publicity that had already been accorded to his views on Herzl's scheme, Chief Rabbi Adler's refusal to conduct a religious service prior to the gathering can hardly have come as a surprise. Consequently, the entire idea of a "prayer meeting" was abandoned.[86] Nevertheless, in a not altogether subtle attempt to impart some religious flavor to the proceedings, the conveners did canvass several other clergymen and requested that they refer to the Clerkenwell Conference during their sermons on the preceding Sabbath. The response, however, was overwhelmingly negative. Hyamson (at Dalston) would add nothing to his previous statements; Fay felt that his congregants had already "had the subject well brought before them"; and Green was afraid of discussing it "ad nauseam." Michael Adler reminded

[84] E.g., 7 April 1899, de Haas to Herzl, CZA, Herzl Papers, H VIII 316; and 8 September 1903 Cowen to Herzl, "P.S.," ibid., H VIII 161.

[85] JC, 21 October 1898, p. 8; 28 October 1898, p. 8; and 4 November 1898, p. 8. Green, on this occasion, opposed Singer, albeit privately; 20 October 1898, Green to Bentwich, CZA, H. Bentwich Papers, A100/71; and 21 October 1898, Green to Gaster, CZA, Gaster Papers, A203/24.

[86] Decision of the conference subcommittee, 27 December 1897, CZA, Files of the Chovevei Zion Association, A2/4.

his correspondents that he had recently declared himself an anti-
Zionist, "and as nothing has happened in the interval to change
my views, I fail to see the advantage of adverting to the subject
again yet." Finally there was Rabbi Dr. Hermann Gollancz (at
Bayswater). By no means antagonistic to Zionism (as his later
sermons revealed), he had "considered the matter and consulted
with those whom I know to be heart and soul in the movement."
Nevertheless, he too had "come to the conclusion that it would
be inadvisable to anticipate in the Pulpit . . . the arguments and
enthusiasm to be brought about at the Conference itself."[87] The
general disposition thus portended remained one of the most
obstinate of clerical barriers to Zionism throughout the period.
As late as 1917 one correspondent (writing under the pseudonym
"Provincial Minister") could still complain: "It is astounding that
during the whole recent discussion concerning Zionism the voice
of spiritual Anglo-Israel has not been heard."[88]

At one level of analysis, such diffidence could be attributed to
the inherent pusillanimity of most of the Anglo-Jewish clergy.
This, indeed, was the explanation upon which the Zionists were
fond of harping. Native ministers, they claimed, were intellectually incapable of responding in a forceful manner to any contemporary issue. Their reticence with regard to political Zionism
reflected their ignorance of Jewish tradition as much as their
inability to resist Adler's will. Both characteristics, in fact, were
consequences of the system in which they had been reared and
of which they formed a part.[89] Tendencious though it was, the
argument did contain more than a grain of truth. Jews' College,
the training ground for many of Anglo-Jewry's native clergy, did
not seem to encourage excellence. Formally, it expected its grad-

[87] The entire correspondence, dated February 1898, in ibid., A2/64, 85, 86.
For an example of Gollancz's later sympathy (although not support) see Hermann
Gollancz, *Sermons and Addresses* (London, 1916), pp. 45-52; and *Fifty Years After*
(London, 1924), pp. 176-83.

[88] *JC*, 14 December 1917, p. 27.

[89] Samuel Daiches, *Judaism in England* (Sunderland, 1907); Isaiah Raffalovich,
"Functions and Status of the Jewish Minister" (1909), in *Our Inheritance* (London,
1932), pp. 1-10; and Y. L. Levin, "Devar Be'ito," *Rashei Alfei Yisrael* 9 (1917):26-
7.

uates to be proficient in various aspects of rabbinic thought and exegesis, and even granted its students "freedom of opinion . . . on the question of Zionism."[90] But its curriculum (which devoted considerable attention to homiletics) was hardly challenging, and permitted no more than a shadow of the give and take of talmudic discourse which was considered *de rigueur* in east European academies of Jewish learning (*yeshivot*). Moreover, the communities to which Jews' College subsequently despatched its alumni invariably regarded even these minimal intellectual qualifications as superfluous. Clerical functions, as set out in most ministerial contracts, were limited to leading the congregation in prayer and collecting synagogue dues. Virtually absent were the traditional tasks expected of spiritual leaders in Jewry—to counsel, teach, adjudicate points of law, and, above all, to further Jewish knowledge by their own learning. Notwithstanding Solomon Schechter's incisive and much-quoted transatlantic admonitions, these functions were generally spurned.[91] Association of any kind with such a controversial subject as Zionism could certainly be considered beyond the bounds of humdrum propriety normally expected of a pastor. As much is indicated by two letters which the Committee of the Liverpool Old Hebrew Congregation addressed to Rev. John S. Harris in 1898. The first instructed him "not to identify yourself with the Zionist or any other similar movement, neither by speeches, publications in the press, attending any meetings or accepting any public position in connection therewith." The second was more explicit:

> With reference to your request [*sic*] that you be permitted to have full liberty of action outside your duties in connection with the Synagogue—the Committee instruct me to say that as long as you remain a minister of this congregation they cannot approve of your having any connection with Zionism.[92]

[90] Israel Cohen, *A Jewish Pilgrimage* (London, 1956), p. 31; in general, Albert M. H. Hyamson, *Jews' College London, 1855-1955* (London, 1955).

[91] Solomon Schechter, "Despising a Glorious Inheritance," *Four Epistles to the Jews of England* (London, 1901), pp. 195-96.

[92] 6 October 1898 and 15 December 1898, Mocatta Library, J. S. Harris Papers, AJ/114. Unlike most of his colleagues, Harris had earlier sent a letter of support

Circumstances such as these lend weight to the conventional comment that the community got the clergy it deserved. At occasional conferences of Anglo-Jewish preachers, the ministers did complain of their lack of autonomy. They also laid intermittent claim to a moderate degree of freedom—from the Chief Rabbi's clerical jurisdiction as much as from the obtuse demands of the lay authorities. Yet their discussions produced no noticeable amelioration.[93] Steadily, the clergy as a whole declined in prestige and status (its salaries were always meager) and "the important debates in society were increasingly conducted by intellectuals in the secular humanities," a category that included many Zionists, as well as such obvious figures as Solomon Schechter, Claude Montefiore, Israel Abrahams, Lucien Wolf, and Israel Zangwill. As at least one observer complained, it was only the "lay preacher" who could possibly be expected to possess the intellectual ability to formulate an original and informative opinion; the nominal clergy, claimed another, could not even begin to understand what Zionism was all about.[94] At the conference of Jewish ministers in June 1914, few of the assembled clergy sympathized with Rev. Joseph Hochman's appeal that "our influential synagogues . . . reconsider their aloofness from the appeal for Palestine. . . . The complete silence of the synagogue, in face of the increasing vigour of that appeal, gives cause for doubting the capacity of the Synagogue to face the problems of the day." Most considered that "they must not exaggerate the importance of the question."[95]

---

to the Clerkenwell Conference, CZA, Files of the Chovevei Zion Association, A2/86.

[93] See, e.g., reports in *JC*, 18 November 1910, p. 19; 27 January 1911, pp. 18-19; 5 January 1912, pp. 21-23; *Jewish Review* 1 (March 1911):481-82 and 2 (July 1911):175-78. In general Isaac Livingstone, *The Union of Anglo-Jewish Preachers* (London, 1944), and Michael J. Goulston, "The Status of the Anglo-Jewish Rabbinate, 1840-1914," *Jewish Journal of Sociology* 10 (June 1968):55-82.

[94] 17 April 1898, A. L. Bernstingle to Zangwill, CZA, Zangwill Papers, A120/54(b); Black, *Shevilei Hayahadut*, p. 35; and Steven Sharot, "Religious Change in Native Orthodoxy in London, 1870-1914," *Jewish Journal of Sociology* 15 (December 1973):183.

[95] Hochman's paper, "Palestine and the Jewish Renaissance," and replies in *JC*, 12 June 1914, p. 30.

Hochman himself undoubtedly represented a type of Anglo-Jewish minister who was different in many ways from the general tepid run. Yet, his career demonstrated the price that such distinction might entail. Appointed to succeed Simeon Singer at the New West End when only twenty-four, Hochman was—as his successor recorded—"an eloquent and forceful preacher . . . a scholar of considerable attainments . . . diligent in promoting Jewish studies."[96] While still a pupil at Jews' College, he wrote an erudite study of *Jewish Temple Festivities* (London, 1908); subsequently, together with Norman Bentwich, he launched *The Jewish Review*, with the "aim of filling to some extent the place left with the dropping of the J[ewish] Q[uarterly] R[eview] in England."[97] Nevertheless, Hochman was almost from the first at odds with his congregants. In part, this was because of his unconventional habits. There is, apparently, good authority for the story that one of his earliest rows with his wardens was occasioned by his appearance at divine service in riding breeches after a canter down Rotten Row. The official minute book of the Synagogue testifies to other clashes caused by his "irregularity and unpunctuality at the synagogue," his support for the Suffragettes, and his apparent tendency to Reform (or, at least, American Conservatism).[98] Finally, and not incidentally, there was his ventilation of Zionism. His views on this subject, it must be stressed, were often expressed in a prolix and complicated style. This, together with his frequent changes of tack, left his audiences in some confusion and led to accusations that his ideas were "half-baked."[99] In fact, Hochman came under as much fire from the

---

[96] Levine, *History of the New West End*, pp. 33-34.

[97] 2 December 1909, N. Bentwich to S. Hirsch, Mocatta Library, Hirsch Papers, AJ/28.

[98] John M. Shaftesly, "Religious Controversies," in Salmond S. Levin, *A Century of Anglo-Jewish Life* (London, 1971), p. 108; and minutes of board meetings, 6 February 1908, 6 April 1910, 6 June 1910 and 9 October 1910; London, United Synagogue Archives, New West End Synagogue, Minute Books.

[99] See, e.g., *Jewish Separatism and Human Progress* (London, 1910); letter to JC, 2 January 1914, p. 28; "The Servant Spirit," ibid., 19 February 1913, pp. 22-23; "Zionism and the Future of Judaism," *Jewish Review* 4 (September 1913):217-42.

(196)

Zionists as from their opponents. But that was little comfort to his congregants. From their point of view, his fault lay in that he had called attention to the Return to Zion. When he finally came to explain his resignation (in the non-Jewish press) he laid particular stress on the fact that the Synagogue had "ignored Zionism."[100]

□

Few immigrant clergymen could have shared Hochman's later opportunities (under the name of Hockman, he left the ministry, joined the armed forces, entered the bar, and eventually became legal adviser to the king of Siam); by and large, they were also immune from the charges of ignorance and weakness levelled against Hochman's colleagues. They, too, of course, had their faults. As the Hebrew, Yiddish, and English press occasionally indicated, individual members of this group could also give the appearance of being intellectually moribund and administratively inept. Some were prone to undignified squabbles; others were apparently so concerned with the fastidious minutiae of traditional practice that they could not wrestle with the larger problems of communal welfare; a third sector—typified by the immigrant appointees to the London Beth Din and by the recipients of Montagu's tight-fisted stipends at the Federation of Synagogues—seemed to have been sucked into the native system and thus shorn of all rituality.[101] As a group, however, they did attempt to remain true to their east European training and milieu and consequently refused to imitate the limited pastoral briefs of their Anglicized colleagues. Instead, they frequently gave vent to their disgust at the scant scholarship and loose manners of the native "reverends." Notwithstanding Chief Rabbi Adler's learn-

[100] *JC*, 3 September 1915, pp. 11-12.

[101] E.g., *Hayehoodi*, 5 March 1903, p. 11; *JC*, 20 March 1903, p. 11; *Idisher Zhurnal*, 14 September 1911, p. 3; *Idisher Ekspres*, 21 May 1913, p. 4; and *Di Tsayt*, 10 June 1914, p. 3; also Black, *Shevilei Hayahadut*, p. 91; and the recollections in Meir Berlin, *Mi-Volozhin ad Yerushalayim*, new ed., 2 vols. (Tel Aviv, 1971), 2:384.

ing and status, they also issued explicit challenges to his claim to be the final arbiter in Britain on all matters Jewish. In 1911, a delegation of immigrant rabbis suggested that Adler's successor virtually be stripped of the late incumbent's powers; the next chief rabbi, they intimated, would only secure immigrant allegiance if designated no more than *primus inter pares*.[102] They had already made some attempts to bring about such a state of affairs. As early as 1892, the Machazike Hadath congregation had asserted its duty to establish an independent and more rigorous *shehitah* authority; subsequently, Adler's exclusive control over licenses to butchers and slaughterers was challenged in the civil courts.[103] Most important of all, dissatisfied spokesmen for immigrant Orthodoxy twice held provincial conferences in order to discuss ways and means of arresting the community's sinful decline into lax observance and wayward behavior. In 1902 twelve rabbis met in Manchester and in 1911 thirty gathered in Leeds; on both occasions, they warned of the pernicious influence of secular education, manners, and entertainment. They also decried "Adlerism" (and in 1911 issued a strongly-worded protest against the Chief Rabbi's controversial evidence before the Divorce Commission), and agreed to establish their own organization—Agudat ha-Rabbanim ha-Haredim be'Angliah.

Significantly, both the Manchester and the Leeds conferences resisted all attempts to get them to pass motions favorable to Herzlian Zionism. Admittedly, after two days of intensive discussions in closed sessions, the Manchester conference did finally patch together an announcement that expressed the rabbis' high regard for the work being undertaken in *Erez Yisrael*. At the same time, however, they issued an injunction against the formation of communal Zionist societies without the express permission of

[102] Minutes of the second meeting of the subcommittee, 4 February 1912, United Synagogue Archives, Conference on the Chief Rabbinate, file 137a, pp. 69-79.

[103] Reports in *JC*, 26 February 1904, p. 7; and 17 February 1911, p. 9; and *Idisher Ekspres*, 15 February 1911, p. 2. Adler's own concern at the threats this posed to his position in his correspondence with his brother, Elkan. New York, Jewish Theological Seminary, E. Adler Papers, Box 1.

the local rabbi. Even more disconcerting to the Zionists were the results of the 1911 conference: its participants demonstratively threw out one resolution which advocated the adoption of "Zionist" educational practice (*Ivrit be-Ivrit*); in scenes of equal emotion they refused to discuss another that expressed support for nationalist work in Palestine.[104]

Proceedings such as these cannot be attributed to an attitude of outright opposition to each and every ideological tenet of political Zionism. Instead, the prevalent tone was equivocal, falling short of support for the Zionist movement and yet not amounting to antagonism to the Zionist idea. The balance of pros against cons induced a degree of self-conscious ambivalence. Admittedly, the very name of the new Jewish national organization aroused intensely messianic associations among immigrant rabbis. Its diagnosis of the present Jewish condition also struck an immediately responsive cord. First-hand experience of conditions in eastern Europe had made them skeptical of the promise of emancipation in the lands of their origin; likewise, contact with the assimilatory habits and ambitions of native Anglo-Jewry had made them doubtful of the possibility of religious regeneration in the land of their adoption. Nevertheless, many members of the Agudat ha-Rabbanim found both the persona and the program of the Zionist Organisation to be profoundly disturbing. On both issues, their position was more complicated—and more interesting—than that of their native counterparts in Orthodox or Reform congregations. As a whole, the Agudat ha-Rabbanim was also more evenly divided where political Zionism was concerned. As one contemporary later noted, even within a single immigrant congregation (the Sunderland Beth ha-Midrash) successive spiritual leaders could express diametrically different opinions on the subject.[105]

---

[104] For reports of the 1902 proceedings see: *JC*, 19 December 1902, p. 26; *Hayehoodi*, 18 December 1902, p. 5; *Beit Va'ad la-Ḥakhamim* 2 (February 1903):3-5. On the 1911 conference see: *JC*, 10 March 1911, pp. 18, 29; and 17 March 1911, pp. 19-22; *Idisher Ekspres*, 15 March 1911, p. 4; *Hayehoodi*, 6, 16, 23, 31 March and 6 April 1911; *Jewish Review* 2 (May 1911):1-2, 55-59. Gaster, who was unable to attend the 1902 conference, was not invited to that of 1911.

[105] I. Cohen, "Some Early Reminiscences and Impressions of Zionism in Sun-

To conclude that "the [immigrant] rabbis supported the Zionist movement"[106] is therefore not quite correct. That broad generalization really fits only a limited—albeit articulate—circle of recent arrivals, most of whom were of a younger generation. Outstanding and influential among this group, even by European standards, were Shemuel Ya'akov Rabinowitz (1857-1921; who came to Liverpool in 1906); Yizhak Herzog (1888-1954; who held posts in Belfast and Dublin); and the latter's predecessor as Ashkenazi Chief Rabbi in mandatory Palestine, Avraham Kook (1865-1935; who was rabbi of the Machazike Hadath community in London from 1916 until 1919). Unlike their older and more restrained colleagues, who had spent more of their formative years in a pre-Herzlian atmosphere, these men were uncommonly effervescent in their advocacy of a religious brand of Jewish nationalism. Writing in the inherited rabbinic mold, their arguments were based on an unconditional commitment to the true faith (and, especially, to the neglected duty of dwelling in the Holy Land). But to this rather defensive structure of argument they added a far bolder, and in Kook's case mystic, emphasis on the oneness of Israel. Explicit in their appeal to the faithful was the notion that a national effort toward Zion was a platform on which non- and anti-religious Jews could stand together with the pious. Thus, they attempted to redirect the secularist tone of mainstream Zionism into traditional channels and—not incidentally—to harness to Orthodox causes the enthusiasms that Herzl had engendered on Zionism's behalf. Increasingly, these themes suffused their writings, speeches, and sermons, which trenchantly proclaimed the message that the emergence of Zionism as a popular movement was a portent of the imminence of divine Redemption.[107] Moreover, these figures of stature were supported,

---

derland," in Arnold Levy, *History of the Sunderland Jewish Community* (London, 1956), pp. 249, 256.

[106] Lloyd P. Gartner, *The Jewish Immigrant in England, 1870-1914*, 2nd ed. (London, 1973), p. 250.

[107] E.g., Shemuel Ya'akov Rabinowitz, *Ha-Dat ve-ha-Le'umiut* (Warsaw, 1900); *Ha-Zionut ha-Datit* (Warsaw, 1917); and for specifically English material, *Litkufot ha-Yamim* (London, 1919). For an example of Herzog's earlier work, *Divrei Yizhak* (London, 1921).

and in some cases preceded, by a cluster of more neglected men who occupied various, and sometimes obscure, provincial posts: Ya'akov Sandelson in Newcastle, Ya'akov Rabinowitz in Edinburgh, Gedalya Silverstone in Belfast and Birmingham, Hirsh Hurewitz in Sunderland, and Yisrael Ya'akov Yoffey in Manchester. Although generally less prolific writers than the main Zionist protagonists, some produced works that faithfully portray their interest and support for the cause. Ya'akov Rabinowitz, for instance, compiled an ardently nationalist commentary to the Passover Haggadah ("our happiness and welfare depends on our speedy return to our land; in strange countries we can never succeed"), and "in view of the times" edited an old manuscript of laws appertaining to the Holy Land.[108]

Precisely what benefits the EZF could reap from such inner-directed sympathizers was never very certain. In part, this was because of the outstanding unconventionality of those rabbis who did give the Zionist movement their blessing. Kook, altogether a man apart, provided one example—as Sokolow became well aware during World War I.

> As much as I would like to induce him to some Zionist propaganda work amongst our orthodox brethren, [he wrote, in reply to various suggestions that more use be made of Kook's outstanding talents] I realize the great difficulty in the way of doing it. Rabbi Kuk [*sic*] . . . has ideas of his own concerning Zionist politics, ideas which may be somewhat interesting and are, undoubtedly, well-meant, but are full of "sancta simplicitas" and impracticable. I would classify him as an individual Zionist who is not induced to co-operate in an Organization like ours.[109]

[108] Ya'akov Rabinowitz, *Shivhei Ya'akov* (London, 1906); and *Sefer Hilkhot Erez Yisrael* (London, 1900); also *Sefer Bikurei Ya'akov* (London, 1899). For an example of Silverstone's views see his *Pirhei Aviv* (London, 1901), especially pp. 60-62; and Yoffey's in *Kenesset Yisrael* (Manchester, 1910).

[109] 6 March 1917, Sokolow to Weizmann, WA, file 213; on subsequent failures to cooperate with Kook see 16 June 1917, J. K. Goldbloom to Weizmann, ibid., file 230, and 2 December 1917, Kook to Weizmann and Sokolow, ibid., file 245.

Other, earlier, attempts to create a climate favorable to concerted Orthodox action on Zionism's behalf had proved equally abortive. Thus, in 1902, no prominent rabbi, native or immigrant, had publicly responded to Rabbi Ya'akov Reines's call to establish a local branch of the Mizraḥi movement of religious Zionists. So few sympathizers attended a conference for this purpose in 1904 that the meeting had to be quickly terminated. Only two Anglo-Jewish representatives attended the first international gathering of Mizraḥi sympathizers at Pressburg in 1904 (James Loewe and a certain Rabbi Epstein, both from Sheffield), but they were clearly uninfluential. There followed what seems to have been a lengthy period of quiescence.[110] Despite the various attempts made to muster rabbinic support during the war, a Mizrachi Federation of Great Britain did not come into existence until December 1918. Moreover, the support of the new body was always conditional—which was why it insisted on retaining its independence of the EZF. From the start, its leaders (who included Chief Rabbi Hertz) insisted on the "importance of spiritual and cultural work in Palestine, as against purely political activities."[111]

Even then, the Mizrachi Federation was never in complete command of the field of Orthodox views on this subject. It had always to contend with the alternative claims of the Agudat Yisrael, an Orthodox movement to its right, which was far less sympathetic to the Zionist Organisation. Although similarly committed to the idea of Jewish reconstruction in *Erez Yisrael*, the Agudah was far more specific in its claim that the Orthodox exercise complete supremacy over the educational and sacerdotal aspects of the endeavor. That was the principal message of the founding conference of the Agudah, held at Kattowicz (Silesia) in 1912, which bitterly attacked the avowedly secular cultural

[110] On which see the various articles on the early history of the Mizrachi Federation in Anglo-Jewry by Z. Plitnick, Sh. Levenberg, and M. Eidelbaum in *Sefer ha-Ẓionut ha-Datit*, ed. Yiẓḥak Raphael and Shlomo Shraga, 2 vols. (Jerusalem, 1977), 2:289-98. Additional material in Y. Chotzner, *Ha-Ẓion*, 12 June 1905, p. 3; JC, 19 August 1904, p. 22 and *Idisher Ekspres*, 13 September 1911, p. 4.

[111] Report in *Jewish Guardian*, 23 July 1920, p. 11.

policy proposed at the tenth Zionist Congress. These were sentiments that evoked a limited, but significant response in Anglo-Jewry. Two of the more prominent immigrant rabbis (Yisrael Ḥayim Daiches, since 1902 of Leeds and Shemuel Hillman, since 1908 of Glasgow) participated in the discussions at Kattowicz. To judge from accounts in the contemporary press, their attacks on established Zionism were somewhat less ferocious than those of their Central and East European colleagues, but the thrust of their arguments was sufficiently similar to allow for a broad measure of agreement.[112] Moreover, together with Yisrael Yoffey and Meyer Jung (an outstanding scholar from Moravia who accepted a "call" to become *Rav* of the Federation of Synagogues in 1912), Daiches and Hillman soon established branches of the Agudah in London and the provinces which, in turn, organized "mass meetings" of their followers. They thus maintained a running fire of criticism that the EZF, precisely because of its ostensible appeal to Orthodox sentiments, had particular difficulty·answering.[113]

The Balfour Declaration of 1917 augmented the intensity of the Agudah's campaign. That document, it was feared, increased the danger that Orthodoxy's viewpoint might be overlooked. At a conference held in Zurich in February 1919, attended by over one hundred European delegates (but not one representative from Anglo-Jewry) an entire batch of resolutions was consequently passed, all of which stressed that "no community in the Holy Land shall be reconstructed except on the basis of the traditional binding form, both written and oral, of Jewish rights." The conference then specifically appealed "to the English section of traditional Jewry" to:

Found local Agudas Yisroel groups all over the British Isles; then combine them all into one British Central Committee; get into contact with the Central Office in Zuerich. . . .

---

[112] Reports which stress the contributions of Daiches and Hillman in *JC*, 31 May 1912, p. 11 and 7 June 1912, p. 10; *Idisher Ekspres*, 5 June 1912, p. 4; *Hayehoodi*, 13 June 1912, pp. 9-10.

[113] *Di Tsayt*, 5 May, 15 July and 28 July 1914; on Jung see Julius Jung, *Champions of Orthodoxy* (London, 1974), pp. 181-254.

Strengthen the chain which will link English traditional Judaism to the Thora-people of the world, for the raising of the horns of our salvation, for the preservation and upholding of our Thora, and for the welfare of Judaism as a whole.[114]

The response was soon forthcoming. Further sections of the Agudah were formed in London and the provinces, several immigrant rabbis recruited as speakers, and a number of demonstrations organized. Less publicly, the Agudah also launched a diplomatic campaign. In an official petition to the Government the organization expressed its heartfelt gratitude for Britain's interest in the welfare of the Jews, but nevertheless begged to "express its fervent hope that the interpretation of the Balfour Declaration will not mean the handing over of Palestine to one section of the Jewish people." Further to guard against that outcome, the leaders of the Agudah in Britain even sought the advice of Lucien Wolf and the Anglo-Jewish Association (to which request the latter eagerly responded).[115]

The Political Committee of the Zionist Organisation, although scornful of this "unholy alliance,"[116] was ill-equipped to respond effectively to the Agudah's main charges and thus counteract its influence within the community. Principally, this was because of the high proportion of manifestly nonobservant Jews within the local and international Zionist movement. Overt associations with men who boasted of their irreligious behavior and atheistic beliefs (as did most of the Zionist Actions Committee and a fair number of the leadership of the EZF), while uncomfortable for some of the native Orthodox clergy, were necessarily an anathema to most immigrant guardians of the tradition. Jewish public affairs,

[114] See the circular, dated 28 July 1919, and encompassing eight pages of English-language type, in New York, Jewish Theological Seminary, E. Adler Papers, Box 1.

[115] 10 November 1919 and 8 February 1920, M. Jung to L. Wolf, London, DEPS General Correspondence, C11/3/15 and Palestine, E3/187(i). During the immediate postwar period, prominent leaders of Agudah in England included Rabbis Bloch, Ferber, Horowitz, Zimmerman, and Schonfeld.

[116] Minutes of EZF executive meeting, 12 April 1920, CZA, Files of the Central Zionist Office (London), Z4/128(ii).

in their view, had to remain the purview of "responsible" individuals, whose qualifications were the ancient attributes of piety and observance. Very few immigrant rabbis, therefore, were prepared to go as far as Meyer Wigoder (of Dublin), who favorably compared the Zionists with the most faithful of the Israelites at the time of the Exodus from Egypt.[117] Far more representative was the view expressed by Victor Schonfeld, the highly articulate guide of German immigrant Orthodoxy in North London, who warned that the Zionist movement would not obtain his complete support until its leaders fostered the required brand of holiness. Their demonstrative unwillingness to do so probably contributed as much as anything else to the opposition of Hayim Zundel Maccoby, whose attacks on the persona of the Zionists were particularly effective since they were uttered by one whose own credentials as a *hovev zion* were beyond question.[118] Similar considerations might affect the perspectives of such other, less immediately rigorous sympathizers as Abba Werner. In an interview that the latter gave to the *Jewish Chronicle* in 1911, he admitted that "some of the leaders have greatly disappointed me in their attitude towards the Jewish religion. Unless the Torah is observed, there is no raison d'être for Zionism."[119]

There was more to this attitude than an insistence on the niceties of rabbinic protocol. Herzl's proposal to establish a Jewish state had raised issues of doctrinal import; the manner in which they would be settled would affect the tenor of the entire Zionist enterprise. Immigrant rabbis were particularly insistent that, in view of Herzl's original inclination to separate Church from State, several such matters had best be settled from the outset. One was the religious injunction to leave the Holy Land fallow every

[117] See his *Sefer Bet Yehudah* (Jerusalem, 1910), pt. 6, pp. 24-31; also *My Life* (London, 1935), p. 75.

[118] *Imrei Hayim*, ed. Max Mansky (Tel Aviv, 1929), p. 12; and minutes of meeting of board, 28 October 1900, London, Federation of Synagogues, Minute Books, 1:282-83.

[119] 8 June 1911, p. 20. Schonfeld's views in *JC*, 26 July 1918, p. 10; and N. Lipschitz, *In Memoriam* (London, 1930), pp. 12-13. Similar statements by Yisrael Yoffey in *JC*, 28 November 1913, p. 23.

Sabbatical year—a vexatious subject which had already caused a hue and cry in *Ere*ẓ *Yisrael* when raised by the Rothschild colonists in 1888. Another was the possibility that, in a restored Jewish state, there might be a move to rebuild the temple and to revive sacrificial worship. Yet a third was the risk that a Jewish government might feel compelled to permit polygamy rather than to prescribe monogamy. On the agenda, in effect, was the entire structure and authority of religion in a modern polity. As a matter of course, traditionalist Jews envisaged uncontested theocratic rule. If that did not suit mainstream Zionist convenience, let alone modern democratic theory, then so much the worse for them.

> Should I be obliged [declared Rabbi Jung] either to consent to our people being a religious society without national characteristics, or to consent to their being a national association without any religious foundations, and should there be no alternative, I frankly confess that I should not hesitate a moment in giving the preference to religion without nationalism.[120]

One conventional retort to many of these criticisms was that the Orthodox could only exert the necessary religious influence on the national movement if they joined forces with it. Moreover, they might thus help preserve the unity of Jewry.[121] But this, too, was debatable. As many immigrant rabbis saw it, there was no justification for an alliance of that sort, if it sanctioned

---

[120] *JC*, 22 June 1917, p. 25. Significantly, such enquiries were not limited to immigrant spokesmen. See e.g., Hermann Gollancz, "The Return to Palestine" (1897), *Sermons and Addresses* (London, 1909), pp. 499-505; Lucien Wolf, "Zionism," *Encyclopaedia Britannica*, 10th ed. (Cambridge, 1903), vol. 9; Albert M. H. Hyamson, "The Present Position of Zionism," *The Empire Review* 6 (December 1903):511; Israel Zangwill, *Speeches, Articles and Letters*, ed. Maurice Simon (London, 1937), p. 161. According to Weizmann, Zangwill preferred East Africa to Palestine "because, in his view, the old Jewish tradition, with its sacrifices and prayers, would have to be re-established and would exclude the building of a secular state there." *Letters*, 3:62-63.

[121] Ya'akov Rabinowitz (Edinburgh), "Mikhtav La-Rabanim," *Beit Va'ad* 2 (May 1903):77-80; and Shemuel Rabinowitz (Liverpool), *Litkufot ha-Yamim*, pp. 78-79, 83, 85. Rabbi M. Jung, letter to *JC*, 3 May 1918, p. 10.

a distinction between physical Return and spiritual Redemption. Jews could not obtain the latter simply by imitating the Italians or the Serbs. People, language, and soil, unless understood in a spiritual context, were alien cults. By preaching them in a secular sense the Zionists were forging an alliance with the most corrupt elements of the gentile environment and assisting the satanic conspiracy against the House of Israel. They were, thereby, betraying the very ideal that they claimed to advance. Under these circumstances, conflict was to be preferred to cooperation with the latter-day prophets of Ba'al.[122] No wonder, therefore, that several of the immigrant rabbis should have posited religious observance as an *alternative* to Zionism, nor that the Manchester conference of 1902 should have enjoined local rabbis to veto any Zionist wishing to propagate Jewish nationalism from synagogue premises. As Yisrael Daiches, the leading spirit at that gathering, informed a public meeting on the eve of the conference, immigrant rabbis could best strengthen Judaism in Britain by leaving Zionism alone and establishing *yeshivot*.

> Even if the Lord will grant the Zionists success in their endeavours to obtain a portion in the land of our fathers, how can we be sure that our children, who are not of our spirit, will remain true sons to their people and religion? . . . Only if we raise our sons to Torah and wisdom, and the next generation will be wise and discerning, can we hope that the children will return to their borders.[123]

Daiches's injunction to delay matters constituted an integral facet of the outlook to which he gave expression. Analogous admonitions to procrastination—even immobilism—are scattered throughout the immigrant and native sermonologies that dis-

[122] See, e.g., Yisrael Yoffey, "Tena'ei he-Shalom," *Beit Va'ad* 2 (July 1903):22-26.

[123] *Beit Va'ad* 2 (May 1903):7-11, and *Derashot Maharyah* (Leeds, 1920), no. 2. Similar albeit less explicit sentiments in Aryeh Leib Levin, *Sefer Bet Yisrael* (London, 1902), p. 81 (a commentary on Genesis 12:1); Yoel Herzog, *Imrei Yoel*, 2 vols. (London, 1921), 2:49-50 (a commentary on Exodus 13:17); and Maccoby, *Imrei Hayim*, pp. 83-84.

cussed Zionism. That such counsels neatly dovetailed with native preferences for the missionary dispersal of the faithful need not detract from their significance. Neither should they be regarded as merely subsidiary expressions of the immigrants' distaste for the secularizing modernity of the Zionists. Complementing, and sometimes justifying these arguments was a deep-rooted belief that any attempt to hasten the End of Days by human means was sinful. Herein, then, lay the third motive for Orthodoxy's resistance to the Zionist rush to statehood.

As traditionally foreseen, the Return to Zion would constitute part of a general messianic panorama; similarly, the prayers for the restoration of Jewish independence had been understood to encompass a wider, eschatological ethos. Exile, it was taught, had been a punishment; the promised Return would signify a return to Grace. Redemption, in fact, was synonymous with a resolution of the spiritual dialogue between the Almighty and the Assembly of Israel; in the very nature of things, it would take place in an otherworldly and almost miraculous atmosphere. Individual decisions to honor the duty to dwell in the Land of Israel were one thing (although the binding force of that injunction at all times was, too, a matter of dispute);[124] carefully orchestrated mass movements organized with the purpose of establishing autonomy in that territory were quite another. At the very least, the impulse to a national Return had to be divinely inspired and to await definitive signs from heaven that the Jews had indeed worked their passage home. Precipitate communal action, unaccompanied by any such omens, was tantamount to rebellion against the divine plan. Post-exilic Jewish history from Bar Kokhba to Shabbetai Zevi was replete with a long series of pseudo-messianic adventurers, whose disobedient impatience had brought physical and spiritual catastrophe to their followers.

To an even greater extent than was the case with other expressions of opposition to Zionism, these opinions were not specifically Anglo-Jewish. They were distilled from centuries of teach-

[124] See e.g., the arguments marshalled at considerable length in Yoel Teitelbaum, *Sefer Va-yo'el Mosheh*, 3 vols., 2nd ed. (Jerusalem, 1974).

ings, some moderate, some radical, which had been developed in the larger and more prolific centers of Jewish settlement on the European continent. In their anti-Herzlian context, they were largely formulated by a distinguished cluster of Central and East European sages and rabbinical authorities whose share of contemporary Jewish hagiography far surpassed that of their Western colleagues. Thus, it was in Hungary, Poland, and Russia that the "battle of books" over political Zionism was most ferocious, and there that Orthodoxy's resistance to the movement attained its most organized form and achieved its greatest impact.[125] Anglo-Jewry's contribution was necessarily minor. At best, Adler could be invited to contribute to one of the most influential and cogent anthologies of rabbinical anti-Zionism; less understandably, his name was also enrolled in a counterproduct issued by Herzl's supporters. To the first he sent a copy of his sermon "Religious versus Political Zionism"; in the second there appeared a letter which, although dated 1891 (and therefore largely irrelevant), was almost equally damning. "Of course the settlement of our Holy Land is a very honourable enterprise," he had written. "But my advice is that our brethren should not go up to the Holy Land *en masse*, for the cost of improving the colonies is unbelievably high. But let the Lord have mercy on the remnants of His people Israel and make us rejoice in the speedy arrival of the righteous redeemer."[126]

More substantial, and significant, were the lines of transmission from Europe to Britain. Several immigrant rabbis regularly corresponded with their Continental counterparts and sought their advice on matters of religious law and talmudic exegesis. Some sought to maintain contact of a more intimate nature, even oral dialogues. As the approbations in several Anglo-Jewish works of

[125] On the earlier period of the struggle see: Yosef Salmon, "Emdatah shel ha-Ḥevra ha-Ḥaredit be-Russia-Polin le-Ẓionut, be-Shanim 1898-1900," in *Eshel Be'er Sheva* (Beersheba, 1976), pp. 377-438, and sources.

[126] Avraham Slutsky, *Shivat Ẓion* (Warsaw, 1900), pp. 54-55; Adler's sermon (in Hebrew) designed, in the words of his own covering letter, to place him "in the distinguished camp of the opponents," in Shlomo Zalman Landa and Yosef Rabinowitz, *Sefer 'Or ha-Yesharim* (Warsaw, 1900), pp. 62-68.

learning of the period indicate, the Zionist congresses and the gatherings of the Agudah council were in this respect particularly useful; they furnished a rendezvous and thus served several ancillary purposes.[127] Hence, the major sources upon which European Orthodoxy built its theological arguments against political Zionism were sufficiently familiar to be cited in Britain. One example is provided by the talmudic interpretation of the three "oaths" in the Song of Songs (2:7; 3:5; 8:4), which were understood to constitute warnings against the use of force to reestablish Jewish national sovereignty and against "excessive supplication" to hasten the End of Days (*Babylonian Talmud*, Ketubot, folio 111a and Rashi's commentary). These injunctions were tendenciously quoted in a number of native and immigrant texts.[128] Although relegated to a parenthesis by Shemuel Rabinowitz and tinkered with by Yisrael Yoffey, they could not be ignored by even the most ardent of Mizrachists.[129] More often, such teachings were taken for what they were: examples of a stream of traditional thought that was at odds with the activism of the Zionists. Indeed, when placed within the magisterial context of the "meaning of the Exile," they could give the entire Zionist thesis a curiously attenuated appearance. As much is implicit in the works of Yoel Herzog, Shemuel Hillman, and Yosef Yoffey— all of whom discussed these themes at some length (and none of whom would appear to have been as uncomplicatedly sympathetic

[127] See, e.g., Daiches, *Derashot Maharyah*, p. 9, and the approbations in Aryeh Leib Levin, *Shivim Panim la-Torah* (London, 1910). For examples of correspondence between immigrant and Continental rabbis, see *Beit Va'ad* 1 (February 1902):35-40; 4 (March 1904):36-50.

[128] H. Adler, sermon, *JC*, 15 October 1897, p. 13; S. Singer, sermon, *JC*, 2 May 1902, p. 29; A. S. Adler, "The Future of Zionism," *JC*, 10 March 1905, p. 31; Hermann Gollancz, *The Targum to the Five Megillot*, ed. B. Grossfeld (New York, 1973), pp. 22-23, 33; Shemuel David Sabel, *Sefer Shir ha-Shirim im Perush Hadash, Migdal David* (London, 1899), pp. 14-21; Yoel Herzog, *Gilyonei Yoel* (Vilna, 1913), p. 144; and "Judaism and Zionism: An Orthodox Point of View," *Jewish Guardian*, 10 October 1919, p. 9.

[129] Shemuel Ya'akov Rabinowitz, *Litkufot ha-Yamim*, pp. 89-90; compare Yosef Yoffe, *Yosef Biur* (Vilna, 1881), pp. 22-23 and Yisrael Yoffey, *Kenesset Yisrael*; see also Gedalya Silverstone's introduction to Hayim Broda's *Sefer Hadash le-Shir ha-Shirim* (London, 1903), and his *Imrei Yosher* (Washington, 1925), pp. 7-8.

to the Zionist program as later hagiographers have attempted to suggest). The Jews, they taught, undoubtedly prayed for national glory as well as spiritual deliverance; they also had a duty to merit both blessings. Nevertheless, since the Return to Zion would perforce be the work of the Messiah, such activities could only take the form of preparations for his coming. Colonizing activities by the few might be one method, but these had to be supplemented by the sanctification of the Divine Name on the part of the many. The prohibition on a premature return to Zion would therefore remain in force until the nations of the world recognized the true God. Redemption, in this sense, had best be attained by displaying unbounded faith in the Almighty's ultimate benevolence, patiently suffering whatever trials He sent, and setting an example of virtuous behavior.[130]

Pushed to their extremes, exhortations such as these might seem to bear distinct affinities with the missionary ethos preached in Reform circles. Appearances, however, are deceptive. For Reform Jews, as has been seen, Dispersion marked the fulfilment of Israel's spiritual destiny; for the Orthodox, it was no more than a painful way station on the road to Return. Complete coalescence between the two wings was thus impossible; the more so when it is remembered that the social and cultural gulf between them was too wide to admit of even the most cursory mutual acquaintance between Rev. Morris Joseph (the minister of the principal Reform congregation in West London) and the leading immigrant rabbis of the East End.[131] Nevertheless, some distinctly recognizable parallels can be discerned in the treatments that even such disparate personalities accorded to particular episodes in Jewish history—a quarry that the immigrants mined with as

[130] The relevant themes in Shemuel I. Hillman, *Sefer 'Or ha-Yashar* (London, n.d.), pp. 9, 10, 12, 40, 54-59, 62-63; Herzog, *Imrei Yoel,* 1:47-49 (on emigration to USA); pp. 206-207 (on Queen Victoria); 3:192-94 (on Kishinev); and *Gilyonei Yoel,* p. 64; Yisrael Yoffey, *Kenesset Yisrael,* pp. 41, 114-15 and 139-40; see also Daiches, *Derashot Maharyaḥ,* nos. 11 and 35 (on the Jewish mission); Mosheh Avigdor Chaikin, *Kelalei ha-Posekim* (London, 1923), p. iii; and Spiers, *Divrei Devash,* pp. 222-23.

[131] E.g., 28 October 1917, Joseph to N. Levy, Mocatta Library, West London Synagogue Archives, AJ/78, Box 2 (1917).

much homiletical assiduity as did the native clergy. One incident found to be particularly apt concerned Rabbi Jochanan ben Zakkai's reaction to the imminent fall of Jerusalem in 70 C.E. Reform preachers were absolutely sure of the moral to be drawn from that ancient sage's disagreement with the "nationalist" Zealots, his flight from the besieged city, and his request that the Roman government grant Judaism a seat of learning in Yavneh rather than the release of the national capital. In so doing, they argued, ben Zakkai had "made Judaism independent of the local Zion" and indicated that Israel's strength lay "not in the attainment of national grandeur, not even in the restoration of the national existence, but the guarding and dissemination of religious truth." The anti-Zionist inference was obvious. "If Judaism is to live and flourish in these latter days of doubt and difficulty, it must continue to build itself upon the imperishable foundations of religious instruction" rather than the momentary glory of national statehood.[132] These were sentiments that would appear to have been shared by several immigrant Orthodox rabbis—albeit in a somewhat guarded, less explicit, and perhaps more recondite fashion. Thus, in the course of an intricate discourse (significantly devoted to the theme of national regeneration), Yisrael Daiches, too, forcibly contrasted Jochanan ben Zakkai's preservation of the true "spirit" of Judaism with his disregard of the less consequential "material" welfare of the land.[133] Meyer Jung referred to the same thought during the course of his induction sermon as chief rabbi of the Federation of Synagogues. Aaron Hyman, in his more systematic and less polemical treatment of the incident, also hinted at the benefits ultimately bestowed upon Israel's religion by the

[132] M. Joseph, *Judaism as Creed and Life*, pp. 197-98, and Rev. I. Harris, sermon at West London Synagogue of British Jews (Berkeley Street), *JC*, 24 March 1911, p. 30. Similar sentiments in I. Abrahams, "Johanan ben Zaccai," *Encyclopaedia Britannica*, 11th ed. (Cambridge, 1911), 15:431; J. M. Myers, *The Story of the Jewish People*, 2nd impress. (London, 1909), p. 66. Throughout, the influence of Heinrich Graetz was obvious; see his *Geschichte der Juden von den altesten Zeiten bis auf die Gegenwart*, 13 vols. (Leipzig, 1897-1911), 4:15-16.

[133] Daiches, *Derashot Maharyah*, no. 19, on *Babylonian Talmud*, Gittin, folio 56b.

destruction of the "bricks and mortar" of Jerusalem.[134] It was his text that others followed when stating: "In the opinion of our venerable Rabbi, the Jewish State was like every other, transitory. The Jewish People, however, was *not* to perish with its existence as a State or Polity. Israel was to be preserved alive; and more so, with a life, even fuller, and more important than ever."[135]

To show such coalescence is not to disfigure the plain differences dividing Orthodoxy from Reform within Anglo-Jewry; it is rather to indicate that, where opposition to political Zionism was concerned, a curious transmutation was possible. On this subject, so-called opposites could sometimes be no more than tints in a spectrum. The social and intellectual variations obtaining between the two wings of the community undoubtedly explain the different emphases that each placed upon certain facets of the Zionists case. But they did not prevent a significant amount of mutual transmission. The appearance of Jewish nationalism raised issues that transcended many boundaries of theological allegiance; opposition to political Zionism, even if it did not yoke together otherwise disparate religious elements, certainly helped to blur some of the distinctions between them. Mingling the scholarly with the demotic, anti-Zionists of these two schools of thought could thus find sufficient in common to effect a tactical alliance which was in many ways as remarkable as the curious coalition of which the EZF was comprised.

As much was appreciated, and put to good effect, by Montefiore, Abrahams, and Wolf, who led the public battle against the Zionists during the war years. For the purposes of that debate, they were prepared to adopt teachings grounded upon the tradition whose authority they were otherwise loath to accept.[136]

[134] *Sefer Toldot ha-Tanaim ve-ha-Amoraim*, 3 vols. (London, 1901-1911), 2:674-81; Jung's views in JC, 21 June 1912, p. 26. See also Schonfeld in *Ben Zakkai* 1 (March 1920):7.

[135] W. Javitz, "Rabbi Jochanon ben Zaccai," *The Sinaist* 1 (February 1917): 11-14.

[136] I. Abrahams, "Palestine and Jewish Nationality," p. 465; Montefiore, "Zionism," *The Inquirer*, 24 November 1917, pp. 463-64; and Wolf, "Statement of

Consequently, they frequently sprinkled their anti-Zionist pronouncements with references to the "spiritual ideas and hopes, the traditions and principles" that they had culled from Orthodox writings. Montefiore was a particularly adept exponent of this tack—not surprisingly, since he had set something of a trend in that sort of exegesis as early as 1892. In an otherwise scathing critique of Michael Friedlander's statement of Orthodoxy, *The Jewish Religion*, he had found only one passage worthy of praise:

> The hopes with which our religion inspires us can never lead us to intrigues, political combinations, insurrection, or warfare for the purpose of regaining Palestine and appointing a Jewish Government. . . . Even if a band of adventurers were to succeed in reconquering Palestine for the Jews by means of arms, or reacquiring the Holy Land by purchasing it from the present owners, we should not see in such an event the consummation of our hopes.[137]

During the war, Montefiore was to be even more explicit; he was then to contend that the anti-Zionist statements that he presented to the Government were based upon opinions which had the sanction of even the most extreme of his Orthodox "allies."[138] It is to the diplomatic and communal circumstances that induced Montefiore to go to such lengths that attention must now be turned.

Objections to the Proposals of the Zionists" (June 1916), CZA, Wolf Papers, A77/3.

[137] Michael Friedlander, *The Jewish Religion* (London, 1891), pp. 161-62, and Montefiore, "Dr. Friedlander on Jewish Religion," *JQR* 4 (1892):226.

[138] Montefiore, "Zionism," *The Inquirer*, p. 464, and "The Dangers of Zionism," p. 3.

6

Zionists and Anti-Zionists, 1914-1917

G ENERALS, IT IS OFTEN
remarked, tend to plan for the previous war; so too, perhaps, do
civilian leaders. At the outbreak of World War I, the Jewish
communal Establishment in Britain emulated the patterns of
thought and behavior laid down during the Boer War. Anglo-
Jewry's philanthropic institutions and political organizations had
managed the strains and stresses of circumstances between 1899
and 1902. The same instruments were presumed sufficiently strong
to accommodate the problems expected to arise after August
1914. Most people anticipated that the forthcoming period of
dislocation would be brief, that the extent of civilian involvement
and damage would be limited, and that Anglo-Jewry could take
war in its stride. In his presidential address to the Board of Deputies in November 1914, David Alexander assured members that
the Conjoint Foreign Committee would cope with the situation.
A "Special Branch" of the committee was established in January
1915, under the direction of Lucien Wolf[1]. Otherwise, there
seemed no need to overhaul the existing institutional machinery
of the community, to review the functions and status of individual
bodies, or—more drastically—to revise received opinions concerning the political and social aims of Anglo-Jewry as a whole.

Such complacency was unwarranted. Only in the very limited
sphere of Jewish military service did matters turn out as the leaders
of the community had hoped and expected. In accordance with
the revered precedent established during the Boer War, significant

[1] Open letter from C. Montefiore and D. Alexander, in JC, 22 January 1915,
p. 8.

numbers of native Anglo-Jewish males did join the armed forces, initially as volunteers and later as conscripts. Some performed deeds of valor considered worthy of mention and decoration; inevitably, many servicemen fell in battle.[2] The community attempted to salvage some virtue from necessity. The casualty lists, published regularly and prominently by the *Jewish Chronicle*, were said to prove that Anglo-Jewry was duly redeeming its pledge to king and country.

This, perhaps, was as predicted; otherwise, however, matters took an unforeseen course which belied many of the assumptions upon which the community's leaders had based their attitudes. The extent of the distress suffered by Jews in the war zones of eastern Europe was greater than had been expected; so too was the wave of xenophobia that affected coreligionists on both sides of the lines. The Conjoint Foreign Committee was initially reluctant to petition the British government or its allies on behalf of such specifically Jewish causes as the plight of the Polish community.

> We think it a most inopportune time to take *any* steps, and if any such steps were taken they would probably do more harm than good; that we shall be occupying our time studying the question in case an opportunity arises, & that it is important not in any case to give any grounds for the proposition that the Jew is cosmopolitan & thinks of his own affairs before those of the country to which he owes allegiance.[3]

Similarly unprecedented, in both scope and importance, were the domestic issues which now confronted Anglo-Jewry's political and charitable institutions. Indeed, the longer the war dragged on, the more obvious became the inadequacy of the existing bodies to meet the needs of the times. In part, the deficiencies were functional—a growing discrepancy between the burdens im-

[2] Michael Adler, *British Jewry: Book of Honour* (London, 1922), recorded that 10,000 Jews volunteered and some 40,000 were later conscripted. Anglo-Jewry sustained 8,925 casualties (2,425 of which were fatal), and won five V.C.'s.

[3] 13 November 1914, C. Emanuel to Wolf, London DEPS, General Correspondence, C11/2/5.

posed on the community and its resources for dealing with them. Equally to blame, however, was the inability of the recognized leadership to reorientate its conceptual framework to fit the bewildering range of novel issues raised by the war. Immigration from eastern Europe did sharply decline, and then virtually cease altogether. But the marginal benefit which thereby accrued to the budget of the Board of Guardians, for instance, could not compensate for the larger outlays of money and energy necessitated by the dislocation of trade (especially the tailoring industry in London and Leeds) and the steep rise in the cost of living index. To many of the Board's critics, the provision of fiscal relief to some afflicted Jews and the encouragement given to others to emigrate—piecemeal measures which the Board had favored before the war—seemed trivial responses to a problem that clearly called for an entirely new approach.[4]

Most particularly was this so since most of those who applied for help had in any case undergone an uncomfortable change in status and standing. On the outbreak of war, unnaturalized immigrants were, for the first time, subject to the disturbing experience of police investigation (a haphazard process, it seems, which could lead to some ironic blunders—Lucien Wolf had himself to suffer the "crudely aggressive indignity" of police enquiries into his origins and status).[5] All unnaturalized immigrants were subject to registration: those from Germany and Austria-Hungary were classified as enemy aliens, and their movements were restricted; those from Russia were ultimately considered liable for military service in the Allied cause, even if this meant deportation to the armies of the tsar.

These new regulations necessarily imposed considerable administrative burdens on the Conjoint Foreign Committee, which

---

[4] See, e.g., the complaints voiced at annual meetings of subscribers in 1915 and 1918, London, Jewish Board of Guardians, Minute Book, 5:78-79 and 158-59, and report of meeting of the United Russian Committee, in JC, 14 October 1917, p. 13.

[5] Wolf's irate letters to the commissioner of police, dated 31 August 1914 and 3 September 1914, in New York, YIVO Institute, David Mowshowitch Collection of Lucien Wolf Papers, nos. 4626-7.

took upon itself the task of mediating between the Government and the immigrants. But that body's responsibilities and discomfort were greatly increased by the marked disinclination of Russian Jews either to return to eastern Europe or to enlist in the British army without first being granted British citizenship. Native Jews were now faced with the awkward alternative of either excusing their coreligionists' actions or supporting the popular charge that the Russian Jews were "shirking their duty." Vladimir Jabotinsky (a Zionist already famous for his organization of Jewish self-defense units in Russia) proposed solving the entire problem by creating a specifically Russo-Jewish battalion in Allied service. But this panacea, although favored by some ministers, was not popular among the immigrants and totally unpalatable to most acculturated members of the community. As several of them pointed out to the Government, behind Jabotinsky's scheme lurked the contentious issue of a specifically Jewish nationality, a specter that could call into question the loyalty of avowedly British Jews, too. That a compromise (principally concerning nomenclature) was not patched up until September 1917, after a deputation of "leading" Jews had appealed to the Government, merely underlined the change in priorities forced upon the Anglo-Jewish Establishment.[6] It was all a far cry from the spacious atmosphere of prewar days, when such deputations were usually concerned with nothing more than congratulatory messages to a new monarch or—in the very worst cases—elegant pleas for intervention on behalf of their less fortunate coreligionists in distant lands.

□

Avowed Zionists, of course, did not share their opponents' fears that a specifically Jewish regiment would raise charges of dual loyalty. Nevertheless, it is indicative of the confusion occasioned

---

[6] The unit was ultimately named the "Thirty-eighth Battalion of Royal Fusiliers"; it was awarded its own badge and privileged destination—Palestine. For the deputation of "leading Jews" to Lord Derby, see minutes of War Cabinet meeting of 3 September 1917, London, Public Record Office, War Cabinet Papers, CAB 23/4, no. 227 (1-2), Secret.

by the war that many of their number did initially find themselves agreeing with the argument that Jabotinsky's plans were impolitic. Not until well into 1917, when the imminence of a British offensive in Palestine was confirmed, did they come to terms with the inevitability of Turkish reprisals against the Jewish population there. Until then, however, the English Zionist Federation had been affected by the uncertainty and irresolution that pervaded most other communal institutions. Zionist progress toward the Balfour Declaration was not premeditated at the outbreak of the war. In 1914, in fact, Zionists in England (and elsewhere for that matter) were as unprepared as any other section of the community to respond to the challenges of wartime circumstances. Initially, some of them seem to have been embarrassed by their association with a movement whose leaders and institutions had such strong ties with Germany. On 17 September 1914, for instance, senior Zionists in London unanimously declined to confer with other members of the Greater Actions Committee in Stockholm on the grounds that to do so "would at this juncture be imprudent"; they also "discouraged the meeting of such an institution in present circumstances" and recommended that the seat of the Zionist executive be transferred from Berlin to New York for the duration of the war.[7] It is of course true that Weizmann did immediately predict that "Palestine will fall within the influence of England"; even before the Ottoman Empire entered the war on Germany's side, and without awaiting Asquith's public announcement that the dismemberment of Turkey-in-Asia was at hand, Weizmann had accordingly begun the "reconnoitering work" which was eventually to pay such handsome dividends. Nevertheless, his early political contacts—although brilliantly conceived—must be placed in their properly modest perspective. In 1914 Weizmann's standing, even within the limited circle of avowed Zionists, was not supreme. Although undoubtedly an influential figure in Anglo-Jewish Zionism, he was not yet in command of the policy and activities of the EZF. In part, this was because he was not considered to possess the political contacts within English society

[7] 2 October 1914, L. Kessler to Weizmann, WA, file 176.

necessary to pursue whatever diplomatic efforts might have been contemplated. (Significantly, the first member of the EZF officially to approach the Foreign Office after the outbreak of war was Leopold Greenberg, whose experience in that sort of activity dated back to 1902.)[8] Equally restraining, however, were internecine dissensions of a more traditional kind. The outbreak of war did little to relax tensions between the local Zionist movement and the parent organization; neither did relations improve within the EZF between the London executive and the provincial membership. The arrival in London (in March 1915) of Yeḥiel Tschlenow and Naḥum Sokolow as delegates of the Inner Actions Committee, seems further to have complicated matters. "The two gents from Russia" struck Cowen as "queer fish," with a disagreeable tendency to poach on preserves that the native leadership of the EZF would have liked to regard as their own. "Our affairs aren't too easy sailing," Cowen complained, "& our own people don't make them less easy. How would you like having to work with people who don't want you?"[9]

Weizmann, who was himself a member of the Actions Committee—and a Mancunian, to boot—seems to have felt the difficulties of the situation particularly keenly. As early as September 1914, he had cause to suspect Greenberg of attempting to undermine his standing in Zionist circles and (perhaps with less justification) of deliberately spoiling his efforts to establish a rapport with non-Zionists in the community. With a lack of modesty which, however justified, must have struck his colleagues as decidedly abrasive, Weizmann maintained that he was the Zionist in Britain best qualified to undertake the delicate task of winning the support of members of the British government and of Anglo-Jewry's elite. Ideally, he would have liked to do this sort of work

[8] 10 October 1914; Greenberg to Weizmann, WA, ibid., Isaiah Friedman, *The Question of Palestine, 1914-1918* (London, 1973), p. 335, n. 3, cites evidence to show that Greenberg had been the first Zionist to interest Lloyd George in Zionism in 1906; Martin Gilbert, *Exile and Return* (London, 1978), p. 74, indicates that he had made an official approach to the Foreign Office in 1913; on his earlier work on Herzl's behalf, see above pp. 81-82.

[9] 26 March 1915, Cowen to de Haas, New York, Zionist Organization of America, de Haas Papers, microfilm 1.

alone; he was certainly averse to subordinating himself to the heavy-handed discretion of the veteran leaders of the EZF. Consequently, his relationship with Joseph Cowen too (even though the latter retained the presidency of the EZF until February 1917) was tense; on at least two occasions after 1914 Weizmann threatened to resign from his own position as vice-president.

Gaster, almost inevitably, caused further difficulties. The Ḥakham maintained his running feud with Greenberg and Cowen throughout the war and yet, with an unerring ability to pick a fight, also managed to fall out with Weizmann's staunchest friends in Manchester. Weizmann himself clearly resented Gaster's attempts to embroil him in various "trivial complaints" and "petty intrigues" from which he was determined to keep fastidiously aloof.[10] The estrangement between the two men, already apparent before the outbreak of war, became progressively pronounced. More especially was this so once Weizmann's scientific work on behalf of the Admiralty brought him to London. There, he enjoyed regular contact with his mentor, Aḥad Ha'am, and managed to build up a wider coterie of his own lieutenants who were quite independent of Gaster. Moreover, at the very hub of the country's social and political life, Weizmann was also able to demonstrate his extraordinary facility for winning important friends and influencing the right people. Besides buttressing Weizmann's reputation, these activities further set him apart from Gaster, whose "pontifical airs" and "egotism," by contrast, tended to annoy some prospective gentile collaborators.[11] As early as 1915, the Ḥakham was beginning to complain that Weizmann was keeping him in the dark on the progress of political developments; subsequently, as his diary reveals, he was left to glean information on these matters from such uninformed sources as Samuel Daiches.[12] Al-

[10] 8 February 1915, Weizmann to Gaster, *Letters and Papers of Chaim Weizmann. Series A. Letters* [hereafter *Letters*], 23 vols. general ed. Meyer Weisgal et al. (Oxford, Jerusalem and London 1969-1980), Vol. 7, *August 1914-November 1917*, ed. Leonard Stein (Jerusalem, 1975), pp. 140-42, and Gaster's angry correspondence with Sieff in CZA, Gaster Papers, A203/212.

[11] The Diary of Aaron Aaronson, as cited in Friedman, *The Question of Palestine*, pp. 120 and 336.

[12] Entries for July and August 1916 in CZA, Gaster Papers, A203/146.

though he did host the first, crucial meeting between the Zionists and Sir Mark Sykes on 7 February 1917, Gaster was clearly not in control of events. It was Sokolow (who was far closer to Weizmann) and not the Ḥakham who was sent to Paris "to accompany Sykes on his errand of diplomacy."[13]

Weizmann, however, did not rely entirely upon his diplomatic accomplishments to place himself in charge of Zionist affairs in Great Britain. He had also managed to overhaul the local organization by a series of bureaucratic reforms. Basically, these involved establishing a viable working relationship between various wings of the EZF and its sister and parent organizations. Two important steps, both largely Weizmann's initiatives, were taken in March 1915. One was the formation of a joint negotiating team between the EZF and the Order of Ancient Maccabeans; the other was an agreement defining the respective spheres of influence of that body and the delegates of the Inner Actions Committee.[14] In 1916 all the parties concerned progressed even further, and established yet another forum "in order to direct the Zionist political activities in England." Consisting, initially, of Sokolow, Tschlenow, Weizmann, Bentwich, Cowen, and Gaster (who cantankerously refused to attend its first meeting), the so-called "Political Committee" thereafter functioned in reasonable harmony. But although nominally chaired by Joseph Cowen, it was decidedly under the control of what had by now obviously become Weizmann's own "circle."[15] By 1917, therefore, Weizmann's Manchester friends (who had meanwhile formed their own "British Palestine Committee" for the purpose of undertaking

[13] 7 February 1917, Rothschild to Gaster, ibid., A203/5. The reasons given for the preference for Sokolow were, firstly, that he was a Russian, and could therefore speak for a large proportion of the Jewish people; secondly, "I felt that it might be preferable if our case were put by a layman, to emphasise the fact that the aspirations of the Jewish masses are national as well as religious."

[14] 10 March 1915, Tschlenow and Sokolow to the EZF, CZA, Sokolow Papers, A18/35 and report of the EZF annual conference in JC, 29 January 1915, pp. 12, 23.

[15] At its second meeting, on 21 January 1917, the committee (present were Cowen, J. K. Goldbloom, B. Goldberg, Greenberg, Simon, P. Goodman, Sokolow and Weizmann) expressed its "full confidence" in the latter; minutes of the Political Committee, CZA, P. Goodman Papers, K11/6/1.

"quiet and more or less subterranean propaganda") could see no reason why the Political Committee should not assume the functions of a cabinet of the entire EZF.[16] Thereafter, Weizmann's election as president of the EZF in 1917 was beyond doubt. Moreover, he was in a position to dictate the terms that would enable him to lead an executive of his own choice. In return for allowing his nomination as president to go forward, Weizmann categorically demanded:

> 1) there can be no competition between Cowen and myself; . . . 2) I would like those friends of mine with whom I have been in close cooperation all these years to come on to the Council. I think they are all nominated and probably stand an excellent chance of being elected on their merits, but it would strengthen the position very much indeed if I would feel that their cooperation as members of the Council is assured. The persons I mean are Messrs. Sieff, Marks, Sacher—Manchester: Benas—Liverpool; Leon Simon, Brodetsky, Tolkowsky—London, and of course all our *true* East End friends.[17]

So commanding was Weizmann's position that these demands were unconditionally accepted at the subsequent Annual Conference of the EZF (held in London on 11 February 1917). Furthermore, Weizmann's nominee, Harry Sacher, also defeated Herbert Bentwich in the elections for the position of grand commander of the Order of Ancient Maccabeans the following May. For the first time in the history of the community, Zionist forces in Anglo-Jewry thus seemed to have attained the unity that had eluded them for so long.

THE ZIONISTS AND THE CONJOINT FOREIGN COMMITTEE, 1914-1917

It is indicative of Weizmann's self-confidence (and perhaps a tribute to his skill as well) that his negotiations on behalf of the Zionists with British government officials had not waited upon

[16] Sieff to Weizmann, 4 December 1916 and 14 February 1917, WA, files 205 and 212.
[17] 1 February 1917, Weizmann to H. J. Morgenstern, *Letters*, 7:323-24.

his formal accession to the highest office in either the EZF or the Actions Committee. As early as the winter of 1914-1915, he had begun to approach Herbert Samuel (the president of the Local Government Board), C. P. Scott (editor of the *Manchester Guardian*) and Henry Wickham Steed (editor of the *Times*); through them he also met Lloyd George (then chancellor of the Exchequer), Winston Churchill (first lord of the Admiralty), Arthur Balfour (who succeeded Churchill in May 1915) and Lord Robert Cecil (parliamentary foreign undersecretary, who entered the Cabinet in July of the same year). The extent to which these approaches incited the jealousy of some of Weizmann's Zionist colleagues has already been mentioned. More serious and far more consistent was the dismay that they caused in anti-Zionist circles. The latter were throughout anxious to discredit the impression that Weizmann spoke for the Anglo-Jewish community at large (a mandate that, incidentally, he never claimed). That privilege, as Lucien Wolf pointed out to Foreign Office officials in December 1914, was the exclusive prerogative of the Conjoint Foreign Committee, "the only responsible body duly authorised by the Jewish Community to represent Jewish interests in regard to His Majesty's Government." With the Zionists specifically in mind, Wolf added:

> The Committee think it necessary to emphasize this at the present moment, as they have heard that several persons representing nobody but themselves or certain phantom organisations holding no mandate from the Community at large, have been making representations to the Foreign Office and are likely to make others in connection with the very large questions which may arise out of the war.[18]

At this early stage of the war, the Conjoint Foreign Committee's own attitude toward Palestine was indeterminate. As was the case with so many other issues of communal concern, its members did not immediately appreciate either the implications or the potentialities of the questions with which they were deal-

---

[18] 18 December 1914, Wolf to Sir W. Tyrrell (private secretary to the foreign secretary), DEPS, General Correspondence, C11/2/5.

ing. Unlike Weizmann and Herbert Samuel, whose minds were independently moving on strikingly parallel lines, the Committee appears to have been particularly slow to see the extent to which British Imperial interests might ultimately converge with Zionist ambitions. Thus, the future of Palestine was only briefly touched upon in November 1914, when representatives of the Conjoint Foreign Committee conferred in Paris with leaders of the Alliance Israelite Universelle. Not until March 1915 was Wolf able to define his Committee's exact policy for the benefit of his French counterpart, Jacques Bigart. ("Special facilities for Jewish immigration and colonisation, and for the free development of Jewish institutions and cultural life. We do not contemplate any special political privileges for Jews.")[19] Weizmann, with his neat sense of timing, was eventually to make his opponents pay dearly for the tactical ineptitude of which such tardiness was characteristic. Nevertheless, as even he realized, at the outbreak of war the Conjoint Foreign Committee possessed sufficient prestige to mask its weaknesses. It was up to the Zionists to put out a line to the "big men" of Jewry or, at the very least, "to know what they are doing."[20]

Harry Sacher, accordingly, had made the first move. As early as November 1914 he requested a frank exchange of views with Lucien Wolf, which was followed by further meetings—in two of which Weizmann participated—and by a brisk correspondence. These exchanges did not constitute formal negotiations between the parties; they were rather in the nature of probes designed to enable each side to gauge the other's position and to establish a set of ground rules for later discussions. Nevertheless, some progress was made. Wolf gave the Zionists to understand that the Conjoint Foreign Committee favored a British protectorate over Palestine, and skirted the issue of a specific national status for the Jewish inhabitants of the country. Sacher had been equally vague. He declared himself principally interested in fostering Jewish culture in Palestine; "political demands or a Jewish State I

[19] 2 March 1915, Wolf to Bigart, YIVO, Mowshowitch Collection of Wolf Papers, no. 4648.
[20] 20 November 1914, Weizmann to L. Greenberg, *Letters*, 7:560.

should not raise if we cd. [*sic*] get Jewish unanimity on such a basis as this."[21] Wolf, of course, was not so naive, or so ignorant of Zionist principles to take such statements at their face value. Hence, he persistently demanded evidence that Sacher and his friends could indeed speak for the great body of Zionists. Nevertheless, he did consider the ground sufficiently well prepared for a fruitful meeting of the principals as soon as Sokolow and Tschlenow (who, as members of the Inner Actions Committee, did possess a formal brief) arrived in England. Sacher, for his part, thought it "reasonable, putting one thing and another together, to conclude that it will be less difficult than we had imagined to get the mighty in Israel to help in Palestine—if we can choose a common ground & programme."[22]

The first full-dress conference between the Zionists and representatives of the Conjoint Foreign Committee, held on 14 April 1915, soon shattered this aura of confidence. Tschlenow's opening speech (even when allowances are made for the fact that only Wolf's record of what he actually said seems to have survived) was uncompromising in tone and content. Speaking in German from a prepared text, he caustically underlined the fallacy of placing any trust in civil emancipation as a solution for the Jewish condition in the Diaspora. The "national" traditions of the Jewish people, he stated, had to be developed in their own "metropolis." The representatives of the Conjoint Foreign Committee do not appear to have responded immediately to this onslaught and, apparently, refused to be goaded even by Gaster's provocative assertion that "special rights [for Jews in Palestine] *would* be asked for." Instead, they drew up a memorandum for presentation to the next round of talks on 29 April. This, however, made their views explicit. Jewish nationalism was "reactionary"; it would do nothing to relieve the distress of the vast mass of Jewry; it would endanger all Jews outside Palestine. The Conjoint Foreign Committee, they repeated at the meeting itself, was prepared to help obtain a measure of local Jewish self-government in Palestine,

[21] As reported in 17 November 1914, Sacher to Weizmann, WA, file 177.

[22] 22 November 1914, Sacher to Weizmann, ibid.; for an equally optimistic account see 17 November 1914, Wolf to Zangwill, DEPS, General Correspondence, C11/2/5.

but this depended on the "ad hoc elimination of national and exclusive rights from [the Zionist] programme." Sokolow, characteristically, attempted to keep the discussions going. His official reply (contained in a memorandum dated 21 May 1915) therefore ended on a conciliatory note. Nevertheless, it conceded nothing on the main point. As far as the Zionists were concerned, the fulfilment of the Basle Program remained their primary object and immediate duty.[23]

The manner in which the two sides thereafter presented their separate cases to the Government has been exhaustively documented by, among others, Stein, Vereté, and Friedman.[24] After the breakdown of the April talks, Wolf (who had been in touch with the Foreign Office throughout) began to draw up a formula on Palestine. In response to Government enquiries, he communicated its substance verbally in the winter of 1915-1916; semi-officially in March 1916; and formally in October 1916 and, again, in March 1917. His version ran:

> In the event of Palestine coming within the spheres of influence of Great Britain or France at the close of the War, the Governments of those Powers will not fail to take account of the historic interest that country possesses for the Jewish community. The Jewish population will be secured in the enjoyment of civil and religious liberty, equal political rights with the rest of the population, reasonable facilities for immigration and colonisation, and such municipal privileges in the towns and colonies inhabited by them as may be shown to be necessary.

[23] Tschlenow, Sokolow, Gaster, Cowen and Bentwich attended for the Zionists. The Conjoint Foreign Committee was represented by Alexander, Montefiore, Wolf and H.S.Q. Henriques. The entire exchange reported in Conjoint Foreign Committee Report No. 2 (20 July 1915), YIVO, Mowshowitch Collection of Wolf Papers, nos. 4671-4814. For evidence of Sokolow's conciliatory approach, compare his draft of the reply with those of Gaster and Cowen, in CZA, H. Bentwich Papers, A100/27.

[24] Leonard Stein, *The Balfour Declaration* (London, 1961); Meir Vereté, "The Balfour Declaration and its Makers," *Middle Eastern Studies* 6 (1970): 48-76; Friedman, *The Question of Palestine*; and idem., *Germany, Turkey and Zionism, 1897-1918* (Oxford, 1977).

Meanwhile, Weizmann, too, went his own diplomatic way. He cultivated his existing contacts with individual ministers and canvassed the sympathy of a large number of their strategically placed advisers and associates in Whitehall and Mayfair. He was undoubtedly much better suited for this sort of lobbying than was Wolf. Besides being an Admiralty employee (as bona fide an introduction as any) Weizmann was also, when he put his mind to it, good company. Wolf, more petulant than ever now that his eyesight had begun to deteriorate badly, was not. Indeed, he seems often to have irritated those with whom he came into contact. His position at the Conjoint Foreign Committee—precisely because it necessitated frequent visits to government departments on a variety of domestic and foreign Jewish affairs— might have increased his handicap. Where Weizmann wooed and excited officials with grandiose visions of prophesies fulfilled, Wolf tended to pester and weary them with a mundane catalogue of rights infringed and calumnies revived.

In 1915, nevertheless, the outcome of the tussle between Weizmann and Wolf for the favors of the Government was still uncertain. However considerable Weizmann's charms—for that matter, however fervent Balfour's Gaelic fundamentalism or Lloyd George's Celtic mysticism[25]—the Balfour Declaration was not yet in sight. That document, as is often pointed out, was the result of an uncommonly propitious concurrence of diplomatic and political circumstances which did not begin to take shape until late in 1916. Not until Lloyd George became Prime Minister in December of that year did Zionist sympathizers in the Government obtain commanding executive authority and influence. (Asquith, the previous premier, had adopted a far more sardonic attitude toward Herbert Samuel's suggestion that the Government reflect upon the advantages of Anglo-Zionist cooperation in Palestine.) Only then, similarly, was Sir Mark Sykes appointed assistant secretary to the War Cabinet, in which capacity he was admirably placed to alter the Palestinian clauses of the agreement he had reached with François Georges-Picot (first secretary at the French

---

[25] Christopher Sykes, *Cross Roads to Israel* (London, 1965), chap. 1, stresses this point.

Embassy in London) in January of that year. Not until 1917 did a policy of "forward" operations in the Middle East recover from the disfavor into which it had fallen after the disasters at Gallipoli and Kut, and thus overcome the traditional objections to an extension of Britain's Imperial responsibilities in the area. Finally, and perhaps most important of all, only in 1917 did Zionism assume in British eyes the status of a pressing military necessity. That year opened with the stalling of General Murray's advance at Gaza; there followed yet another round of carnage on the Western Front, mutiny in the French army, revolution at Petrograd, and, once the U-boats had been unleashed, heavy losses to Allied shipping in the Atlantic. The Jews were not responsible for these calamities, but their support might help to offset them. Jewish propaganda on Allied behalf, the official pundits gradually persuaded themselves, could help hasten America's military entry into the war and postpone Russia's exit. Moreover, Jewish intelligence services, such as were provided by the Nili spies, might help Allenby to overcome Turkish resistance in Palestine itself. If, in return for all this, the Jews wanted little more than an official approbation of Zionist ambitions in the Holy Land (such as the Germans were incorrectly rumored to be promising), then the price seemed fairly cheap.

Relations between the Conjoint Foreign Committee and the Zionists (upon which somewhat less attention has been lavished) had begun to deteriorate long before this extraordinary sequence of events had run its full course. Indeed, the "spirit of conciliation and moderation" that had characterized their initial contacts had always been somewhat deceptive. Zionists and anti-Zionists had clashed often enough before the war for each side to regard the other as its adversary by 1914. That was why Aḥad Ha'am, for instance, had always doubted whether any meaningful agreement could emerge from the conversations between Wolf and Sacher. Although regularly consulted on the negotiations, he pointedly refused to take any part in an exchange that he believed could never bridge the gulf between two entirely different outlooks.[26]

[26] 12 January 1915, Aḥad Ha'am to Simon, *Igrot Aḥad Ha'am*, 6 vols., 2nd ed. (Tel Aviv, 1956-1960), 5:313.

Sokolow, who had got to know Wolf during his visit to London in 1913, was altogether more conciliatory. But Wolf himself was soon provoked by the deliberately self-righteous attitude adopted by other Zionists, and it was only by a commendable exercise of self-restraint that he resisted the temptation to reply in kind to Sacher's threatening declaration of "the spirit and purpose with which we approach your friends."[27] Further umbrage was caused by the collapse of the talks on 14 April 1915. Weizmann refused to participate in the second round (held on 29 April), considering the entire charade a waste of time. In the event, he was not displeased to hear that these conversations, too, had borne no fruit. ("Of course they spoke two different languages and arrived at no conclusions.") Only by sacrificing their principles, he feared, could the Zionists ever hope to patch together a compromise with the Conjoint Foreign Committee.[28]

It is indicative of the extent to which individuals on both sides nevertheless continued to entertain hopes of some agreement that the door to further contacts was deliberately left ajar. Wolf, for instance, "noted with pleasure the friendly sentiments with which the discussions with the Zionists had ended"; in March 1916 a majority of the recently constituted Political Committee of the Zionist executive voted to try and resume the discussions. By then, moreover, Herbert Samuel gave Wolf to understand that "when it comes to the point" the Zionists would accept the Conjoint Foreign Committee's formula for Palestine.[29] Both sides, accordingly, accepted James de Rothschild's somewhat prefectorial summons to yet a third meeting at his house in August 1916. But this too was a disaster; it merely emphasized (in Wolf's words) their "vital and irreconcilable differences of principle and

[27] Thus, in reply to Sacher's letter of 1 December 1914 (quoted at length above, pp. 14-15), Wolf merely noted that "much of it, if you will allow me to say so, was quite superfluous." 2 December 1914, to Sacher, DEPS, Zionism, 1914-1916, E3/204(1).

[28] 3 May 1915, Weizmann to Dorothy de Rothschild, *Letters*, 7:196-98.

[29] 7 April 1916, Wolf to Alexander, YIVO, Mowshowitch Collection of Wolf Papers, no. 1773, The Zionist Political Committee, meeting on 23 March 1916, voted by five votes to three to renew discussions; minutes in CZA, P. Goodman Papers, K11/6(1).

method." Wolf pressed the priority of a "liberal" solution to the Russo-Jewish question; he intransigently opposed the grant of special Jewish rights in Palestine and repudiated the existence of a Jewish nationality. Weizmann ignored this invitation to a theoretical discussion, bluntly stating that "there could be no question of dropping Jewish nationality, or even of passing it over in silence." Under these circumstances, the two men did not even begin to work on a joint formula for Palestine (which Baron Edmond de Rothschild, the man who had thought up the meeting, had considered to be the main point of the exercise).[30] Instead, they sparred on the Conjoint Foreign Committee's possible reaction to an independent Zionist approach to the Foreign Office. Later in the autumn, their contacts were reduced to a run of lengthy memoranda which pursued—with considerable ingenuity—the different meanings and scope of the term nationality. A "quibble" was reportedly the term used to describe the exchange by Mrs. James de Rothschild, whose husband and cousin-in-law (Leopold) had the unenviable task of acting as circumlocutory postmen. But both Weizmann and Wolf thought differently. The former refused to compromise his "essential principles"; Wolf informed James that "my friends regard the situation . . . as one of very serious gravity, and I am afraid it will be necessary very soon to declare an end to the negotiations. . . . In that case, the rupture will not be a private one."[31]

Wolf's warning of a public controversy was not occasioned by the latest series of Zionist memoranda. Interesting though they were, they went over ground that had been pretty thoroughly covered before the war. They contained no new Zionist idea, and very little new information concerning Zionist intentions. This is not to imply that they therefore served no useful purpose at all; on the contrary, the exchange did enable the two sides to discover their points of agreement as well as of discord. Some

[30] Wolf's record of his conversations with Baron Edmond in Paris in his "Diary" (1916), pp. 10-13, Jerusalem, Archives of the Israel Historical Society, HM 2765.

[31] 12 December 1916, Wolf to James de Rothschild, YIVO, Mowshowitch Collection of Wolf Papers, no. 7868. The run of memoranda in ibid., nos. 5724-61.

sort of accord, indeed, was possible. Left to themselves, Wolf and Sokolow might even now have found the way to a standoff arrangement, which would have distinguished between the nationality of Jews in Palestine and the status of those who chose to remain in the Diaspora. Significantly, both men wished to continue negotiations even after the fiasco at James de Rothschild's house. Their motives were not altogether complementary: Wolf clearly thought it politic to remain on good terms with the Rothschilds; Sokolow wished to keep tabs on the progress of Wolf's negotiations with the Foreign Office.[32] Nevertheless, a sincere desire to bring the parties closer together also seems to have played a part. By November 1916 Wolf and Sokolow had achieved "an appreciable approximation" of views which gave both reason to think that agreement was at hand. Whether or not a Jewish nationality existed admittedly remained a crucial bone of contention; so too did the possibility that Jews in Palestine might be granted a privileged status vis-à-vis the non-Jewish population. But, as Friedman points out, "a working compromise was not beyond reach. . . . On practical matters the differences were only of emphasis and degree." In January 1917 Wolf was to speak to Balfour in terms which suggested that the gap between his formula and that ultimately obtained by the Zionists was not very wide.[33]

By then, however, the acrimony between the Zionists and the Conjoint Foreign Committee appears to have attained a momentum of its own. Their attitude toward each other, which had always been predicated on suspicion, was between the summer of 1916 and the spring of 1917 embittered by outright—and mutual—animosity. The occasion of the explosion, and of Wolf's warning to Rothschild of a public controversy, was the publication of *Zionism and the Jewish Future* in July 1916. This medium-sized volume (234 pages; edited by Harry Sacher and partly financed by Edmond de Rothschild) was by and large an innocuous collage.

[32] 30 September 1916, minutes of Political Committee, CZA, P. Goodman Papers, K11/6(i) and 11 October 1916, Wolf to Leopold de Rothschild, YIVO, Mowshowitch Collection of Wolf Papers, no. 7869.

[33] Friedman, *The Question of Palestine*, p. 230.

Many of its articles added little to what could have been garnered from a close reading of the lengthy reports presented to prewar Zionist Congresses ("The Jews and the Economic Development of Palestine" by Samuel Tolkowsky; "Cultural Work in Palestine" by Selig Brodetsky; "The Meaning of a Hebrew University" by Bertram Benas; and "The Hebrew Revival" by Leon Simon). Only marginally more rigorous were its various synoptic pieces ("A Century of Jewish History" by Harry Sacher; "Anti-Semitism" by Albert Hyamson; and "The Future of Palestine" by Norman Bentwich). Its theoretical essays, however, were—for an English audience—both novel and pugnacious. Weizmann ("Zionism and the Jewish Problem") insisted that even the emancipated Jew was, and must always be, an alien in the land in which he dwelt; his efforts to assimilate himself to his surroundings "deceives nobody but himself." Gaster ("Judaism—a National Religion") was even more provocative. "The claim to be Englishmen of the Jewish persuasion—that is English by nationality and Jewish by faith—is an absolute self-delusion."[34] These were doctrines which, as he informed James de Rothschild, Wolf had "spent the larger part of my life in combatting." The fact that they had been allowed to appear in print at the very moment when the Conjoint Foreign Committee and the Zionists were ostensibly negotiating was tantamount to an insult that Wolf and his associates could not ignore. Claude Montefiore, by now convinced that Zionists "want to make all Gentiles anti-Semites," had already decided to pick up the gauntlet.

> I think the Conjoint will sooner or later have to consider whether we are to sit silent at the awful things which the Zionists print. That Sacher book is *too* bad. . . . Are we to allow our whole position and the whole case of emancipation to be ruined & given away?[35]

[34] Compare with earlier Zionist statements: "The individual Jew is no doubt 'at home' in those countries which tolerate Jews and allow them the right of citizenship." Leon Simon, *Zionism and the Jewish Problem* (London, 1915), reprinted in Leon Simon, *Studies in Jewish Nationalism* (London, 1920), p. 44.

[35] 11 July 1916, Montefiore to Wolf, DEPS, General Correspondence, C11/2/3/9; as early as March 1915, when Sacher first projected his book, Sir Philip Magnus

The controversy that followed was entirely different in character and content from the earlier negotiations. Indeed, it was largely the tone of the exchange that finally dissipated the hope of any productive dialogue between the parties. In private, charges of conceit and deception sped back and forth; the Zionists sharpened their caricatures of the Conjoint Foreign Committee as Establishment toadies; Montefiore and Wolf responded that the Zionists were a pack of uncouth louts, whose lack of manners could probably be attributed to the fact that "they are all foreign Jews, bearing no quality to speak for the native Jews of the United Kingdom with whom, for the most part, they do not cooperate in the affairs of the community."[36] More serious, and only slightly more restrained, was the public row that erupted. Encouraged by Montefiore and goaded by Sacher, Wolf was determined to broadcast the anti-Zionist point of view to as wide an audience as possible. As an "opening step" he approached William Courtney, editor of the *Fortnightly Review*, who—after some difficulty—was persuaded to accept for publication a hostile tract that Montefiore had written in June. Entitled "Zionism," and attributed anonymously to "An Englishman of the Jewish Faith," the article appeared on 1 November 1916. An immediate storm was provoked by its claim that Jewish nationalism was "a very dangerous movement . . . which, unless checked, may hinder [Jewish] emancipation in countries where this emancipation is yet to seek, and even imperil its continuance . . . in countries where that emancipation has already been attained."[37] Charging that such state-

---

had warned: "It will add to the Anti-Semitism in this country and can do no good to the cause you have in view. . . . I assure you it sickens me to feel that at the present time when England and her allies are engaged in the greatest struggle the world has ever known for the victory of *ideals* which Jews and Christians equally prize, to find Jews agitating for what they consider their own special interests." 23 March 1915, letter to Simon, WA, file 182.

[36] 10 November 1916, Wolf to Zangwill, DEPS, Zionism 1914-1916, E3/204(3); compare with an earlier letter in which Wolf had agreed with Zangwill about the German preponderance in the Zionist leadership "though perhaps it is not wise to press the point"; 28 July 1915, CZA, Zangwill Papers, A120/49.

[37] "Zionism," *Fortnightly Review* 100 (November 1916):820. Wolf's negotiations with Courtney lasted throughout the late summer and autumn of 1916; see DEPS, General Correspondence, C11/2/9.

ments were "wicked and malicious," the *Jewish Chronicle* ran a series of counterattacks throughout the entire month of November until, in the December issue of the *Fortnightly Review*, fuller replies appeared from Herbert Bentwich and Chief Rabbi Hertz. (The latter, however, characteristically concluded: "It is not my intention or my desire to defend Zionism.") Nevertheless, Wolf refused to retract; instead he reiterated his well-known views in the April 1917 issue of the *Edinburgh Review* which carried his piece on "The Jewish National Movement." Individual members and supporters of the Conjoint Foreign Committee had this article reprinted and distributed as part of a series to which Claude Montefiore and Sir Philip Magnus also contributed. But this, in turn, prompted retorts from the Zionists: Leon Simon's *The Case of the Anti-Zionists: A Reply* and Harry Sacher's *Jewish Emancipation: The Contract Myth.*

While thus breaking the conventionally restrained bounds of intra-Jewish debate, both sides also hardened their respective bargaining positions. When further negotiations were resumed in March 1917, Sokolow demanded unconditional recognition of the Basle Program, and Wolf its prior retraction.[38] Sokolow must have known that he was on stronger ground. In February the Zionists had had their crucial meeting with Sykes at Gaster's house. With official connivance, Sokolow had then begun to lobby for French and Italian assurances to the Zionists. Wolf did not suspect the extent of the collusion between Sykes and Sokolow, still less that Jules Cambon (the French minister for foreign affairs) would soon be prepared to issue a statement that in many respects was an indispensable precondition to the Balfour Declaration. But, through his contacts at the Alliance Israelite Universelle, Wolf did learn enough to realize that something

[38] 15 March 1917, Sokolow to Wolf, and 26 March 1917, Wolf to Sokolow, YIVO, Mowshowitch Collection of Wolf Papers, nos. 5801-5804. It is an indication of the shift in the balance of power between the Zionists and the Conjoint that it was the latter who initiated the new round of correspondence; it is also indicative of Sokolow's tact that he pressed his own colleagues to give the approach due consideration. See, e.g., 9 March 1917, Sokolow to Gaster, CZA, Gaster Papers, A203/131.

serious was afoot.[39] The suddenly suspicious reticence of the Zionists to renew negotiations contributed to his nervousness; so too did repeated warnings from the Foreign Office that "there should be no public polemic"—an admonition that totally ignored the ongoing pamphlet campaign and that struck Wolf as an unusual instance of official interference in a matter of internal Jewish concern. Silence, especially at a time when the Conjoint's "constituents" (so Wolf claimed) were "clamouring" for information, would leave the Zionists in command of the field.

> We were apparently being kept in the dark as what was taking place . . . we were all much disturbed at the probability of some transaction with the Zionists which would be extremely detrimental to the general interest of the Jewish community. . . . We had been astonished to discover that the Zionists had . . . been trying to place us in the presence of a *fait accompli*.[40]

Wolf thought the air could best be cleared by the publication of the entire correspondence with the Zionists (supplemented by a written official assurance that the Government would take no action on Palestine without consulting the Conjoint Foreign Committee). Others, however, were less sanguine. Leopold de Rothschild and Lord Swaythling had since early April 1917 been "clamouring" for a manifesto by the leading British Jews in the community repudiating and reprobating the bad influence of the Zionists.[41] Claude Montefiore, after a frustrating conversation with Lord Milner on 16 May, was equally convinced of the need for drastic action. Milner had trotted out standard Zionist replies

[39] 16 April 1917, Bigart to Wolf, informing him "in strict confidence" of Sokolow's contacts with the French government and enclosing a purported memorandum of Zionist contacts with HMG; YIVO, Mowshowitch Collection of Wolf Papers, no. 5948.

[40] 1 May 1917, Wolf's memorandum of a telephone conversation with L. Oliphant of the F.O. in DEPS, Correspondence on Palestine 1916-1920, C11/12/54, file 2. Wolf, it seems, had been mollified by the Government's assurance to act "with a due regard to the wishes and opinions of all . . . sections" of Anglo-Jewry. 27 April 1917, R. Graham to Wolf, ibid.

[41] 9 April 1917, Wolf to Montefiore, YIVO, Mowshowitch Collection of Wolf Papers, no. 2981.

to most of Montefiore's objections to the establishment of Jewish political autonomy in Palestine; other problems, he had re-marked, "could be left to settle" themselves. Altogether, recorded Montefiore with obvious alarm, "he clearly thought that, in our dislike of Zionism, we greatly exaggerated its importance and dangers."[42]

Thereafter, an explosion could hardly have been avoided. Montefiore summoned a meeting of the Conjoint Foreign Com-mittee for the following day (the 17th); the fifteen members present (out of twenty-one) were asked to approve a "Statement on Palestine" which had clearly been prepared in advance. Twelve did so; two dissented: Joseph Prag, whose past services in the cause of the Chovevei Zion Association seem at the crucial mo-ment to have overcome his more recent sense of loyalty to Claude Montefiore; and Elkan Adler (the late Chief Rabbi's half-brother and a noted bibliophile and Semitic scholar), who had long main-tained unofficial contact with several Zionist groups and person-alities.[43] These were defections that the presidents of the Conjoint Foreign Committee tried, unsuccessfully, to overcome by some textual emendations to their statement.[44] More damage was caused by the opposition of Chief Rabbi Hertz "who was present by invitation but without a vote." Having said his piece, Hertz walked out of the meeting and informed Leopold Greenberg of what had transpired. That weekend, Hertz and Greenberg im-plored Wolf to reconsider, but in so doing they merely increased the chances of a split. Wolf was now afraid that the Zionists would "betray" the secret of the Conjoint's decision; conse-quently, he also disregarded his own promise to show the Foreign

[42] Montefiore's memorandum of the interview in CZA, papers relating to the Balfour Declaration, K11/46, no. 171.

[43] Thus, Adler had addressed Zionist cultural groups in London, Manchester, and Liverpool before the war (New York, Jewish Theological Seminary, E. Adler Papers, boxes 7 and 10); and had some correspondence with Weizmann in 1910 and Sokolow in 1915 (boxes 12 and 11). Nevertheless, he had refused membership of the EZF "as I am not a Zionist nor an adherent of Zionism," 19 January 1909, to M. Rosenberg, CZA, H. Rosenberg Papers, A150/104.

[44] 18 May 1917, Wolf to Adler, private, Jewish Theological Seminary, E. Adler Papers, box 12; and Adler's letter of resignation, 24 May 1917, ibid., box 3.

Office a copy of the manifesto prior to its publication. Lord Cecil's request to be consulted arrived too late. The statement appeared in the *Times* on 24 May.[45]

□

Entitled "Palestine and Zionism—Views of Anglo-Jewry," the document can be regarded as a *locus classicus* of its own brand of anti-Zionism. As such, it deserves to be bracketed with the resolutions passed at the Central Conference of American Rabbis in July 1897 and the statements published and promoted by the *Antizionistiches Komitee* in Germany between 1912 and 1914. The Conjoint's manifesto opened with a preliminary bow to Allenby's current campaign in the Middle East, and closed with a perfunctory offer "to co-operate in securing for the Zionist organisation the united support of Jewry." The intervening matter, however, constituted a sustained and "earnest" (a recurring word) attack on Zionism in the best tradition of the Reform school of thought. The Jews, claimed the signatories, were not "a homeless nationality"; indeed, in no political sense could they be described as a nationality at all. They had "no separate national aspirations"; as members of nothing more distinct than a "religious community . . . they hold Judaism to be a religious system" and maintain that "as citizens of the country in which they live, they are fully and sincerely identified with the national spirit and interests of those countries." To establish a Jewish nationality in Palestine, the manifesto claimed, would stamp Jews everywhere "as strangers in their native lands"; it would also hopelessly compromise their demands for equal rights elsewhere, and would inevitably give rise to bitter feuds with the members of other races and religions who constituted the majority of the Palestinian population. "A competition"—conceived in the best liberal traditions of fair play and equal opportunity—was all the Jews should seek.

[45] Conjoint Report for period 17 May 1917 to 15 July 1917 (entitled "A Breach of Confidence"), YIVO, Mowshowitch Collection of Wolf Papers, nos. 6039-6051.

Quite properly, the appearance of the Conjoint Foreign Committee's manifesto became a communal *cause célèbre*. It provoked angry and immediate responses in the *Times* from Lord Walter Rothschild, Chaim Weizmann, and Chief Rabbi Hertz, to which the Conjoint responded with a canvassed letter of accord from an impressively prestigious roll of its own supporters.[46] An unprecedented element of bitterness was thus injected into communal life. By June 1917, Anglo-Jewry appeared to have become polarized as never before. Several congregations were called to extraordinary meetings of members in order to discuss the manifesto; so too were members of the B'nai B'rith and the United Council of Jewish Friendly Societies.[47] The Committee's unrepentant defense of its actions incited further outbursts. The Zionists, of course, were furious: Weizmann brusquely rejected the Conjoint Foreign Committee's belated and indirect offer of further negotiations; Gaster introduced a motion condemning the manifesto at the Anglo-Jewish Association. Out of personal respect for Montefiore, he later withdrew, but then did much to encourage the presentation of a similarly worded condemnation at the Board of Deputies on 17 June.[48] After a long, tense, and often unpleasant debate (after which two divisions were called), a majority of deputies expressed their "profound disapproval of the views of the Conjoint Foreign Committee," and called upon the Board's representatives to resign their offices "forthwith." Without hesitation, they did so.

[46] On 29 May 1917 Alexander and Montefiore had asked their supporters to telegraph their agreement to the letter which was published in the *Times* on 1 June, DEPS, Correspondence on Palestine 1916-1920, C11/12/54. file 5.

[47] See, e.g., the list of synagogue meetings in Naḥum Sokolow, *History of Zionism, 1600-1918*, 2 vols. (London, 1919), 2:65-66.

[48] 1 June 1917, Weizmann to H. Lewis, *Letters*, 7:422-24, and Stein, *The Balfour Declaration*, p. 458.

PART FOUR

Zionism and the Politics of
Anglo-Jewry, 1914-1920

7

Anglo-Jewry and Zionism, 1914-1917

THE CENSURE OF THE CON-joint Foreign Committee's manifesto by the Board of Deputies has been treated as a milestone in the history of Anglo-Jewish Zionism—perhaps the only such milestone of the community's own making. Admittedly, the victory then attained by the critics of the committee was not decisive; in fact, they only just scraped home by fifty-six votes to fifty-one, with six abstentions. Nevertheless, the result altered the delicate balance of the triangular relationship among the British government, the Zionists, and the anti-Zionists. Hitherto the latter (as represented by the Conjoint Foreign Committee) had negotiated with the Government from an assumed position of strength. Their opposition to the designation of Palestine as the national home of the Jews, they had been able to claim, represented the views of the main body of Anglo-Jewry; the Zionists wielded no comparable influence. That position became untenable once the community's so-called parliament had apparently voted otherwise. Henceforth, Weizmann could claim supremacy in this particular field. It was futile for Lucien Wolf to point out that the warring parties were "evenly balanced" at the Board of Deputies and that a similar motion of censure against the manifesto had not been supported at an earlier meeting of the AJA.[1] Special pleading of that sort cut no ice at all in official circles. On the contrary, now that the Board of

[1] 18 June 1917, Wolf to L. Oliphant, London, Public Record Office, Foreign Office Files, Turkey (War), 1917, FO 371/3053, no. 121745. For the meeting of the AJA Council on 3 June 1917, see London, Mocatta Library, University College, Archives of the AJA, Council Minute Book, 4:140-41.

Deputies had spoken the Government felt itself to be relieved of any prior commitments it had made to the anti-Zionists. As one Foreign Office clerk frankly minuted on the morrow of the debate: "This vote means the dissolution of the Conjoint Committee and it will no longer be necessary to consult that body." Instead, the Government could move deliberately, albeit cautiously, toward an even closer association with Weizmann and in the direction of the Balfour Declaration. Significantly, it was only two days after the vote that the foreign secretary himself asked Rothschild and Weizmann to submit a "formula" on Palestine for his consideration.[2]

It is understandable that Zionist historiography has tended to invest the proceedings at the Board of Deputies with momentous importance. Retrospective panegyrics, however, have not been limited to the diplomatic implications of the vote of 17 June and of the opportunities that it gave Weizmann to press home his advantage at the Foreign Office. Equal emphasis has been placed on a somewhat different, although related, aspect of the episode—the meaning of the vote at the Board of Deputies in terms of internal Jewish communal politics. This was the feature that apparently exercised the greatest immediate impact on contemporaries. "Ending a System" was the snap judgment of the *Jewish Chronicle* and the *Jewish World*; a "Breach in the Bastille" that of *Di Tsayt*, each of which newspapers devoted entire pages of report to the debate and several succeeding issues to joyful comment on its importance and implications.[3] The EZF despatch to the Copenhagen bureau, although deliberately more matter-of-fact in tone, was unmistakably tinged with enthusiasm. "This resolution is a significant turning point in the history of the Jews

---

[2] Minute by R. Graham, in Foreign Office Files, FO 371/3053, no. 121745; see also Isaiah Friedman, *The Question of Palestine, 1914-1918* (London, 1973), pp. 244-58.

[3] To which might be added the *Zionist Review* 1 (July 1917):37. The vote "means the destruction of a regime, the oligarchic system which enabled a handful of self-elected persons to arrogate to themselves the name of Anglo-Jewry." But note the more laconic account presented in the *Times* of 18 June 1917, and blandly entitled "Zionist Controversy."

in England," ran the official telegram. Gone were the days when
Zionism could be dismissed with benign condescension. Adherents of the movement now seemed to constitute the majority of
the community.[4]

This "radical" interpretation of the vote at the Board of Deputies has entered the realm of Anglo-Jewish folklore. In the standard version, the rejection of the Conjoint Foreign Committee's
manifesto wrought a fundamental revolution in Anglo-Jewish politics. It did not merely reflect a change of heart on the part of
the hundred or so individuals who sat on the Board, although
that in itself was a substantial achievement. More significantly,
the vote represented a decisive stage in the Zionist campaign to
win the community away from the control of the antinationalist
plutocracy. Indeed, after 1917 the entire leadership of the community is said to have been "radically altered." This was as much
a matter of tone as of personnel. "The spirit that henceforth
animated the Board," runs the most recent and fullest account,
"marked a definite break with the past."[5] Ultimately, the censure
of the manifesto seemed also to open the floodgates elsewhere
too. After the vote at the Board, increasing numbers of pro-
Zionist resolutions were passed (often without demur) in a large
number of communal bodies and in congregations affiliated to
the United Synagogue and the Federation of Synagogues. Without the support of these institutions, the Zionists might have

---

[4] 18 June 1917, Boris Goldberg telegram to Copenhagen in CZA, Files of the
Central Zionist Office (Berlin), Z3/648. See also 21 June 1917, Weizmann to
Raffalovich, *Letters and Papers of Chaim Weizmann. Series A. Letters* [hereafter
Letters], 23 vols., general ed. Meyer Weisgal et al. (Oxford, Jerusalem and London,
1969-1980), Vol. 7, *August 1914-November 1917*, ed. Leonard Stein (Jerusalem,
1975), p. 448.

[5] E.g., Friedman, *Question of Palestine*, pp. 239-40; Naḥum Sokolow, *History
of Zionism, 1600-1918*, 2 vols. (London, 1919), 2:69; Israel Cohen, "British
Jewry's Reaction," in *The Jewish National Home*, ed. Paul Goodman (London,
1943), p. 43; "Board of Deputies of British Jews," in *Encyclopaedia of Zionism and
Israel*, ed. Raphael Patai, 2 vols. (New York, 1971), 1:147; and (citing Leonard
Stein's *The Balfour Declaration* [London, 1961]), Chaim Bermant, *The Cousinhood*
(London, 1971), p. 261, Walter Laqueur, *A History of Zionism* (London, 1972),
p. 194. Stein himself, however, was more judicious (pp. 567-68).

found it difficult to lobby the Great Powers, and the British government in particular, as hard as they did in later decades.

As other such Whig interpretations of history are, this view of the significance of the proceedings at the Board in June 1917 is too tendencious. Open to criticisms of both substance and detail, it must be placed in a somewhat less climactic perspective. Principally, and most obviously, this is because the vote did not suddenly put an end to the long period of communal strife on the merits of Zionism. On the contrary, to some extent the vote at the Board merely emphasized and deepened the divisions within Anglo-Jewry on the subject. Instead of retracting their anti-Zionist statements, convinced supporters of the manifesto reiterated their views; confronted with the *fait accompli* of the Balfour Declaration in November 1917, they then founded the League of British Jews with the express object of ensuring that their viewpoint would be brought to public attention. It is therefore fallacious to assert that, by their victory at the Board of Deputies, the Zionists conquered the community in one fell swoop. All claims that they did so telescope a fairly protracted process. For one thing, intense debates on Palestine were still held at the Board itself as late as 1943; for another, comparatively few of those deputies who voted to condemn the Conjoint Foreign Committee's manifesto in June 1917 agreed to become members of the Zionist movement thereafter. Instead, some pointedly cautioned the Zionists not to put too biased an interpretation on their votes. Simon Rowson, who had himself sided with the majority against the manifesto, was perhaps the most explicit. The vote, he claimed, was a victory for the contention that the members of the Board had a right to be consulted by their leaders, and thus also a victory for communal democracy. "I sincerely hope," he commented, "the decision will not be strained to represent support for the principles of the Zionist Organisation."[6]

[6] Letter to the JC, 22 June 1917, pp. 21-22. As late as 1922 Rowson described himself as, at best, "lukewarm" in his attitude toward Zionism and therefore refused to take an active part in the movement's campaign during the parliamentary elections of that year. 16 February 1922, Rowson to P. Goodman, CZA, Files of the Central Zionist Office (London), Z4/1845 (1).

(246)

Paradoxically, perhaps, the standard Zionist interpretation of the vote would be easier to accept had the censure of the Conjoint's policy been less unexpected, in the sense of being the undisputed result of a steady growth of pro-Zionist sympathy at the Board. Such evidence, however, is hard to find. A hard core of about a dozen Zionist sympathizers did sit on the Board as deputies for individual synagogues; some of them were duly vociferous. But their weight has to be offset by other (and larger) interest groups, such as those deputies who were members of the B'nai B'rith, the United Council of Jewish Friendly Societies (which was officially neutral in matters Zionist), and the members of the Conjoint Foreign Committee itself. That was why two earlier avowedly "Zionist" resolutions, tabled at the Board as recently as October 1916 and May 1917, had been easily defeated.[7] Those results had emphasized that most deputies were non-Zionists, perhaps even anti-Zionists. It is clear that without the support of a substantial contingent of previously unsympathetic deputies, the June 1917 motion of censure against the Conjoint Committee's manifesto on Palestine would never have been passed. The undisguised surprise with which Zionist leaders themselves greeted the result suggests that their "victory" was not a well-planned move.[8] In fact, most members of the EZF did not foresee the eventual alignment at the Board; neither could those Zionists who were themselves deputies claim sole responsibility for bringing it about.

[7] Indeed, in October 1916 Sidney Newman (deputy for Stamford Hill) had been forced to withdraw altogether his motion that "the Conjoint Committee be urged to use its best endeavours towards the acquisition of Palestine as an internationally and legally safeguarded home for the Jews after the War." In May 1917, the Board of Deputies rejected (by thirty-three votes to twenty-six) Rabbi Dr. Samuel Daiches's motion that: "The President convene a Special Meeting of Deputies for the purpose of considering the issuing of a declaration to the effect that the British Jews hope that the historical claims of the Jewish people on their ancient homeland will be recognised and that Palestine will be made a Jewish Centre." See reports in JC, 27 October 1916, pp. 16, 17 and 25 May 1917, pp. 11-12.

[8] 17 June 1917, Walter Rothschild to Weizmann, telegram, WA, file 230.

(247)

COMMUNAL STATUS AND COMMUNAL STRATEGY

Several alternative explanations might be advanced to account for the vote of 17 June 1917. One, first suggested by Naḥum Sokolow, is that the result obtained on that day represented a response on the part of most deputies to popular pressure. The publication of the manifesto, he notes, aroused considerable resentment throughout the community; extraordinary meetings of protest were convened at several of the provincial and metropolitan congregations represented at the Board.[9] These manifestations of popular feeling, he implies, were neither unprecedented nor unexpected; they were merely a dramatic outpouring of emotions that had long sought suitable expression. Sokolow's claims are not entirely unfounded. Attacks on the Conjoint Foreign Committee, and on every other established communal body, had undoubtedly been increasing in ferocity and frequency throughout the war. With the growing urgency and magnitude of several problems of Jewish concern (of which the future of Palestine was certainly one), the native and immigrant Anglo-Jewish press had launched what amounted to a campaign of criticism against the native community's handling of foreign and domestic affairs. The press was seconded by a spate of public meetings held in the immigrant quarters of London and the larger provincial centers of Jewish population. In each case, comment had been unfavorable and scrutiny censorious, to the extent that new organizations (bearing such high-sounding titles as the "Jewish Workers' Relief Emergency Fund," or the "National Union for Jewish Rights") had been founded in immigrant quarters, with the purpose of virtually taking over the functions of the Conjoint Foreign Committee itself. The damaging import of these proceedings was not, of course, lost on the members of the Anglo-Jewish Establishment and their associates. As early as October 1915, for instance,

---

[9] Sokolow, *History of Zionism*, 2:65-66; for a somewhat different list see reports in JC, 8 June 1917, pp. 20-21; 15 June 1917, p. 10; and 22 June 1917, pp. 19-20. For specific descriptions of local feeling in Manchester and Glasgow see June 1917, Marks to Weizmann, CZA, S. Marks Papers, A247/18; and 19 June 1917, S. Grasse to Gaster, CZA, Gaster Papers, A203/53, respectively.

Lucien Wolf had been warned that "by not getting the East End elements into your Committee, you encourage them to their unorganised activities."[10] In partial response to such pressure, the United Council of Jewish Friendly Societies and the executive of the National Union for Jewish Rights were in 1916 invited to appoint to their own representatives to the Conjoint.[11] That these condescending palliatives did not avert criticisms of the Board cannot be attributed simply to the fact that they were not considered generous enough (although that, too, was true). Far more crucial, Sokolow suggests, were undercurrents of a specifically ideological kind. So compelling was the Zionist cause, and so overwhelming the popular support that the movement could arouse, that the ultimate demise of the anti-Zionists on the Conjoint Foreign Committee was inevitable. Those deputies who voted to condemn the manifesto merely acknowledged the fact.

□

This analysis of events rests upon two assumptions. One is that the Board of Deputies (as constituted in 1917) was sufficiently sensitive to such public opinion as was expressed in mass meetings or newspaper comment to be converted from its previous stand of antagonism to political Zionism. The other is that the Zionists (as officially represented by the EZF) were responsible for whatever agitation can be discerned and that they were its principle, if not the sole, beneficiaries. On both counts the evidence is unconvincing. Allegedly "popular" resentment against the publication of the manifesto was not universal, and comparatively few deputies seem to have been susceptible to such as there was on this issue.[12] Furthermore, and more crucially, the leaders of

[10] 6 October 1915, Zangwill to Wolf, New York YIVO Institute, Mowshowitch Collection of Lucien Wolf Papers, file 211; Wolf had for some months been considering something of the same kind; see his letter to Alexander of 8 June 1915, in London, DEPS, General Correspondence, C/11/2/11.

[11] Report of meeting of the Conjoint Foreign Committee on 17 May 1916, in DEPS, Conjoint Foreign Committee, 1916, A3/1; see also below, pp. 268-69.

[12] Thus, several of the deputies who had voted in defense of the manifesto, despite the expressed wishes of their constituents, were nevertheless returned

the EZF were not in any position to pose as the celebrants of a communal consensus as far as Zionism was concerned. The outbreak of war had not brought about an immediate and dramatic influx to the ranks of organized Zionism in Britain. National Jewish feeling of a sort did, undoubtedly, run high at various times between 1914 and 1917, but the occasions on which the EZF could mobilize all the urgent clamor for their own purposes were few and far between.[13] Far more significant were the numerical gains recorded by other and newer bodies of protest, reform, and Jewish defense (the nomenclature, and doubtless much of the membership too, was interchangeable), especially since these did not formally adhere to the tenets of political Zionism and were not willing to work in conjunction with the EZF. Thus, despite several direct and indirect approaches, accredited representatives of the EZF failed to establish a productive working relationship with the United Council of Jewish Friendly Societies (whose membership exceeded 31,000 and whose annual budget was over 80,000 pounds) which had been established under the honorary presidency of Sir Stuart Samuel in the spring of 1915.[14] More discreet attempts to secure the backing of Jewish socialist groups and trade unions (with a combined membership in the region of 6,000 males) for a program of Jewish nationalism seem to have produced equally disappointing results. A "Workers'

---

when they stood for reelection to the Board of Deputies in 1919; others, who complied with such wishes and voted to condemn the manifesto, were not returned in 1919. See my article, "The Conquest of a Community? The Zionists and the Board of Deputies in 1917," *Jewish Journal of Sociology* 19 (December 1977):172-73.

[13] Not untypical is the prominence given in the *Encyclopedia Judaica*, 16 vols. (Jerusalem, 1971), 16, col. 1117, to the petition, reportedly signed by 77,000 adults in 1915, advocating "the establishment of a publicly recognised and legally secured Home for the Jewish People in Palestine." That was undoubtedly a considerable achievement, but the effort was never repeated nor was the momentum sustained.

[14] Friendly Society statistics in *JC*, 17 December 1915, p. 26; the upwardly mobile composition of their membership in *Jewish Guardian*, 27 August and 3 September 1920. On EZF attempts to secure their backing, *JC*, 14 January 1916, p. 16; 11 February 1916, p. 21; 18 February 1916, pp. 14-17; and 26 May 1916, p. 18.

League for Jewish Emancipation," founded early in the war at
the instigation of adherents of the Poalei Zion, was soon disbanded for lack of support; successive conferences of Jewish trade
unions, held in Manchester in 1915 and 1916, rejected all motions advocating the establishment of a National Home in Palestine (their only concession was a vague resolution advocating
the colonization of the country); and the entire strength of all
Poalei Zion societies in Britain at one point dwindled to a membership of merely 700 stalwarts.[15]

To some extent, the absence of popular support for the EZF
and its affiliated bodies can be attributed to factors that were older
than the war. Long before 1914, it will be recalled, the public
image presented by official Zionism in Britain had been severely
tarnished by perenniel displays of internecine strife and by the
apparent bankruptcy of its ideology. Moreover, the "West End"
leaders of the movement had not scored a single diplomatic success that might have excused, let alone justified, the persistence
of their high-handed attitude toward their potential following
among the immigrants. These deficiencies were not substantially
repaired during the first three years of war. Then, as before, the
EZF presented a picture of organizational disarray and doctrinal
flabbiness; and in both respects it suffered from a comparison with
such equally small, but more robust, advocates of social and political reform as the Jewish Social Democratic Organisation. As
even the EZF's own supporters and members admitted, throughout
the first half of the war the local Zionist movement suffered from
a debilitating absence of an attractive program capable of evoking
a responsive chord among the majority of Anglo-Jewry. Public
enthusiasm, it was remarked, could not be aroused simply by the
ritual repetition of the hope that "next year" Jewry would somehow find its way to Jerusalem. Neither could existing sympathy

[15] Reports on the fate and fortunes of the P.Z. during the war, dated 6 December
1917, and 28 January 1918, in CZA, Files of the Central Zionist Office (London),
Z4/674; see also M. Myer's articles in *Di Tsayt*, 2, 3, 4, and 23 May and 2 June
1916. The situation very much improved later in 1917, after the Labour Party's
resolutions sympathetic to Zionism, see Friedman, *Question of Palestine*, pp. 254-
55.

for the plight of the Palestinian *yishuv* be effectively tapped by carefully worded appeals for warm clothing. Most immigrant Jews (according to the Yiddish press), desperately wondered what sort of future awaited their friends and relations in Central and eastern Europe; their principal emotional need was for a decisive program of action which might infuse a gleam of practical hope into their otherwise despondent lives.[16] Leaders of British Zionism appeared incapable of satisfying these requirements and aspirations (unlike their colleagues in the United States and even in Austria, it was reported), least of all by their repeated appeals for the support of the immigrants' religious guides or left-wing mentors. Indeed, the very frequency of such approaches seemed to indicate the extent of the EZF's own weakness. Many rabbis, as has been seen, continued to harbor doubts concerning the propriety of a hybrid form of religious nationalism; contributors to the *Arbayter Fraynd* simply scoffed at what they considered to be the Poalei Zion's "feeble attempts to introduce into the life of progressive London society a brand of Polish chauvinism in the guise of Jewish Nationalism."

> The solution to the Jewish question [readers were advised just before the newspaper was closed by a court order in the summer of 1916] is not to be found in an antediluvian formula of nationalism, but in the struggle for the unity of Jewish and gentile forces in the fight against exploitation. Anti-Semitism will cease to exist in a society in which the oppressed are united against the oppressors. . . . Jewish workers must realise that the struggle for Jewish national rights—even if successful—will only lead to the establishment of a Jewish state under the domination of the Jewish bourgeoisie.[17]

More immediate damage, albeit of a less fundamental kind, was caused by the EZF's unpopular attitude toward the nonen-

[16] Comments and critisms in *Di Tsayt* by, e.g., Y. Pomerantz, 23 November 1914; A. D. Romanovsky, 2 January 1916; and M. Myers, 22 February 1916; in *Idishe Shtime*, 22 September 1916; and 19 September 1915, A. Steinacre to Sokolow, CZA, Sokolow Papers, A18/35.

[17] *Der Arbayter Fraynd*, 9, 15, and 30 June 1916; cf. M. Myer in *Di Tsayt*, 22 and 23 May 1916.

listment of Russian immigrant Jews. This, to judge from a variety of sources, was the burning issue of immigrant concern, provoking more grandstand agitation and backroom debate than Zionism and socialism combined. The Government's offer (of April 1916, when Asquith finally introduced compulsory conscription) that Russian refugees volunteer for service in the British army in return for a promise of British citizenship aroused deep suspicions; out of a potential catchment of some 25,000 Russian immigrant Jews of military age, only 700 took the authorities at their word. The warning (of August 1917) that the remainder either fight under the British flag or return to Russia for military duty aroused anger. The majority of immigrants rejected both proposals, as well as several halfway measures suggested in the interim. Instead, they formed themselves into such vociferous groups as the "Foreign Jews' Protection Committee against Conscription, Deportation to Russia, and Compulsory Military Service" which (according to the reports surreptitiously submitted to the Special Branch of the Criminal Investigation Department) grew "by leaps and bounds" after June 1916.[18] Effusions such as these, accompanied as they were by severe oscillations of the Jewish public mood, produced no tangible benefits for the Zionists, especially since many of the more prominent leaders of the EZF ostentatiously dissociated themselves from the antienlistment feelings which were all the rage. Cowen and Greenberg, in particular, merely alienated even further much of the immigrant community by their repeated references to the "swarms of shirkers" who were giving Jews everywhere a bad name; so too, although less abruptly, did Weizmann, who in September 1916 suggested a compromise whereby Russian Jews would be persuaded to enlist for civil defense or herded into "labour battalions" in Britain or France. Finally, and as is well-known, there was the opposition to Jabotinsky's scheme—that the Zionist Mule Corps be expanded to allow for the establish-

[18] Confidential report, dated 23 October 1916, in Public Record Office, Home Office Files, CID Reports, 1916-1917, HO 45/10819, file 318095/132; for an example of the complaints against compulsory service see *Idishe Shtime*, 15 September 1916. That newspaper was edited by A. Bezalel and Y. M. Zalkind, both members of the executive of the Foreign Jews' Protection Committee.

ment of a specifically Jewish "Legion." Although opposed by Greenberg and Cowen (and initially by Weizmann, albeit for different reasons), Jabotinsky's persistent advocacy of his proposal tended to discredit each of the organizations with which he was connected, including the Zionist movement. The EZF, in particular, seems to have suffered from being associated in the public mind with such an unpopular figure. Jabotinsky himself was hounded off several platforms in the East End, and on at least one occasion had to seek police protection; other Zionist leaders were howled down at *shekel*-day meetings.[19]

From the Zionists' point of view, the appearance of an immigrant-based National Union for Jewish Rights increased the difficulties of an already complex situation. This organization (in effect a federation of some thirty new Jewish groups in the East End of London, with a combined membership of about 15,000 males) was not especially anti-Zionist in outlook. Indeed, although few of its leaders were *shekel*-paying members of the Zionist Organisation, they expressed no objections to the principles of Jewish nationalism. Neither did they disagree with the EZF's standard charge that the Conjoint Foreign Committee was "insufficiently representative" to speak on behalf of immigrant Anglo-Jewry. Nevertheless, their spokesman explicitly rejected the Zionists' own claims to communal preeminence; by implication, their actions further frustrated whatever hopes may have been entertained that immigrant activists would throw their weight behind the EZF in a trial of strength with the native Establishment. Thus, at a series of foundation meetings in the autumn of 1915, the executive committee of the National Union reportedly turned down a suggestion that it combine forces with the EZF in

[19] Special Branch reports, dated 16 September, 16 October, and 18 October 1916, Public Record Office, Home Office Files, HO 45/10819, file 318095/132; *Di Tsayt*, 29 July 1916; *Idishe Shtime*, 27 September 1916 (reporting that the EZF had decided to refrain from all comment on enlistment), and 11 October 1916. For a recent, and fully documented account of the entire episode, David Yisraeli, "The Struggle for Zionist Military Involvement in the First World War, 1914-1917," in *Bar-Ilan Studies in History*, ed. Pinḥas Artzi (Ramat-Gan, 1978), pp. 197-213.

a campaign to undermine the prestige and authority of the older communal bodies. Instead, the Union preferred to ensure the defense of Jewish interests "wherever and whenever they are en-dangered or assailed" by "cultivating a friendly understanding with existing institutions having similar aims." To that end, the founders offered the presidency of their organization to Lucien Wolf, whose social credentials (and official contacts, for that matter) were far more solid than those most Zionist leaders could at that time parade. Wolf, once he had sought the necessary nod from Claude Montefiore, accepted the post with alacrity. Political sense, so he informed his superiors in the Establishment, left him with no choice.

> The organisation of these people to do the work the Conjoint is now doing is inevitable. If we do not avail ourselves of the opportunity they are themselves offering us of working with them, practically on our terms, they will certainly work apart from, and perhaps against us, and they will fall into the hands of demagogues, who will in the end seriously compromise the Jewish cause.[20]

Whether or not Wolf had the Zionists specifically in mind is not made clear from the surviving documents. But his actions suggest that this might be so. From the first, he stipulated that the Union refrain from "unfurling the Nationalist flag" (and therefore vetoed the suggestion that it call itself the "Jewish *National* Union"); he also insisted that the entire question of Zionism "has no relevancy to the serious work we have in hand, and you will incur a very heavy responsibility if you impede and prejudice that work by dwelling upon it."[21] Once assured that the Union had agreed "to drop, or, at any rate, to reserve this dangerous question" (and it is indicative of the attitude of the founders of the Union that they agreed to do so), he determined to press home his advantage. He quickly arranged for a mass meeting of the Union to be held

[20] 21 January 1916, Wolf to Alexander, DEPS, General Correspondence, C11/2/8; compare M. Myer in *Di Tsayt*, 5 January 1916.

[21] 11 January 1916, Wolf to Z. W. Dywien (hon. sec. of the Union), YIVO, Mowshowitch, Collection of Wolf Papers, nos. 2166-67.

in the East End on 12 March 1916, and pressed the Conjoint Foreign Committee to undercut the Zionists by inviting additional immigrant associations to join its ranks. As he gleefully reported to Zangwill, "although the Zionist Federation have been trying to get up a rival concentration they have, I believe, completely failed." In fact, nine of the societies affiliated to the EZF agreed to join the National Union.[22]

As was often the case in communal matters, Wolf overplayed his hand. Not content with the Union's acceptance of a mild Palestinian formula, he demanded, in the spring of 1916, that its executive committee adhere more explicitly to the Conjoint Foreign Committee's line. Specifically, he called for a declaration that the National Union disavow any claim to exclusive privileges for the Jews, that by "national rights" they had in mind "communal and non-especially educational autonomy, wherever such rights may be proved to be necessary." These conditions, together with Wolf's widely reported criticisms of the "foreign" Jews during a meeting of the AJA, proved too much for his erstwhile collaborators. So, too, did his threat that if the Union did not accept the terms of affiliation offered by the Conjoint Foreign Committee, he would have nothing further to do with the new organization. Thereafter, tempers became frayed and mutual antagonisms more noticeable. After a spate of typically ill-tempered letters to all and sundry—and an unsolicited accusation that "many of them are Socialists, very close to the Anarchist wing"—Wolf eventually severed his connection with the Union.[23] But his resignation, although possibly attributable to a revulsion of Union feeling against his extreme anti-Zionism, left little impression on the communal fortunes of the EZF. When seeking a replacement for Wolf, the organizing committee of the National Union once again ignored the official leadership of Zionism in Britain. Instead, its members turned to Zangwill (who declined "to accept a po-

[22] 17 January 1916, Wolf to Zangwill, CZA, Zangwill Papers, A120/60; and 3 March 1916, Wolf to Zangwill, DEPS, General Correspondence, C11/2/8.

[23] 4 July 1916, Wolf to Dywien, DEPS, General Correspondence, C11/2/3/9, and 26 October 1916, Wolf to Zangwill, ibid. Wolf's remarks at the AJA reported in JC, 7 April 1916, pp. 15-16, and *Di Tsayt*, 6 April 1916, p. 2.

sition which my friend, Mr. Lucien Wolf, has been unable to hold"), and to Gaster. This was a predictable choice but, as far as the EZF was concerned, an unfortunate one. The Ḥakham, as was well known, was already at odds with most leaders of the EZF and hence in no mood to lend his name and reputation to whatever communal strategy its spokesman might have envisaged. On the contrary, he seems to have played with the idea that he could use the National Union as a means of bolstering his own position. He did insist that the Union declare its unequivocal adherence to the Basle Program (a stand that, incidentally, did not prevent the organization's subsequent demise),[24] but he refused to associate himself with any other plank in the platform adopted at wartime conferences of the EZF. Instead, he devoted many hours to devising a nationalist formula of his own which, he was careful to point out, was "somewhat different" from Weizmann's. Even during the testy days of June 1917, when Gaster did propose some form of "working cooperation" with the EZF, he demanded that his own organization be accorded a position of precedence.[25] This was a condition that neither Weizmann, Cowen, nor Sokolow were prepared to accept. The latter, the previous April, had already reached the conclusion that the National Union was merely a tool in Gaster's campaign against the official Zionist leadership. "If you should find any news of this 'Organisation' in the newspapers," he warned his colleagues in the United States, "please attach no importance to it whatsoever."[26]

[24] Another factor was Gaster's earlier refusal to touch the enlistment question; 31 August 1916, Dywien to Gaster, Mocatta Library, Gaster Papers, Letter Book, 1916-1917, and 27 June 1918, J. Slivko (hon. sec. of the Union) to Gaster, CZA, Gaster Papers, A203/245.

[25] 12 June 1917, Gaster to Weizmann, and 20 June 1917 to M. Shire, Mocatta Library, Gaster Papers, Letter Book, 1916-1917, nos. 697, 748. His earlier discussion with the Union representatives in his correspondence with Dywien between November 1916 and January 1917 (ibid.), and his diary entries for the same period (CZA, Gaster Papers, A203/146 and A203/162).

[26] April 1917, Sokolow to the Provisional Executive in the USA, WA, file 214; alarming reports on the Union's activities had earlier reached Moscow, CZA, Sokolow Papers, A18/41/2/8.

There was more to such strictures than a distaste for Gaster's unwelcome claims to preeminence in Zionist affairs. Weizmann, who shared and prompted Sokolow's disparagement of the National Union, was already far too secure in the EZF saddle to be unduly concerned with a challenge of that nature. Far more fundamental, at this stage, was his disagreement with the radical strategy of communal action on which the Ḥakham (through the Nation Union) seemed to be embarking with barely disguised relish. At that level, the differences were over both ends and means. Gaster, driven by egoistic convictions and purposes which had something demonic about them, gave the impression of wishing to use the National Union as a weapon with which to challenge not only the EZF but the communal Establishment. Weizmann, by contrast, had been working at a different speed and in a different direction. His sights were set on securing an official declaration of diplomatic support for Zionist aims in Palestine, and from that perspective there could be little point in a slanging match with the accredited officers of the community's senior institutions. On the contrary, open conflict would merely reveal the extent of communal differences over Zionism and provoke a wrangle for which he had little stomach and less time. Instead, he had been determined to "attempt everything to rope in these Jews and work with them harmoniously."[27]

Conciliation rather than confrontation had been the keynote of Weizmann's activity. He had himself pursued this tactic with some success ever since 1913, when canvassing support for the establishment of a Jewish University in Jerusalem.[28] With the outbreak of war it seemed to be even better suited to his wider purposes and diplomatic abilities: hence his deliberately flattering approaches to Walter and James de Rothschild (which were reciprocated with genuine esteem);[29] hence too his fawning, but

[27] 28 November 1914, Weizmann to Sacher and Simon, *Letters*, 7:57-60.

[28] *Trial and Error* (London, 1949), pp. 177-81; and, e.g., 16 December 1913, Weizmann to L. Stein, *Letters*, 6:180-81.

[29] E.g., 22 November 1914, Weizmann to Dorothy de Rothschild, *Letters*, 7:51-54. The entire relationship is warmly described in Simon Schama, *Two Rothschilds and the Land of Israel* (London, 1978), pp. 190-209.

unsuccessful, advances to Claude Montefiore, Sir Philip Magnus, and—most interestingly in the light of later developments at the Board—Simon Rowson.[30] Throughout the strategy was clear; instead of challenging members of the native communal Establishment, Weizmann wished to persuade them to allow the Zionists to reach as good an arrangement as possible with the British government. Whatever the pitfalls of this course, it had seemed feasible enough in 1915 for him to reject the suggestion that local Zionists attempt to "put the screws on the Conjoint Committee," whose members he still thought might be won over.[31] Even when these hopes proved unfounded, he attempted to neutralize some of the senior critics of Zionism by invoking the name of Rothschild. As late as October 1916 Weizmann believed (mistakenly) that James had persuaded the Conjoint Foreign Committee

> to leave Zionism alone. They have, I understand, agreed to keep their hands off Zionism, not to interfere with our negotiations with the Government. Moreover, they have agreed to refer the Govmt. to us in case the latter asks for the opinion of the C.C. on matters Zionist. After all is said and done, this is the maximum we can expect from the C.C. We don't want them to help us, we don't expect them to act against their own "convictions." We wish them to leave us strictly alone.[32]

Even in April 1917 he was confident (again, mistakenly) that the Conjoint Committee's members would simply "not dare" to cause the Zionists any further trouble.[33]

Weizmann's attitude toward the Board of Deputies had throughout been of a piece with that line of thought. Consequently, he took no steps whatsoever before the spring of 1917 to ensure the sort of result that was ultimately achieved on 17 June of that year. Indeed, he seems to have been slow to appre-

[30] 16 December 1914, Weizmann to Harry Lewis, *Letters*, 7:89-90; 6 January 1915, Simon to Weizmann, WA, file 179; and 23 June 1915, Sacher to N. Bentwich, WA, file 183.

[31] 7 February 1915, Weizmann to Sacher, *Letters*, 7:137-39.

[32] 17 October 1916, Weizmann to I. Sieff, ibid., 305-306.

[33] 29 April 1917, Weizmann to Tschlenow, ibid., 387-89.

ciate the possibility that a vote favorable to Zionism at that institution would serve any purpose. As late as October 1916 he specifically rejected suggestions that the EZF officially adopt the motion which one Zionist member of the Board wished to present for the deputies' consideration.

> Supposing the unexpected happens and by some sort of miracle such a resolution is carried, I would not be happy. It would mean that we leave the honour of asking for Palestine to the Board of Deputies. Surely no Zionist would like to see the Board of Dep. entrusted with such a mission. . . . But let us take the more probable case. The resolution will fail and then . . . the B. of D. stands committed *against* Zionism, a position which may be utilised by some of our enemies.[34]

Significantly, Weizmann did not seek information on the structure and privileges of the Board until after the publication of the Conjoint Foreign Committee's manifesto; neither did he himself obtain nomination as a deputy until after a full-scale debate on the issue of Jewish nationalism had been provoked by groups and individuals who possessed no nominal allegiance to the EZF or any other Zionist body.[35] Both moves, it transpired, were too late to be influential in the sense of determining the form and shape of the resolution ultimately passed on 17 June. As far as the vote of that date was concerned, the leading Zionists in the community did not foresee the alignment at the Board, and neither were they altogether responsible for bringing it about.

THE BOARD OF DEPUTIES AND THE CONJOINT FOREIGN COMMITTEE

In the absence of convincing evidence that the leading Zionists of Anglo-Jewry were responsible for the censure of the Conjoint

---

[34] Above, n. 32.

[35] Even then, he did not eventually stand. 21 June 1917, Weizmann to Raffalovich, *Letters*, 7:448; and Isaiah Raffalovich, *Ẓiyunim ve-Tamrurim* (Tel-Aviv, 1952), pp. 144-45. On his enquiries concerning the Board, 14 June 1917, Greenberg to Weizmann, WA, file 230.

Foreign Committee's manifesto on 17 June 1917, alternative explanations must be sought for the alignment at the Board of Deputies on that day. The vote cannot be understood by concentrating exclusively on the affiliations of those few deputies who were avowed Zionists. Instead, attention must be turned to a wider range of thematic and institutional correlates. Particularly, some note must be taken of the structure of the Board in 1917 and (as far as can be ascertained) of the background and communal affiliations of the individual deputies who participated in the division.

Any analysis of the division figures must begin by noting the terms of the motion. Significantly, it did not call for an emphatic declaration of Anglo-Jewry's support for the Zionist program. As proposed by Elsley Zeitlin (the deputy for Dublin, who described himself as being "outside the Zionist Organisation"), it took the negative and less forthright course of asking the Board to demonstrate its "profound disapproval" of the publication of the Conjoint Foreign Committee's manifesto. That was why some Zionists grumbled that the motion "did not go far enough."[36] During the debate itself, the principal charge to emerge was the failure of the Board's representatives on the Conjoint Foreign Committee to consult with the parent organization before issuing the manifesto. At issue, therefore, were the authoritarian practices, not necessarily the anti-Zionist principles, of the executive. For many deputies, Zionism per se was a subject of peripheral importance; their decision to oust the executive was less the expression of a belief in Jewish nationalism than an attempt (in the words of one account) "to show the community who were the masters."[37]

A previous study of the division list has already attempted to

[36] 11 June 1917, I. Sieff to Weizmann, WA, file 230, and Gaster's speech to the National Union in JC, 29 June 1917, p. 23. On the clutch of other—more explicitly Zionist—motions originally presented for discussion see; 13 June 1917, Emanuel to Alexander, DEPS, Letter Book, B3/31:165, and agenda list in DEPS, Agenda and Reports, 1916-1920, A3/1.

[37] As indicated by one account of the meeting of the B'nai B'rith caucus at the Russell Hotel on the morning of the Board's meeting see: Elsley Zeitlyn, *A Paragraph of Anglo-Jewish History* (London, 1936), pp. 5-6.

verify that claim;[38] its conclusions can therefore be briefly summarized here. Three principal items appear worthy of note. First, attendance at the meeting of the Board on 17 June 1917 was the highest ever recorded in the life of that particular parliament, which was itself the largest in the Board's history hitherto (elections to the Board were held triennially; the most recent having taken place in May 1916). Of the 143 deputies entitled to vote in June 1917, no less than 113 (79 percent) did so—more than twice as many the number (55—38 percent) who usually turned up for Board meetings. A breakdown of the June 1917 division list into frequent and infrequent members showed that the balance against the incumbent executive was tipped by deputies who did not usually attend the Board's monthly meetings. Of the fifty-six deputies who voted to condemn the Conjoint's manifesto, thirty-eight had hitherto turned up for less than 40 percent of the Board's regular meetings; for ten of them this was to be their only appearance throughout the 1916-1919 session. Not surprisingly, therefore, soon after the vote some spokesmen for the defeated camp suggested a reform in the Board's constitution that would entail the disenfranchisement of those congregations whose deputies were irregular in their attendance.[39]

A second characteristic that separated the two parties in June 1917 was their respective experience at the Board. The side that voted against the Board's leadership in 1917 was a relatively inexperienced body. This was true in terms of both the congregations represented and the deputies themselves. Over fifty new single-member congregations had been granted representation at the Board since the turn of the century (eighteen of them since the general election to the Board in 1913); 60 of the 113 deputies who voted in June 1917 had not begun to attend Board meetings until the outbreak of World War I. A correlation of these figures with those relating to frequent and infrequent attendance further distinguishes the two blocs of voters. Most of those who voted in defense of the Conjoint Foreign Committee's manifesto on

[38] See my article, "The Conquest of a Community? " pp. 157-84.
[39] Ibid., p. 166, Table I, and 14 September 1917, Emanuel to Wolf, DEPS, Letter Books, B3/34:458.

Palestine (said to represent the views of the Old Guard), were both frequent attenders at the Board and more experienced members. Conversely, the document was principally condemned by infrequent and inexperienced deputies.[40]

To attendance and inexperience must be added a third criterion—that of constituency representation. In this respect, the statistics supplied by the Board's official *Annual Reports* are misleading. Nominally, of the 143 members of the Board in 1917, 45 represented congregations in London and its environs; 9 sat for congregations in the colonies; and the remaining 89 represented provincial congregations. In effect, however, the electoral practices of the Board permitted—and even encouraged—a number of anomalies. The constitution of the Board, when defining the eligibility of prospective deputies, contained no residence qualification clause. Candidates were only required to be male Jews over the age of twenty-one who had rented a seat in the congregation of their choice for at least one year before election. They had not necessarily to be residents of the area that they aspired to represent. As a result, and not surprisingly in view of the exigencies of travel in wartime, several provincial congregations deliberately elected Londoners as their representatives to the Board. In fact, no less than 110 of the 143 deputies in 1917 came from London. Moreover, most of those 110 were members of (and in some cases officeholders in) the wealthy synagogues of the West End.[41]

There were only two general exceptions to this rule of metropolitan and Establishment dominance. One consisted of those deputies who represented congregations in the north and east of London; the other of deputies for provincial congregations in the northeast (Liverpool-Manchester area) and northwest (Yorkshire-Durham) of the country. Invariably, these men were discovered to have been active in the local affairs of the communities whom they represented. Although not themselves immigrants, they had usually also staked claims to the affections of the immigrant pop-

---

[40] Cohen, "The Conquest of a Community? " p. 168, Table II.
[41] Ibid., pp. 169-71, Table III.

ulations that comprised much of their individual constituencies. Judged by the previously noted scale of "newer-older" deputies, they certainly lacked experience in the arena of central Jewish government: the majority had not been returned to the Board before 1913. They were also often remiss in their attendance at regular Board meetings (hence falling into the "infrequent" segment of the attendance scale). Both factors must largely explain why their numerical capacity to influence the Board's affairs was, for much of the war, largely unfulfilled.

It was the influence of this group of deputies that seems to have been more decisive than that of any other in determining the outcome of the vote on 17 June 1917. Ultimately, it has been argued, it was largely the newer London and resident provincial deputies who on that day gave the ayes their victory. For one thing, they then voted as a clearly discernible *bloc* (thirty-four to six, with three abstentions, against the manifesto); for another, they turned up in far greater force than usual for the vote. Consequently, they were able to play a proportionately more important part in the proceedings on that day than had usually been the case hitherto, and they ultimately controlled 40 percent of the total votes cast. (This was particularly so in the case of the native provincial representatives: they usually averaged an attendance of ten deputies, but on this occasion totalled thirty-one). The fact that far fewer members of this group had attended the previous meeting of the Board of Deputies (in May) must largely account for the failure of the pro-Zionist motion that had been presented on that occasion. They had then commanded only 29 percent of the attendance.[42]

No single cause can be expected to explain why such a large proportion of the provincial and newer London deputies decided to condemn the Conjoint Foreign Committee's manifesto. Some (but not more than a dozen or so) were active Zionists, who had long taken a prominent part in the movement's affairs; others (but very few, it seems) may have been reacting to pressure from

---

[42] Eighteen deputies in all. Of the thirty-four members of this group who voted against the manifesto in June, only fourteen had attended in May: five from London and nine from the provinces.

their local congregations;[43] in yet a third category, some individual deputies may have been swung by the arguments adduced during the course of the debate itself. But overriding each of these considerations, influences of a more generally constitutional character seem to have been at work. The *novi homines* who tipped the balance against the incumbent Conjoint Foreign Committee were responding to convictions that exceeded the formal boundaries of the motion on the agenda. Specifically, they were acting in accordance with their own perceptions of the need for greater representation in Anglo-Jewish government. Although often imprecisely defined, this demand had long proved to be of greater interest to most deputies than had discussions on Zionism. Their behavior on 17 June 1917 did not, therefore, represent a sudden reversal of their previous attitudes and voting patterns. Rather, it constituted an extension of their earlier campaign for a larger share in the management of communal affairs. Most dissident deputies seem to have voted with the purpose of influencing a pronounced, and pragmatic, tug-of-war for influence in Anglo-Jewry.

Some of the background to this struggle has been related in chapter 4. Ever since the turn of the century (at least), various groups of deputies representing interests which stood in no direct relation to Zionist concerns or immigrant aspirations had been exerting persistent pressure for change at the Board. Those from Manchester had been particularly forward in pressing the need for greater provincial representation and influence; those who were active in the London-based B'nai B'rith had likewise advocated that the Board of Deputies widen the base of its support by granting representatives of newer bodies a larger share in the management of affairs. Demands such as these had already led to some changes at the Board before the outbreak of war, but their extent was apparently insufficient. Consequently, criticisms of the executive remained rife. There continued to be a widespread feeling (which was quite independent of occasional Zionist irruptions into communal councils) that the Board of Deputies,

---

[43] Cohen, "The Conquest of a Community? " p. 182, n. 43.

as presently constituted, was out of step with the realities of twentieth-century Anglo-Jewry. Arrangements which might have been adequate in the Georgian, or even mid-Victorian age were not suitable in the more turbulent economic, political, and demographic circumstances of Edwardian life.

Initially, the outbreak of war threatened to smother these claims. Times of unprecedented passions and prejudices, it was said, were not those most conducive to dramatic changes in the traditional methods of communal government. On the contrary, they had to be continued and extended. Distinguished members of inner Establishment circles put the case most explicitly. At the AJA and the Board of Deputies, Claude Montefiore and David Alexander declared that the discussions and decisions of the Conjoint Foreign Committee were now, more than ever, "too confidential" to permit the free-wheeling inspections of their reports which many members of the community frequently demanded.[44] The president of the Board of Guardians, Sir Leonard Lionel Cohen, administered equally frosty doses of stricture and sneers. In 1915, for instance, he publicly denigrated those "irresponsible busybodies with high sounding titles" who obsessively criticized his policies and attempted relief work for which they possessed neither the required training nor the necessary competence.[45] Elsewhere, the tone adopted was frankly abrasive. Sir Francis Montefiore was merely echoing views already current in some select circles when advising that "the strictest enquiry into nationality should be made before admitting, or appointing, persons to the various Jewish institutions in this country." As his own contribution to the effort, he had already renounced his former adherence to the Zionist movement.[46]

[44] See, e.g., minutes of AJA meeting of 29 October 1916 in Mocatta Library, Archives of the AJA, Council Minute Book, 4:131, and of Board of Deputies meeting of 21 March 1915 in DEPS, Minute Book, A16, p. 224.

[45] Speech to the Board of Guardians in JC, 15 October 1915, p. 11; omitted from Board of Guardians Minute Book, 5:88-89. The same phrase occurs in H. Landau to Stephany (secretary of the Board of Guardians) in Board of Guardians Letter Book, vol. 5, p. 196, and 13 December 1914, Sir P. Magnus to Weizmann, WA, file 178.

[46] Speech at the annual meeting of Sephardi Elders in JC, 9 February 1917,

The advocates of communal reform had generated far too much momentum before the war to be thus easily slapped down. Principally, this was because the war itself raised the issues of communal management and policy-making in a particularly acute form. Loose and highly personalized methods of government, such as had been practiced in Anglo-Jewry during conditions of relative stability, were clearly unsuitable in times of unprecedented turmoil. If they were to deal effectively with several pressing questions (of which the future of Palestine was only one; the status of enemy aliens, the conscription of Russian Jews, and the effect of the March 1917 Revolution in Russia being far more prominent), the community's institutions would have to act more decisively and more efficiently.[47] For different reasons, they might also have to replace some of their personnel. The war, after all, was having a progressively dissolving effect on the hierarchical structure of English society in its entirety; the status and deference hitherto enjoyed by the political elite were being undermined by elements which were both economic—taxation especially—and emotional: the sense of "topsy-turvydom." Several barriers of class lingered on, but many others became increasingly blurred and thereby accelerated the liquefaction of the Anglo-Jewish political system. Native Anglo-Jewry (the immigrants were in a somewhat different category) was clearly not immune to such influences. By the end of the war it was apparent that

the old rich have become the new poor and the old poor have become the new rich . . . and as the new poor cling to the advantages of the implied communal bargain—the offices, and the honours, and (so-called) 'leadership'—the new rich do not see why they should take upon themselves the burden of paying

p. 12; a comparable motion by A. E. Franklin had provoked an acrimonious debate at the annual meeting of the governors of Jews' College, JC, 29 October 1915, p. 15. On Montefiore's denunciation of Zionism, JC, 24 December 1915, p. 22.

[47] As Charles Emanuel admitted, the Conjoint Foreign Committee's bureaucratic procedures were deficient: he "scrambled down" notes at its meetings, which were "cut about" by Alexander and then referred to Wolf. 29 June 1916, Emanuel to Wolf, DEPS, General Correspondence, C11/2/3.

for the institutions without the compensating advantage of calling the tune from an honorary official position in connection with them[48]

It has been suggested that there existed a connection between the subsequent "change from oligarchic to democratic control" in the community and the "growth and spread of Zionism."[49] But the relationship between these two trends seems to have been one of parallelism rather than causation. After 1914, discussions at the Board of Deputies (in particular) were frequently punctuated by testy exchanges over internal and external affairs. During this period too, however, the predominant demand was for structural alterations rather than shifts of ideological perspective. As has been seen, those motions that did advocate a pro-Zionist orientation in the Board's policies between 1914 and 1917 were defeated. On the other hand, many of the concessions forced upon the reluctant executive (to whom Lucien Wolf was able to give even more support after his election as deputy for Woolwich in 1915) were won without any specifically Zionist instigation, and sometimes in the teeth of expressed Zionist opposition. The most striking example is provided by the campaign that brought about the enlargement of the Conjoint Foreign Committee in 1916. Early in 1915, Joseph Cowen (speaking at the AJA) had demanded special representation on that body for "those Jews who represent the Zionist spirit and the Zionist ideal."[50] But his enthusiasm for reform noticeably slackened as soon as he appre-

---

[48] "The New Plutocracy," in *JC*, 28 December 1917, p. 5; and Mentor, "From My Note Book," *JC*, 2 July 1920, p. 11. In general Vivian D. Lipman, *Social History of the Jews in England* (London, 1954), chap. 8; Arthur Marwick, *The Deluge: British Society and the First World War* (London, 1961); Norma Branson, *Britain in the 1920's* (London, 1975), chap. 5; and William D. Rubinstein, "Jews Among Top British Wealth Holders, 1857-1969: Decline of the Golden Age," *Jewish Social Studies* 34 (1972):73-84.

[49] Redcliffe N. Salaman, "Whither Lucien Wolf's Anglo-Jewish Community?" *Lucien Wolf Memorial Lecture, 1953* (London, 1953), p. 21.

[50] Minutes of 10 January 1915 in Mocatta Library, Archives of the AJA, Council Minute Book, 4:102. The motion was easily defeated; the only alteration made to the composition of the Conjoint Foreign Committee being the cooption (in a nonvoting capacity) of Chief Rabbi Hertz.

ciated that the EZF would not be the only, nor indeed the main beneficiary of an enlarged Conjoint Foreign Committee to which several non-Zionist groups (supposedly representative of immigrant feeling) would also be invited. Officially, the EZF was content merely to decline invitations to further discussions on the topic. Individually, however, Zionist deputies explicitly opposed a motion at the Board that the Conjoint Foreign Committee be brought "into closer touch with elements in the East End" by the co-option of two representatives from the United Council of Jewish Friendly Societies.[51] As Samuel Daiches, to cite but one example, correctly foresaw, changes of this sort could not possibly further the cause of Jewish nationalism: a condition of the appointment of the two new members was that they previously agree to the broad outlines of the Conjoint's antinationalist policy with regard to Palestine.[52]

To search for the roots of native communal change solely, or even predominantly, in the Zionist Organisation is, it seems, to look in the wrong place. The shift of power away from the Establishment, as represented by the members of the Conjoint Foreign Committee, owed its momentum to other groups and individuals, with interests and ambitions that moved along a different axis from those explicit in Zionist ideology. In the provinces, the development was expressed in the establishment of local communal councils ("soviets" to their opponents), often—but not always—in response to local feeling that Anglo-Jewry's existing institutions were not sufficiently diversified to meet uniquely regional requirements. Among the newer London bourgeoisie, it

[51] Cowen's speech at the 1915 annual conference of the EZF in *JC*, 29 January 1915, pp. 12, 23; and report of a council meeting of EZF in *JC*, 30 June 1916, p. 21. For discussions at the Board in March and April 1915, see minutes in DEPS, Minute Books, A16, pp. 223-24; and for reactions to parallel talks at the AJA, *Di Tsayt*, 3 April 1916.
[52] The selected Friendly Society representatives were M. Cash and B. Fersht. But any influence they might have had was neutralized by the simultaneous co-option of Lord Swaythling, Sir Mathew Nathan, Lionel Cohen, and Sir Philip Magnus. See minutes of Conjoint Foreign Committee meeting of 23 February 1916 in DEPS, C11/1/1. For one account of East End reactions, see *Di Tsayt*, 28 March 1916.

took the form of greater support for the B'nai B'rith. The officers of the Board of Deputies regarded neither development favorably. They criticized Manchester deputies for acting as a "lobby," and refused to recognize either the prerogatives or influence claimed by the Manchester Jewish Representative Council.[53] Relations between the Board of Deputies and the B'nai B'rith were still more tense, principally because the latter once again appeared to be poaching on the Board's traditional preserves. In 1915, the First London Lodge of the B'nai B'rith established a bureau for advising interned Jewish enemy aliens on their rights, an organization for the supply of kosher food to internees on the Isle of Man, and a hostel for homeless Belgian refugees. By the end of the year, it had obtained Alexander's grudging admission that the B'nai B'rith was the communal organization best placed to petition the Government on these matters.[54] Admittedly, in 1916 Lucien Wolf did brusquely reject an offer to cooperate and exchange information with the London Lodge's council on the international Jewish situation. But his action merely precipitated an even more ominous development. It was during the course of that year that those members of the B'nai B'rith who were members of the Board of Deputies began to form themselves into an "Actions Group," and that the First Lodge established a "Jewish Emergency Committee" with a brief "to keep a watchful and critical eye on the proceedings and acts of the Conjoint Committee" itself.[55]

[53] E.g., 7 September 1916, Alexander to Wolf, DEPS, General Correspondence, C11/2/9. In May 1917, Emanuel bluntly told one correspondent that "the Board does not recognise the 'Manchester Jewish Representative Council' either officially or otherwise." 21 May 1917, to A. Goldstone (sec. S. Manchester Synagogue), DEPS, Letter Book, B3/34, p. 193. At Glasgow and Leeds embryonic communal councils had been formed as early as 1913; see JC, 3 December 1913, p. 21, and 17 December 1913, p. 10.

[54] See Seventh Annual Report of the Independent Order of B'nai B'rith (signed by S. Rowson, President), in CZA, Sokolow Papers, A18/36; and correspondence between the Board of Deputies and the B'nai B'rith in JC, 18 June 1915, p. 13. Also *Di Tsayt*, 25 July 1915.

[55] 18 October 1916, Nathan Laski to Gaster, Mocatta Library, Gaster Papers; and confidential report of the Council on the International Jewish Situation, submitted to a meeting of the Lodge on 7 May 1916 by S. Rowson, CZA, Sokolow Papers, A18/36.

Proceedings such as these had exerted a progressively discernible effect on the structure and tone of debates among the rank and file of deputies. Specifically, they contributed—some time before June 1917—to the formation of a recognizable cadre of alienated provincial and newer London members of the Board of Deputies. The fact that many of these future collaborators were infrequent attenders at Board meetings naturally tended to reduce their effectiveness, but it did not entirely obscure their potential influence. Certain portents of changes to come had long been in the air. As early as December 1914, they had combined to defeat the executive's motion to postpone the annual general meeting of the Board of Deputies, the attendant "froth and bubble" of which H.S.Q. Henriques wished to avoid; in June 1915 they supported the claims of the Order Achei B'rith (affiliated to the B'nai B'rith) to approach the Government on the inconveniences suffered by interned Jewish aliens; and in November of that year insisted that Alexander submit a copy of his annual report to the rank and file before its publication.[56] These skirmishes whetted appetites for more substantial advances. The sessions of 1916 opened with two extraordinary conferences of congregational delegates at which several changes in the constitution were broached. One was that smaller provincial congregations be allowed to retain the right to combine and thus attain representation at the Board of Deputies; another that the executive co-opt "fifteen representatives of leading Jewish institutions . . . to be members under the designation of Elders"; a third that London's representation on the Board's various committees not exceed 50 percent. The fact that each of these suggestions was defeated did not dissipate the enthusiasm of those who proposed them. Simon Rowson, in particular, claimed to have derived much encouragement from the substantial size of their minorities. He also cited the letters of support that regularly appeared in the Jewish press as evidence of his ability to call upon the allegiance of an increasing proportion of his constituents.[57]

[56] Minutes of 19 December 1914, 3 June 1915 and 21 November 1915 in DEPS, Minute Books, A16, pp. 213, 231-34, and A17, p. 16.

[57] Minutes of the special conference in DEPS, A1/2/2; and report of debates in JC, 14 January 1916, pp. 13-14 and 28 January 1916, p. 13.

In the latter argument, Rowson was obviously on shaky ground. Dissent makes notoriously good—but often notoriously inaccurate—copy, and Leopold Greenberg's relish for the knocks of communal warfare (quite apart from his Zionism) undoubtedly influenced his selection of the comments and correspondence that appeared in the *Jewish Chronicle* and *Jewish World*. Nevertheless, the reform agitation which matured at the Board of Deputies in 1916 was not altogether artificial. In April 1915, the annual general meetings of several synagogues passed motions to the effect that "in view of the serious questions now affecting Jews," deputies at the Board should "meet the members of the congregation at least once a year to report and consult."[58] These pledges were invariably honored when triennial elections to the Board of Deputies were held in May 1916, with the result that (sometimes for the first time in living memory) an opportunity was officially provided for some serious discussion of the state of Anglo-Jewry.[59] Whether or not any of this spirit would rub off on the Board itself remained to be seen. As had previously been the rule, most of the incumbent deputies were reelected unopposed; even where contests did occur, they were often occasioned by trivial personal rivalries of no apparent relevance to the overarching issues of the day.[60] But the number of new faces who assembled for the "parliament" of 1916 was large enough to excite comment and speculation. At the first meeting of the new Board (in June) a buoyant Rowson—fresh from provoking a minor row at Hammersmith Synagogue and firmly in charge at the B'nai B'rith—again proposed that the deputies terminate their conjoint agreement with the AJA.[61]

[58] Reports of annual general meetings in JC, 23 April 1915, p. 11, 30 April 1915, pp. 18-22, and 21 May 1915, p. 17; and *Jewish World*, 28 April 1915, p. 9.

[59] Reports in JC, 19 May 1916, p. 18.

[60] See, e.g., the correspondence concerning the Stamford Hill election in JC, 26 May 1916, p. 16, and 2 June 1916, p. 18. The case is an interesting one since S. Newman, who was eventually elected, tabled his pro-Zionist resolution of October 1916 "in the name of his congregation." DEPS, Agendas and Reports, 1916-1920, A3/1; agenda list of 17 July 1916.

[61] Defeated by 61 votes to 19; minutes of 25 June 1916 in DEPS, Minute Books,

Sniffing a change in the communal wind, several Zionists did attempt to exploit the situation. Some, as early as April 1915, had tried to tag a "recognition of Jewish interests in Palestine" on to the more general instructions issued to deputies at individual congregations. Others in 1916 became members of provincial communal councils. Sokolow, Weizmann, Sieff, and Israel Cohen all joined the B'nai B'rith of which Paul Goodman (also the secretary of the EZF) became secretary. As individuals, but not necessarily as integral contributions to the same effort, Sidney Newman (in October 1916) and Samuel Daiches (in May 1917) proposed specifically Zionist motions at the Board of Deputies. But this scurry of activity neither generated nor reflected a surge of Zionist strength. On the contrary, it merely emphasized the extent of Zionism's weakness. Unable to conquer the community with their own program, or even by their own efforts, the members of the EZF felt themselves to be increasingly dependent upon the enthusiasms engendered by other, non-Zionist interests that were better placed to embody native Anglo-Jewry's abstract feelings of unease and better equipped to serve as vehicles for its expression. It is because they were equally capable of seeing this that the more important of the groups courted by the Zionists refused to adopt a wholeheartedly nationalist program. Instead, they went some way toward manipulating their assumed allies. The Manchester Community Council, for instance, rejected a motion to include "the acquisition of Palestine for the Jews" in its list of objectives; although accrediting the representation of two members of the local Zionist Association, it contented itself with a less decisive pledge to "defend Jewish national interests when and where they are endangered or assaulted."[62] Similarly, the B'nai B'rith declined Weizmann's suggestion that it "set up an organisation in this country to deal with the Jewish Question *vis-à-vis*

A17, p. 25; for Rowson's criticisms of his local board of management see minutes of annual general meeting, 15 May 1916, London, United Synagogue Archives, Hammersmith Synagogue, Minute Book, p. 430. No elections to the offices in the First Lodge were held in 1916; the entire council, over which Rowson presided, was simply asked to remain in office.

[62] Report in JC, 2 June 1916, p. 19.

the British Government." While requesting the benefit of So-
kolow's expertise on the future Jewish situation in an independent
Poland, the Lodge took no action on Goodman's paper on "The
Special Jewish Interests in Palestine."[63]

This discouraging attitude was not abruptly modified in June
1917. Sacher's hope that, after the publication of the Conjoint
Foreign Committee's manifesto, Zionism would suddenly flourish
was not fulfilled. He did persuade Weizmann to abandon the
aversion to an open fight at the Board of Deputies that had
hitherto characterized his policy. But the hastily contrived efforts
that Weizmann subsequently made to rustle up a pro-Zionist motion at the Board were awkward and inadequate.[64] Perhaps, like
many members of the Conjoint Foreign Committee, he was still
inclined to dismiss his putative supporters there as "firebrands"
who, when it came to a vote, would be overawed and falter.[65]
Perhaps (and this seems more likely) he was out of touch with
the roots of the resentments that the manifesto had aroused; his
insistence on the overriding importance of a diplomatic success
(and his immersion in his scientific work) had dulled his senses
to the motives of those whom he now wished to be his transient
accomplices. His speech to a special conference of London Zi-

[63] Annual report for 1917; Goodman's paper (dated 22 December 1916); and
24 November 1916, Goodman to Sokolow (asking for his assistance on the Polish
and other questions), in CZA, Sokolow Papers, A18/36. As early as January
1915, Mr. L. Benjamin (then secretary of the B'nai B'rith) had voiced doubts
about the injection of too much Zionism into the Lodge's program. "He is afraid
that the Manchester people will favour and give preference to acquiring Palestine
on an autonomous basis rather than trying to obtain freedom for the Jews in
Russia," 23 January 1915, S. J. Cohen to Gaster, CZA, Gaster Papers, A203/208.

[64] 30 May 1917, Sacher to Weizmann, WA, file 219; see also Greenberg's
letter to Weizmann, "in reply to your enquiry," on the powers and prerogatives
of the Board of Deputies, 14 June 1917, WA, file 230.

[65] The expression occurs in 3 August 1915, Wolf to Zangwill, DEPS, General
Correspondence, C11/2/7 and 16 October 1916, Alexander to Wolf, New York,
YIVO Institute, Mowshowitch Collection of L. Wolf Papers, no. 1740. For an
early attempt to overawe, or at least intimidate, "a man who seems to hold
somewhat advanced views & might otherwise be somewhat difficult to manage"
(a reference to H. S. Alexander), see 12 June 1907, Emanuel to D. Alexander,
DEPS, Letter Books, B3/29:321.

onists on 20 May, in which he ignored the state of the community and hinted at the value of Whitehall's philo-Zionism, certainly struck a discordant note. So too did his offer to give the B'nai B'rith caucus of deputies the benefit of his advice.[66] The first seemed blithely to ignore, even denigrate, the complex communal forces that, for almost two decades, had acted as stimulants to change within Anglo-Jewry. The second, likewise uncharitably, assumed that those members of the community who had done much to undermine public confidence in the entrenched leadership would willingly transfer whatever credit they had accumulated into the Zionist account. If anything, the leaders of the B'nai B'rith (who had called a meeting of their Emergency Committee to discuss a protest at the Board against the manifesto as early as 25 May) had quite the opposite in mind. The general feeling at the First Lodge, they informed Weizmann, was

> that any outside pressure on the Deputies would defeat its object and that it would . . . not be advisable for you to intervene.
>
> As a matter of fact, it is thought best that the Opposition should concentrate itself on the *manner* rather than the *matter* of the C.C. manifesto. It is considered that, broadly speaking, there is no very widespread or vehement opposition to the terms of the manifesto but that the general objection is rather to the way in which the C.C. have acted.[67]

☐

A "Communal Revolution" of sorts did ultimately take place at the Board of Deputies in June 1917 (the phrase, incidentally, was first applied to the vote by Simon Rowson in an address to the B'nai B'rith). But its form and objectives were not specifically Zionist. Those deputies who happened to be members of the movement constituted a small band, and they had never been

[66] Reported in JC, 25 May 1917, p. 21; 8 June 1917, Goodman to Weizmann, WA, file 230.

[67] 12 June 1917, Goodman to Weizmann, WA, file 230; for the circularized invitation to a meeting of the Jewish Emergency Committee, see Mocatta Library, Gaster Papers, "in" letters, May 1917.

anything more than accomplices or adjuncts, at best stimulants, in a struggle between larger and better-organized forces at the Board. The defeat of the Conjoint Foreign Committee, then, was not simply the climax of a well-orchestrated campaign of communal conquest originally initiated by Herzl in 1898. At the most it can be described as the fortunate fulfilment of a more haphazard program of institutional infiltration, which his leading Anglo-Jewish followers had been constrained to modify and reform. Even then, it did not constitute a clear-cut Zionist victory, with repercussions and implications of exclusively Zionist interest. The rejection of the manifesto was less the expression of a new-found belief in Jewish nationalism on the part of the deputies than an extension of their older demand for more representative government. Neither can the vote be portrayed as the result of the exercise of communal power on the part of Anglo-Jewry's immigrant and proletarian classes. Their spokesmen (who were not noticeably and actively supportive of organized Zionism in Britain before 1917) played what amounted to no more than a spectatorial role. The true protagonists of the contest were groups of more fortunate elites, already in possession of the means to translate sentiments of presumed "popular discontent" into the language of political action. As the record of ubiquitous conflict within the Board of Deputies itself before 1917 indicates, these forces were not dependent upon external pressure for inspiration or justification. They had already demonstrated their ability and determination to be masters of their own communal fate. Their strong sense of regionalism, combined with their fierce antagonism to the exaggerated influence of a privileged coterie, had largely conditioned the terms of reference of their rebellion. Mounting political tensions (of which Zionism, of course, formed a part) merely supplied the immediate cause. In terms of immediate political gains, the Zionists clearly benefited from the censure of the manifesto. But they had no guarantee that the interests that had brought about the revolution at the Board of Deputies would always remain on their side.

(276)

8

English Zionists and British Jews, 1917-1920

In the euphoric aftermath of the vote of 17 June 1917, several leading Zionists in Britain overestimated the extent of their communal strength. The clutch of congratulatory resolutions showered on the Board of Deputies later in the month by congregations throughout the country gave them the unwarranted impression that the barriers of hostility and indifference to the movement had begun to fall. Ignoring explicit warnings that the vote against the Conjoint Foreign Committee had not necessarily been a vote for Zionism, leaders of the EZF contemplated further advances. "The successful fight at the Board of Deputies and the open adhesion of Lord Rothschild have paved the way for an onward sweep," wrote Leon Simon. The opportunity was too good to squander.[1] In general, the communal climate seemed conducive to precisely the kind of conquest envisaged by Herzl almost two decades earlier, and the Zionists had to take their chance. "Doubtless the Antis will not give up the struggle yet," warned Sacher, "but we ought now to take possession of the Board and use it for our purposes." Many of his friends agreed. They accordingly bombarded Weizmann with staccato memoranda. "We must capture the Board entirely. The change of personnel is not sufficient. We must have an assured and preponderating majority. . . . In these cases strike and spare not is a sound motto."[2]

[1] 15 August 1917, Simon to Kellen, CZA, L. Simon Papers, K11/200.
[2] 20 June 1917, Sacher to Simon; 20 June 1917, Raffalovich to Weizmann; 21 June 1917, Sieff to Weizmann; and 22 June 1917, Sacher to Weizmann; WA, files 230-31; see also 18 June 1917, Gaster to S. J. Cohen, London, Mocatta Library, University College, Gaster Papers, Letter Book 1916-1918.

Initially, Weizmann stayed his hand. He had always been averse to becoming too deeply involved in the internal politics of Anglo-Jewry, preferring to invest his energies in gaining the sympathy of gentile British politicians. After June 1917, his mind remained set on a decisive diplomatic coup rather than a ponderous communal struggle. Convinced that the essential task was to elicit a public declaration of the British government's support for Zionist aspirations, he and his colleagues on the Political Committee concentrated almost exclusively during the ensuing months on composing a formula acceptable to the War Cabinet. The complexities of this task were themselves daunting. The Zionists, as Weizmann later confessed, were no more than a "group of amateur state builders," barely competent to define their desiderata in a manner and language acceptable to all shades of their own opinion. That was one reason why Rothschild could not present Balfour with a draft formula until 18 July 1917. Soon thereafter, however, Edwin Montagu (Lord Swaythling's brother and, like the rest of the family, an intransigent anti-Zionist) was appointed secretary of state for India. Admittedly, the post did not carry a seat on the War Cabinet; neither, apparently, did most of Montagu's ministerial colleagues attach much significance to his barrage of rebarbative memoranda—the most stinging of which was unabashedly entitled "The Anti-Semitism of the Present Government." Nevertheless, the timing of his appointment was disconcerting from the Zionists' point of view. They believed Montagu to be the source of many of the objections raised in the Cabinet to successive drafts of the Balfour Declaration, and considered his opposition responsible for the delays in its eventual ratification.[3] For Weizmann, in particular, these were frustrating and frantic months during which he had to put in a full day at the laboratory and still find time to orbit the corridors of Whitehall. Thus occupied, he seems to have been inhibited from in-

[3] E.g., 18 September 1917, Rothschild to Weizmann: "Do you remember I said to you in London as soon as I saw the announcement in the papers of Montague's [sic] appointment that I was afraid we were done." WA, file 237; and Isaiah Friedman, *The Question of Palestine, 1914-1918* (London, 1973), pp. 254-69.

volvement in more parochial affairs. He declined an invitation to join the Board of Deputies (although he did take the preliminary step of becoming a member of the Birkenhead Synagogue), and took no part in the discussion held to consider the composition of that body's new executive. His communal strategy, such as it was at this time, seems to have been based on one of the assumptions originally favored by Herzl: whatever opposition to political Zionism remained in Anglo-Jewry would inevitably crumble once the British government had pledged its support to the movement.

Subsequent events seemingly vindicated Weizmann's deliberately cavalier approach. Between 1917 and 1920 he was indeed in a position to dazzle the community with a string of unprecedented triumphs: the Balfour Declaration of November 1917, the despatch of the Zionist Commission to Palestine in 1918, his own appearance at Versailles in 1919, and the inclusion of the Balfour Declaration in the terms of the San Remo mandate agreement of 1920. Primarily, of course, each of these diplomatic moves hastened the realization of Zionist ambitions in Palestine, but they also served a local and auxiliary purpose. By fostering the impression that, at long last, the tide of history had turned in the Zionists' favor, they acted as powerful inducements to a growth of Zionist influence and prestige within the Anglo-Jewish community. Understandably, therefore, the publicity department of the EZF insisted that it be given ample opportunity to tap the spontaneous spasms of popular support to which each success gave rise. The monster demonstration held at the London Opera House in December 1917 established a pattern: the large audience was roused to a semblance of respectable enthusiasm by carefully selected Zionist speakers ("You must at all risks prevent Dr. Tschlenow from speaking *German*," warned Lord Rothschild);[4] it was then treated to the impressive spectacle of congratulatory messages from Lord Robert Cecil, Herbert Samuel, Sir Mark Sykes, and, in absentia, from Viscount Grey of Fallodon, Walter Long,

[4] 17 November 1917, Rothschild to Weizmann, WA, file 241; and the memorandum by L. J. Stein of the publicity department, dated April 1920, in CZA, Files of the Central Zionist Office (London), Z4/16022.

and Arthur Henderson.[5] Similarly flamboyant gatherings were orchestrated in order to welcome Weizmann home from Palestine (in 1918), Versailles (in 1919), and San Remo (in 1920); an entire series of fêtes was arranged in order to greet the arrival in London of the American Zionist Medical Unit en route to Palestine in 1918. In the latter case, Reform Jews too felt that "their Synagogue cannot well do less for Jewish Soldiers"—even if they were Zionists—"than has been done by others."[6]

In terms of communal influence, such manifestations produced two tangible consequences, both of which proved beneficial to the status of Zionism within Anglo-Jewry. First, they induced several of the more influential men in the community to come to terms with the new situation, and therefore to reconsider their previous reserved attitude toward cooperation with the Zionist movement. Adolph Tuck was one early sympathizer of this sort; Joseph Prag, wistfully recalling his days in the Chovevei Zion Association, another.[7] By November 1918, even such a convinced opponent of the idea of Jewish nationalism as Robert Waley Cohen was advising some of his friends to temper their ire. Once he had been assured, in writing, that "no claim is made, or will be made, that the Jews constitute a separate political nationality all over the world," he suggested that they cooperate in Weizmann's proposed "Advisory Committee" of Anglo-Jewish leaders. This, after all, was the lesser of two evils:

> The policy of leaving the Zionists alone to devise the scheme for the Government of Palestine, and for the carrying out of the Allied Governments' declarations of policy in regard thereto,

[5] An exhaustive report of this, and other meetings in Naḥum Sokolow, *History of Zionism, 1600-1918*, 2 vols. (London, 1919) 2:99-127. The publication in 1919 of Sokolow's work, with its prefatory note by Balfour, was itself a significant propaganda success.

[6] Circular, dated 15 July 1918, signed by the secretary of the West London Synagogue, in Mocatta Library, West London Synagogue Archives, AJ78/29, Correspondence, 1918, box 2.

[7] 13 November 1917, A. Hyamson to Weizmann, WA, file 241; and 10 December 1918, J. Prag to Weizmann, CZA, Files of the Central Zionist Office (London), Z4/106/29.

seems an exceedingly dangerous one. It leaves the entire control of constructive policy for Palestine in the hands of those
who are believed to be much tempted to make some sacrifices
of what we regard as vital principles in their desire to secure
the consummation of Zionist policy. Far better, therefore, for
"all those who care for the position of British Jews and of Jews
of all other nationalities . . . [to] co-operate to the utmost of
their power in constructing a National Home of the Jews in
Palestine in such a way as to safeguard . . . the position and
interest of Jews throughout the world. . . . It is necessary that
that policy should be pursued with as much publicity as possible, so that the forces of the Community may be united . . .
instead of being dissipated in a controversy upon a 'chose ju-
gee.' "[8]

Waley Cohen's plan for a unifying "Anglo-Jewish Conference"
was not accepted; as will be seen, the more prominent—and
important—anti-Zionists in Anglo-Jewry continued to reprehend
association of any sort with the Zionists whom they considered
to have "tricked, calumnied and intrigued against [them] most
shamefully."[9] Some of the less committed adversaries, however,
were more forthcoming. Thus Alfred Mond (subsequently Lord
Melchett) and Anthony de Rothschild, both of whom had hitherto held aloof from Zionist work, contributed handsomely to the
"Preparation Fund." Throughout 1920, they also played an indispensable part in the laborious establishment of the "Economic
Council," from which the Keren Hayesod eventually evolved.[10]
These, like Waley Cohen, were recruits whom the Zionists were
justly proud to have attracted, and for whose support they were
accordingly prepared to pay a high price. Thus, in 1920 Weiz-

[8] 13 November 1918, memorandum by R. Waley Cohen and F. Stern to the
League of British Jews, copy in CZA, Wolf Papers, A77/3c.

[9] 17 October 1918, Wolf to Montefiore, New York, YIVO Institute, David
Mowshowitch Collection of Lucien Wolf Papers, no. 3011. On the League's
reaction to Waley Cohen's suggestion: 15 November 1918, Wolf to Montefiore,
CZA, Wolf Papers, A77/3c.

[10] On which see Evyatar Friesal, *Ha-Mediniut ha-Zionit le-Ahar Hazharat Balfour,
1917-1922* (Tel-Aviv, 1977), pp. 180-86.

mann readily acceded to Waley Cohen's request that he publish a letter supporting the campaign to raise 1 million pounds for a Jewish War Memorial. The objection that the scheme (of which Waley Cohen was cochairman) would siphon off funds that might otherwise be donated to Palestine was rejected as subordinate to a different set of priorities. In the long run, argued Weizmann, association with Waley Cohen would prove more beneficial than confrontation, which was why he also invited Waley Cohen to join the Zionist Executive.[11] The same logic influenced the Political Committee's decision to accept (in 1920) Anthony de Rothschild's demand that his chairmanship of the Zionist executive be made conditional on his simultaneous presidency over "a larger and more influential gathering." Weizmann admitted the inconvenience of this approach, but advised his colleagues of the importance of maintaining the novel link between the Zionists and such prestigious names.[12]

Complementing these somewhat aristocratic gains was a more widely distributed increase in the size of the EZF and the scope of its activities. This was the second benefit that Weizmann's diplomatic successes bestowed on the local movement. Nominal membership of the various Zionist groups in Britain rose dramatically from about 4,000 in 1917 to over 30,000 in 1921; the number of affiliated societies from 61 to 234; and the sums contributed to various funds from just over 500 pounds in 1916 to just under 120,000 pounds in 1918. No less gratifying was the stimulus that such quantitative gains provided for an improvement in the quality of the organization's communal activity. Between 1918 and 1920 the Executive demonstrated unprecedented

[11] For the Waley Cohen-Weizmann exchange on the Jewish Memorial scheme see *Jewish Guardian*, 25 June 1920, p. 6; on earlier Zionist opposition to the scheme: I. Cohen, "Our London Letter," *The Maccabean*, August 1919, p. 232; the discussion at a meeting of the B'nai B'rith in *JC*, 21 November 1919, p. 15. For Weizmann's invitation to Waley Cohen to join the Zionist Executive, *Letters and Papers of Chaim Weizmann. Series A. Letters* [hereafter *Letters*], 23 vols., general editor Meyer Weisgal et al. (Oxford, London, and Jerusalem, 1969-1980), Vol. 9, *October 1918-July 1920*, ed. Jehuda Reinharz (Jerusalem, 1978), p. 366.

[12] Minutes of the Zionist executive meeting of 17 May 1920, CZA, Files of the Central Zionist Office (London), Z4/302(ii).

energy and initiative: it authorized the appearance of a respectable *Bulletin* in English and of a Zionist miscellany in Yiddish; made provisions for the employment of a "synagogue propagandist" (at a weekly wage of three pounds); and established properly constituted, and active, Literary, Hebrew, Palestine, and Financial Committees.[13] Gone, so it seems, was the mood of defensive modesty that had tended to characterize Zionist communal activity before the war. To judge from the EZF's records for the years 1917-1920 (which, unlike their predecessors, have largely survived intact), the leaders of the movement in Britain appeared to be girding themselves for a substantial breakthrough to positions of indisputable preeminence in Anglo-Jewish life. Their long struggle for recognition, so they claimed, was over: Zionists had become "fashionable" and Zionism "which had hitherto looked like a step-child, was in the course of becoming a social stepping-stone."[14]

This forecast was not fulfilled. Despite their enlarged following, the Zionists did not reap the expected harvest of communal authority as easily and as speedily as they had hoped. In 1920 the main body of politically articulate Jews still appeared to be substantially unaffected by the swirl of momentous tidings and high rhetoric. Indeed, once the cheering had subsided and the crowds had dispersed, it was difficult to detect substantive innovations in the corporate behavior of the community. The supposed changes of communal attitude incorrectly observed in June 1917 ultimately reflected minor realignments of perspective, not fundamental shifts of interest. Zionist progress and Zionist problems had undoubtedly moved to the center of the stage, but the Zionists themselves still constituted only a chorus—capable of making a good deal of noise but not of dominating the plot.

This was true even at the Federation of Synagogues and the

[13] Minutes of the executive committee of the EZF in ibid., Z4/692(1); membership and financial statistics in ibid. and Z4/1785. Donations to the "Preparation Fund" were particularly large (see report by S. Marks, 3 November 1918, in ibid., Z4/617); although, it should be noted, not large enough to match the sums collected during the next year on behalf of the Jewish War Memorial scheme.

[14] "Annus Mirabilus," *The Zionist Review*, November 1917, p. 109.

Sephardi congregation, both of which witnessed scenes of un-precedented turmoil after 1917. At the former, Lord Swaythling was loudly hectored for supporting the Conjoint Foreign Committee's manifesto and for refusing to allow discussion on a motion of thanks for the Balfour Declaration; at Bevis Marks a "League of Yehidim" was formed in protest against the Elders' allegedly "unconstitutional" dismissal of Ḥakham Moses Gaster. But both incidents proved to be temporary, and not altogether effective, outbursts; they neither reflected specifically Zionist strength on these bodies nor increased Zionist influence over them. As had been the case before 1917, Zionism (or the anti-Zionism of the incumbent leadership) appears to have played a less important role in these proceedings than did a broader and older demand for reforms in their structure. Swaythling's eventual removal from the Federation of Synagogues in 1925, although undoubtedly foreshadowed in the earlier protests, was not instigated by them. He easily managed to suppress the revolts of 1917 and 1918 by threatening to resign. Similarly, the Elders of the Sephardi con-gregation smoothly calmed tempers within their community by allowing for changes in the *Ascamot* (congregational ordinances) which entitled *Yehidim* to elect their own representative Elders. In neither case were specifically Zionist candidates for office either promoted or seriously considered.[15] The Board of the Federation and the Sephardi *Mahamad* in fact adhered to the tradition of resistance to Zionist control steadfastly maintained by other more quiescent bodies. At the United Synagogue, for instance, Lionel de Rothschild was unanimously elected president in 1918, with-out his well-publicized support for the Conjoint Foreign Com-mittee's manifesto apparently influencing the choice one way or the other; at the Anglo-Jewish Association, Claude Montefiore

[15] On the Gaster affair and the eventual constitutional changes at Bevis Marks, see minutes for 1918 in London, Sephardi Congregation Archives, Elders Minute Book, 1912-1918; and *JC*, 4 April 1919, p. 12. On the Federation, see minutes for 20 November 1917 and 14 January 1918 in London, Federation of Synagogues, Minute Book, 2:230-38 and *JC*, 18 January 1918, p. 13. For Gaster's own view of the extent to which Zionism was "mixed up" in his dismissal, see 27 February 1919, Gaster to Landau, CZA, Gaster Papers, A203/264.

continued to dominate proceedings; and at the Jewish Board of Guardians, Sir Leonard Lionel Cohen (before handing over the reins of office to Sir Arthur Stiebel) was roundly applauded when he admonished "certain propagandists" (meaning the Zionists) for their "personal invective, directed against those who have borne hitherto the burden of the day . . . imputation of motives . . . and other sinister methods."[16]

This is not to suggest that anti-Zionism constituted the dominant communal tone after 1917. It did not. But in terms of political affiliations matters did remain much as they had been ever since Herzl's first appearances in London: relatively small groups of inveterate antagonists continued to struggle for the support of larger numbers of nonpartisans, and the latter remained persistently and overwhelmingly apathetic. The implications and results of this situation were disheartening. From the Zionist point of view, the postwar period cannot be regarded as a suitable prologue to the climactic successes of the 1940s; rather, it emerges as a fitting sequel to the era that preceded the censure of the Conjoint Foreign Committee's manifesto. As such, it does not seem to merit the aura of triumph conveyed in Paul Goodman's *Zionism in England*. At several important points in the narrative there in fact exists a serious dichotomy between his image of a movement maturing in these years toward the threshold of communal power, and the grimmer reality of what amounted to a prescriptive and continuing equilibrium in Anglo-Jewish public life. Zionism did not, firstly, supersede all other items on the communal agenda after 1917. As a topic of Anglo-Jewish concern, the Zionist ideology remained subordinate to such lingering subjects as the alleged inequality of institutional representation and the inefficiency of communal management; as a vehicle for communal change, the Zionist movement was still less effective than provincial protest and customary institutional bargaining. Consequently, Zionist progress and Zionist problems did not during these years generally dictate attitudes toward more local—

---

[16] Presidential address at annual meeting of the Board of Guardians, 24 March 1918; in *Annual Report of the Jewish Board of Guardians* (London, 1918), p. 3.

and sometimes individual—ambitions; rather, and as had previously been the case, traditional interests and objectives continued to influence the fortunes of Anglo-Jewish Zionism. Secondly, the Zionists were not in a particularly favorable position to wrestle with this situation after 1917. The English Zionist Federation did not then achieve a degree of doctrinal and organizational cohesion which might have enabled it to pose as a well-knit force, led by a cadre of responsible leaders sufficiently united to heal the communal rifts of the day. In fact, during the immediate postwar period English Zionism seemed to suffer from a baneful recurrence of the disarray that had previously done much to discredit the EZF's founders, and from various exhibitions of tactlessness on the part of their equally ungracious successors.

> Will you permit me to say [wrote an irate Lord Northcliffe to Israel Cohen] plainly and bluntly, that this pressing to see me, immediately after I have been away for eight months, and before I have had time to see my own relatives, is somewhat typical of the tactlessness of the extreme Zionists.
>
> This kind of thing explains a good deal of the intense dislike in which they are held in many Jewish circles.
>
> You are overdoing it with this telephoning and general pushfulness, just as you are overdoing it in Palestine.[17]

Finally, opposition to Zionism of a more ideological kind did not entirely disappear during this period. Despite the haemorrhages caused by the censure of the Conjoint Foreign Committee's manifesto and the publication of the Balfour Declaration, it became, in some respects, even more aggressive and organized than hitherto.

Chronologically, these three trends were simultaneous; in terms of cause and effect they were to some extent related. Nevertheless, since each reflected a distinctive aspect of the status of Zionism in postwar Anglo-Jewry they will, in the following account, be treated separately.

[17] 27 February 1922, Northcliffe to Cohen, CZA, I. Cohen Papers, A213/17/26.

English Zionists and British Jews

Zionism at the Board of Deputies, 1917-1920

The corporate attitude of the Board of Deputies toward political Zionism between 1917 and 1920 deserves particular attention. Partly, this was because it remained the most prestigious of the community's representative institutions. For all its faults, the public standing of the Board seems to have risen as a result of the upheaval of 1917. By dismissing the Conjoint Foreign Committee, the Board had allegedly demonstrated its ability to respond to changes in the pace and style of Anglo-Jewish life; arguably, that action had allowed it to append the virtues of flexibility to its traditional assets of experience and official recognition. Thus, the vote of 17 June 1917 did not leave a vacuum of authority, which might have paved the way for a shift of communal power away from the Board of Deputies and toward such newer political bodies as the B'nai B'rith, the National Union, the provincial councils, various East End committees, the United Council of Jewish Friendly Societies, or even the EZF. These claimants still had to work through or (where possible) with the Board; they could not simply usurp its functions and prerogatives. As a result, the opinions and votes of deputies continued to influence communal policy and—albeit more obliquely—to reflect much of communal opinion.

To an extent, the Zionists welcomed this situation; they blithely assumed that they had in any case already captured the Board of Deputies. As early as 22 June 1917, Sacher presumed that Lord Rothschild would "assume" the presidency, with Weizmann as vice-president "& say Laski as Treasurer." Within a fortnight, Sokolow was wondering whether he might not "offer" the presidency to A. M. Langdon.[18] Such arrangements were both premature and ill-advised (particularly since neither Sacher, Weizmann, Sokolow, nor Langdon were at the time deputies). Ultimately, the extent of Zionist influence on the formation and composition of the Board's new executive was much more modest than they had hoped. Lord Rothschild was indeed elected senior

[18] 22 June 1917, Sacher to Weizmann, WA, file 231; 4 July 1917, Sokolow to Rothschild, CZA, Files of the Central Zionist Office (London), Z4/117.

vice-president and Nathan Laski treasurer, but neither owed their appointments entirely to Zionist support. Rothschild had, quite independently, established himself as an outstanding figure on the Board of Deputies, and Laski had for some time been a recognized spokesman for the provincial interest. Significantly, the Zionists were unable to ensure the election of the presidential candidate of their own choice. That position eventually went to Sir Stuart Samuel, who, although less hostile toward Zionism than his predecessor, was not a supporter of the movement (which was why an earlier approach had been made to Herbert, his brother).[19] Even more disconcerting was the fact that the junior vice-presidency was retained by Sir Philip Magnus. Of the latter's attitude there could be no doubt. In thanking the deputies for their confidence, Magnus provocatively announced that, where Zionism was concerned, "my views are unchanged. . . . I can take no part, for reasons which I have stated, in encouraging the establishment of Palestine as an autonomous Jewish State. . . . I accept my election, therefore, as an indication on the part of the Deputies that my views on Zionism are not inconsistent with my tenure of this office."[20]

Some significant changes of attitude did occur in the Board of Deputies after June 1917. Most notably, its debates appear to have become far more robust and wide-ranging than they had generally been during the period that preceded the censure of the Conjoint Foreign Committee's manifesto. Several deputies deliberately abandoned the conventions of solid decorum and deliberate prudence that had hitherto tended to limit discussion; meetings—so it was said—were often informative, if rowdy, occasions to which the community as a whole could look forward with interest and even excitement.[21] In part, the change of tone merely reflected the controversial nature of the subjects on the Board's agenda during this period. The plight of Jews in eastern Europe,

[19] 18 June 1917, H. Samuel to Gaster, CZA, Gaster Papers, A203/4.

[20] Minutes of meeting of 15 July 1917, and 28 July 1917, Magnus to Emanuel, London, DEPS, Minute Book, A17, pp. 69-73.

[21] See e.g., *Jewish Guardian*, 25 June 1920, p. 7 and H. Chesney's report to the Grand Order of Israel Friendly Society, JC, 13 August 1920, p. 27.

the debates at Versailles, the anti-Semitic references to the "Bolshevism" of the immigrant community published in the *Morning Post*, as well as the future of Palestine, were all topics that invited the articulation of various, and often unprecedented, points of view.

But to this must be added an avowed wish on the part of the provincial and newer London deputies (in particular) to demonstrate that their recent revolt against "bigotry and autocracy" had not been an aberration; rather, it was to mark the beginning of an entire era of more originality and responsiveness in communal government. For representatives of this group (who increased in number by nineteen deputies between June 1917 and June 1919 and who retained their tradition of independent action),[22] the dismissal of the Conjoint Foreign Committee had marked only one stage in a long campaign which they were determined to continue. Accordingly, Jacobs and Laski prodded the Board to embark upon a fundamental revision of its own constitution. After four full debates between August and December 1918, two extraordinary conferences of synagogue delegates in January 1919, and a series of intricate negotiations with the United Synagogue thereafter, the majority of deputies eventually agreed to most of the reforms suggested by the Constitution and Bye-Laws Committee. Thus, they allowed for the admission of female deputies (as nominees of the Union of Jewish Women); altered the distribution of seats allotted to the United Synagogue and Federation of Synagogues; and, most important of all, consented to forego the Board's traditional insistence on exclusively synagogal representation. Instead, they empowered the election of deputies by certain specified secular societies and associations, the Jewish members of the Universities of Oxford and Cambridge, and any other body whose credentials might subsequently be approved of by a two-thirds majority of deputies at any one meeting. (They also voted to exclude moneylenders from the Board, and to admit as deputies only those persons who had been reg-

[22] See e.g., the remarks appertaining to the Manchester Committee of Deputies in 12 September 1918, Emanuel to Neville Laski, DEPS, Letter Book, B3/37: 193 and minutes of 20 October 1918, DEPS, Minute Book, A17, p. 116.

istered members of the synagogues or societies which they represented for one full year prior to their election.)[23]

These changes did not result in recognizable Zionist gains. The EZF was notably absent from the list of nonsynagogal bodies newly entitled to representation (although the Order of Ancient Maccabeans, as a Friendly Society, did receive one seat). On the other hand, the United Synagogue and Federation of Synagogues actually increased their weight, since their constituents were granted corporate representation in addition to the right of returning separate deputies for individual congregations. (Thus, the loss of five seats entailed in the reduction of the Great, Central, Bayswater, New West End, and Hampstead Synagogues to single-member constituencies was offset by the clause that granted the United Synagogue, as a body, twelve additional deputies to be nominated by its own council.) Sacher's complaint against this "blatant attempt to perpetuate an oligarchic clique" of anti-Zionist safe seats was easily defeated;[24] not surprisingly, since the original momentum for the constitutional changes had not originated with the Zionists on the Board. In fact, those deputies who were Zionists had deliberately—if with some embarrassment—declined to initiate changes in the structure of the institution. The defeat of the Conjoint Foreign Committee had been attained under existing circumstances. They could not be sure that they would do any better by changing the system; they might even do worse. In the provinces, as they admitted, the influence of the EZF was far too slight to make itself felt. Moreover, formal Zionist influence over the communal bodies newly entitled to representation could, they appreciated, only be tenuous. In 1918, the friendly societies had still not officially committed themselves to cooperation with the EZF, while the B'nai B'rith was seriously

[23] The alterations are most conveniently listed in the revised *Constitution of the Board of Deputies*, published in January 1920. For the debates at the Constitution and Bye-Laws Committee and at the full meetings of the Board in 1918 and 1919, see minutes in DEPS, Constitution and Bye-Laws Committee, C/5 and Minute Book, A17 respectively.

[24] By 41 votes to 13; JC, 17 January 1919, p. 13.

divided on the entire topic of Jewish nationalism.[25] Accordingly, most Zionists preferred to repeat the attitude of immobilism toward reform (for outright opposition was clearly out of the question) that they had adopted when the expansion of the Conjoint Foreign Committee had been broached two years earlier. Now, as then, even Gaster poured cold water on suggestions that the Zionists declare themselves in favor of a radical program of reconstruction.[26]

Precisely the same sort of calculation, however, influenced the contrasting behavior of the defeated Old Guard. They were afraid that, as formerly constituted, the Board of Deputies might compound the disaster of June 1917 and succumb to "a panic resolution . . . which would simply get the Board converted into a Zionist organisation."[27] Reform, on the other hand, might obviate this danger. These were the reasons for a new strategy of accommodation, which might best be implemented by bending before the forces of reform agitation or even by stealing some of their thunder. Significantly, it was Lucien Wolf who first spoke to Stuart Samuel about "the very defective constitution of the Deputies" as early as September 1917; three months later he, H.S.Q. Henriques, and Ellis Franklin voiced some of the loudest complaints against the fact that the Board of Deputies "had long ceased to be a truly representative body"; many of the more drastic reform kites were subsequently flown in the anti-Zionist press.[28]

[25] Not until 1919 did the friendly societies begin to alter their attitude (A. Romanovsky in *Di Tsayt*, 8 January 1919, p. 2). Even then, they insisted on retaining a free hand (correspondence in CZA, Files of the Central Zionist Office [London], Z4/1845[i]). On the B'nai B'rith's division over Zionism see P. Goodman's pro-Zionist memorandum (marked "not adopted by the Lodge," in CZA, Goodman Papers, K11/6/2) and J. Gilbert's defense of the League of British Jews, dated 6 June 1918, in CZA, Sokolow Papers, A18/36. On Zionism in the provinces see below pp. 299-300.

[26] Gaster's correspondence with J. C. Fine, in Mocatta Library, Gaster Papers, November 1917.

[27] 2 October 1917, C. Emanuel to B. A. Fersht, confidential, DEPS, Letter Book, B3/33:3-4.

[28] Wolf's letters to C. Montefiore of 20 November 1917 and 12 March 1919 in YIVO, Mowshowitch Collection of Wolf Papers, no. 3000 and folder 210; E. L. Franklin in JC, 14 December 1917, p. 11; and articles on the Board in

Thus, of all the constitutional changes promulgated by the deputies during this period only one—the July 1917 decision to disband the old Conjoint Foreign Committee—can properly be considered a specifically Zionist achievement. Otherwise, a spirit of caution prevailed. An extraordinary meeting of deputies was immediately thereafter called (for a weekday) in order to discuss the manner in which the traditional relationship with the AJA might be retained. Eventually, the few deputies who met on that occasion voted overwhelmingly in favor of a fresh *modus vivendi*. Despite the publicized and unrepentant anti-Zionism of the AJA, they passed a limp resolution that merely "hoped" that the AJA would be "agreeable" to terminating the old arrangement and invited its suggestions for the development of a new one.[29] Ultimately, the new combined "cabinet" of the Board of Deputies and the AJA—now called the Joint Foreign Committee—was remarkably similar to its disgraced predecessor; in matters of procedure, prerogatives, and even personnel, the differences were not substantial. The Zionists failed, successively, to foist their own nominees onto the Board's negotiating team with the AJA and to bring about significant changes in the structure and administration of the new body. Two avowed Zionists, S. J. Cohen and Bertram Benas, were appointed to the Joint Foreign Committee, but their influence was limited. They were outnumbered by new non-Zionist appointees, who consistently recorded a higher rate of attendance at the committee's meetings.[30] Moreover, their room for manoeuver was, a priori, limited by Stuart Samuel's early concession to the majority of Claude Montefiore's demands. Most of the proceedings of the committee were to remain "confidential"; Lucien Wolf's services were to be retained; and—after

---

Jewish Guardian, 10 December 1919, pp. 10-11 and 25 January 1920, p. 1; *Jewish Opinion*, April 1919, p. 1; and *Jewish Religious Union Bulletin*, February 1919, p. 2.

[29] JC, 17 August 1917, p. 12.

[30] Not least because both Benas and Cohen lived in the provinces, whence they found it difficult to travel for every meeting. Benas's request to be sent an agenda before the meetings, so that he might be present at the "most interesting," was rejected. Correspondence for January 1919 in DEPS, General Correspondence, C11/4/3.

a more protracted debate—Palestinian questions were to be considered within its purview.[31] Weizmann's attempts to neutralize Montefiore's influence by an extended correspondence of his own with Sir Stuart Samuel were unavailing. So too were subsequent attempts on the part of other EZF officers to persuade individual deputies to vote against the renewal of the Board's treaty with the Anglo-Jewish Association. Samuel continued to support the arrangement, and threatened to resign the presidency of the Board unless it was adopted by a clear majority of deputies. In both 1919 and 1920, accordingly, the motion for renewal was carried overwhelmingly.[32] Of Samuel, Weizmann soon reached the conclusion: "He is not a friend of ours and must be left alone . . . he has no notion about Zionism and is full of slander."[33]

Zionist attempts to sway the Board on specific matters of substance were equally unsuccessful. When, in November 1917, the Board voted to express its gratitude to the Government for the Balfour Declaration, the majority of deputies rejected a motion that would have pledged "cooperation with the English Zionist Federation and other bodies" in promoting the establishment of a Jewish National Home. As finally carried, the resolution merely thanked the authorities for their "sympathetic interest" in Jewish affairs, without specifically mentioning national aspirations at all.[34] A similarly unwelcome compromise was forced upon Zionist sympathizers at the Board during two highly charged and acrimonious debates in April 1919. At issue was a letter that ten members of the anti-Zionist League of British Jews had recently addressed to the *Morning Post*, in which they implicitly accepted

[31] Minutes of the Foreign Committee of the Board, December 1917 and January 1918, in Mocatta Library, Anglo-Jewish Association Correspondence with the Board of Deputies, 1917-1918, AJ 37/6(i); and 19 December 1917, Montefiore to Samuel, DEPS, Anglo-Jewish Association and Board of Deputies Negotiations, 1916-1918, C11/1/2.

[32] Minutes of 21 June 1919 and 18 April 1920 in DEPS, Minute Book, A17, pp. 63 and 172; for the Weizmann-Samuel correspondence see CZA, Files of the Central Zionist Office (London), Z4/69; an example of an EZF circular against renewal of the treaty, dated 20 June 1919, in CZA, Gaster Papers, A203/244.

[33] Postscript to 12 April 1919, Weizmann to Sieff, *Letters*, 9:134.

[34] *JC*, 23 November 1917, p. 17.

the argument that immigrant Jews harbored "Bolshevik" tendencies not shared by their native coreligionists. After some initial hesitation (which allowed League sympathizers on the Board to muster their supporters), the majority of deputies ultimately deprecated the letter. But they were not prepared to issue a blanket condemnation of the League, or to accuse that body of "casting the stigma of Bolshevism on the Nationalist [Zionist] section of the community."[35] Instead, the Board adopted a policy of appeasement. In 1920, deputies voted to accept Lord Rothschild's suggestion that they cooperate with the League of British Jews in the establishment of a Press Committee to counter anti-Semitic propaganda. Once again, the Zionists (and particularly Samuel Daiches) failed to convince the Board to withhold its "hallmark of approval from a body whose very name was objectionable to large numbers of Jews in the community." After yet another appeal for "unity" from Stuart Samuel, and a considerable amount of pressure from Lord Rothschild, the suggestion was carried by fifty-one votes to thirty.[36]

Only once, in February 1919, could Daiches legitimately claim to have broken the conventional pattern of Zionist defeat. He then managed to carry the rejection of one clause in the Joint Foreign Committee's suggested program for Palestine (clause 5: "that no political or economic privileges or preferences be created in favour of any race or religious community"; the Zionists, of course, *did* desire such exclusive privileges). However, at the very next meeting, that decision was reversed. Sympathetic to allegations that the initial vote had somehow not been "representative," Sir Stuart Samuel exercised his presidential prerogatives to have the clause in question amended to allow for "the fullest equality" for all races and religions. At the same time, and despite

---

[35] Minutes of 27 and 29 April 1919, in DEPS, Minute Book, A17, pp. 136-38; for an example of a hasty summons to League supporters see Emanuel's telegram to Philip Magnus of 28 April 1919 in DEPS, Letter Book, B3/39:202. After the debate, Sir Philip Magnus did resign from the Board; but he was replaced as deputy for the West London Synagogue by his equally anti-Zionist son, Laurie. *Jewish World*, 28 May 1919, p. 5.

[36] JC, 20 November 1920, p. 11.

noisy Zionist complaints, he also advised deputies not to "en-
dorse" the program for Palestine that Weizmann proposed to
present at Versailles; instead he supported the Joint Foreign Committee's suggestion that Lucien Wolf (who was already in Paris)
be instructed "not to agree to, or support, the demand for Jewish
National Rights."[37] In view of the manner in which Sir Stuart
handled that particular debate, and its outcome, many Zionists
understandably felt that their supposed victory of June 1917 had
turned somewhat sour. As early as January 1918 some complained
that the "revolution" of the previous summer "had been undone";
by February 1920 they generally agreed that "the change of the
Conjoint Foreign Committee (of unhappy memory) into the Joint
Foreign Committee has been of no avail."[38]

The unfavorable climate thus in evidence at the Board brought
about a change in the Zionist attitude toward that institution.
Hopes of an early or easy conquest were abandoned. Deputies
were not going to succumb to the pressure of either Zionism's
alleged popularity or its assumed official favor. Instead, the Zionists would have to wage a lengthier and less glamorous campaign for influence. Basically, this involved a reversion to the
old policy of infiltration. As much was apparent, as early as April
1918, to Harry Sacher; he accordingly urged Simon Marks to

> carry through and organise all Zionist forces on the Board of
> Deputies. . . . We must form a Zionist party with Whips and
> endeavour to fill every vacancy with Zionists. . . . My idea
> about the party is that it should quite definitely declare that
> its organisation is not intended to affect the ordinary work of
> the Board or to introduce any kind of party vote but to create
> an organisation which would secure proper representation in
> full force on the Board when Palestine and related questions
> come up for discussion. We must have a central organisation

[37] Minutes of Board meeting of 23 March 1919 in DEPS, Minute Book, A17,
p. 132; and of Joint Foreign Committee on 4 February 1919, in DEPS A3/1(5).

[38] *JC*, 26 January 1918, p. 11 and 27 February 1920, p. 29; and *Di Tsayt* 22
July and 18 November 1919. Compare these complaints with Lucien Wolf's
buoyant report of Zionist defeats at the Board in YIVO, Mowshowitch Collection
of Wolf Papers, nos. 3003 (1917), 3574 (1920), and 2128 (1921).

for that and you have in London the material for it. There should be a provincial whip or whips and a London whip or whips and we should keep an account of the names of every member of the Board who is in sympathy and who is summoned to a special meeting.[39]

After some delay, these suggestions were implemented; a "Communal Organisation Committee" of the EZF began to function in May 1919 (on the eve of triennial elections to the Board of Deputies) with the promise to "issue special whips, . . . circularize and educate the waverers on the Board . . . bring pressure to bear on deputies from the Zionists in the institutions they represent . . . devote ourselves to encouraging all congregations eligible to elect candidates in the Colonies to do so."[40] But, even with the assistance of that body, Zionist achievements were limited. The committee, although active, was manifestly unable to exert a substantial influence on the elections of 1919. Neither could it put together a cohesive party out of those of its nominal candidates who were returned.[41] Thirty such deputies did attend a private meeting on Thursday, 19 June 1919, called by Col. William Schonfield (the chairman of the committee who was himself unanimously elected deputy for Hull), but the only point upon which they could all agree was that they should *not* form a distinct lobby. Any other course, seems to have been the feeling, would at this stage merely reveal the extent of Zionist weakness at the Board. When, contrary to Schonfield's advice, Samuel Daiches nevertheless stood as a specifically Zionist candidate for

[39] 12 April 1918, Sacher to Marks, CZA, H. Sacher Papers, Z4/120.

[40] 15 May 1919, W. Schonfield and J. L. Cohen to S. Landman, CZA, Files of the Central Zionist Office (London), Z4/618.

[41] In May 1919 the committee addressed a "Call to Arms" to all Zionists through the Jewish press (e.g. JC, 9 May 1919, p. 10 and 23 May 1919, p. 2); and made careful enquiries as to the nomination procedures at Board elections (e.g., 23 May 1919, C. Emanuel to J. L. Cohen, DEPS, Letter Book, B3/39:403). In June it approached individual prospective candidates, and in July circularized all members of the Board with a list of its own nominees for seven of the executive committees (special meeting of EZF executive, 15 July 1919, CZA, Files of the Central Zionist Office [London], Z4/631). Compare Paul Goodman, *Zionism in England, 1899-1949* (London, 1949), pp. 52-53.

the vice-presidency of the Board in August 1919, he received only twenty-one votes.[42]

THE EZF, 1917-1920

Scrupulously observing their own folklore, many senior Zionists attributed their lack of success at the Board to the workings of the community's oligarchic system of government. Their successive defeats, they maintained, were the work of "a small governing class, who have been able to usurp positions of authority chiefly owing to their wealth."[43] This, in all fairness, was one side of the picture; Anglo-Jewry's Establishment did still possess sufficient reserves of influence to resist blatant nationalist encroachments on its traditional demesnes. Thus, Weizmann was denied an opportunity to address the Jewish Historical Society of England; the secretary of the EZF was refused employment at the Board of Deputies; and Gaster's election as deputy for the West End Talmud Torah (in 1919) was disallowed on a technicality.[44] But, as was indicated by the cantankerous squabble over Daiches's nomination to the vice-presidency of the Board of Deputies in August 1919, much of the trouble also lay with the Zionists themselves. In general, one great weakness of the strategy of infiltration was that its successful implementation would have demanded a greater degree of organizational cohesion and unity of purpose than the EZF had yet managed to attain. In this respect, too, 1917 did not represent a watershed. Despite the diplomatic successes of

[42] Lord Rothschild received 123 votes and Anthony de Rothschild, 105: *JC*, 27 June 1919, p. 17 and 25 July 1919, p. 17.

[43] Col. W. Schonfield at the Board on 22 June 1919, in DEPS, Minute Book, A17, p. 140. To which Stuart Samuel retorted: "Were the Deputies, which for over 170 years had been the representative body of Anglo-Jewry, to be ruled by a policy dictated by the newly arrived in this country.?"

[44] 12 December 1918, H. Morgenstern (EZF) to Weizmann, CZA, Files of the Central Zionist Office (London), Z4/617; on the absence of an invitation to Weizmann from the JHS see 31 October 1918, Zangwill to Salaman, CZA, Zangwill Papers, A120/50; on Gaster's invalidated election to the Board of Deputies see 18 June 1919, Emanuel to Gaster, Mocatta Library, Gaster Papers; and 9 July 1919, Emanuel to S. Samuel, DEPS, Letter Book, B3/40, p. 220.

the succeeding years, the movement continued to be racked by an embarrassing range of personal antagonisms and local jealousies. These continued to tarnish its public image and thereby to impede its communal progress.

In Weizmann the EZF did, of course, possess a leader whose contribution to the cause was unquestionable and whose authority was therefore largely supreme. After San Remo, even Greenberg, whose previous exchanges with Weizmann had often been bitter, took pains to emphasize that his loyalty would thereafter be unswerving.[45] Other old emnities, however, died somewhat harder. Joseph Cowen, for instance, "sulked" in opposition throughout 1918 and 1919; Herbert Bentwich, possibly because he had been slighted by the Zionist delegates at Versailles, refused to accept nomination as vice-president of the EZF under Weizmann in 1921.[46] Gaster, almost obsessionally one feels, continued to play his customary embattled role. His residence in Brighton during most of the latter part of the war initially muzzled him, as did his subsequent dispute with the Sephardi Elders (which was, itself, occasioned by the *Ḥakham*'s frequent absences from London). By early 1919, however, Gaster had returned to the fray. He claimed that his past services to the movement were being ignored (why, he wanted to know, was his portrait not included in Sokolow's *History of Zionism*?); more important, his entire life's work was being undone (why had Weizmann accepted merely "a small colony under most abject conditions"?). It was, so he informed the Jewish press, all the result of "hole and corner meetings conducted with a curious secrecy which is in flagrant contradiction with the fundamental principles of an open, free and dem-

[45] 14 May 1920, Greenberg to Weizmann, CZA, Files of the Central Zionist Office (London), Z4/16022.

[46] 17 August 1919, Weizmann to D. Eder, *Letters*, 9:200, no. 201; and 21 July 1921, H. Bentwich to E. Mayer, CZA, H. Bentwich Papers, A100/50. Bentwich went to Versailles as the representative of the B'nai B'rith, and often complained that "the intervention of the Order seems to be resented . . . in quarters . . . where its assistance was previously welcomed." 12 June 1919, Bentwich to Goodman, CZA, P. Goodman Papers, K11/6/4.

ocratic Zionism."[47] If the movement was to be rebuilt on a "true and solid foundation," the present bunch of "self-appointed representatives" would have to be ousted. Gaster himself ostentatiously refused to participate in the various Zionist demonstrations held in 1919 and 1920; more ominously, he invited some of his old cronies in the Order of Ancient Maccabeans, the National Union, and the provinces to support his efforts to establish a rival organization.[48]

In thus fermenting dissention, Gaster was able to take advantage of a different set of already-existing tensions within the Zionist camp. Thus, several of the "petty, potty, piffle partisan" jealousies which so embarrassed the Zionists[49] (and which Gaster undoubtedly wished to exploit) could be attributed to the long-standing provincial mistrust of the London leadership. This was one of the difficulties hardly affected by Weizmann's assumption of the presidency in February 1917. In fact, as early as May 1917 Sacher and Simon had felt that Weizmann was himself being unduly influenced by the "London group" and, in the name of the Manchester-based British Palestine Committee, complained that the provinces were not being kept fully informed of the Executive's ambitions, propaganda, and political progress.[50] The publication of the Balfour Declaration, and the subsequent desire to exploit the occasion in communities up and down the country, brought forth a predictable crop of similar charges. Throughout 1918, the Executive of the EZF was accused of treating provincial societies in a perfunctory and slipshod manner, and of surrendering its influence to the newly-established London bureau of

---

[47] Gaster's letters to the JC in 25 February 1919, CZA, Gaster Papers, A203/264, no. 4; his complaints to Sokolow in ibid., no. 11 and to Moser in ibid., no. 15.

[48] E.g., 5 February 1918, S. J. Cohen (Manchester) to Gaster, CZA, Gaster Papers, A203/243; 3 March 1919, Gaster to S. Goldberg (E. London Zionist Society), ibid., A203/264, no. 8; 3 March 1919 Gaster to M. Myers (National Union) ibid., no. 9, and 12 June 1919 Gaster to N. Sarna (North London OAM), ibid., no. 33. Gaster consistently declined invitations to official EZF gatherings, e.g., ibid., A203/265, nos. 3, 23, 36, and 40.

[49] The phrase in 1 February 1918, B. Benas to Weizmann, WA, file 1918(2).

[50] 11 May 1917, Sacher to Simon, WA, file 216; and 17 May 1917, Sieff to Weizmann, WA, file 217.

the World Zionist Organisation at 77 Great Russell Street. At the Annual Conference of that year, representatives from Manchester and Leeds presented motions demanding that the council hold special quarterly meetings in order to accommodate its provincial members and objecting to the practice whereby London proxies were appointed for provincial societies. Both motions were carried but, as was later discovered by a specially appointed Provincial Advisory Committee, neither was put into effect. The results, reported the committee, were "deplorable": the London office of the EZF did not even possess a list of members of all provincial societies and was generally out of touch with their fortunes.

Even where statistics did exist, their message of healthy growth was often deceptive. In the country at large, the EZF retained the image of a disparate conglomeration of individualistic cells, which recruited their followers almost exclusively from the poorer classes of Anglo-Jewry and which were therefore unattractive to "the more influential and most desirable persons" in the community. This situation could only be remedied by the employment of a highly-paid provincial organising secretary (at a salary of no less than 500 pounds per annum) and considerable investment in a comparably expensive press campaign.[51] Until these recommendations were adopted (and neither of them were), the EZF could not hope to pose as a truly national organization fully in command of communal sympathy. On the contrary, it appeared to be losing the intellectual and material support of the provincial societies upon which its initial development had in part depended. Samuel J. Cohen (one of Gaster's Mancunian friends who resigned from the EZF) had as early as 1917 drawn an uncomfortable parallel: "The English Zionist Federation as it stands today is suffering from the same disease as the Board of Deputies suffered before the last change."[52]

[51] Report of the Provincial Advisory Committee, dated 7 November 1918, in CZA, Files of the Central Zionist Office (London), Z4/5069. See also J. Cohen, "Organisation Problems of the EZF," *Zionist Review* 3 (January 1920):141-43 and minutes of the 1918 annual conference in CZA, Files of the Central Zionist Office (London), Z4/692(2).

[52] 16 August 1917, S. J. Cohen to Weizmann, WA, file 235.

In one sense, the very pace of Zionist progress tended to exacerbate such dissensions. Every advance, particularly on the diplomatic front, imparted immediacy to problems that had hitherto seemed remote and theoretical, and thereby enlarged the scope of possible disagreement. Internal Zionist differences over the attitude to be adopted toward the Jewish Legion had provided one early example of this process. The Balfour Declaration and the British conquest of Palestine supplied many others. The imminence of an autonomous form of Zionist administration in Palestine, for instance, necessarily raised the question of the content of the religious instruction to be imparted in Jewish schools; the prospect of large-scale land purchase and selective immigration invited debates on the social and administrative framework that would best ensure equality of opportunity and expression for the immigrants; the prospective existence of a *"Jewish* National Home" prompted discussions of the manner in which its inhabitants might properly cope with the hopes and aspirations of their Arab neighbors, whose violent attacks on Jewish settlements increased in ferocity throughout 1920. As the Zionist leadership in Britain soon discovered, it was impossible to provide one section of the community with satisfactory answers to such questions without antagonizing other groups whose support was considered equally important. Agreement on the minimal basis of the Basle Program and the Balfour Declaration was possibly, but not consistently, attainable; a more coherent and composite platform was an entirely different matter. Ultimately, as they confessed, the Zionists found themselves speaking in a number of different and, at times, competing voices.[53]

Differences over the nuts and bolts of life in Palestine were not, of course, exclusive to the EZF. In many respects, the debates on these matters within and between English Zionists and their fellow travellers did little more than mirror similar—and more

---

[53] 2 September 1917, Rothschild to Weizmann, WA, file 236; and 7 January 1918, Jabotinsky to Weizmann, CZA, Files of the Central Zionist Office (London), Z4/106/16. See also "Dr. Weizmann's Zionist Policy" by "A Jewish Nationalist," in JC, 5 September 1919, pp. 15-17; and the reports of conflicting Zionist statements in *Jewish World*, 1 October 1919, p. 3. Also 6 April 1919, Zangwill to I. Cohen, CZA, I. Cohen Papers, A213/17/15.

intensive—discussions on the Continent, in the United States, and at the extraordinary conference of the World Zionist Organisation, held in London in 1920. But the cumulative effect of such wrangles on the image of the EZF was nevertheless particularly debilitating. In particular, they frustrated the plan to establish an all-embracing Zionist Organisation of the United Kingdom, which would have included every wing of nationalist thought within the country. Schemes of this sort were regularly discussed between 1917 and 1919 by the Executive Council of the EZF, which took appropriate steps to hold *pourparlers* with representatives of the Mizrachi Federation, the Order of Ancient Maccabeans, the Jewish trade unions, and—in a more delicate and deliberately "informal" manner—with the Ito.[54] But not one of the organizations approached immediately agreed to forego its independence; each claimed that the special interests of its own constituents would not be satisfied by submersion with a larger conglomeration. At best, the OAM and the Mizrachi agreed to elect representatives to the council of the EZF; Ito and the trade unions refused to do even that. Instead, all of the bodies approached took advantage of the EZF's invitation to publicize the extent to which they were at variance with each other.[55] As an exercise in public relations, the entire episode was therefore unfortunate. Instead of creating a novel impression of purposeful unity, Zionists in Anglo-Jewry had demonstrated their persistent ideological confusion. As late as 1922 Laurie Magnus could still

[54] Minutes of Executive Council meetings in CZA, Files of the Central Zionist Office (London), Z4/692(1-2); and minutes of constitutional subcommittee of the EZF, 15 October 1918, ibid., Z4/6051. On the negotiations with Zangwill see minutes of the Political Committee of the Zionist Bureau, 14 November 1918, CZA, files of the Zionist Commission, Jerusalem, 1918-1921, L3/310; and 29 November 1918, Zangwill to Lucien Wolf, private and confidential, CZA, Ito files, A36/113.

[55] On the OAM, see memorandum by D. Lewis, 20 November 1917, CZA, Files of the Central Zionist Office (London), Z4/674; on the Mizrahi, "Report of the First Mizrachi Conference in the UK" (Manchester, 28-29 December 1918), pp. 9-10, copy in WA, file 1918(12); on trade unions, memorandum by M. Shire, 28 January 1918, Files of the Central Zionist Office (London), Z4/692(2) and 24 December 1918, R. Stiebel to L. Wolf, DEPS, General Correspondence, C11/2/11.

chide Israel Cohen for being more concerned with the conversion of his "friends" than his "adversaries."[56]

THE LEAGUE OF BRITISH JEWS, 1917-1920.

One of the factors that lent weight to such criticisms was the contrasting image of obstinate decisiveness projected by the various opponents of political Zionism. Admittedly, they too did not work in unison; as had always been the case, critical differences of interests, values, and backgrounds prevented, almost entirely, overt cooperation between those members of the community who supported the Agudah, the Reform movement, and— at a later stage—the Communist Party.[57] Nevertheless, the combined effect of their continued opposition was sufficiently powerful both to cause concern to the Zionists and to make some impression on different groups within Anglo-Jewry. Most obviously was this the case where the Reform school of native opposition to Zionism was concerned. Despite their discomfiture at the Board of Deputies in 1917, the instigators and supporters of the Conjoint Foreign Committee's manifesto had adamantly refused to abandon their cause. If anything, that defeat had merely increased their determination to publicize their views as widely as possible. Accordingly, in June, opponents of Zionism were persuaded to remain on the Board of Deputies (where proceedings "are sure to have a sequel, and it would be well we think to wait and see what happens");[58] in October they eagerly accepted the Government's suggestion that three prominent anti-Zionists pass comment on its draft "Declaration on Palestine." Secretly coached by Edwin Montagu, Claude Montefiore presented a particularly impressive case. Without questioning the importance of Jewish

[56] 8 March 1922, L. Magnus to I. Cohen, CZA, I. Cohen Papers, A213/17/27.

[57] "Almost entirely," since the Agudah did, on at least one occasion, appeal for help to the avowedly Reform members of the Joint Foreign Committee; see above p. 204.

[58] 26 June 1917, M. Levy (secretary, West London Synagogue of Reform Jews) to Sir P. Magnus, Mocatta Library, West London Synagogue Archives, AJ/78 1917, box 2.

colonization in Palestine, he stressed that recent events in Russia had strengthened his conviction that the Zionist program was redundant. "For the true well-being of the Jewish race, eman-cipation and liberty in the countries of the world are a thousand times more important." If the Government felt some declaration to be necessary, for reasons of state, then it had best be made as mild and ineffectual as possible. His advice was to strike out all mention of a "national home" and to substitute an innocuous reference to "free and unimpeded Jewish immigration into Pal-estine," to promise "such municipal and local autonomy for the Jews as may be possible," and to stress that most Jews "have no desire to relinquish their existing nationality and citizenship."[59]

Milner's efforts to accommodate some of these sentiments in the final version of the Government's announcement did nothing to allay Montefiore's fears.[60] Less than a week after the publication of the Balfour Declaration, he and his colleagues organized a gathering of their sympathizers at New Court, the London head-quarters of the Rothschild concerns. The meeting was brisk and—as befitted its location—businesslike. The assembly soon agreed to establish a "League of British Jews"; a provisional committee was elected, office space obtained, and a plan of campaign agreed upon. In its subsequent announcement to the press, the League proclaimed its determination to combat the Zionist caveat that "the Jew is an alien in the land of his birth." It called upon all Jewish citizens in Britain (irrespective of their place of birth) to support its own platform:

[59] C. Montefiore to Sir M. Hankey, 12 October 1917, London, Public Record Office, War Cabinet Papers, 1917, CAB 21/58. Altogether eight Jews were consulted by the Government; the other two anti-Zionists being Lionel Cohen and Sir Philip Magnus. For Edwin Montagu's influence on their replies, see his letter (dated 4 October 1917, and marked "secret") to Claude Montefiore: "I . . . write in order to help you to be in readiness to advise and act, as I am sure that you would wish to do, at and after the time at which the draft declaration is circulated." DEPS, Correspondence on Palestine, 1916, C11/12/54, no. 2.

[60] See Ben Halpern, "The Drafting of the Balfour Declaration," *Herzl Year Book* 7 (1971):255-84.

(i) To uphold the status of British subjects professing the Jewish religion.

(ii) To resist the allegation that Jews constitute a separate Political Nationality.

(iii) To facilitate the settlement in Palestine of such Jews as may desire to make Palestine their home.[61]

This program was formally adopted at the first General Meeting of the League of British Jews, held in London midway through March 1918 and attended by over 400 members. There, Lionel de Rothschild was elected president and Lord Swaythling vice-president. In his speech of thanks, the latter explicitly proclaimed that the League's object was to establish a "party" within Anglo-Jewry, "bound together for the sake of defending our rights and taking a larger part in the government of the community."[62]

It is tempting to dismiss the League of British Jews as an inconsequential affair. Only eighteen Jews "British by birth and nationality, actively engaged in public work in the Anglo-Jewish community" participated in the foundation meeting at New Court. There is evidence to indicate that over twenty others, privately summoned by telegram, declined to do so.[63] Furthermore, attendance at the body's public gatherings and at annual general meetings was always to remain slight; less than thirty members turning up to hear the chairman's report in 1920. Whether or not this sorry state of affairs was attributable to the general apathy of the community, to its failure to comprehend the League's arguments, or—in a more sinister fashion—to "organised opposition," remained a matter of debate at the League's offices in Finsbury Circus, but there was general agreement that for whatever reason "the actual total of Members has to date not reached

[61] *The League of British Jews: Prospectus* (London, 1918); on the foundation meeting see *JC*, 16 November 1917, p. 6.

[62] *Report of the First General Meeting of the League of British Jews, 14 March 1918* (London, 1918), pp. 5-6.

[63] Memorandum by L. Wolf (1917) in DEPS, Correspondence on Palestine, 1916, C11/12/54.

expectations."[64] All attempts to drum up wider support by a concerted series of drawing-room meetings, public lectures, and even Lionel de Rothschild's personal signature to 500 letters, produced disappointing results. Numerically, the League of British Jews was never a match for the EZF; any mathematical comparison of their respective memberships should have prompted the rational conclusion that the former had best cut its losses and retire from the fray.[65]

A mere count of heads does not, however, provide a true gauge of the importance and influence of the League of British Jews. Despite its numerical weakness, the body managed to create a surprisingly powerful impression upon both Jews and gentiles in postwar Britain. In part, this was due to the composition of its executive, which was almost exclusively drawn from families that had stood at the summit of Anglo-Jewish affairs for several generations. In many eyes (including, of course, their own), the Montefiores, Montagus, Rothschilds, and Cohens *were* Anglo-Jewry. Their emblematic presence on the League's platform was still sufficient to foster the impression that the organization represented "the most responsible and respected members of the community."[66] That was one reason why the Zionists felt that their adversaries were opponents whom it would be impolitic to underrate. Admittedly, Weizmann's initial inclination had been to strike a deliberately disdainful pose, designed to belittle the League as a gang of isolated lightweights. But this attitude could not long be sustained. Lord Walter Rothschild, as early as January 1918, insisted on the need for a serious discussion on the League's

[64] "Private and confidential" report to the executive committee of the League (dated 1919), by M. A. Green and J. Gluckstein, DEPS, League of British Jews, 1918, E3/208(2).

[65] 4 May 1920, L. Wolf to C. Montefiore, DEPS, General Correspondence, C11/2/15.

[66] M. A. Green (the first secretary of the League), letter to the editor, JC, 4 January 1918, p. 11. The *Times* reported that "all the leading names in Anglo-Jewry are represented on its provisional committee" (13 March 1918, p. 3) and the *Westminster Gazette* that "it includes in its membership the lay heads of all the sects of the Jewish community in this country and the presidents of the principal charitable and representative institutions" (2 April 1918, pp. 1-2).

activities; Weizmann soon became equally concerned. Writing from the Zionist Commission in Palestine, he pestered his colleagues at the London bureau for details of the League's work and their own response. Throughout the spring of 1918, he anxiously cabled that "alarming rumours about anti-Zionist activities in London have been received here. Considerable importance attached to them in official circles. An immediate detailed report very necessary for our work."[67] He never seems to have shared the sanguineness of Israel Sieff, who would have preferred to "let them suffocate in their own———."[68]

But there was more to the League of British Jews than its impressive muster of names. In the final analysis, the vigor and tone of its activities and arguments was equally important. It ensured that the antinationalist cause would not go by default. As much was admitted, in an internal memorandum, by the Zionists themselves.[69] That, too, was what made its members formidable opponents. Unlike the Ito, for instance, the League was not content merely to hurl the odd brick of carping criticism, which ultimately called into question nothing more than the alleged exuberance of Zionist claims. More conspicuously still, it threw off the mantle of indifference and ambivalence toward Zionism worn by the majority of the community. Instead, the League attempted to erect a cogently structured alternative theory which scrutinized and challenged the Zionist thesis in its entirety. To this end, Montefiore, Wolf, and Abrahams (who throughout remained the League's guiding spirits) committed their talents, their status, and their time. Marshalling all the arguments that they had developed during the previous quarter of a century, they prodded their colleagues into a display of activity. By the end of

[67] 6 January 1918, Rothschild to Weizmann, WA, file 1918(i); and e.g., 22 March 1918, telegram to Sokolow, no. 2 and 27 March 1918, telegram to Sokolow, no. 6, CZA, Files of the Central Zionist Office (London), Z4/305/1. Sokolow's replies on, e.g., 9 April 1918, CZA, Files of the Zionist Commission, Jerusalem, 1918-1921, L3/370.

[68] 24 April 1918, I. Sieff to I. Cohen, CZA, Files of the Central Zionist Office (London), Z4/242.

[69] Unsigned note, 1919, ibid., Z4/5014.

1918, the League had begun to publish a monthly commentary on communal affairs (*Jewish Opinion*); it had presented its case to the British government;[70] and it was in a position to contemplate the establishment of an international network of sister societies. Wolf assiduously maintained his contacts with Sylvain Levi and the anti-Zionist Alliance Israelite Universelle in France. In a flutter of transatlantic correspondence, he and Lionel de Rothschild also attempted to foster the foundation of a League of American Jews in the United States.[71] These efforts did not redress the balance in favor of anti-Zionism; judged by the standards of practical results they were all flops. But from the communal perspective they nevertheless fulfilled one essential function: by demonstrating that opposition to Zionism was still vigorous, they combatted the impression that Anglo-Jewry had no alternative to the program that the EZF had to offer.[72]

More successful from every point of view were the League's attempts to establish an independent weekly of its own. Once again, the initiative was Lucien Wolf's. It was he who persuaded the executive of the League of British Jews to support the estab-

[70] E.g., memorandum to Lloyd George, 18 December 1918 in London, Public Record Office, Foreign Office Files, FO 371/3388, file 856, no. 208514; and to Balfour, 25 October 1918, ibid., FO 371/3366, file 1495, no. 178317; and further drafts in CZA, Wolf Papers, A77/3c.

[71] On the French connection see, e.g., 30 September 1918, Wolf to Bigart, CZA, Wolf Papers, A77/3c; for the USA see the correspondence between D. Philipson and leading American Jews in Cincinnati, American Jewish Archives, D. Philipson Papers; the circular addressed to similar persons by Max Senior, dated 16 October 1918, and his correspondence with Louis Marshall, in New York, Jacob Blaustein Library, Archives of the American Jewish Committee; and the exchange between Lionel de Rothschild and the committee (initiated in June 1918), published in *Jewish World*, 18 December 1918, pp. 5-6.

[72] As much was admitted in the USA, even by American Jews who declined to join the projected League of American Jews. "It is sad but true, that the Jews in England showed finer form. And it is a sad commentary on Reform Judaism in this country, that whereas in England, Orthodox Jews did not hesitate to join their Reform brethren in the presence of the Balfour Declaration, and their rejection of its formula, in our country we cannot get the laymen who, as I know, really do agree with us, to make a clear and dignified statement of their position." 26 September 1918, Sam Schulman to Philipson, American Jewish Archives, D. Philipson Papers, file 2/1.

lishment of the *Jewish Guardian* as a rival to the pro-Zionist *Jewish Chronicle* and *Jewish World*.[73] Not all of those who gave their financial and moral support to the enterprise necessarily had altruistic motives at heart; personal animosity also seems to have played some part. As Isidore Spielmann admitted to Israel Zangwill, he, for one, saw the *Guardian* as a stick with which to beat "Master Greenberg, who has run the community long enough & it seems to me that he tries to 'boss it' with his J.C. & J.W. as Northcliffe tries to 'boss' the country with his *Times & Mail*."[74] This, however, was only one of the venture's results. Skilfully edited by Laurie Magnus, the *Guardian* provided an attractive and successful platform for non-Zionist opinion throughout the next decade. Most obviously was this so because the paper did not limit itself (as its first edition threatened to do) to a series of attacks on the "chauvinistic" aspects of political Zionism or to a turgid repetition of the League's litanies. Instead, it soon developed into a medium of Anglo-Jewish opinion which invited views from various quarters and addressed itself to a wide spectrum of subjects (Chief Rabbi Hertz was among the first contributors, Habil Hotfallah Bey of the Syrian Union an early correspondent, and a special supplement on Jewish Friendly Society affairs was for some years one of its unique features). Altogether, the newspaper ensured that the community was supplied with a perspective on current events that was not exclusively Zionist; in so doing, it prevented the anti-Zionism of the League from becoming a subject of peripheral concern.

The gritty determination of the League of British Jews to withstand the Zionist tide did not, however, wait upon the success of the *Guardian*. From the outset, its senior members had fully demonstrated their determination to stick to their ideological guns. That is certainly the impression to emerge from the proceedings of what was inelegantly dubbed "the Provisional Committee of the Balfour Declaration Committee." This ad hoc collection of Anglo-Jewish leaders (Zionist, non-Zionist, and anti-

[73] Minutes of meeting of the literary subcommittee of the League, held on 18 March 1918, DEPS, League of British Jews, E3/208(1).

[74] Spielman to Zangwill, n.d., CZA, Zangwill Papers, A120/63.

Zionist) was first convened late in 1917 by Sir Lionel Abrahams, whose membership in the Ito was thought to give him a foot in every camp.[75] His avowed purpose, as he wrote to both Lucien Wolf and Chaim Weizmann, was to find some common ground between the parties and thereby end the strife that was doing neither any good and the community as a whole considerable harm. Admittedly, he conceded, "the facts render impossible any complete unity in the community"; nevertheless, the leaders of the two factions ought to possess sufficient pragmatism to see the advantages in some joint effort at accommodation. By demonstrating their willingness to embark on a process of "reconciliation," members of the League might be able to wriggle off the hook of apparent intransigence and isolation.[76] The Zionists, on the other hand, might benefit from the impression that they were being consulted as equals by their principal aristocratic opponents. This would produce (so it was hoped) a particularly striking effect on the so-called "Anglo-Jewish bourgeoisie," that "flock of sheep, idolators of names & titles," without whose assistance the leaders of the EZF could not hope to capture the most important communal offices.[77]

Initially, all the desired effects seemed attainable. Abrahams and Hyamson (respectively chairman and secretary of the committee) were both imbued with a strict sense of civil-service form, and their impeccable impartiality did much to foster a mood of mutual confidence at its meetings. Convinced that an atmosphere

[75] 28 November 1917, Abrahams to Zangwill, CZA, Ito files, A36/113; the other members of the committee were Lord Rothschild, Sokolow, M. Spielman, F. H. Harvey-Samuel, and H. M. Kirsch. The original minute book of the Provisional Committee is preserved in the Mocatta Library, AJ/82; other reports of proceedings in CZA, Files of the Central Zionist Office (London), Z4/1591 and Z4/106(i).

[76] 6 January 1918, Abrahams to Weizmann, WA, file 1918(1); and 15 February 1918, Abrahams to Wolf, CZA, Wolf Papers, A77/3c; Abrahams had mooted the idea of the committee even before the publication of the Balfour Declaration, see JC, 26 October 1917, p. 24.

[77] 27 October 1917, A. M. Hyamson to Weizmann, WA, file 1917(x); and minutes of meeting of the honorary officers of the EZF, held on 9 April 1918, CZA, Files of the Central Zionist Office (London), Z4/692(ii).

of "silent discussions" would most be conducive to progress, the other members of the committee likewise eschewed provocative statements; instead, they invited position papers from the Zionists and their opponents, which they then attempted to reconcile. Land reclamation, urban construction, and even education presented few problems. These were the sorts of practical activities that had originally interested the Chovevei Zion Association and that most of the anti-Zionists considered to be the only legitimate sphere of Jewish operations in Palestine. After only two months of meetings, dicussions on these matters had produced a definite impression of communal harmony. As Lord Walter Rothschild gratefully exclaimed:

> If only the extremists of both parties could be persuaded to leave all decisions . . . in the hands of people for whom the present fourteen delegates stand, I am convinced that the breach in the Community would be healed and the settlement in Palestine would be recognised as a boon for Anglo-Jewry and the world at large.[78]

Sokolow (who in Weizmann's absence in Palestine acted as the chief Zionist advocate) was, as ever, cordial. Provided he had the committee's sanction for a formula that specifically asserted the "national status" of the Jewish population in Palestine, he was prepared to agree to several limiting provisos: the Jews would respect the regulations already in force in the country; they would not demand an exclusive right to immigration; and they would render the entire package "subject to such conditions as the Suzerain Government may consider necessary." But the representatives of the League of British Jews were far less accommodating. First, they insisted on a preamble that explicitly affirmed that the Jews "do not form a separate political nation"; then, they demanded a new clause, barring the Suzerain Power from sanctioning "anything being done to make religious belief a test of citizenship or of political or civic rights." Finally, they made it a

[78] Minutes of 21 January 1918, Mocatta Library, Provisional Committee of the Balfour Declaration Committee, AJ/82.

(311)

condition of agreement that "any document to be accepted by them should further include a specific proviso against any religious tests for membership of the Jewish nationality or Jewish unit."[79] There, as had always been the case, lay the supreme—and in-surmountable—difference between the two sides. Whichever way the Zionists looked at things, they found it to be "self-evident that there must be some special qualification for the membership of the Jewish National Unit." Deny that, and the entire Jewish claim to any special interest in Palestine would appear ridiculous. From the League's point of view, however, there could clearly be no other qualifications for nationality in Palestine "than those which are needful for admission to, say, the British or Indian nationality." To deny *that* was to make nonsense of the Jews' lengthy struggle for religious and political equality in the lands of their dispersion.[80]

☐

With the positions of the two sides at such variance, there seemed little point in continuing the discussions. Amidst a welter of mutual recriminations, the committee finally disbanded in Oc-tober 1918 (Lionel Abrahams died the following year) and the grand Communal Conference for which it was supposed to have prepared never took place. As has been seen, several subsequent attempts to find a community of interest at both the Board of Deputies and such forums as the "Economic Council" were equally unsuccessful. Instead, some other means had to be found of trans-forming the Zionists into the spokesmen for a communal con-sensus. Mass meetings and demonstrations could not entirely serve the purpose: at best, they could only impress those who already supported the movement; at worst, they might further antagonize its critics. In order to attract the sympathies of the uncommitted ballast of Anglo-Jewry, the Zionists could not restrict their appeal to the first or even second generation of immigrants. They would

[79] Minutes of 21 February 1918, ibid.
[80] 26 April 1918, Hyamson to Lionel de Rothschild; and 7 May 1918, Lionel de Rothschild to Hyamson, ibid.

also have to demonstrate the extent to which their own ambitions and interests complemented those of the established section of the community.[81] Consequently, as the Political Committee was informed, Zionist tactics would once again have to become more obviously political in form and content. They would have to be designed to cultivate the influential and institutionally articulate groups within the community and to repair "the lack of confidence with which rightly or wrongly the Zionist Organisation was (still) regarded in many quarters."[82] To this end, the EZF would have to increase its involvement in such contingent concerns as the Jewish War Memorial, to intensify the work of the Communal Organisation Committee of the EZF, and in general to continue to infiltrate every area of Anglo-Jewish life.[83] Notwithstanding the diplomatic success of the years 1917-1920, the Zionists would thus have to prolong the arduous campaign of communal conquest which Herzl had initiated in 1898.

[81] J. Cowen at meeting of Executive Committee, 8 May 1919, CZA, Files of the Central Zionist Office (London), Z4/302(i).

[82] 1st meeting of Political Committee, 9 March 1920, ibid., Z4/16007; 17th meeting 11 May 1920, ibid., Z4/1281(ii); and 26th meeting, 16 September 1920, ibid., Z4/1281(iv), and memorandum by A. Hyamson, 28 April 1920, ibid., Z4/1281(ii).

[83] Minutes of EZF executive, 4 February 1921, ibid., Z4/302/4(i).

Conclusions

Nᴏᴛ ǫᴜɪᴛᴇ ᴀ ǫᴜᴀʀᴛᴇʀ ᴏꜰ ᴀ century separated Herzl's initial address to the Maccabeans in November 1895 from Weizmann's triumphant return to London from San Remo in April 1920. During the intervening period, the English Zionist Federation had become one of Anglo-Jewry's most conspicuous organizations. By any standards, the achievement was immense. On the eve of the twentieth century, political Zionism had appeared to be nothing more than "the harebrained delusion of a few mad fanatics," the outcome of a kind of delirium which would soon burn itself out. Herzl's ambitions were hopelessly romantic, his program was altogether impractical, and his melodramatic attempts to lobby the great and near-great of Europe were sadly misplaced. As for the recently founded EZF, its future seemed uncertain. By 1920, the Zionist movement and its local branch could no longer be thus dismissed. As all sections of the community noted, Weizmann was ceremoniously bowed in and bowed out of confidential meetings with the world's most powerful statesmen; Zionist programs for Palestine's future were placed, as a matter of course, on the agendas of important international conferences. Equally telling were the EZF's own successes. The Zionists possessed branches in every sizable Jewish community in Britain, and sympathizers at the apex as well as at the base of Anglo-Jewish society. Their annual budget had grown impressively; so too had the range and extent of their publications and activities. Above all, their leaders had apparently proven their ability to act independently of the community's entrenched patriciate. That, at least, was the impression sedulously fostered by Weizmann. The Balfour Declaration, he claimed, had been secured despite "all the might and all the prestige and all the bank

(314)

accounts of those established leaders of the British Jewish community."[1]

This book has attempted to identify the influences that enabled the English Zionist Federation and its leadership to attain a position of such prominence. The story, it appears, was more intricate than is conventionally thought and the development of the EZF's communal influence less linear than much Zionist historiography suggests. Within Anglo-Jewry (as elsewhere) political Zionism was not enthusiastically and immediately adopted by the predominantly immigrant masses, who are sometimes presumed to have been universally fired by a conviction that Herzl's analysis of the Jews' predicament was correct and his solution to their problem therefore imperative. Conversely, neither was anti-Zionism simply the preserve of a clique of native aristocrats, concerned solely with the protection of their own social privileges and accumulated wealth. Differences of background, occupation, and communal status certainly affected the compositions of the two camps; so too, over the long haul, did education and age (compare the support given to Zionism by Lord Walter and James de Rothschild with the earlier circumspection of Lord Nathan). But in neither party were these the only determinants; within each class, other lines of tension could blur such superficially simple classifications. Standard Zionist obloquies, to the effect that their opponents were motivated solely by particularism and selfishness, are as unhelpful as the implication that the concerns of the EZF were entirely idealistic in intent and public, if not cosmic, in dimension. Had that indeed been the case, the struggle between the two sides might have been concluded somewhat earlier, and in a more clear-cut fashion.

In fact, however, the wrangle was prolonged and—as late as 1920—yet to be concluded. One influence that must largely account for both phenomena is the organizational ineptitude of Zionism in Britain. This was a recurrent theme, which persistently invited doubt of the wisdom and propriety of granting communal

[1] Speech to a specially organized conference of British Zionists at Cannon Street Hotel, London; 21 September 1919, transcript in CZA, Files of the Central Zionist Office (London), Z4/1833(1).

authority to a group which could not maintain its own unity. Another, which reflects no more credit on the EZF, was the strength and variety of the ideological case put forward by those members of the community who were opposed to, or resisted, political Zionism. That the leaders of the movement in Britain generally tended to disparage the force of this factor (indeed, that it has largely been condemned to obscurity ever since World War II) reflects the comparative weakness of most Anglo-Jewish Zionists in the same field. When confronted by arguments that appealed to the minds rather than to the customs of the community, the leaders of the EZF seemed more often to wax platitudinous than philosophical. In so doing, they can be said to have misrepresented their antagonists. Anti-Zionists in Britain said little that was entirely original. Their contribution, rather, was to adapt to specifically Anglo-Jewish circumstances arguments developed earlier, and more fully, by their coadjutators in the United States, Central Europe, and the Pale of Russian-Jewish settlement. Within those limits, however, Reform, Orthodox, and (albeit less directly) radical left-wing spokesmen in the community presented their case with a vigor and determination that merits both attention and credit. It was their expositions that fueled a lengthy debate on the merits of Herzl's scheme, and their presentations that occasionally endowed the communal battle with the character of an intellectual dialogue. The fact that a large portion of their separate cases seemed to have collapsed by 1948 (although not necessarily for the same reasons) must not be allowed to obscure the extent of the influence that their arguments exerted until some time after World War I. Their literary and verbal outputs sufficed to make it clear that separating the anti-Zionists from the Zionists was a gulf clearly demarcated by a range of divergent premises and aspirations. They also suggest that the content of the anti-Zionist mind (like that of the Zionist mind, for that matter) was as relevant to their respective cases as was the sociological contexts in which those minds were alleged to be operating. Reflection and conviction, even if occasionally jolted by social instinct and irritation, provided the spur to action on both sides, and thus helped to influence the communal alignments with which this book has been concerned.

Conclusions

Nevertheless, the ideological debate between the Zionists and the anti-Zionists was confined to but a very small slice of the total population of Anglo-Jewry. However noteworthy the range and intensity of the exchange, its influence on the political affiliations of the community at large must not be exaggerated. Writings and speeches on the doctrinal aspects of political Zionism were the preserve of a few highly vocal intellectuals; most Jews in Britain did not express themselves one way or the other on such theoretical matters. In terms of convinced devotees, the situation in 1920 did not therefore differ very much from that which had prevailed ever since Herzl's first appearance in London: relatively limited groups of inveterate antagonists contested the rights and wrongs of the Zionist idea, while the overwhelming majority of the community remained persistently (and given the nature of the subject, perhaps understandably) nonpartisan. This situation was necessarily harmful to the Zionists. After all, it was they who wished to alter the status quo by converting Jewry to a doctrine of radical political action. They appreciated that their proposals went against the conservative grain of received Jewish traditions and, specifically, that their proposals contradicted the optimistic assumptions that had underpinned the political behavior of Anglo-Jewry. Their dilemma, therefore, was tactical. They had to find some means of translating Zionism from an opinion on the state of Jewry into a program capable of altering the course of Jewish life. That was why the foundation of the League of British Jews in 1917 caused them less concern than did their failure to convert Zionism into a decisive issue in the elections to the Board of Deputies in 1919. Arguably, the League could be relegated to the level of a collection of diehards, anachronistically consoling each other with memories of happier days. But the reluctance of the vast majority of the politically active community to select its deputies on the basis of their attitude toward Zionism (or, in 1922, to elicit messages of support for Zionism from prospective parliamentary candidates)[2] represented a more insidious threat. Such reticence might indicate

[2] 30 October 1922, Rev. A. Cohen (Birmingham) to Hawkins, ibid., Z4/1845(2); 22 November 1922, B. B. Benas to Hawkins, ibid., Z4/1878(1).

(317)

that the Zionists themselves still constituted something of a fringe faction in a community largely characterized by its mood of ideological noncommitment.

The problem, as has been seen, was not new. Reserve was the reaction that Herzl had himself most often encountered in Anglo-Jewry, and that which he had found most disconcerting. Accordingly, as early as the turn of the century he and his local followers had plotted a plan of campaign whereby it might be overcome. Broadly speaking, the leaders of the English Zionist Federation considered two possible methods of creating an impact on the community and thereby winning its members (especially those who wielded some communal influence) to their cause. One was to demonstrate unequivocally that political Zionism was fully supported by the British government; nothing, ran the argument, would impress Anglo-Jewry more than categorical, and public, evidence that the movement possessed the blessing of the gentile rulers of the land. The alternative was to reverse the order of the campaign. Attention was to be concentrated on a conquest of the Anglo-Jewish community; once that was accomplished, the Zionists could approach the Government as the recipients of a communal mandate for their claims and aspirations. These two policies did not have to be mutually exclusive; indeed, for most of the period covered by this book the course of events hardly allowed English Zionists the luxury of a feasible choice between them. Instead, they had to pursue both options concurrently, with only such shifts of emphasis as circumstances would occasionally allow. Nevertheless, in terms of implications and desired consequences, they clearly led in different directions; each therefore demanded the pursuit of separate targets and the adoption of different tactics.

Considered retrospectively, the first course, an aggressive diplomatic campaign, seems to have been the more daring and the more decisive. Consequently, historical research has largely been directed toward uncovering the drama of the negotiations between the Zionists and the British government which were initiated by Herzl and consummated by Weizmann. That, without question, was one strand necessarily affecting the progress of Zionism within Anglo-Jewry. But it was not the only such influence. In fact, from a communal perspective the diplomatic option proved to be neither the more effective strategy nor (retrospectively) the distinguishing characteristic of Zionism's impact upon Anglo-Jewry. Weizmann's triumphs of statemanship did not automatically confer communal power on the EZF; neither did they ensure the Zionists of the unwavering support of the entire community in their future dealings with the British government. They could have the opposite effect. Several opponents of the movement retrenched and reorganized; they also presented the government with counterclaims that the British mandatory authorities in Palestine were glad to exploit.[3] Proceedings at the Board of Deputies between 1917 and 1920 further confirmed that occasional diplomatic flourishes were, of themselves, of only marginal and momentary importance to Anglo-Jewry's political classes. They had to be supplemented, and thereby secured, by a more ponderous campaign for local communal influence.

Such a campaign, however, might also have taken two different forms. One was a virtually exclusive appeal to the immigrants in Anglo-Jewry, that largely submerged section of the community that was supposed to supply the movement with the necessary numerical buoyancy. A "revolt of the masses," it was sometimes believed, would frighten the overwhelmingly anti-Zionist native leaders; they would either have to bend before the storm by endorsing the Basle Program or relinquish the reins of communal office. Alternatively, and less flamboyantly, the Zionists could embark upon a policy of gradual infiltration. Designed to create an effective Zionist lobby at Anglo-Jewry's principal institutions (the senior compositions of which were hardly affected by the waves of immigration), this strategy implied the manipulation of the electoral procedures for the selection of the most important communal offices. Here, too, both policies could be—and sometimes were—combined, but, once again, their requirements were clearly distinct. An attempt at communal "revolution" (such as

[3] 21 August 1921. Ormsby-Gore to N. Bentwich, CZA, N. Bentwich Papers, A255/256.

was once envisaged by Herzl, for instance), ultimately depended upon the existence of several postulates: overwhelming immigrant support for Zionism; effective Zionist control over such political action as the immigrants were capable of sustaining; and a perceived identity of communal interests between the leaders of the EZF (most of whom were not first-generation immigrants) and the rank and file (most of whom were). For a variety of reasons, some of which coalesced, these conditions were not fully obtained. Immigrant political sympathies, when expressed, were not wholeheartedly Zionist; furthermore, corrosive organizational deficiencies within the EZF undermined its ability to coordinate whatever popular support it possessed. Finally, (and most critically, it has here been argued), the communal aims of the EZF's leading officers did not altogether coincide with those of the immigrant followers. In significant respects, they diverged.

In terms of social backgrounds, professional pursuits, and places of residence, the distinctions between the two wings of the movement were readily apparent. The differences in their communal ambitions were not more subtle. The leaders of the EZF, after all, were already associated with the mainstream of Anglo-Jewry's political elite. By dint of their personal achievements they had won some communal recognition; occasionally they also wielded some communal influence that was quite independent of their position within the Zionist Organisation. Admittedly, they still stood on the periphery of the decisive inner sanctum of Anglo-Jewish government; but they had, as a group, undoubtedly arrived. The immigrants, by contrast, had merely landed. (The fact that Gaster and Weizmann, both technically immigrants, were at various times presidents of the EZF does not contradict this analysis; the range of their professional pursuits was obviously atypical, as was the extent of their professional success.) The men who had founded the EZF in 1899, and who dominated the tone of its communal activities thereafter, were not insensitive to the plight of the immigrants. There is, therefore, no need to ascribe to political opportunism either their attachment to the principles of Zionism or their quest for a rapport with their immigrant followers through the medium of various Zionist societies. But, as communal politicians, they generally adopted a policy of caution. In seeking to extend the influence of their movement, they deliberately employed methods that had already brought them some public success and that continued to be commensurate with their private interests. They did not consider it possible to overthrow the existing structure of Anglo-Jewish government by an indiscriminate appeal for mass support (quite rightly, given the divisions within immigrant society); neither did they think it wise to do so. Despite the personal antipathies and antagonisms that divided them, they almost all shared a fundamental desire to pursue communal power within the boundaries set by the accepted conventions of Anglo-Jewish political debate.

□

Thus perceived, the Zionist strategy of communal infiltration was obviously restrictive. It deliberately concentrated the EZF's attention on the attainment of a limited objective: influence at the major institutions of Anglo-Jewry. Ultimately, moreover, it involved the conversion and cooperation of only a small circle of activists willing and able to play an effective part in the regular business of those bodies. Implicit in the preference was the unspoken contention that responsibility for that aspect of Zionist work lay with the more acculturated segments of the movement. The immigrants were clearly cast in a supporting role. Within those parameters, however, the strategy had implications that were much more far-reaching. Precisely because it advocated nothing more than the incubation of a nationalist party within native Anglo-Jewry and the orderly transfer to that interest of the more powerful communal offices, the strategy presented Zionism as a responsible program of incremental reform, not a reckless movement of destabilizing activism. The communal campaign enabled the EZF to pose as the vehicle of tolerable institutional change and its leaders as the advocates of respectable communal regeneration. In that guise, they could attach themselves to various other waves of native protest and discontent. Specifically, they could associate their cause with the progressively successful struggle being waged against the incumbent leadership of the community by uncoordinated elements in the provinces and the London districts of bourgeois Jewish settlement. That those manifestations of dissent had no organic connection with the tenets of the Zionist movement (whose advent they had in fact preceded) did not preclude the possibility of some programmatic cooperation. Most obviously was this so at a personal level. Some of Herzl's earliest supporters (notably Bentwich, de Haas, and Greenberg) had served their communal apprenticeships in the service of the older causes, whose interests they still claimed to have at heart. Others (particularly the Manchester group of second-generation Zionist leaders), rose to prominence in the EZF on the crest of a wave of provincial disaffection toward anything that smacked of metropolitan predominance.

As an exercise in political mobilization, the strategy of institutional infiltration was thus innovative. It was also remarkably consistent. Individual leaders of the EZF rose and fell with a regularity that gave their organization the appearance of a cast of warring prima donnas. But the underlying principles of Zionist communal activity which they adopted hardly changed at all. What remained constant from the Clerkenwell Conference to San Remo was a deliberate attempt to diversify the interests of the EZF and thereby to enlist behind it an articulate Jewish public capable of making Zionism a force in the politics of the entire community. Ultimately, therefore, the history of the Zionist movement in Britain is to a large extent a history of the community that it attempted to conquer. Altogether, the period covered by this book was one of perceptible shifts in the demographic, economic, and managerial equilibrium that had characterized Anglo-Jewry for most of the nineteenth century. At every stage in its story, the EZF can be seen to have reacted to those developments and, in some cases, to have acted as a catalyst on them. Thus, the organization became one of the links between the recent Jewish arrivals to the British Isles and those whose parents and grandparents had made the journey some time earlier. More to the point, it also participated in the process whereby the community's ruling class came to enlarge its ranks by accepting the participation in Anglo-Jewish government of native elements that had hitherto been excluded. In both instances, the EZF contributed to the gradual—but nevertheless perceptible—reconstruction of the mores and structure of the community during the early twentieth century.

Nevertheless, the theme must not be exaggerated. It is a measure of the EZF's success that debates on the future of Palestine had permeated every major Anglo-Jewish forum by 1920, and that by then some of its officers had also risen to positions of communal prominence. Equally, however, it is a measure of the limitations of the organization's accomplishments that Zionism had not become the undisputed arbiter of communal fortunes and reputations. The strategy of infiltration had not entirely served its purpose. In some respects, it seems to have been self-defeating. The search for communal influence induced the Zionists, as a group, to underwrite causes (such as the Jewish War Memorial scheme) that were only marginally relevant to the central issues of their corporate concern. Sometimes it also necessitated collusion with the leaders of other organizations (such as the B'nai B'rith) who, in ideological terms, can only be described as fellow travellers. One result of this situation was that the Zionists themselves helped to unite some of their opponents, many of whom objected as much to the brazen manner in which the EZF pursued communal power as to its Palestinian ambitions. Another consequence, arguably of more importance, was that the progress of the movement came to depend upon the readiness of its allies to convert what was basically a temporary act of collaboration into a more lasting affiliation. Hence Zionist influence within the community could not advance steadily after 1897. Rather, it had to jerk and stumble forward (or back) in accordance with the local ambitions of those who occasionally saw fit to use it.

Bibliography

PRIMARY SOURCES

Archives

Jerusalem. Central Zionist Archives.

INSTITUTIONAL RECORDS.

Z1. Files of the Central Zionist Office, Vienna, 1897-1905.
Z2. Files of the Central Zionist Office, Cologne, 1905-1911.
Z3. Files of the Central Zionist Office, Berlin, 1911-1920.
Z4. Files of the Central Zionist Office, London, 1917-1920.
L3. Files of the Zionist Commission, Jerusalem, 1918-1921.
K11/46. Papers relating to the Balfour Declaration, 1917.
A2. Files of the Chovevei Zion Association of England, 1890-1902.
A36. Files of the Jewish Territorial Organization, 1905-1920.

PRIVATE PAPERS.

A100. H. Bentwich Papers.
A255. N. Bentwich Papers.
A213. I. Cohen Papers.
A203. Gaster Papers (copies).
K11/6. P. Goodman Papers.
A224. J. de Haas Papers.
H. T. Herzl Papers.
K11/1. E. Ish-Kishor Papers.
A143. L. Kessler Papers.
K11/96. S. Levy Papers.
A247. S. Marks Papers.
A150. M. Rosenberg Papers.
Z4/120. H. Sacher Papers.
K11/200. L. Simon Papers.
A18. N. Sokolow Papers.
A77. L. Wolf Papers.
W. D. Wolffsohn Papers.
A120. I. Zangwill Papers.

Bibliography

Jerusalem. Archives of the Israel Historical Society. HM 2765. Lucien Wolf, "Diary" (1916).

Reḥovot. The Weizmann Archives. Letters received by Weizmann (1905-1920).

London. The Board of Deputies of British Jews. (For a detailed catalogue see Roberta A. Routledge, *Report on the Records of the Board of Deputies of British Jews* [London, 1978].)

A1. Annual Meetings, 1903-1914.

A2. Attendance Registers, 1912-1922.

A3. Agenda and Reports, 1916-1920: Conjoint Foreign Committee, 1916; Foreign Committee, 1917; Joint Foreign Committee, 1918-1921.

A14-17. Minute Books of the Board, 1903-1921.

B3/2-49. Letter Books, 1903-1920.

C5. Constitution and Bye-Laws Revision Committee.

C11. Foreign Affairs:

(1) Anglo-Jewish Association and Board of Deputies negotiations; Foreign Committee, 1916-1918.

(2) General Correspondence, 1895-1920.

(3) World War I.

(4) Joint Foreign Committee.

(5) Lucien Wolf Personal Correspondence.

(12) Correspondence on Palestine, 1916-1920.

E3. General Correspondence:

(187) Palestine, 1916-1918.

(204-207) Zionism, 1914-1916.

(208) League of British Jews, 1918.

London. Federation of Synagogues.

Minute Books of the Board, Vols. 1-2, 1895-1920.

Letter Books, 1895-1920.

London. Jewish Board of Guardians (Jewish Welfare Board).

Minute Books, Vols. 3-5, 1895-1920.

Letter Books, Vols. 3-5, 1895-1920.

London. Mocatta Library, University College.

INSTITUTIONAL RECORDS.

AJ/37/1-4. Archives of the Anglo-Jewish Association.

AJ/37 and AJ/95 ADD. Council Minute Books, Vols. 3-4, 1895-1920; Executive Committee Minutes, Vols. 4-5, 1895-1920.

AJ/37/6. Correspondence with the Board of Deputies, 1917-1918.

AJ/12. Union of Jewish Literary Societies, Minute Book, 1905-1914.

AJ/78. West London Synagogue Archives, 1916-1920.

AJ/82. Provisional Committee of the Balfour Declaration Committee, Minutes, 1917-1918.

AJ/133. English Zionist Federation, Archives, 1909-1910.

PRIVATE PAPERS.

G. M. Gaster Papers (originals).

AJ/94. P. S. Goldberg Papers.

AJ/114. J. S. Harris Papers.

AJ/28. S. A. Hirsch Papers.

AJ/9. Miss R. Phillips, Diary.

London. Public Record Office.

    CAB 21. War Cabinet Papers, 1917.

    FO 371/991-92. Foreign Office Files. Turkey (Political), 1910.

    FO 371/3042-3062. Foreign Office Files. Turkey (War, Political), 1917.

    FO 371/3380-3418. Foreign Office Files. Turkey (War, Political), 1918.

    HO 45/10819. Home Office Files. CID Reports, 1916-1917.

London Sephardi Congregation Archives. Elders Minute Books, 1891-1911; 1912-1918.

London. United Synagogue Archives, Woburn House.

    Conference on the Chief Rabbinate, 1912-1913, files 137 a-b.

    Bayswater Synagogue, Minute Books, 1895-1920.

    Borough Synagogue, Minute Books, 1896-1920.

    East London Synagogue, Minute Books, 1895-1914.

    Hammersmith Synagogue, Minute Books, 1895-1920.

    New West End Synagogue, Minute Books, 1908-1915.

    Stoke Newington Synagogue, Minute Books, 1895-1920.

Cincinnati. United States. American-Jewish Archives.

    C. Adler Papers.

    S. Blank Papers.

    G. Deutsch Papers.

    R. Gottheil Papers.

    D. Philipson Papers.

    J. Schiff Papers.

    F. Warburg Papers.

Bibliography

New York. Jacob Blaustein Library. American Jewish Committee, Correspondence Files, 1918.

New York. Jewish Theological Seminary.

    E. Adler Papers.

    B. Richards Papers.

    S. Schechter Papers.

New York. YIVO Institute for Jewish Research. David Mowshowitch Collection of Lucien Wolf Papers (for a detailed catalogue, see Zosa Szajkowski, "Jewish Diplomacy. Catalogue of the David Mowshowitch Collection in the YIVO." *YIVO Bletter* 43 [1966]:283-96).

New York. Zionist Organization of America. J. de Haas Papers, microfilms 1 and 40.

Newspapers and Periodicals

ENGLISH LANGUAGE

Ben Zakkai (1920)

The Jewish Chronicle (1895-1920).

The Jewish Guardian (1918-1920).

Jewish Opinion (1917-1919).

The Jewish Religious Union: Bulletin (1914-1919).

The Jewish Review (1910-1914).

The Jewish World (1895-1920).

The Jewish Year Book (1895-1920).

Palestina. The Chovevei Zion Quarterly (1892-1898).

The Sinaist (1917-1918).

The Zionist Review (1917-1920).

HEBREW

Beit Va'ad la-Ḥakhamim (1902-1904).

Ha-Me'orer (1907-1908).

Ha-Yehoodi (1897-1913).

Ha-Zion (1903).

Rashei Alfei Yisrael (1917-1919).

YIDDISH

Der Arbayter Fraynd (1895-1916).

Di Idisher Shtime (1916).

Der Idisher Ekspres (1908-1918).

Idisher Treyd Yunionist (1910-1911).

Der Idisher Zhurnal (1908-1911).

Di Tsayt (1913-1920).

Bibliography

Published Primary Sources

Abrahams, Israel. *Festival Studies*. London, 1906.

———. (with S. Levy) *Macaulay's Essays and Speeches on Jewish Disabilities*. London, 1908.

———. *The Union and the Festivals*. London, 1909.

———. *The Future of Palestine*. London, 1918.

———. *Jewish Life Under Emancipation*. London, 1918.

———. "Palestine and Jewish Nationalism," *Hibbert Journal* 16 (April 1918):455-66.

Addresses Delivered at the Services of the Jewish Religious Union. London, 1904.

Adler, Alfred S. *The Discipline of Sorrow*. London, 1911.

Adler, Hermann. *A Pilgrimage to Zion*. London, 1885.

———. *Religious Versus Political Zionism*. London, 1898.

———. *Our Provincial Brethren*. London, 1901.

———. *Anglo Jewish Memories*. London, 1909.

Aḥad Ha'am [Asher Ginzberg]. *Igrot Aḥad Ha'am*. 6 vols. 2nd ed. Tel Aviv, 1956-1960.

Benas, Bertram, B. *Zionism*. London, 1919.

Benjamin, Lewis S. "The passing of the English Jew." *The Nineteenth Century and After* 72 (September 1912):491-504.

Black, Isaac I. *Shevilei ha-Yahadut be-Angliah*. London, 1903.

Board of Deputies of British Jews. *Annual Reports*. London, 1895-1920.

Burgin, Hertz. *Die Geshikhte fun der Yiddisher Arbeiter Bavegung in Amerika, Russland un England*. New York, 1915.

Chaikin, Avigdor. *The Celebrities of the Jews*. Sheffield, 1899.

Daiches, Samuel. *Judaism in England*. Sunderland, 1907.

———. *Essays and Addresses*. Edited by Maurice Simon and Isaac Levy. London, 1955.

Daiches, Yisrael Ḥayim. *Derashot Maharyaḥ*. Leeds, 1920.

Emanuel, George. *The Mission of Israel*. Birmingham, 1897.

English Zionist Federation. *Constitution*. London, 1901 and 1910.

———. *Opinions of Parliamentary Candidates on Zionism*. Rev. ed. London, 1901.

Fuchs, Joseph S. *Merkaz Ivri: An Hebrew Centre. A Critical View of English Judaism*. London, 1909.

Gerber, Pinḥas. *Yad Pinḥas*. London, 1928.

———. *Sefer Ra'ui le-Vilah*. London, 1929.

Gollancz, Hermann. *Sermons and Addresses*. London, 1909.

———. *Sermons and Addresses*. London, 1916.

(329)

Bibliography

Gollancz, Hermann. *Fifty Years After*. London, 1924.

Goodman, Paul, ed. *Zionism: Problems and Views*. London, 1916.

Green, Aaron Asher. *Sermons*. Edited by M. Adler. London, 1935.

Herzl, Theodor. *The Jewish State*. Translated by Sylvie D'Avigdor. 5th ed. London, 1967.

———. *Igrot Herzl. 1895-1899*. Edited by A. Bein et al. 3 vols. Jerusalem, 1958.

———. *The Complete Diaries of Theodor Herzl*. Edited by Raphael Patai. Translated by Harry Zohn. 5 vols. New York, 1960.

Herzog, Yiẓḥak. *Divrei Yiẓḥak*. London, 1921.

Herzog, Yoel Leib. *Gilyonei Yoel*. Vilna, 1913.

———. *Imrei Yoel*. London, 1921.

Hillman, Shemuel. *Sefer 'Or ha-Yashar*. London [1910?].

Hirsch, Samuel A. *A Book of Essays*. London, 1905.

Hochman, Joseph. *Orthodoxy and Religious Observance*. London, 1910.

———. *Jewish Separatism and Human Progress*. London, 1910.

———. "Zionism and the Future of Judaism." *Jewish Review* 4 (September 1913):217-42.

Hyamson, Moses. *The Oral Law and Other Sermons*. London, 1910.

Joseph, Morris. *Judaism as Creed and Life*. London, 1903.

———. *The Message of Judaism*. London, 1906.

Kook, Avraham Yiẓḥak. *She'eolot u-Teshuvot Mishpat Kohen*. Jerusalem, 1966.

Levin, Aryeh Leib. *Sefer Bet Yisrael*. London, 1902.

———. *Shivim Panim la-Torah*. London, 1910.

Levine, Ephraim. *Judaism*. London, 1913.

———. *The Mission of the Jew*. London, 1917.

Levy, Solomon. *Zionism and Liberal Judaism*. Edinburgh, 1911.

Maccoby, Ḥayim Zundel. *Imrei Ḥayim*. Edited by Max Mansky. Tel Aviv, 1929.

Magnus, Laurie. *Aspects of the Jewish Question*. London, 1902.

———. *Zionism and the Neo-Zionists*. London, 1917.

———. *Old Lamps for New: An Apologia for the League of British Jews*. London, 1918.

Mazin, Raphael. *Geshikhte fun der Yidden in England*. London, 1915.

Montagu, Lily H. *Thoughts on Judaism*. London, 1904.

———. *Samuel Montagu, First Baron Swaythling*. London, 1913.

Montefiore, Claude G. M. *The Bible for Home Reading*. 2 vols. London, 1896.

Bibliography

—————. "Nation or Religious Community?" *Transactions of the Jewish Historical Society of England* 4 (1903):1-15.

—————. *Liberal Judaism: An Essay*. London, 1903.

—————. *Outlines of Liberal Judaism*. London, 1905.

—————. "Assimilation: Good and Bad." *Papers for the Jewish People*, no. 9 (1909).

—————. *Truth in Religion and Other Sermons*. London, 1909.

—————. *Liberal Judaism*. London, 1911.

—————. "What Would you Have us Do? " *Papers for the Jewish People*, no. 7 (1913).

—————. ["An Englishman of the Jewish Faith."] "Zionism." *Fortnightly Review* (November 1916):819-26.

—————. "Liberal Judaism and Jewish Nationalism." *Papers for the Jewish People*, no. 16 (1917).

—————. "The Dangers of Zionism." *Papers for the Jewish People*, no. 20 (1917).

—————. "Zionism." *The Inquirer*, 24 November 1917, pp. 463-64.

—————. (with B.L.Q. Henriques), *The English Jew and His Religion*. London, 1918.

Montefiore, Leonard G. "Anglo-Jewry at the Cross-Roads." *Jewish Review* 5 (July 1914):128-35.

Rabinowitz, Shemuel Ya'akov. *Ha-Dat ve-ha-Le'umiut*. Warsaw, 1900.

—————. *Litkufot ha-Yamim*. London, 1919.

Rabinowitz, Ya'akov. *Sefer Bikurei Ya'akov*. London, 1899.

—————. *Sefer Hilkhot Erez Yisrael*. London, 1900.

Raffalovich, Isaiah. *Our Inheritance*. London, 1932.

Rosenbaum [Rowson], Simon. "A Contribution to the Study of the Vital and Other Statistics of the Jews of the U.K.," *Journal of the Royal Statistical Society* 68 (1905):526-66.

—————. "The Jewish Question in England," *Jewish Review* 2 (1911):106-119.

Russel, C. *The Jew in London*. London, 1900.

Sabel, Shemuel David. *Sefer Shir ha-Shirim im Perush Ḥadash, Migdal David*. London, 1899.

Sacher, Harry. *Jewish Emancipation: The Contract Myth*. London, 1917.

—————, ed. *Zionism and the Jewish Future*. London, 1916.

Schechter, Solomon. *Four Epistles to the Jews of England*. London, 1901.

Schonfeld, Victor. "The Rabbinical Conference of 1911 (in London)." *Jewish Review* 2 (May 1911):55-59.

Silverstone, Gedalya. *Pirḥei Aviv*. London, 1901.

Bibliography

Silverstone, Gedalya. *Lishu'ah Gedolah*. London, 1904.

———. *Imrei Yosher*. Washington, 1925.

Simon, Leon. *Zionism and the Jewish Problem*. London, 1915.

———. *The Case of the Anti-Zionists: A Reply*. London, 1917.

———. *Studies in Jewish Nationalism*. London, 1920.

Simon, Oswald. "The Return of the Jews to Palestine," *The Nineteenth Century* (September 1898):437-47.

Singer, Simeon. *The Literary Remains of Simeon Singer*. Edited by I. Abrahams. 3 vols. London, 1905.

Slutsky, Avraham. *Shivat Zion*. Warsaw, 1900.

Sokolow, Naḥum. *History of Zionism, 1600-1918*, 2 vols. London, 1919.

Spiers, Baruḥ. *Divrei Devash: Ethical Sermons Delivered to Working Classes at the Great Synagogue and Other Places of Worship*. London, 1901.

———, ed. *Haggadah for Passover*. London, 1897.

Spiers, F. S. *Zionism and the Jewish Religion*. London, 1919.

Strauss, Joseph. *Essays*. London, 1911.

Suvalski, Isaac. *Ma'amar Beteilin u-Mevutolin*. London, 1903.

Wasserzug, David. *Why I Am Orthodox*. London, 1913.

———. *The Messianic Idea and its Influence on Jewish Ethics*. London, 1913.

Weizmann, Chaim. *The Letters and Papers of Chaim Weizmann. Series A Letters*. Edited by Meyer Weisgal et. al. Oxford, London, and Jerusalem, 1969-1980. Vol. 3, *September 1903-December 1904*, edited by Gedalya Yogev, 1972; Vol. 4, *January 1905-December 1906*, edited by Camillo Dresner and Barnet Litvinoff, 1973; Vol. 5, *January 1907-February 1913*, edited by Hanna Weiner and Barnet Litvinoff, 1974; Vol. 6, *March 1913-July 1914*, edited by Barnet Litvinoff, 1974; Vol. 7, *August 1914-November 1917*, edited by Leonard Stein, 1975; Vol. 8, *November 1917-October 1918*, edited by Dvorah Barzilay and Barnet Litvinoff, 1977; Vol. 9, *October 1918-July 1920*, edited by Jehuda Reinharz, 1977.

Wigoder, Myer Yoel. *Sefer Bet Yehudah*. Jerusalem, 1910.

Wolf, Lucien. "The Zionist Peril." *Jewish Quarterly Review* 17 (1904): 1-25.

———. "The Jewish National Movement." *Edinburgh Review* 225 (April 1917):1-17.

———. "Anti-Semitism." In *Essays in Jewish History*, edited by Cecil Roth. London, 1934.

World Zionist Organisation. *Stenographisches Protokoll des Zionisten—Kongresses*, I-XI (Vienna, 1897-1913).

Bibliography

Wortsmann, Yeḥezkel. Vos Villen die Tsionisten? London, 1901.
———. Vos Villen die Sotsial-Demokratien? London, 1902.
Yoffey, Yisrael Ya'akov. Kenesset Yisrael. Manchester, 1910.
Yoffey, Yosef. Yosef Biur. Vilna, 1881.
———. Ahavat Ẓion Virushalayim. Vilna, 1890; 2nd ed. Tel Aviv, 1946.
Zangwill, Israel. Speeches, Articles and Letters of Israel Zangwill. Edited by M. Simon. London, 1937.

SECONDARY SOURCES

Abrahams, Phyllis. "The Letters of Israel Abrahams from Egypt and Palestine in 1898," Transactions of the Jewish Historical Society of England 24 (1975):1-23.
Adler, Michael. The History of the Hammersmith Synagogue. London, 1950.
———. British Jewry: Book of Honour. London, 1922.
Agus, Jacob. Banner of Jerusalem. London, 1946.
Alderman, Geoffrey. "The Anti-Jewish Riots of August 1911 in South Wales." Welsh History Review 6 (1972):190-200.
Alsberg, Pinḥas A. "Ha-Orientaẓiah shel Mediniut ha-Hanhalah ha-Ẓionit erev Milkhemet ha-Olam ha-Rishonah." Ẓion, n.s. 22 (1957):149-76.
Apple, Raymond. The Hampstead Synagogue, 1892-1967. London, 1967.
Baron, Salo W. Modern Nationalism and Religion. New York, 1947.
Barzilay, Dvorah. "The Ormsby-Gore Reports from Palestine, April-May 1918." Ha-Ẓionut (English ed.) 1 (1975):383-437.
Battersea, Constance. Reminiscences. London, 1922.
Bayme, Steven. "Jewish Leadership and Anti-Semitism in Britain, 1898-1918." Ph.D. dissertation, Columbia University, 1977.
Beilin, A. "Y. Ḥ. Brenner be-London." Ha-Tekufah 14-15 (1922):646-71.
Bein, Alex. Theodore Herzl: A Biography. Philadelphia, 1943.
Benas, Bertram B. "A Survey of the Jewish Institutional History of Liverpool and District." Transactions of the Jewish Historical Society of England 17 (1951-52):23-38.
Bentwich, Norman. Early English Zionists. Tel Aviv, 1940.
———. (with Margery Bentwich) Herbert Bentwich: The Pilgrim Father. Jerusalem, 1940.
———. The Social Transformation of Anglo-Jewry, 1883-1960. London, 1960.

Bibliography

Bentwich, Norman. *My First Seventy Years: An Account of My Life and Times, 1883-1960*. London, 1962.

————. *Claude Montefiore and His Tutor in Rabbinics*. London, 1966.

Bermant, Chaim. *The Cousinhood: The Anglo-Jewish Gentry*. London, 1971.

Best, Garry D. "Jacob H. Schiff's Galveston Movement. An Experiment in Immigrant Deflection." *American-Jewish Archives* 30 (April 1978):43-79.

Bolitho, Hector. *Alfred Mond, First Lord Melchett*. London, 1933.

Brodetsky, Selig. *Memoirs: From Ghetto to Israel*. London, 1960.

Chotzinoff, Samuel. *A Lost Paradise: Early Reminiscences*. New York, 1955.

Cohen, Israel. *A Jewish Pilgrimage*. London, 1956.

————. "300 Years of Anglo-Zionism." In *Aspects of Jewish Life, 1656-1956*, edited by B. Buill and W. Perry. London, 1956.

Cohen, Lucy. *Some Recollections of Claude Goldsmid Montefiore, 1858-1938*. London, 1940.

Cohen, Norman. "Dayan Bernard Spiers." *Jewish Monthly* 5 (January, 1952):588-97.

Cowen, Joseph. "My Conversion to Zionism." In *Theodor Herzl: A Memorial*, edited by Meyer Weisgal. New York, 1929.

Daiches, David. "My Father and His Father." *Commentary*, December 1955, pp. 522-33.

————. *Two Worlds*. New York, 1956.

D'Arcy Hart, Ronald. *The Samuel Family of Liverpool and London*. London, 1958.

Domb, Israel. *The Transformation*, London, 1966.

Dunbrow, M. *They Docked at Newcastle and Wound up in Gateshead*. Jerusalem, 1972.

Eliav, Mordekhai. *David Wolffsohn: Ha-Ish u-Zemano*. Tel Aviv, 1978.

Ettinger, Philip. *'Hope Place' in Liverpool Jewry*. Liverpool, 1930.

Faris, Hani "Israel Zangwill's Challenge to Zionism." *Journal of Palestine Studies* 4 (1975):74-90.

Finestein, Israel. "The New Community, 1880-1915." In *Three Centuries of Anglo-Jewish History*, edited by Vivian D. Lipman. London, 1961.

————. "Arthur Cohen, Q.C. (1892-1912)." In *Remember the Days: Essays in Honour of Cecil Roth*, edited by John M. Shaftesley. London, 1966.

————. "The Lay Leadership of the United Synagogue since 1870." In *A Century of Anglo-Jewish Life*, edited by Salmond S. Levin. London, 1971.

Fisch, Harold. *The Zionist Revolution: A New Perspective.* Oxford, 1978.

Fishman, William J. *East End Jewish Radicals, 1875-1914.* London, 1975.

Fraenkel, Josef. "Colonel Albert E. W. Goldsmid and Theodor Herzl." *Herzl Year Book* 1 (1958):145-53.

————. "The Jewish Chronicle and the Launching of Political Zionism," *Herzl Year Book* 2 (1959):217-27.

————. "Lucien Wolf and Theodor Herzl." *Transactions of the Jewish Historical Society of England* 20 (1964):161-88.

Freedman, Maurice, ed. *A Minority in Britain.* London, 1955.

Freisel, Evyatar. *Ha-Mediniut ha-Ẓionit le-Aḥar Hazharat Balfour, 1917-1922.* Tel Aviv. 1977.

Friedman, Isaiah. *The Question of Palestine, 1914-1918: British-Jewish-Arab Relations.* London, 1973.

————. "Dissensions over Jewish Identity in West European Jewry." In *The Role of Religion in Modern Jewish History*, edited by Jacob Katz. Cambridge, Mass., 1975.

————. *Germany, Turkey and Zionism, 1897-1918.* Oxford, 1977.

Fyvel, T. R. "Weizmann and the Balfour Declaration." In *Chaim Weizmann: A Biography by Several Hands*, edited by Meyer Weisgal and Joel Carmichael. New York, 1963.

Gainer, Bernard. *The Alien Invasion: The Origins of the Alien Act of 1905.* London, 1972.

Garrard, John A. *The English and Immigration, 1880-1910.* London, 1971.

Gartner, Lloyd P. *The Jewish Immigrant in England, 1870-1914.* 2nd ed. London, 1973.

Goldfine, Marvin J. "The Growth of Zionism in England up to the World War." Master's thesis, Columbia University, 1939.

Goodman, Paul. *Zionism in England, 1899-1949.* London, 1949.

Goulston, Michael J. "The Status of the Anglo-Jewish Rabbinate, 1840-1914." *Jewish Journal of Sociology* 10 (June 1968):55-82.

————. "The Theology of Reform Judaism in Britain." In *Reform Judaism: Essays on Reform Judaism in Britain*, edited by Dov Marmur. London, 1973.

Haas, Jacob de. *Theodor Herzl: A Biographical Study.* 2 vols. Chicago, 1927.

Halpern, Ben. *The Idea of the Jewish State.* 2nd ed. Cambridge, Mass., 1969.

————. "The Drafting of the Balfour Declaration." *Herzl Year Book* 7 (1971):255-84.

Hein, Virginia H. "The British Followers of Theodor Herzl: English

Zionist Leaders, 1896-1904." Ph.D. dissertation, Georgia State University, 1978.

Henriques, Robert. *Sir Robert Waley Cohen*. London, 1968.

Hertzberg, Arthur, ed. *The Zionist Idea*. New York, 1959.

Heymann, Michael, ed. *The Uganda Controversy*. 2 vols. Jerusalem, 1970; Tel Aviv, 1973.

Holmes, Colin, ed. *Immigrants and Minorities in British Society*. London, 1978.

Homa, Bernard. *A Fortress in Anglo-Jewry: The Story of the Machzike Hadath*. London, 1953.

Hyamson, Albert M. H. *Israel Abrahams: A Memoir*. London, 1940.

————. *The Sephardim of England*. London, 1951.

————. *Jews' College, London, 1855-1955*. London, 1955.

Jabotinsky, Vladimir. *The Story of the Jewish Legion*. New York, 1945.

Jaffe, Benjamin. "The British Press and Zionism in Herzl's Time." *Transactions of the Jewish Historical Society of England* 24 (1975):89-100.

Jung, Julius. *Champions of Orthodoxy*. London, 1974.

Kaplan, Stanley. "The Anglicization of the East European Jewish Immigrant as seen by the London *Jewish Chronicle*, 1870-1897." *YIVO Annual of Jewish Social Science* 10 (1955):267-78.

Klausner, Israel. *Ha-Opoziziah le-Herzl*. Jerusalem, 1960.

Krausz, Ernest. *Leeds Jewry: Its History and Structure*. Cambridge 1964.

Landman, Samuel. "Origins of the Balfour Declaration: Dr. Hertz's Contribution." In *Essays in Honour of the Very Rev. Dr. J. H. Hertz*, edited by Isidore Epstein, Ephraim Levine, and Cecil Roth. London, 1942.

Laqueur, Walter. *A History of Zionism*. London, 1972.

Leftwich, Joseph. *Israel Zangwill*. London, 1957.

Leigh, Michael. "Reform Judaism in Britain (1840-1970)." In *Reform Judaism: Essays on Reform Judaism in Britain*, edited by Dov Marmur. London, 1973.

Levine, Ephraim. *The History of the New West End Synagogue*. London, 1929.

Levy, Arnold. *History of the Sunderland Jewish Community*. London, 1956.

Lewis, Chaim. *A Soho Address*. London, 1965.

Lipman, Vivian. *Social History of the Jews in England, 1850-1950*. London, 1954.

————. "Synagogal Organisation in Anglo-Jewry." *Jewish Journal of Sociology* 1 (1959):80-93.

Bibliography

————. *A Century of Social Service, 1859-1959: The History of the Jewish Board of Guardians.* London, 1959.

————. "The Age of Emancipation, 1815-1880." In *Three Centuries of Anglo-Jewish History,* ed. Vivian D. Lipman. London, 1961.

————. "The Rise of Jewish Suburbia." *Transactions of the Jewish Historical Society of England* 21 (1968):78-103.

————. "The Development of London Jewry." In *A Century of Anglo-Jewish Life,* edited by Salmond Levin. London, 1970.

Litvinoff, Barnet. *Weizmann: Last of the Patriarchs.* New York, 1972.

Livingstone, Isaac. *The Union of Anglo-Jewish Preachers, A Retrospect.* London, 1949.

Loewe, Basil. "Prolegomenon" to *A Rabbinic Anthology* by Claude Montefiore and Herbert Loewe. New York, 1974.

Loewe, Herbert. *Israel Abrahams: A Biographical Sketch.* London, 1944.

Loewe, Lionel. *Basil Henriques: A Portrait.* London, 1976.

Marmor, Kalman. *Mein Lebens-Geshikhte.* 2 vols. New York, 1959.

Marmorstein, Emil. *Heaven At Bay: The Jewish Kulturkampf in the Holy Land.* Oxford, 1969.

Masliansky, Zvi Hirsch. *Ketavim.* 3 vols. New York, 1929.

Mathew, W. R. *Claude Montefiore: The Man and His Thought.* London, 1956.

Montagu, Lily H. *The First Fifty Years: A Record of Liberal Judaism in England,* London, 1950.

Namier, Julia. *Lewis Namier, A Biography.* Oxford, 1971.

Newman, Aubrey. *The United Synagogue, 1870-1970.* London, 1976.

Orlan, Haiyim. "The Participants in the First Zionist Congress." *Herzl Year Book* 6 (1965):133-152.

Orren, Elhanen. *Hibat Zion be-Britanyah, 1878-1898.* Tel Aviv, 1974.

Patai, Raphael. "Herzl's Sinai Project—A Documentary Record." *Herzl Year Book* 1 (1958):107-144.

Prager, Leonard. "A Bibliography of Yiddish Periodicals in Great Britain (1867-1967)." *Studies in Bibliography and Booklore* 9 (1969):3-32.

Rabinowicz, Oskar K. "Herzl and England." *Jewish Social Studies* 13 (1951):25-46.

Raffalovich, Isaiah. *Ziyunim ve-Tamrurim.* Tel Aviv, 1952.

Rocker, Rudolph. *The London Years.* Translated by Joseph Leftwich. London, 1956.

Roth, Cecil. "The Court Jews of Edwardian England." *Jewish Social Studies* 5 (October 1943):355-66.

————. *The Federation of Synagogues.* London, 1937.

Bibliography

Roth, Cecil. *The Jewish Chronicle, 1841-1941*. London, 1941.

———. *The Rise of Provincial Jewry*. London, 1950.

Rubinstein, William D. "Jews Among Top British Wealth Holders, 1857-1969: Decline of the Golden Age." *Jewish Social Studies* 34 (1972):73-84.

Sacher, Harry. *Zionist Portraits*. London, 1959.

Salaman, Redcliffe N. "Whither Lucien Wolf's Anglo-Jewish Community?" *Lucien Wolf Memorial Lecture, 1953*. London, 1953.

Salmon, Yosef. "Emdatah shel ha-Hevrah ha-Haredit be-Russia-Polin le-Zionut be-Shanim 1898-1900." In *Eshel Be'er Sheva*. Beersheba, 1976.

Schama, Simon. *Two Rothschilds and the Land of Israel*. London, 1978.

Schisha, A. "Hermann Adler, Yeshiva Bahur, Prague, 1860-1862." In *Remember the Days: Essays in Honour of Cecil Roth*, edited by John M. Shaftesley. London, 1966.

Schwab, Walter M. *B'nai B'rith, The First Lodge of England: A Record of Fifty Years*. London, 1960.

Shabtai, N. "Ahavat Zion Bein Yehudie Angliah, mireshit ha-She'eilah ha-Mizrahit ve'ad le-Kongres Berlin." Masters thesis, Tel Aviv University, 1969.

Shaftesly, John M. "Religious Controversies." In *A Century of Anglo-Jewish Life*, edited by Salmond S. Levin. London, 1971.

Shapiro, Yonathan. *The Leadership of the American Zionist Organization, 1897-1930*. Urbana, 1971.

Sharot, Stephen. "Religious Change in Native Orthodoxy in London, 1870-1914." *Jewish Journal of Sociology* 15 (December 1973):167-87.

Sieff, Israel. *Memoirs*. London, 1971.

Silberner, Edmund. "British Socialism and the Jews." *Historica Judaica* 14 (1952):27-52.

Stein, Leonard. *The Balfour Declaration*. London, 1961.

Teitelbaum, Yoel. *Sefer Vayo'el Mosheh*. 3 vols. 2nd ed. Jerusalem, 1974.

Vereté, Meir. "The Balfour Declarations and its Makers." *Middle Eastern Studies* 6 (1970):48-76.

———. "The Restoration of the Jews in English Protestant Thought, 1790-1840." *Middle Eastern Studies* 8 (1972):3-50.

Vital, David. *The Origins of Zionism*. Oxford, 1975.

Weisbord, Robert G. *African Zion: The Attempt to Establish a Jewish Colony in the East Africa Protectorate, 1903-1905*. Philadelphia, 1968.

Weizmann, Chaim. *Trial and Error*. London, 1949.

Bibliography

Wiener, Max. "The Conception of Mission in Traditional and Reform Judaism." *YIVO Annual of Jewish Social Science* 2-3 (1947-48):9-24.

Wigoder, Meyer J. *My Life*. London, 1935.

Williams, Bill. *The Making of Manchester Jewry, 1740-1875*. Manchester, 1976.

Wohlgelernter, Maurice. *Israel Zangwill: A Study*. New York, 1964.

Wright, Dudley. "Select Bibliography of the Writings of Israel Abrahams." In *Jewish Studies in Memory of Israel Zangwill*, ed. B. Kohuth. New York, 1927.

Yisraeli, David. "The Struggle for Zionist Military Involvement in the First World War, 1914-1917." *Bar-Ilan Studies in History*, edited by Pinhas Artzi. Ramat Gan, 1978.

Zangwill, Lewis. "Herzl Invades England." In *Theodor Herzl: A Memorial*, edited by Meyer Weisgal. New York, 1929.

Zeitlyn, Elsley. *A Paragraph of Anglo-Jewish History: The Board of Deputies and the B'nai B'rith*. London, 1936.

Index

Abrahams, Israel, 30, 195, 213; character, 164-66; and Chovevei Zion Association, 38; and League of British Jews, 307; opposition to Zionism, 163-83 *passim*; visit to Palestine, 31, 166

Abrahams, Sir Lionel: and Ito, 95; and Provisional Committee of the Balfour Declaration Committee, 310-12

Adler, Rev. Alfred S., 196

Adler, Elkan, 237

Adler, Chief Rabbi Hermann, 9, 25; and Chovevei Zion Association, 186; and clergy, 71, 189-90, 193; and Herzl, 61, 188; and immigrant rabbis, 197-98; opposition to Zionism, 47, 130n, 188, 209; and Reform Judaism, 184-85

Adler, Rev. Michael, 189, 192

Agudat ha-Rabannim ha-Haredim be'Angliah, 198-99

Agudat Yisrael, 202-203; and Zionism, 203-204, 303n

Ahad Ha'am: and Conjoint Foreign Committee, 229; and emancipation, 175; in London, 108-109; and Weizmann, 122, 222

Alexander, David, 69, 73, 136, 144, 215, 266; and B'nai B'rith, 270

Aliens Act, 18, 71, 132, 142. *See also* immigration

Alkalai, Judah, 13

Alliance Israelite Universelle, 19, 225, 308, 478

Altneuland, 89

anarchism, 74, 125

Anglo-Jewish Association, 20, 41n, 165, 256, 266, 268, 284; and Conjoint Foreign Committee's manifesto, 239, 243; and Kishinev protest meeting, 73-74; target of Zionist strategy, 55, 67-68; tensions within, 139-40; Zionism at, 47, 55, 68, 292

Anglo-Jewry: ambience, 5, 28, 71; institutional structure, 19, 297; population, 18; tensions within, 131-43, 215-18, 322-23; Weizmann's views of, 108; World War I and, 215-18

Angola, 104

anti-Semitism, 12, 63, 90, 167, 171, 189; in Britain, 18, 132, 289, 293-94; motif in communal debate, 84, 157, 178-81

anti-Zionism, 16, 315; left-wing, 58-61, 250-52; orthodox, 184-214; reform, 163-83

Anti-Zionistisches Komitee, 238

anti-Zionists: caricatures of, 49, 160-61, 234, 315; character of, 155-57, 162; and East Africa, 83-84

Arbayter Fraynd, 59, 125, 252

Asquith, Herbert H., 228, 253

assimilation: motif in communal debate, 169-70

Association of Jewish Literary Societies, 31-32, 165

Ayrton, Edith, 97

Index

Balfour, Arthur, 228, 232, 280n; and
Weizmann, 84, 224
Balfour Declaration, 4, 79, 171, 174,
203, 219, 278-79, 286, 314-15;
background, 228-29, 243-46; com-
munal impact, 291-93
Barnett, Zerah, 6, 8
Baker, D. G., 143n
Bar Kokhba, 208
Basle Program, 55, 118, 150, 160,
227, 235, 257, 301
Beilis trial, 132, 139, 147
Belisha, Barrow, 46n, 140
Ben Gurion, David, 3
Benas, Bertram, 223, 233, 292
Bentwich, Herbert, 17, 79, 90, 110-
11, 113, 116, 132, 146-47, 223,
225, 298, 322; character, 70n;
communal strategy, 47, 66-67,
150; diplomacy, 80; and Maccabean Pilgrimage, 30-31; and Order
of Ancient Maccabeans, 118
Bentwich, Norman, 128, 147, 196,
233
Bialystok pogrom, 97
Bible, cited in communal debate,
167, 172, 177, 181-82, 185, 207n,
210
Bigart, Jacques, 225
B'nai B'rith, 265, 287, 323; and
Board of Deputies, 136, 247, 270-
71; and Conjoint Foreign Committee's manifesto, 239, 275; and Zionists, 150-51, 273-75, 290-91
B'nei Zion tent, 10-11, 39, 71
Board of Deputies: and Conjoint Foreign Committee's manifesto, 239,
243-48, 261-63, 275-76; elections
to, 250n, 272, 296, 317; foundation, 19; and Kishinev protest, 73-
74; reforms of, 132, 143, 289-90;
structure and composition, 261-64;
target of Zionist strategy, 55, 67-

68, 121, 287-96; tensions within,
134-37, 142-43, 265-72 passim;
Weizmann and, 259-60; Zionism
at, 48, 55, 268-69, 287-96
Brenner, Yosef Hayim, 108
British Government: and Balfour
Declaration, 228-29; and East Af-
rica, 81-83; and El Arish, 81; and
Mesopotamia, 101-102
British Palestine Committee, 222-23,
229
Brodetsky, Selig, 128-29, 223, 233

Cambon, Jules, 235
Cassel, Sir Ernest, 100-101
Cecil, Lord Robert, 224, 238, 279
Central Conference of American
Rabbis, 156, 238
Chaikin, Rabbi Avigdor, 189
Chamberlain, Joseph, 80-81, 134
Chief Rabbi, election of, 132, 138,
141, 145
Chovevei Zion Association, 7-12,
75, 80, 158; aims, 10-12, 17-18;
communal influence, 18-19, 28;
decline, 44-46; and EZF, 41-42,
46; leadership, 10-11; membership,
8, 11-12, 17-18; and political
Zionism, 22-46
Churchill, Winston: and East Africa,
4n, 92; North-West Manchester
by-election, 142; and Weizmann,
224
clergy, 141; status, 193-95; and
Zionism, 189-97 passim. See also
rabbinate
Clerkenwell Conference, 41-42, 44,
47, 66, 192-93, 322
Cohen, Sir Benjamin Louis, 9
Cohen, Israel, 118, 147, 273, 286,
303
Cohen, Leonard Lionel, 266, 285;
and Balfour Declaration, 304n; and

Index

Conjoint Foreign Committee, 269n; and Mesopotamia, 100, 102

Cohen, Samuel J., 292, 300

Communist Party, 303

Conder, Col. Claude, 44n, 89n

Conference of Anglo-Jewish Ministers, 141

Conjoint Foreign Committee, 83, 128; communal status, 20, 134, 224; disbanded, 292; enlargement, 256, 268-69; and Kishinev protest, 73; negotiations with Zionists, 226-39; Weizmann and, 259; and World War I, 215-17, 249, 266

Conjoint Foreign Committee's manifesto: censure of, 243-48, 261-63, 275-77; influence, 239; origins, 236-37; theme, 238

"conquest" of community, 51-55, 70-73, 126-29, 148-52, 275-76, 323

conscription of immigrants, 216-18, 251-54

Cowen, Joseph, 64-65, 74, 111, 113, 115-16, 119, 122, 128, 147, 151, 158, 221, 223, 298; communal strategy, 66-73 passim, 268; and conscription, 253-54; introduction to Zionism, 53; and Zangwill, 104-105

Cromer, Lord Evelyn, 81-82

cyrenaica, 101, 103

Daiches, Rabbi Salis, 69, 147

Daiches, Rabbi Samuel, 147, 221, 247n, 294, 297; and Board of Deputies, 269, 273, 296

Daiches, Rabbi Yisrael Ḥayim, 203, 207, 212

D'Avigdor-Goldsmid, Osmond, 95

Diaspora, 12; motif in communal debate, 173, 181-83

Dreyfus, Charles, 72, 116, 121

Dreyfus Affair, 178

dual loyalty, 174-75, 216-18

Duhlberg, Joseph, 140

East Africa offer, 82-85, 110, 159, 168

Edward VII, 53

El Arish scheme, 43, 81

Emanuel, Rev. George, 30

emancipation, in Britain, 72; motif in communal debate, 173-79, 199, 312

Englander, Alfred, 67, 69, 74

English Zionist Federation: and Chovevei Zion Association, 41-42, 46, 80; communal influence of, 20, 107, 113, 130, 144-47, 249-54, 283-96, 315-18; communal strategy, 51-76, 124-29, 151-52, 277-79, 318-23; foundation, 42, 110; ideological poverty, 158-59, 316; leadership, 63-73, 127-28, 147-48, 320-22; negotiations with Ito, 97, 100, 102, 302; and Orthodoxy, 186; size, 56-57, 282, 314; structure, 105-110, 222-23, 283, 300-303, 315-16; tensions within, 110-23, 299-302; wartime diplomacy, 219-20

enlistment, see conscription

Erez Yisrael: colonies in, 6, 36-38, 206, 209, 304; in Jewish thought, 3, 91, 185-86, 198, 202; Muslim inhabitants, 88, 301; physical deficiencies, 89-90. See also Palestine

exile: in orthodox thought, 208, 210-11; in reform thought, 172-73

Fay, Rev. Steven, 189, 192

Federation of Synagogues, 9, 19, 132; and Board of Deputies, 289-90; and Conjoint Foreign Committee, 245; tensions within, 138; and Zionism, 49, 68, 284

Index

Franklin, A. Ellis, 267, 291
Friendly Societies, Jewish, 52, 60.
    See also United Council of Jewish
    Friendly Societies
Fuchs, J. S., 106

Galveston scheme, 93, 103
Gaster, Ḥakham Moses, 9, 79, 106,
    128, 146-47, 156, 158, 222n, 226,
    298, 300; character, 112-13; com-
    munal strategy, 47, 64-75, 150-51,
    258, 297; and Conjoint Foreign
    Committee, 233, 239; and con-
    scription, 257n; and East Africa,
    110-11; and EZF, 110-13, 257-58,
    298-99; and Greenberg, 110-13,
    124, 221; and Herzl, 27, 191; and
    Ito, 96; and Maccabean Pilgrim-
    age, 30; and National Union for
    Jewish Rights, 257-58; and rabbini-
    cal conference, 199n; and Sephardi
    congregation, 48, 145, 191-92,
    284; visit to Erez Yisrael, 112; and
    Weizmann, 114-15, 122, 221-22
General Election (1900), 62-63
Georges-Picot, François, 228
Goldberg, Boris, 222n
Goldbloom, Rev. J. K., 107, 222n
Goldsmid, Col. A.E.W.: and Clerk-
    enwell Conference, 193; and foun-
    dation of Chovevei Zion Associa-
    tion, 7-8; and Herzl, 26-29, 35-36,
    53, 117; and Maccabean Pilgrim-
    age, 30
Gollancz, Rabbi Hermann, 71, 74-75
Goodman, Paul, 112, 147, 222n,
    273, 285
Graetz, Heinrich, 212n
Green, Rev. A. A., 151, 188-89,
    192
Greenberg, Leopold, 64, 109, 115,
    118-19, 128, 222n, 272, 332; and
    Board of Deputies, 150; communal
    strategy, 66-70; and Conjoint For-

eign Committee, 237; and con-
    scription, 237; and East Africa, 83,
    110-11; and foundation of EZF, 42;
    and Gaster, 110-13, 124, 221; and
    Herzl, 81; and Jewish press, 106,
    150, 309; and Weizmann, 298;
    and Zangwill, 94, 104; and Zionist
    diplomacy, 81-83, 220

Haas, Jacob de, 186, 322; and Cho-
    vevei Zion Association, 39-40, 45;
    communal strategy, 60, 66-69; and
    EZF, 67, 101, 106; and Herzl, 27,
    50-51, 117
Hanukah, 172
Harris, Rev. John, 194
Hartog, Philip, 96
Hebrew, 106-109, 233
Henriques, H.S.Q., 94, 291
Hertz, Chief Rabbi Joseph: and Con-
    joint Foreign Committee, 190,
    237-39, 268n; election as Chief
    Rabbi, 138, 145; and Zionism,
    190-91, 235
Herzl, Theodor, 3, 5, 69, 79, 84, 89,
    111, 155-57, 180, 183-86 passim,
    276, 279, 285, 309, 313-14; and
    Anglo-Jewry, 25-30, 56, 61; Brit-
    ish diplomacy of, 80-82; and Brit-
    ish parliamentary elections, 62-63;
    and Chovevei Zion Association,
    34-38; and communal strategy, 50,
    92, 276-77; and Jewish religion,
    205-206; and Mesopotamia, 100;
    and C. Montefiore, 166; and polit-
    ical Zionism, 12-13, 85; and Royal
    Commission on Alien Immigra-
    tion, 64
Herzog, Rabbi Yoel, 96n, 200, 216
Hess, Moses, 13
Hillman, Rabbi Shmuel, 203, 210
Hirsch, Baron Maurice, 7, 93
Hirsch, Dr. Samuel A., 10, 35, 37,
    42, 119

Index

history, as motif in communal debate, 170-73, 179
Hochman, Rev. Joseph, 151, 195-97
Hurewitz, Rabbi Hirsh, 201
Hyamson, Albert, 148, 150, 233, 310
Hyamson, Dayan Moses, 189, 192
Hyman, Aaron, 212

ideology, as factor in communal struggle, 16
immigrant clergy, see rabbinate
immigrants: and Anglo-Jewry, 52, 248; and Ito, 93, 96; status during World War I, 217-18, 253-54; Weizmann's attitude toward, 108; and Zionism, 56-58, 125-26, 312, 315, 320
immigration, 18, 71, 134
Ish-Kishor, Ephraim, 27, 39, 117
Ito: aims of, 85-87; and Anglo-Jewry, 92-104; and East Africa, 87; and EZF, 97, 100, 102, 302; wound up, 97

Jabotinsky, Vladimir, 218, 253-54
Jacobson, Victor, 100, 103
Jewish Board of Guardians, 9, 67-68, 217, 266, 285
Jewish Chronicle, 20n, 30, 68, 88, 216, 244, 272, 309; and Herzl, 26, 32; and Zionism, 106, 188, 235
Jewish Colonisation Association (Ica), 11, 37, 41n, 86-87, 93, 165; and Mesopotamia, 100-102, 104
Jewish Guardian, 309
Jewish Historical Society of England, 165, 175, 297
Jewish Opinion, 308
Jewish Quarterly Review, 164
Jewish Review, 196
Jewish Religious Union, 164, 167, 184
Jewish Social Democratic Association, 251
Jewish State, The, 32, 89
Jewish Territorial Organisation, see Ito
Jewish University, 112, 122, 183, 233, 258
Jewish War Memorial scheme, 282, 283n, 313, 323
Jewish Working Men's Club, 8, 27, 42, 191
Jewish World, 39, 106, 244, 272, 309
Jews' College, 193-94, 196
Joḥanan ben Zakkai, 212-13
Joint Foreign Committee, 292-93
Joint Zionist Council of Great Britain, 119, 121-22
Joseph, Rev. Morris, 130n, 167, 211
Joseph, N. S., 34
Jung, Rabbi Meyer, 203, 206, 212

Kadimah Society, 8
Kalischer, Zevi Hirsch, 13
Kattowicz Conference (1884), 8
Kattowicz Conference (1912), 202-203
Kessler, Leopold, 116
Kishinev pogrom, 71, 86-87, 132, 180; demonstration of protest, 73-76, 139
Kletz, Louis, 142-43, 150
Kook, Rabbi Abraham Isaac, 200-201

Langdon, A. M., 287
Lansdowne, Lord Henry, 81-82
Laski, Nathan, 72, 287-88
League of British Jews, 156, 165, 168, 317; and Board of Deputies, 293-94; character, 305, 306; foundation, 246; influence, 306-309; program, 304-305
Leven, Narcisse, 102, 104
Levin, Shemaryahu, 107
Liberal Judaism, 164
Lieberman, Aaron, 58

(345)

Index

Lloyd George, David, 224, 228
Lousada, George, 100

Macaulay, Thomas Babington, 176
Maccabean Pilgrimage, 30-31, 90
Maccabeans, 20, 26, 29-30, 35, 41n, 88, 314
Maccoby, Rabbi Ḥayim Zundel, 8, 19, 205
Machazike Hadath Congregation, 186, 198, 200
Magnus, Lady Kate, 96, 167
Magnus, Laurie, 95, 167, 296n, 302, 309
Magnus, Sir Philip, 235, 296n; and Balfour Declaration, 304n; and Conjoint Foreign Committee, 269n; and Ito, 95; and Zionism, 167, 288; and Weizmann, 259
Maimonides, 173n
Manchester (North-West) by-election, 142, 146
Manchester Community Council, 273
Manchester "group" of Zionists, 121, 322
Manchester Jewish Hospital, 72
Manchester Shechitah Board, 146
Marks, Simon, 223, 295
Marmor, Kalman, 60, 65, 126
Marmorek, Oscar, 112
Mendelssohn, Moses, 12
Mesopotamia, Ito project for Jewish settlement in, 98-104
messianism, 156-57
Middle East, British strategic interests in, 6, 229
millenarianism, 5
Milner, Lord Alfred, 236-37, 304
"Mission of Israel," as motif in communal debate, 182-83, 189
Mizraḥi movement, 202, 302
Mocatta, Frederic, 26, 29
Mond, Alfred, 281

Montagu, Edwin, 175n, 278, 303
Montagu, Lily, 167
Montagu, Sir Samuel: communal status of, 9, 186n; and Federation of Synagogues, 138, 197; and Herzl, 26; and Ito, 94; as target of Zionist strategy, 62, 71; and Zionism, 49, 88-89, 156
Montefiore, Claude, 73, 135, 144, 171n, 188, 195, 255, 266, 284, 292; and Balfour Declaration, 174-75, 303-304; character of, 164-66; communal influence of, 166-72, 184; and Conjoint Foreign Committee's manifesto, 237; and Herzl, 27, 61, 180; and Ito, 94; and League of British Jews, 307; and Mesopotamia, 100, 102; opposition to Zionism, 47, 163-83 passim, 233-35; and Orthodoxy, 213-14; and Weizmann, 259
Montefiore, Sir Francis, 48-49, 62, 64, 67-68, 110-11, 125-26, 145, 150, 266
Montefiore, Sir Moses, 6, 165
Morning Post, 289, 293-94
Moser, Jacob, 118
Myer, Mauriss, 106
Myers, Asher, 26, 32

Namier, Lewis, 166
Nathan, Sir Mathew, 269n
National Union for Jewish Rights, 249, 254-57, 287, 299
nationalism, as motif in communal debate, 172-73
Newman, Sidney, 247n, 273
Nili spies, 229
Nordau, Max, 25, 28, 52, 112
Northcliffe, Lord Alfred, 286
Nossig, Alfred, 100

Order of Ancient Maccabeans, 117-18, 222-23, 290, 299, 302

Index

Orthodoxy: and political Zionism, 186, 206-207; and Reform, 213-14, 308n

Palestina, The Chovevei Zion Quarterly, 10
Palestine, British offensive in, 219, 229, 301. See also Erez Yisrael
Palestine Colonisation Association, 8
Passover, as motif in communal debate, 181-82, 187, 201
Petaḥ Tikva, 6
Pinsker, Leon, 13
Poalei Zion, 59-60, 125-26, 251
Prag, Joseph, 17, 29, 36, 42, 237, 280
protestrabbiner, 156, 188
provinces: and Anglo-Jewry, 132, 139-43, 209-210; and Board of Deputies, 263-64, 289n; and Chovevei Zion Association, 18, 44-45; and EZF, 119-21, 290, 299-300
Provisional Committee of the Balfour Declaration Committee, 309-312

rabbinate: character of, 196, 209-210; and Chief Rabbi, 198; and political Zionism, 187, 198-213, 252. See also clergy
rabbinical conferences, 198-99, 207
Rabinowitz Shemuel Ya'akov, 200, 210
Rabinowitz, Ya'akov, 96n, 201
redemption, as motif in communal debate, 207-211
Reform Judaism, 184; and Orthodoxy, 213-14, 308n; and Zionism, 163-83
return to Zion: in liturgy, 184, 186, 208; as motif in communal debate, 185, 208-211
Rhodes, Cecil, 53
Rocker, Rudolf, 125
Rosebery, Lord Archibald, 10, 53

Rothschild, Anthony de, 281-82
Rothschild, Baron Edmond de, 36, 231-32
Rothschild, James de, 230-32, 258, 315
Rothschild, Leopold de, 95, 231, 236
Rothschild, Lionel de, 284, 306
Rothschild, Lord Nathaniel, 315; communal status of, 9, 138; and Herzl, 53, 61, 81; and Ito, 94, 101; Zionists and, 71, 89
Rothschild, Lord Walter, 239, 244, 258, 277-79, 287-88, 306, 311, 315
Rowson (Rosenbaum), Simon, 134-36, 151, 246, 259, 271-72, 275
Royal Commission on Alien Immigration, 53, 61, 64, 110
Rubinstein, S. B., 33n, 40, 64-65, 146
Russia, revolutions in, 181
Russo-Jewish Committee, 19

Sacher, Harry, 116, 120-21, 232-33, 235, 237, 287, 295, 299; and Board of Deputies, 290; and Conjoint Foreign Committee, 229-30, 274; negotiations with Wolf, 225-26; and Order of Ancient Maccabeans, 223
Salaman, Clement, 99
Salisbury, Lord Robert, 10, 53
Samuel, Herbert, 224-25, 228, 230, 279
Samuel, Sir Stuart, 250, 288, 291, 294-95
San Remo Conference, 20-21, 279, 322
Schechter, Solomon, 30, 38, 164, 184, 195
Schiff, Jacob, 93, 100-104 passim
Schonfeld, Rabbi Victor, 205
Schonfield, William, 296
Scott, C. P., 224

Index

Sephardi Congregation, 19, 48, 67, 139, 284
Shabbetai Ẓevi, 157, 208
Sieff, Israel, 121, 223, 273, 307
Silverstone, Gedalya, 201
Simon, Leon, 120-21, 129, 222n, 223, 235, 277, 299
Simon, Oswald John, 167
Singer, Rev. Simeon, 9, 89n, 165, 192, 196; and Herzl, 26, 33, 56; and Zionism, 188
socialists, 74; influence in Anglo-Jewry, 59; and Zionism, 59-61, 251
Sokolow, Naḥum, 6, 107, 191, 201, 222n, 287, 311; and communal institutions, 128, 257-58, 273; and Conjoint Foreign Committee's manifesto, 248; negotiations with anti-Zionists, 226-35 passim; and Zionist diplomacy, 222, 235
Solomon, Solomon J., 29
Spielman, Isidore, 309
Spielman, Meyer A., 95
Spiers, Dayan Barukh, 189
Stein, Leonard, 128
Stern, Rev. David, 189
Stiebel, Arthur, 285
Straus, Oscar, 104
Suvalsky, Isaac, 106
Swaythling, Lord Edwin Samuel, 138, 236, 269n, 284, 305
Swaythling, Lord Samuel, see Montagu, Samuel
Sykes, Sir Mark, 122, 222, 228, 235, 279
synagogues, Zionist campaigns in, 127, 186-87

Talmud, cited in communal debate, 170, 182n, 210
territorialism, 90-91. See also East Africa; Ito; Zangwill

Tolkowsky, Samuel, 222-23, 233
trade unions, Jewish: immigrants and, 125; and Zionism, 52, 60, 251, 302
Tsayt, Di, 106, 244
Tschlenow, Yeḥiel, 222, 225-26, 279
Tuck, Sir Adolph, 138, 151, 280

Uganda, see East Africa
Umanski, Jack, 45
Union of Jewish Literary Societies, 128
United Council of Jewish Friendly Societies, 247, 249, 287; and Conjoint Foreign Committee, 239, 269; and Zionism, 250
United Synagogue, 19; and Board of Deputies, 289-90; and Conjoint Foreign Committee, 245; tensions within, 132, 137-38; and Zionism, 48, 69, 145-46, 284
universities, Zionism at, 128-29

Waley Cohen, Sir Robert, 280-82
Warburg, Otto, 119
Weizmann, Chaim, 3, 79, 84, 92, 111, 116, 121, 156, 191, 310, 314; and Aḥad Ha'am, 221; and B'nai B'rith, 273, 275; and Board of Deputies, 274-76, 287; caricature of anti-Zionists, 161; communal strategy, 79, 127-28, 258-60, 278-79; and Conjoint Foreign Committee, 230, 233, 239; and conscription, 253-54; diplomacy, 219-20, 223-25, 279, 318; and EZF, 113-15, 118, 123-24, 219-23, 298; first years in Britain, 72n, 108; and Gaster, 114-15, 121-25; and Hertz, 191; and Jewish University, 150; and League of British Jews, 306; and S. Samuel, 293
Werner, Rabbi Abba, 186, 205

Index

West London (Reform) Synagogue, 19, 185
Wickham Steed, Henry, 224
Wigoder, Rabbi Meyer, 205
Winchevsky, Morris, 59
Wolf, Lucien, 30, 143, 162n, 195, 213, 215, 217, 292, 310; and Agudah, 204; and B'nai B'rith, 270; and Board of Deputies, 268, 291; diplomacy, 224, 227-28; and East Africa, 83-84; and Herzl, 27, 30, 168; and immigrants, 249; and Ito, 95, 97; and League of British Jews, 307-308; and National Union, 255-57; negotiations with Zionists, 225-31, 235-38; opposition to Zionism, 168-83 passim, 230-31, 235
Wolffsohn, David, 70, 84-85, 104, 106, 112, 118-20, 128, 140
World War I, impact on Anglo-Jewry, 215-18, 265-67
Wortsmann, Yehezkel, 65

Yoffey, Rabbi Yisrael, 201, 203, 210
Yoffey, Rabbi Yosef, 210

Zangwill, Israel, 21, 53, 62, 69-70, 111, 195, 309; character, 87-88; early attitude toward Erez Yisrael, 87; and EZF's communal strategy, 54; and Herzl, 25, 29; and Ito's communal strategy, 85-86, 92-104; and Maccabean Pilgrimage, 30; and National Union, 256-57; and Orthodoxy, 206n
Zionism: gentile, 61-63, 80, 99, 228; "political," 112; "practical," 112; revolutionary nature, 12-13, 157-58
Zionist Commission to Palestine, 279, 307
Zionist Congresses: first, 31n, 32n, 33, 39-40, 50, 186, 188; second, 50, 54; third, 114; fourth, 33, 56; sixth, 84; seventh, 84; eighth, 115; ninth, 118; tenth, 38, 119
Zionist Organisation, as force for communal change, 13-15
Zionists: at Board of Deputies, 247; character, 155; as communal faction, 16, 70-73; communal strategy, 186-87

LIBRARY OF CONGRESS CATALOGING IN PUBLICATION DATA

Cohen, Stuart.
  English Zionists and British Jews.

  Bibliography: p.
  Includes index.
  1. Zionism—Great Britain—History. 2. Jews—
Great Britain—Politics and government. 3. Great
Britain—Ethnic relations. I. Title.
DS149.C638   305.8'924'041   82-47588
ISBN 0-691-05361-8   AACR2

Stuart A. Cohen is a professor in the Department of Political Studies, Bar-Ilan University, Israel. He is the author of *British Policy in Mesopotamia, 1903-1914* (1976).

DATE DUE